# THE PHOTOSHOP
# USER'S
# ENCYCLOPEDIA

Peter Cope

# THE PHOTOSHOP
# USER'S ENCYCLOPEDIA

With 653 color illustrations

FRIEDMAN/FAIRFAX
PUBLISHERS

This edition published by
**FRIEDMAN/FAIRFAX** PUBLISHERS
by arrangement with Ilex Press

2002 **FRIEDMAN/FAIRFAX**

ISBN 1-5866-3460-7

For bulk purchases and special sales, please contact:
Friedman/Fairfax Publishers
Sales Department
230 Fifth Avenue
Suite 700-701
New York
NY 10001
Tel: 212/685-3916
Fax: 212/685-3916

01 02 03 04 05 MC 10 9 8 7 6 5 4

This book was conceived, designed, and produced by
**The Ilex Press Limited**
Cambridge CB2 4LX
England

*Art Director:* Alastair Campbell
*Design Manager:* Kevin McGeoghegan
*Managing Editor:* Kim Yarwood
*Production Editor:* Jannie Brightman

A Cataloguing in Publication record
is available from the Library of Congress

Printed and bound in China

# CONTENTS

## FILE MANAGEMENT

## COLOR MANAGEMENT

## DOCUMENT STRUCTURE

## IMAGE MANIPULATION

## IMAGEREADY & **WEB**

## **PHO**TOGRAPHY

## **PRI**NTING

## **GEN**ERAL

# HOW TO USE
# THIS BOOK

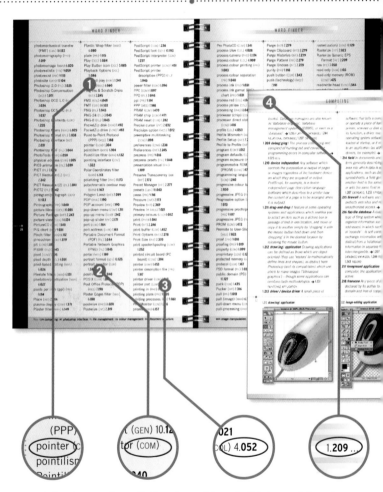

**Word finder** To look up
the meaning of a term,
first refer to the Word
Finder, where all
3,000 terms in the
Encyclopedia are listed
in alphabetical order.

**Category** Next to each
term in the Word Finder
is a category
abbreviation. Category
names are listed in
full at the bottom of
each Word Finder page.

**Entry number** This gives
the location of the
explanation of the term.
Each number features
the chapter number
first, then the specific
entry number.

**Entry numbers** run
consecutively within
each category. Much
like a thesaurus, the
span of entry numbers
is indicated at the
head of each page.

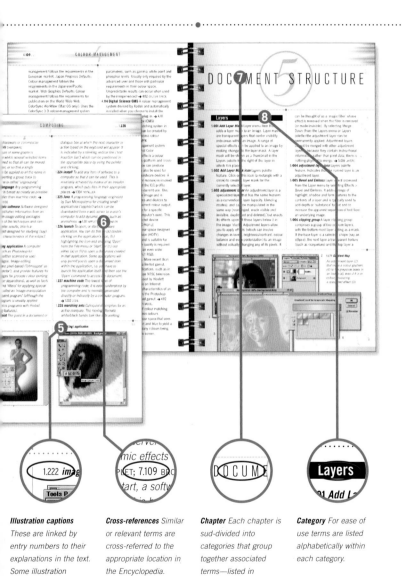

**Illustration captions**
These are linked by entry numbers to their explanations in the text. Some illustration captions may refer to more than one term.

**Cross-references** Similar or relevant terms are cross-referred to the appropriate location in the Encyclopedia.

**Chapter** Each chapter is sud-divided into categories that group together associated terms—listed in alphabetical order.

**Category** For ease of use terms are listed alphabetically within each category.

Part 1

# WORD FINDER

Key: **COM** computing; **INT** photoshop interface; **FIL** file management; **COL** color management; **DOC** document structure;

13

Blur More filter (MAN) 6.**088**
BMP (FIL) 3.**006**
Bookmark (WEB) 7.**108**
boot disk (COM) 1.**113**
boot/boot up/booting up
(COM) 1.**022**
bootstrapping (COM) 1.**022**
bot (WEB) 7.**197**
bounce lighting (PHO) 8.**194**
bounding border/box (INT)
2.**003**
Bounding Box Optimization
(WEB) 7.**053**
bps (COM) 1.**126**
bracketing (PHO) 8.**002**
brick (MAN) 6.**144**
brightness (MAN) 6.**005**
brightness range (PHO) 8.**061**
Brightness/Contrast (INT)
2.**295**
Bring Forward (INT) 2.**346**
Bring to Front (INT) 2.**346**
browser (WEB) 7.**109**
brush creation (INT) 2.**004**
Brush Options (INT) 2.**118**
Brush Strokes filters (MAN)
6.**100**
Brushes Option palette (INT)
2.**119**
Brushes/Color/Swatches
(INT) 2.**127**
bubblejet printer (COM) 1.**442**
Bucket tool (INT) 2.**094**
buffer (COM) 1.**460**
bug (COM) 1.**023**
bulb (setting) (PHO) 8.**062**
bulleted list (WEB) 7.**110** .
bulletin board service (BBS)
(WEB) 7.**111**
bump maps (MAN) 6.**137**
burn (PHO) 8.**003**
Burn tool (INT) 2.**069**
bureau (PRI) 9.**123**
burlap (MAN) 6.**144**
burn-in (monitor) (COM)
1.**385**
Button mode (INT) 2.**120**
Byline (INT) 2.**223**
byte (COM) 1.**024**

# C

c (1) (COL) 4.**006**
c (2) (COL) 4.**028**

C format (PHO) 8.**110**
C/C++ (COM) 1.**201**
cache (COM) 1.**461**
Calculations (INT) 2.**269**
calibrate, calibration (GEN)
10.**015**
Calibration Bars (PRI) 9.**080**
cameo coated paper (PRI)
9.**076**
camera (PHO) 8.**143**
camera angle (PHO) 8.**063**
camera-ready art (PRI)
9.**006**
camera shake (PHO) 8.**004**
cancel/abort (COM) 1.**294**
candids (PHO) 8.**005**
canvas (INT) 2.**005**
Canvas Size (INT) 2.**297**
Caption (INT) 2.**215**
capture (GEN) 10.**016**
Carbon (COM) 1.**269**
card reader (COM) 1.**419**
carriage return (COM) 1.**346**
cartridge (PHO) 8.**111**
cartridge, removable (COM)
1.**491**
Carve (MAN) 6.**051**
Cascade (WEB) 7.**002**
case sensitive (GEN) 10.**170**
cassette (PHO) 8.**112**
cast (COL) 4.**004**
catadioptric lens (PHO) 8.**144**
Categories (INT) 2.**216**
cathode ray tube (CRT)
(COM) 1.**365**
CAV (COM) 1.**501**
CCD (PHO) 8.**208**
CCD array (PHO) 8.**207**
CCD pitch, CCD element
pitch (COM) 1.**364**
CCITT encoding (FIL) 3.**061**
CD (COM) 1.**494**
CD format specification (FIL)
3.**022**
CD-I (COM) 1.**495**
CD-R (COM) 1.**498**
CD-ROM (COM) 1.**496**
CD-ROM/XA (COM) 1.**497**
CD-RW (COM) 1.**499**
cell (GEN) 10.**004**
center-aligned (GEN) 10.**171**
center line (text) (GEN) 10.**168**
center-weighted exposure
(PHO) 8.**064**

central processing unit
(CPU) (COM) 1.**392**
CGI (1) (WEB) 7.**116**
Chalk & Charcoal filter (MAN)
6.**141**
Charcoal filter (MAN) 6.**142**
channel (WEB) 7.**112**
Channel Mixer (INT) 2.**298**
channels (DOC) 5.**036**
Channels palette (INT) 2.**121**
Channels/Paths/Layers (INT)
2.**146**
Character palette (INT) 2.**122**
character set (GEN) 10.**172**
character shape player
(CSP) (WEB) 7.**113**
character shape recorder
(CSR) (WEB) 7.**114**
character space (GEN) 10.**173**
character width (GEN) 10.**174**
charge-coupled device
(CCD) (PHO) 8.**208**
charge-injection device
(CID) (COM) 1.**420**
checkbox (COM) 1.**295**
chemical reversal (PHO) 8.**024**
chemical transfer (GEN)
10.**122**
chip (COM) 1.**393**
chisel-tipped brush (MAN)
6.**106**
chroma (COL) 4.**005**
Chrome filter (MAN) 6.**143**
chrominance (c) (COL) 4.**006**
Cibachrome (PHO) 8.**065**
CID (COM) 1.**420**
CIE (COL) 4.**007**
CIE L*a*b* color space (COL)
4.**079**
CIE RGB (COL) 4.**107**
circle of confusion (PHO)
8.**066**
circuit board (COM) 1.**394**
circular polarizer (PHO)
8.**173**
circular selection (INT) 2.**077**
CISC (COM) 1.**396**
CIX (WEB) 7.**115**
Classic (environment) (COM)
1.**267**
clean install (COM) 1.**296**
Clear (1) (INT) 2.**259**
Clear (2) (COL) 4.**087**
Clear Actions (DOC) 5.**064**

15

database (COM) 1.**207**

database engine (COM) 1.**208**

database management system (DBMS) (COM) 1.**208**

database manager (COM) 1.**208**

Dataviz Conversions Plus (FIL) 3.**079**

Date Created (INT) 2.**239**

datum (GEN) 10.**031**

daughterboard (COM) 1.**398**

DBMS (COM) 1.**208**

DCS (FIL) 3.**009**

DDCP (PRI) 9.**094**

DDES (GEN) 10.**044**

De-Interlace filter (MAN) 6.**173**

Debabilizer (FIL) 3.**079**

debug(ging) (COM) 1.**209**

deckle edge (PRI) 9.**069**

decompressor (FIL) 3.**062**

decryption (GEN) 10.**032**

dedicated flash (PHO) 8.**196**

Default Colors icon (INT) 2.**073**

defaults (GEN) 10.**063**

defective pixels (INT) 2.**070**

Define Brush (1) (INT) 2.**264**

Define Brush (2) (INT) 2.**129**

Define Custom Shape (INT) 2.**265**

Define Pattern (1) (INT) 2.**266**

Define Pattern (2) (INT) 2.**267**

definition (GEN) 10.**033**

defragment(ing) (COM) 1.**503**

Defringe (INT) 2.**331**

degauss(ing) (COM) 1.**367**

degrade/degradation (GEN) 10.**034**

Delete Brush (INT) 2.**130**

Delete Channel (1) (INT) 2.**131**

Delete Channel (2) (WEB) 7.**011**

Delete Current Channel icon (DOC) 5.**038**

Delete Current icon (DOC) 5.**070**

Delete Current Layer icon (DOC) 5.**012**

Delete Current Path icon (DOC) 5.**045**

Delete Current State (DOC) 5.**071**

Delete Layer (1) (INT) 2.**347**

Delete Layer (2) (INT) 2.**132**

Delete Path (DOC) 5.**046**

Delete Selection (DOC) 5.**013**

Delete Slices (WEB) 7.**012**

delimit 1.**035**

delimited file (COM) 1.**035**

delta frames (GEN) 10.**097**

dense (PHO) 8.**069**

densitometer (GEN) 10.**035**

density (GEN) 10.**036**

density range (GEN) 10.**037**

deprecated (WEB) 7.**119**

depth of field (PHO) 8.**070**

depth of focus (PHO) 8.**071**

desaturate (COL) 4.**029**

Desaturate (INT) 2.**303**

desaturated color (COL) 4.**030**

descreen (MAN) 6.**032**

descreen(ing) (PRI) 9.**090**

deselect (COM) 1.**305**

Deselect (INT) 2.**332**

desensitize (PRI) 9.**091**

desk copy (PRI) 9.**009**

DeskJet (COM) 1.**443**

desktop (COM) 1.**306**

desktop computer (COM) 1.**399**

desktop publishing (DTP) (COM) 1.**036**

desktop (publishing) system (COM) 1.**037**

desktop scanner (COM) 1.**421**

Despeckle filter (MAN) 6.**121**

destination (COM) 1.**117**

destination image (MAN) 6.**006**

detail (GEN) 10.**038**

Deutsche Industrie-Norm (DIN) (GEN) 10.**039**

developer (PHO) 8.**028**

developing tank (PHO) 8.**029**

device (COM) 1.**038**

device driver (COM) 1.**213**

device independent (COM) 1.**210**

device-independent color (COL) 4.**031**

dfi (PRI) 9.**089**

DHTML (WEB) 7.**123**

dial-up (WEB) 7.**120**

Diamond Gradient (INT) 2.**074**

diaphragm (PHO) 8.**150**

diapositive (PHO) 8.**116**

DIF (FIL) 3.**008**

Difference (COL) 4.**092**

Difference Clouds filter (MAN) 6.**135**

difference frames (GEN) 10.**097**

differencing (PHO) 8.**008**

diffraction (PRI) 9.**092**

diffuse (PHO) 8.**197**

Diffuse filter (MAN) 6.**155**

Diffuse Glow filter (MAN) 6.**107**

diffuse highlight (PRI) 9.**093**

diffuse lighting (PHO) 8.**198**

diffuser (GEN) 10.**040**

Diffusion dither (WEB) 7.**057**

diffusion transfer (GEN) 10.**122**

Digimarc (MAN) 6.**069**

digit (GEN) 10.**041**

digital (GEN) 10.**042**

digital audio tape (DAT) (COM) 1.**504**

digital camera (PHO) 8.**212**

digital data (GEN) 10.**043**

Digital Data Exchange Standard (DDES) (GEN) 10.**044**

digital device (GEN) 10.**045**

digital domain (GEN) 10.**046**

digital image (GEN) 10.**047**

digital photography (PHO) 8.**213**

Digital Science CMS (COL) 4.**114**

digital switch port (DSP) (COM) 1.**132**

digital versatile disc (DVD) (COM) 1.**505**

digital versatile disc random access memory (DVD-RAM) (COM) 1.**506**

digital versatile disc read-only memory (DVD-ROM) (COM) 1.**507**

digital versatile disc recordable (DVD-R) (COM) 1.**508**

digital versatile disc video (DVD-Video) (COM) 1.**509**

digital video interactive (DVI) (COM) 1.**400**

digitize (GEN) 10.**048**

digitizer (COM) 1.**422**

---

**MAN** *image manipulation*; **WEB** *imageready & web*; **PHO** *photography*; **PRI** *printing*; **GEN** *general* digitizing tablet/pad (COM) 1.**423**

DIMM (COM) 1.**463**

dimmed command (COM) 1.**307**

dimmed icon (COM) 1.**308**

DIN (GEN) 10.**039**

dingbat (GEN) 10.**175**

diopter/dioptre (PHO) 8.**072**

DIP (COM) 1.**401**

DIP SIMM (COM) 1.**462**

DIP switch (COM) 1.**401**

direct access (GEN) 10.**049**

direct digital color proof (DDCP) (PRI) 9.**094**

direct entry (COM) 1.**039**

direct reading (PHO) 8.**009**

Direct Selection tool (INT) 2.**098**

directory (FIL) 3.**075**

directory structure (FIL) 3.**076**

Disable Layer Mask (INT) 2.**348**

disabled (COM) 1.**307**

disc (COM) 1.**510**

disc drive (COM) 1.**512**

discrete value (GEN) 10.**050**

disk (COM) 1.**510**

disk buffer (COM) 1.**460**

disk crash (COM) 1.**511**

disk drive (COM) 1.**512**

disc film (PHO) 8.**122**

disk image (FIL) 3.**077**

disk operating system (DOS) (COM) 1.**336**

disk optimizing (COM) 1.**535**

disk track (COM) 1.**557**

disk/disc drive (COM) 1.**512**

diskette (COM) 1.**517**

Displace (COL) 6.**108**

Displace filter (MAN) 6.**108**

displacement map (MAN) 6.**035**

Display (INT) 2.**010**

Display & Cursors (INT) 2.**245**

display device (COM) 1.**402**

disposable camera (PHO) 8.**151**

Dissolve (COL) 4.**093**

Distort (INT) 2.**268**

Distort filters (MAN) 6.**109**

Distribute Linked (INT) 2.**349**

Ditherbox™ Filter (MAN) 6.**174**

dither(ing) (MAN) 6.**007**

dithered bitmap (WEB) 7.**052**

diverging/divergent lens (PHO) 8.**152**

Divide Slices (WEB) 7.**013**

dock (COM) 1.**133**

Dock (COM) 1.**270**

docking station (COM) 1.**133**

document (WEB) 7.**121**

Document Type Definition (DTD) (WEB) 7.**122**

Document Window (WEB) 7.**058**

dodge/dodging (PHO) 8.**030**

dongle (COM) 1.**040**

donor sheet (PRI) 9.**060**

DOS (COM) 1.**336**

dot matrix printer (COM) 1.**444**

dot pattern (PRI) 9.**095**

dot/stripe pitch (COM) 1.**368**

dots per inch (dpi) (GEN) 10.**051**

dots per square inch (dpsi/dpi2) (GEN) 10.**052**

double exposure (PHO) 8.**014**

double image (PRI) 9.**096**

double-black duotone (MAN) 6.**064**

double-click (COM) 1.**309**

double-dot halftone (PRI) 9.**097**

double-tone ink (PRI) 9.**024**

Down state (WEB) 7.**087**

download (COM) 1.**041**

downsampling (MAN) 6.**008**

downsize (MAN) 6.**009**

downtime (GEN) 10.**053**

dpi (GEN) 10.**051**

dpi2 (GEN) 10.**052**

dpsi (GEN) 10.**052**

draft (GEN) 10.**054**

drag (COM) 1.**310**

drag-and-drop (COM) 1.**211**

drag-copy (INT) 2.**075**

DRAM (COM) 1.**465**

draw(ing) application (COM) 1.**212**

drive (COM) 1.**512**

drive head (COM) 1.**513**

driver/device driver (COM) 1.**213**

Drop Shadow (1) (DOC) 5.**014**

Drop Shadow (2) (MAN) 6.**063**

drop-down menu (COM) 1.**311**

Droplet (WEB) 7.**059**

drum (PRI) 9.**098**

drum scanner (COM) 1.**424**

Dry Brush filter (MAN) 6.**074**

dry litho (PRI) 9.**049**

dry mounting (PRI) 9.**070**

dry proof (PRI) 9.**050**

DSP (1) (COM) 1.**132**

DSP (2) (COM) 1.**132**

DTD (WEB) 7.**122**

DTP (COM) 1.**036**

dual inline memory module (DIMM) (COM) 1.**463**

dual inline package (DIP) (COM) 1.**464**

dumb terminal (COM) 1.**402**

duotone (MAN) 6.**064**

Duotone (INT) 2.**304**

dupe (GEN) 10.**055**

duplex halftone (MAN) 6.**064**

Duplicate (INT) 2.**305**

Duplicate Channel (INT) 2.**133**

Duplicate Layer (1) (INT) 2.**134**

Duplicate Layer (2) (INT) 2.**350**

Duplicate Optimized (WEB) 7.**014**

Duplicate Path (DOC) 5.**047**

Duplicate Slices (WEB) 7.**015**

DuPont (PRI) 9.**048**

Dust & Scratches filter (MAN) 6.**122**

DVD (COM) 1.**505**

DVD-R (COM) 1.**508**

DVD-RAM (COM) 1.**506**

DVD-ROM (COM) 1.**507**

DVD-Video (COM) 1.**509**

DVI (COM) 1.**400**

Dvorak keyboard (COM) 1.**425**

DX (PHO) 8.**211**

dye diffusion (PRI) 9.**051**

dye sub(limation) (PRI) 9.**051**

dye-based ink (PRI) 9.**025**

dynamic effects (MAN) 6.**010**

dynamic HTML/DHTML (WEB) 7.**123**

dynamic RAM (DRAM) (COM) 1.**465**

dynamic range (GEN) 10.**056**

# E

e-commerce (WEB) 7.**124**

e-mail (WEB) 7.**125**

## F

MAN *image manipulation*; WEB *imageready & web*; PHO *photography*; PRI *printing*; GEN *general*

22

Key: **COM** *computing;* **INT** *photoshop interface;* **FIL** *file management;* **COL** *colour management;* **DOC** *document structure;*

Key: **COM** computing; **INT** photoshop interface; **FIL** file management; **COL** color management; **DOC** document structure;

**MAN** image manipulation; **WEB** imageready & web; **PHO** photography; **PRI** printing; **GEN** general

## S

Key: **COM** *computing*; **INT** *photoshop interface*; **FIL** *file management*; **COL** *color management*; **DOC** *document structure*;

**MAN** *image manipulation;* **WEB** *imageready & web;* **PHO** *photography;* **PRI** *printing;* **GEN** *general*

Key: **COM** *computing*; **INT** *photoshop interface*; **FIL** *file management*; **COL** *color management*; **DOC** *document structure*;

Key: **COM** *computing;* **INT** *photoshop interface;* **FIL** *file management;* **COL** *color management;* **DOC** *document structure;*

35

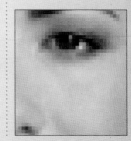

MAN *image manipulation;* WEB *imageready & web;* PHO *photography;* PRI *printing;* GEN *general*

# Part 2
# PHOTOSHOP TERMS

# COMPUTING

## General computer terms

1.**001 access time** The time taken by a disk drive to access data. This is measured as an average of the "seek" time (the time the drive head takes to find the data), and the "latency" time (the time the data sector takes to rotate under the head). Also known as "average access time". → 1.548 SECTOR

1.**002 active** In computer interfaces and applications, items selected for editing or other modification are described as being "active". Active items are indicated by, for example, highlighting (text) or the appearance of "handles" on boxes (graphics). → 1.003 ACTIVE ICON; 1.004 ACTIVE WINDOW

1.**003 active icon** The currently selected icon in a window or on the desktop; its status is indicated by highlighting, usually so that it appears as a negative of its inactive image. → 1.055 ICON

1.**004 active window** The currently selected desktop or document window. Usually the active window is the only one in which the content can be modified, although with some types of window (such as floating palettes) editing of one window simultaneously updates others. The active window is usually indicated by a bold title bar and active scroll bars. → 1.354 TITLE BAR; 1.349 SCROLL BAR

1.**005 address (1)** The number or code identifying the location of data in a computer's memory. It can be "logical"— used when an instruction is executed—or "physical"—when the computer translates the logical address into a physical location on a disk drive, for example.

1.**006 AFK** Acronym for "away from keyboard".

1.**007 alert** An audible or visible warning on a computer alerting you to a specific situation. Usually used to alert the user to a required input or action, or an error. → 1.008 ALERT BOX

1.**008 alert box** An onscreen message box with information or a warning that usually requires no action by the user other than an acknowledgement. → 1.007 ALERT

1.**009 algorithm** A predetermined mathematical procedure for solving a specific problem. Computer programs comprise groups of (often interlinked) algorithms.

1.**010 append** The facility within some applications to import user-defined formatting into one document from another. → 1.520 FORMATTING

1.003 *active icon*

Folder 01

Active icon

Folder 02

Inactive icon

1.008 *alert box*

This cannot be undone. Continue?

Cancel    OK

1.012 *application/application program*

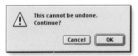

:52:12 pm     Finder

Hide Finder
Hide Others
Show All

☞ Eudora
✓ Finder
Palm™ Desktop
Photoshop®
QuarkXPress™
StuffIt Deluxe™

1.016 *bit*

| | | | | | |
|---|---|---|---|---|---|
| *1 bit:* | 1 | = | on | = | ■ |
| | 0 | = | off | = | ❑ |
| *2 bit:* | 00 | = | | | ❑ |
| | 01 | = | | | ▨ |
| | 10 | = | | | ■ |
| | 11 | = | | | ■ |
| *8 bit:* | 01000001 | = | | | A |
| | 01100001 | = | | | a |
| | 01000010 | = | | | B |
| | 01100010 | = | | | b |
| | 01000011 | = | | | C |
| | 01100011 | = | | | c |
| | 01000100 | = | | | D |
| | 01100100 | = | | | d |

**1.011 applet** A general term that can be applied to any small application that performs a specific task, such as the calculator. More specifically the term applet is also used to describe a small application, written in the Java programming language, which is downloaded by an Internet browser to perform specific tasks. → 7.158 INTERNET; 1.005 JAVA; 7.109 BROWSER

**1.012 application / application program** A software program written to enable the user to create and modify documents for a specific purpose, thus distinguishing it from operating system software and utilities (software that improves the functioning of your computer rather than enabling you to create anything). Typical application groups include those for page layout, graphics, word processing, and spreadsheets. Often called, imprecisely, simply a "program." → 1.259 SYSTEM SOFTWARE; 1.259 UTILITY (PROGRAM)

**1.013 attribute (1)** The specification applied to a character, box, or other item. Character attributes include font, size, style, color, shade, scaling, kerning, etc.

**1.014 background processing** The ability of a computer to process commands from one program or application in the background while simultaneously performing another (usually in response to user input) in the foreground. → 1.460 BUFFER; 9.078 BACKGROUND PRINTING

**1.015 batch processing** Programming a computer to process several documents (usually images) as computer resources become available.

**1.016 bit** A commonly used acronym for binary digit, the smallest piece of information a computer can use. A bit is expressed as one of two values – a 1 or a 0, on or off, something or nothing, negative or positive, small or large, etc. Each alphabet character requires eight bits (called a "byte") to store it. → 10.011 BINARY; 10.041 DIGIT; 1.024 BYTE; 1.017 BIT DENSITY; 1.018 BIT DEPTH; 7.107 BIT RATE; 1.019 BITMAP

**1.017 bit density** The number of bits occupying a particular area or length—per inch of magnetic tape, for example. → 1.016 BIT

**1.018 bit depth** The number of bits assigned to each pixel on a monitor, scanner or image file. One-bit, for example, will only produce black and white (the bit is either on or off), while eight-bit will generate 256 grays or colors (256 is the maximum number of permutations of a string of eight 1s and 0s) and twenty-four-bit will produce 16.7 million colors (256 x 256 x 256). → 1.016 BIT; 10.011 BINARY; 4.001 16-BIT COLOR

**1.019 bitmap** Strictly speaking any text character or image comprised of dots. A bitmap is a "map" of "bits" that describes the complete collection of the bits that represent the location and binary state (on or off) of a corresponding set of items, such as pixels, which are required to form an image, as on a display monitor. → 1.016 BIT; 10.011 BINARY; 1.095 PIXEL; 10.169 BITMAPPED FONT; 1.020 BITMAPPED GRAPHIC

**1.020 bitmapped graphic** An image made up of dots, or pixels, and usually generated by "paint" or image-editing applications, as

1.018 *bit depth*

1.020 *bitmapped graphic*

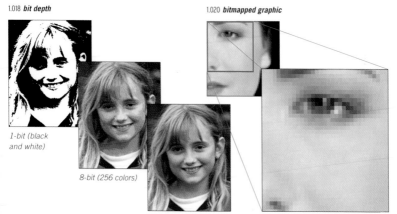

*1-bit (black and white)*

*8-bit (256 colors)*

*24-bit (16.7 million colors)*

39

COMPUTING

distinct from the vector images created by object-oriented drawing applications. → 10.160 VECTOR; 1.082 OBJECT-ORIENTED

**1.021 bitstream** A sequence of binary digits representing a flow of information being transferred from one digital device to another.

**1.022 boot / boot up / booting up** To start a computer (or computer-based device) loading the operating system and checking and allocating resources (disks, memory, and, where appropriate, peripherals). Short for "bootstrapping." More commonly called "startup" or "starting up," the process is sometimes called a "cold boot," as distinct from a "warm boot," which refers to rebooting ("restarting") the computer once it is already switched on. Restarting a computer by physically switching off the power and then switching it back on is also called a cold boot. → 1.112 STARTUP

**1.023 bug** A programming error in software that can cause the program to behave unexpectedly, erratically, or can even crash the computer. Although bugs are errors, they do remind us of the complexities of writing computer programs and the difficulties of testing every possible sequence of commands and circumstances that is likely to occur during its use. The term refers to early computing architecture when cloth insulation tended to be eaten by real bugs, causing short circuits. → 1.012 PROGRAM; 1.088 PATCH

**1.024 byte** A single group of eight binary bits (0s and 1s) that is processed as one unit. It is possible to configure eight 0s and 1s in only 256 different permutations, so a byte can represent any value between 0 and 255—the maximum number of ASCII characters, one byte being required for each. → 1.016 BIT; 3.002 ASCII

**1.025 client** In a "client/server" arrangement, such as on a network or on the Web, the client is the end-user (your computer). On the Web, your browser is a "client program," which talks to web servers. → 1.026 CLIENT/SERVER; 1.107 SERVER; 7.234 WORLD WIDE WEB (WWW); 1.152 NETWORK

**1.026 client / server** An arrangement that divides computing into two separate functions, connected by a network. The "client" is the end-user (your computer), while the server is a centralized computer

that holds and manages information or multi-user applications which other computers can access when necessary. → 1.025 CLIENT; 1.107 SERVER; 1.152 NETWORK

**1.027 clock speed** The rate at which a central processing unit (CPU) communicates with its associated circuitry and components. A processor will run at a fixed rate governed by a clock pulse generated within the unit. Measured in megahertz (MHz).

**1.028 cold boot** → 1.022 boot/boot up/booting up

**1.029 composite video** A video "bus," or signal, in which all the color information is combined, such as in the "video out" RCA jack on older VCRs (video cassette recorders). This results in loss of quality. On computer monitors quality is maintained by keeping each of the RGB color signals separate. → 4.055 RGB

**1.030 computer** An electronic device that can process data (usually binary) according to a predetermined set of variable instructions— a "program." → 10.011 BINARY; 1.012 PROGRAM

**1.031 computer-generated image (CGI)** Generic term for any artwork, image or visual composed using a computer.

**1.032 computer graphics** Generically any graphic item generated on or output by a computer, such as page layouts, typography, illustrations, etc. The term is more specifically used to refer to a particular genre of computer-generated imagery.

**1.033 computer language** The language, or code, devised to make computers work. These may be "high level"—those used for writing application programs and written so that the user (or, at least, the programmer) can understand them—or "low level" (usually binary), which only the computer can understand. → 1.012 PROGRAM; 10.011 BINARY

**1.034 data** Although strictly speaking the plural of "datum," meaning a piece of information, "data" is nowadays used as a singular noun to describe—particularly in the context of computers—more or less anything that can be stored or processed, whether it be a single bit, a chunk of text, an image, audio, and so on.

**1.035 delimit** To separate items of information, such as words, lines of text, or—in databases, for example—fields and records. This is done by placing a character (a "delimiter") at the end ("limit") of each item. Commonly used characters are generated by the tab and comma keys (to separate fields) and the return key (to separate records). Files formatted in this way are described as "delimited."

1.**036 desktop publishing (DTP)** The entire computer-based process of generating text, laying it out on a page with images, and then printing the result—in other words, publishing it. The term was originally coined when the first personal "desktop" computers to use a GUI (the Apple Lisa, which evolved into the Macintosh) were introduced, before the potential of desktop computers in the professional design and graphic arts industries was fully realized, and was thus used somewhat derogatorily by professional designers to indicate amateurism. However, the massive advances in the capabilities of the technology have consigned such views to the trash can. Also called "electronic publishing," usually to imply a more sophisticated process. → 1.399 DESKTOP COMPUTER; 1.066 MACINTOSH

1.**037 desktop (publishing) system** A collection of standard desktop hardware devices and off-the-shelf software applications capable of handling the entire desktop publishing process. As distinct from specialist equipment, such as drum scanners, used in high-end prepress systems. → 1.036 DESKTOP PUBLISHING (DTP); 1.399 DESKTOP COMPUTER

1.**038 device** An alternative term that describes any piece of hardware, but usually used to describe a piece of equipment that is peripheral to the computer itself (a "peripheral device"). → 1.044 EXTERNAL DEVICE; 1.092 PERIPHERAL DEVICE

1.**039 direct entry** Any matter which is entered into a computer directly, such as via a keyboard, rather than indirectly by some other means, such as via a scanner.

1.**040 dongle** A hardware "key" that plugs into a computer port to enable its associated software to run. Once a common method of copy-protecting software, dongles now generally accompany only very expensive, high-end applications. They tend to be frowned on by many users since they consume connection ports and can lead to consequential problems.

1.**041 download** To transfer data from a remote computer—such as an Internet server—to your own. The opposite of upload. → 1.107 SERVER; 1.188 UPLOAD

1.**042 eight-bit / 8-bit** Of display monitors or digital images—the allocation of eight data "bits" to each pixel, producing a display or image of 256 grays or colors (a row of eight bits can be written in 256 different combinations: 00000000, 00000001, 10000001, 00111100, etc.). → 1.016 BIT

1.**043 error message** A message box that automatically appears if you have attempted to do something that your computer or an application won't permit or cannot do, or, at worst, if your computer crashes. → 10.061 ERROR/RESULT CODE

1.**044 external device** Any item of hardware that is connected to a computer but resides externally—a disk drive, for example, may reside internally or externally.

1.**045 Fkey** A contraction of "function key." Fkeys have nothing to do with the special function keys on some keyboards ("F1," "F2," etc.); they are the keyboard equivalents for basic functions such as copying and pasting. → 2.026 KEYBOARD SHORTCUT; 1.429 FUNCTION KEYS

1.**046 file server** A computer that serves a network of other computers and provides central storage of files and programs. → 1.152 NETWORK

1.**047 four-bit / 4-bit** This term describes the allocation of four bits of memory to each pixel, giving an image or screen display of 16 grays or colors (a row of four bits can be written in 16 different combinations: 0000, 0001, 1001, 0110, etc.). → 1.016 BIT; 1.042 EIGHT-BIT/8-BIT

1.**048 garden wall** A security feature that can be implemented on computers to restrict Internet access to preferred sites. Normally used to prevent children from accessing sites that are deemed unsuitable, but provide them with easy access to appropriate sites. → 1.215 FIREWALL

1.**049 generic** Hardware devices, such as disk drives and printers, whose mechanisms are common to other brands.

1.**050 gigabyte (G, GB, gig)** One gigabyte is equal to 1,024 MB (megabytes). → 1.063 KILOBYTE; 1.073 MEGABYTE; 1.118 TERABYTE

1.**051 hardware** A term that describes any physical piece of equipment, generally in a computer environment; as distinct from firmware (programs built into hardware) and software (application programs). → 1.250 SOFTWARE; 1.320 FIRMWARE

1.**052 hotspot, hot spot** The specific place on the mouse pointer icon that activates the item on which it is placed.

1.**053 IBM PC** IBM personal computer; usually describes a PC made by IBM but also often used as a generic term for any PC that is "IBM compatible" (actually meaning—usually—one that runs either Microsoft's "DOS" or "Windows" operating systems), thus distinguishing them from other computers, such as Apple Computer's "Macintosh" series. → 10.082 IBM; 1.066 MACINTOSH; 1.336 MS-DOS; 1.288 WINDOWS

1.**054 iBook** Portable computer from Apple Computers, designed for the "consumer" rather than the professional market. The original iMac-inspired model was curvy and somewhat heavy but more recent models have introduced a more compact design along (depending on model) CD-R and DVD. FireWire connectivity is now standard on all models.

1.**055 icon** A graphical representation of an object (such as a disk, file, folder, or tool) or of a concept or message used to make identification and selection easier. → 1.322 GUI

1.**056 iMac** Computer produced by Apple Computers and first launched in the summer of 1998. The single-unit design houses all the principal components—monitor, processor, CD drive (latterly a DVD drive)—in one case. The advent of the iMac broke several computer "traditions." There was no floppy drive, just a CD drive, and traditional Apple connectors were rejected in favor of newer alternatives. Apple Desktop Bus connectors (for mouse and keyboard) were replaced with USB connectors, which also provide connectivity for other peripherals. Later versions also feature FireWire connections. The industrial design (variously ascribed as "futuristic" and "retro") drew controversy but also led to a high profile for the iMac. The computer was joined a year later by a portable version, the iBook.

1.**057 import / export filter** Translating a file from the host, format another format, and vice-versa. → 10.062 EXPORT; 10.089 IMPORT

1.**058 information technology (IT)** Anything to do with computers and/or telecommunications, particularly networking and databases.

1.**059 interactive mode** The ability of an application to process data as it is input, as distinct from that which is processed in batches (batch mode). For example, spelling is checked as it is input rather than later as a batch. Also called "real-time" processing. → 10.091 INTERACTIVE; 10.130 REAL-TIME

1.**060 interrupt button** On Macintosh computers, a hardware button that allows programmers to debug software.

1.**061 kilobit (kb, kbit)** One kilobit is equal to 1,024 bits. An upper case "K" represents "kilobyte" while the lower case form means "kilobit," although correct usage is inconsistent. Modem speed, for example, is often described as e.g. 65 K, when what is actually meant is 65 kilobits—which should accurately be expressed as 65 kbps. → 1.016 BIT; 1.063 KILOBYTE

1.**062 kilobits per second (Kbps)** A measurement

1.052 *hotspot, hot spot*

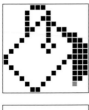
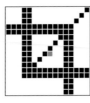

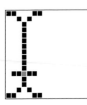

of the speed at which data is transferred across a network, a kilobit being 1,024 bits, or characters.

**.063 kilobyte (K, KB, Kbyte)** One kilobyte is equal to 1,024 bytes (8,192 bits). Since one byte represents a single character, a kilobyte is roughly equivalent to 170 words. Correctly, an upper case "K" represents "kilobyte" while the lower case form means "kilobit." → 10.098 KILO; 1.073 MEGABYTE; 1.050 GIGABYTE; 1.118 TERABYTE

**.064 laptop (computer)** A small, portable computer, as distinct from the larger "desktop" variety. The smallest examples are often called notebooks.

**.065 locked file** A data file which cannot be modified or deleted.

**.066 Macintosh** The brand name of the Apple Computer's personal computers. It was the first commercially available computer to utilize the "graphical user interface" (GUI) pioneered by Xerox Corporation's Palo Alto Research Center (PARC), although the concept was first seen in the unsuccessful "Lisa" computer. The Macintosh heralded the concept of "plug and play" computing, while the use of a GUI provided a platform for software applications which gave rise to the phenomenon of "desktop publishing" (DTP), thus revolutionizing not only the graphic design profession but the entire graphic arts industry—all in the space of 10 years. Original processors (the Motorola 68000 series) have now given way to the PowerPC RISC processors, which are faster and more powerful. The iMac introduced legacy-free technology (eschewing SCSI and serial connectors for USB, and abandoning the increasingly feeble floppy disk). Mac OS X incorporates a UNIX core for improved performance and stability. → 1.272 MAC OS; 1.322 GUI; 1.036 DESKTOP PUBLISHING (DTP)

**.067 macro** A single command (usually a keystroke or keystroke combination) that actions a series of other commands. A macro can be predefined or can be created by the user (by "recording" a sequence of commands or keystrokes and assigning it to a key or perhaps a button). Some applications have similar "events" (such as actions in Photoshop). → 1.429 FUNCTION KEYS; 5.062 ACTIONS

**.068 mainframe** A large computer system used mainly to manage vast databases where simultaneous processing of transactions is required, such as in banks or insurance companies.

**1.069 mapping** Converting data between formats, particularly databases.

**1.070 media** A plural term now accepted as covering any information or communications medium, such as "broadcast media" (television, radio, etc.) and "print media" (newspapers, magazines, etc.).

**1.071 megabit (Mb, Mbit)** 1,024 kilobits or 1,048,576 bits of data.

**1.072 megabits per second (Mbps)** A measure of data transfer speed.

**1.073 megabyte (MB, Mbyte, meg)** One megabyte is equal to 1,024 KB (kilobytes) or 1,048,576 bytes of data. → 1.063 KILOBYTE; 1.050 GIGABYTE; 1.118 TERABYTE

**1.074 megahertz (MHz)** One million hertz (or cycles, occurrences, or instructions per second), often used as an indication (not necessarily accurate) of the speed of a computer's central processing unit (CPU), and thus sometimes referred to as "clock speed."

**1.075 mouse event** The action ("event") initiated by pressing the button on your mouse. This can happen at the moment you press the button down ("mouse-down"), or when you release it ("mouse-up"). → 1.432 MOUSE

**1.076 multi-user** A qualification of a license agreement that allows more than one person to use a single piece of software.

**1.077 multimedia personal computer (MPC)** A "standard" set by the manufacturers and resellers of multimedia-capable PCs to define minimum performance capabilities.

**1.078 multitasking** The ability of a computer to do many things at once, such as run several applications simultaneously. Most PCs aren't true multitasking machines although they can usually work on several tasks or applications simultaneously by switching very rapidly from one to another (sometimes called "time-slicing"). → 1.098 PREEMPTIVE MULTITASKING

**1.079 navigate** The process of finding your way around a multimedia presentation or web site by clicking on words or buttons.

**1.080 noise** In imaging terms undesirable fluctuations or interference that (usually) affects the whole image, reducing detail representation and giving an effect similar to film grain. Small amounts of noise can be artificially added to images for creative and compositional purposes, such as with Photoshop's noise filters.

**1.081 object linking and embedding (OLE)** Microsoft technology in which a linked object—an image created in a graphics application, for example—that has been placed ("embedded") into another application, such as a page-layout, will be updated each time it is altered in the source application. An embedded object will, when "double-clicked," fire up the source application in anticipation of further editing.

**1.082 object-oriented** A software technology that uses mathematical points, based on "vectors" (information giving both magnitude and direction), to define lines and shapes, these points being the "objects" referred to. As distinct from a graphic shape as an object (an "object" in computer programming is a database of mathematical formulas). The data for each shape is stored in these points, which in turn pass information from one to another on how the paths between them should be described—as straight lines, arcs, or Bézier curves. The quality of the line between each point is determined entirely by the resolution of the output device—a line produced by an imagesetter at 2,400 dpi will be very much smoother than the same line output on a laser printer at 300 dpi or viewed on a monitor. The alternative technology for rendering computer images is that of "bitmapped" graphics, which are edited by modifying individual pixels or by turning them on or off.

**1.083 one-bit / 1-bit** Term used for display monitors and digital images. The allocation of only one "bit" to each pixel; hence an image is composed of only white or black pixels; such images have a bit depth of 1 and are often called 1-bit images (or bitmapped 1-bit images). → 1.016 BIT; 1.019 BITMAP; 1.042 EIGHT-BIT/8-BIT

**1.084 online help** A file that gives help and advice, always available while that application is being used. Also describes help available via Internet connections.

**1.085 open architecture** The facility, in the design of a computer system, for unrestricted modification and improvement of the computer and its system. Macintosh computers are not "open" in as much as the ROM chip used as the basis of the

operating system can only be used in non-Apple-manufactured machines ("clones") under license.

**1.086 original equipment manufacturer (OEM)** The manufacturer of an item that may be marketed under a different name, a common practice with disk drives. Sometimes called a "third-party" supplier. The practice is sometimes called "badge engineering."

**1.087 out-of-memory message** A message that tells you there is not enough memory (RAM) available to perform the task that you require. Typical out-of-memory messages relate to reasons such as having too many system files open (such as fonts) or a particularly memory-intensive task (especially those involving bitmapped images) exceeding available RAM. → 1.457 APPLICATION HEAP/MEMORY

**1.088 patch** A small piece of program code supplied for fixing bugs in software. → 1.023 BUG

**1.089 path (1)** The hierarchical trail through disks and folders to a particular file. → 1.090 PATHNAME

**1.090 pathname** A string of words identifying the entire path from disk to file, such as "mydisk: myfolder:myfile," indicating that the file named "myfile" is inside the folder named "myfolder" which is on the disk called "mydisk." Colons (Mac computers) or forward slashes "/" (PCs) are generally used to separate each name in the path, which is why colons or slashes should not be used in file names.

**1.091 PC** Personal computer. The name originally used to describe IBM PCs but now used to describe any personal computer that is IBM-compatible or that runs the Windows operating system. This is distinct from computers running the Mac OS although, strictly speaking, they are also personal computers.

**1.092 peripheral device** Any nonessential device attached to a computer. Scanners, digitizing tablets, and film recorders would be obvious examples. Printers and backup devices, though pretty much essential, are also usually classed as peripheral devices. → 1.038 DEVICE

**1.093 Personal Computer Memory Card International Association (PCMCIA)** A standard format for a type of expansion card used mainly in portable computers for adding features such as external devices, modems, and memory. Some digital cameras use PCMCIA cards, or adaptors that permit SmartMedia or CompactFlash cards to be used with them. Also known as "PC cards." → 1.552 SMARTMEDIA; 1.500 COMPACTFLASH

1.**094 pit** A tiny cavity burned by a laser in the surface of an optical disc. It equates to one bit of digital information.

1.**095 pixel** Acronym for picture element. The smallest component of a digitally generated image, such as a single dot of light on a computer monitor. In its simplest form, one pixel corresponds to a single bit: 0 = off, or white, and 1 = on, or black. In color or grayscale images or monitors, one pixel may correspond to several bits: An eight-bit pixel, for example, can be displayed in any of 256 colors (the total number of different configurations that can be achieved by eight 0s and 1s). → 10.139 RESOLUTION

1.**096 power filter** → 1.111 spike suppressor

1.**097 PPC** Power PC. Chip from the Apple/IBM/Motorola alliance, used in Power Macintosh computers and elsewhere. The PPC is a RISC chip, and the latest variants used by Apple are the G3 and G4 models.

1.**098 preemptive multitasking** A form of multitasking wherein the processor periodically passes control to a waiting application, preventing any single process from monopolizing the processor. Tasks are prioritized to ensure every task gets the appropriate resources at the right time. → 1.078 MULTITASKING

1.**099 property** The attributes of a digital object, size, position, color, orientation, etc.

1.**100 QWERTY** The standard typewriter-based keyboard layout used by most computer keyboards. The name comes from the first six characters of the top row of letter keys.

1.**101 random access** Digital data that can be retrieved at random, such as from a disk or from memory, as distinct from data, which can only be retrieved sequentially, such as from a tape.

1.**102 raster image processor (RIP)** A hardware device or software that converts data generated by a page description language, such as PostScript, into a form that can be output by an (often) high-resolution imagesetter for use in commercial printing. RIPs can also allow midrange bubblejet printers (for example) to output PostScript pages. → 10.129 RASTER(IZATION)

1.**103 read only** Disks, memory, and documents which can only be read from.

1.**104 reboot** To reload a computer's operating system (or an application) into memory. This can be achieved by either switching the power off ("shutting down") and switching it on again ("cold boot"), or by using the "Restart" command, if available ("warm boot"). Also referred to as a "restart." → 1.022 BOOT/BOOT UP/BOOTING UP; 1.112 STARTUP

1.**105 scalar processor architecture (SPARC)** A powerful microprocessor developed by Sun Microsystems. Forms the basis of the UNIX operating system and is embodied in Sun's SPARCstation computer workstations. → 1.357 UNIX

1.**106 scan mode** Option offered by most scanners (and, in particular, virtually all flatbed scanners). Choose between black-and-white line art (for diagrams and illustrations with no intermediate gray tones), grayscale (for monochrome images and diagrams), or color. Note that a color image file will be around three times the size of a grayscale one.

1.**107 server** A networked computer that serves client computers, providing a central location for files and services, and typically handling such things as e-mail and web access. → 1.026 CLIENT/SERVER; 1.025 CLIENT

1.**108 shut down** To switch off your computer in a safe manner. Any open application will prompt you to save any unsaved documents.

1.**109 source (1)** Any document, file, disk, etc., which is original, as opposed to a copy.

1.**110 source (2)** Documents, files, disks, etc., from which copied, transmitted, or linked data originates. As distinct from the "target," or destination, of such data. → 1.117 TARGET

1.**111 spike suppressor** A device installed in the inline power supply of computing equipment. Its function is to eliminate power surges and voltage fluctuations. Also called a "surge suppressor" or "power filter."

1.**112 startup** The process of turning on the power to a computer, and the startup procedure it goes through during which a number of checks are made—such as checking the RAM—and in which the operating system is loaded into memory. If there is a fault it will be reported accordingly, or the computer may fail to start altogether. Also called "booting up." → 1.022 BOOT/BOOT UP/BOOTING UP; 1.104 REBOOT

1.**113 startup disk** Any hard drive, floppy disk, Zip disk, or CD containing an operating system and used to start up a computer. Also called a "boot disk." In contemporary computers this is normally the hard disk. → 1.112 STARTUP

1.**114 style sheet** In applications such as those used for page-layout and the construction of HTML pages, the facility to apply a range of specific, frequently-used attributes such as typographic or graphic formats to text and graphic elements in a document.

1.**115 syntax** In programming languages, such as those used for creating multimedia presentations and HTML documents for the Web, syntax describes the correct use of the programming language according to a given set of rules. → 7.151 HTML; 1.254 SYNTAX CHECKER

1.**116 system** The complete configuration of software and hardware components necessary to perform electronic processing operations. Also a now-redundant term for operating systems in Macintosh computers.

1.**117 target** A description of where documents, files, disks, etc., are being copied, transmitted, or linked to, as distinct from the source from whence they originated. Also known as the "destination." → 1.110 SOURCE (2)

1.**118 terabyte** One terabyte is equal to 1,024 GB (gigabytes) or 1,048,576 MB (megabytes) of data. → 1.063 KILOBYTE; 1.073 MEGABYTE; 1.050 GIGABYTE

1.**119 upgrade** To modify or enhance the performance or capabilities of a computer either by adding more memory or an accelerator card, for example, or by installing a newer version of the operating system or application software.

1.**120 virus** A computer program that is deliberately (and illegally) written to alter or disrupt the normal operation of a computer. Viruses are spread from computer to computer across networks, via the Internet (increasingly), or simply via floppy disks. A virus may infect some files, but not others (an application, perhaps, but not documents), and they manifest themselves in different ways, sometimes innocuously by, for example, simply beeping, displaying a message, or causing strange behavior, or sometimes cataclysmically by deleting files or even an entire hard disk. → 1.260 VIRUS PROTECTION UTILITY/PROGRAM

1.**121 word** A term used to describe a number of bits (usually two bytes). → 1.016 BIT; 1.024 BYTE

1.**122 workstation** Any single computer that may or may not be on a network but which is dedicated to one person's use. Also used specifically for a powerful computer—often UNIX-based—which is typically used for applications such as advanced image editing, CAD/CAM and 3D applications. High processor speeds and large RAM memory allocations often characterize these computer systems.

## Hardware and communications

1.**123 Apple Desktop Bus** (**ADB**) The standard connection bus on Macintosh computers, until the advent of the iMac and G3

1.114 *style sheet*

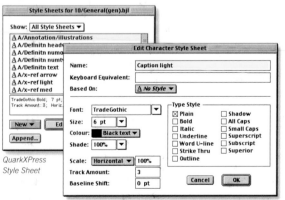

*QuarkXPress Style Sheet*

*Photoshop Styles*

desktops, for connecting input devices such as the mouse, keyboard, digitizing tablets, etc. Surplanted in more recent machines by Universal Serial Bus (USB) connectors. ➔ 1.187 UNIVERSAL SERIAL BUS (USB)

**1.124 AppleTalk** Apple's machine-to-machine networking standard, which is built into the Mac OS and enables a computer to communicate with other computers, or with hardware devices such as printers, across a network. The hardware cabling used to connect computers via AppleTalk can be LocalTalk or Ethernet. ➔ 1.152 NETWORK; 1.147 LOCALTALK; 1.136 ETHERNET

**1.125 asynchronous transfer mode (ATM)** A very fast communications technology in which data can be transferred at rates of up to 24 gigabits per second.

**1.126 bandwidth** The measure of the speed at which information is passed between two points, which may be between modems, across a "bus," or from memory to disk—the broader the bandwidth, the faster data flows. Bandwidth is usually measured in cycles per second (hertz) or in bits per second (bps).

**1.127 daemon** Special networking software, used mostly on computers running the UNIX operating system, which handles requests from users, e.g. for e-mail, the World Wide Web, and other Internet services. ➔ 1.357 UNIX; 1.339 OPERATING SYSTEM; 7.125 E-MAIL; 7.234 WORLD WIDE WEB (WWW); 7.158 INTERNET

**1.128 daisy-chain** The linking together, in a line, of computer hardware devices. Networked devices such as printers and disk drives are typically daisy-chained to a computer, usually using SCSI, USB, or FireWire interfaces. ➔ 1.152 NETWORK

**1.129 data bits** An expression used in data transmission to distinguish bits containing the data being transmitted from bits giving instructions on how the data is to be transmitted. ➔ 1.016 BIT; 7.218 TRANSMISSION CONTROL PROTOCOL (TCP)

**1.130 data bus** The path, or circuitry, along which data is transmitted by a processor, as distinct from the circuitry used by the processor to handle memory. ➔ 1.468 MEMORY

**1.131 data transfer rate** The speed at which data is transferred between devices, but generally referring to its transfer from a disk drive into computer memory; usually measured in megabytes per second. ➔ 1.468 MEMORY; 1.073 MEGABYTE; 1.522 INTERLEAVE RATIO

**1.132 digital switch port (DSP)** A port that can be switched between peripheral devices on command from a computer. As opposed to a manual switch port, which needs manual intervention; and physical switching between connections. ➔ 1.164 PORT

**1.133 dock** To connect one device—usually a computer—to another. Usually used to described the connection of a laptop to a desktop system or a laptop to a "base unit" (also often called a docking station).

**1.134 error correction (code)** The transmission of a data code using an encoding method that enables errors that occur en-route to be detected and (usually) corrected. Error correction techniques are used in conventional modems that are prone to electronic interference that can corrupt data.

**1.135 error correction (protocol)** A method of checking the integrity of modem data transmission. A "parity" error check is typical, where seven bits of data are transmitted, followed by an eighth, which indicates whether the sum of the previous seven should be odd or even. If a discrepancy occurs the data will be retransmitted.

**1.136 Ethernet** A hardware connection standard used on local area networks (LANs) which offers fast data transfer. ➔ 1.152 NETWORK; 1.146 LAN

**1.137 file transfer** The transmission of a file from one computer to another either over a network or telecommunication lines, using a modem. ➔ 1.152 NETWORK; 1.150 MODEM

**1.138 FireWire** Apple Computer's name for the IEEE 1394 bus standard. FireWire allows high-speed communications between the computer and peripherals, such as external hard disks, CD writers, and digital movie cameras. Sony (and others) include FireWire links on many of their cameras. Sony refer to the connector as iLink. Data transfer rates as high as 400 Mbps are possible.

**1.139 flow control** A method of organizing the flow of data as it is transmitted via a modem or across a network.

**1.140 gateway** A device or program used to connect disparate computer networks. ➔ 1.152 NETWORK; 1.169 ROUTER

**1.141 global system for mobile communications (GSM)** A telecommunication standard used increasingly throughout the world.

**1.142 handshake** The procedure whereby two networked computers or other devices

47

introduce themselves to each other when initial contact is made. this means that each device can establish data transmission protocols. → 1.167 PROTOCOL

**1.143 high-definition television** (**HDTV**) Nominally defined as television pictures featuring twice the conventional number of horizontal scanning lines (i.e. around 1,100), and a similar increase in horizontal resolution, compared with conventional television pictures. → 4.061 SMPTE

**1.144 iLink** Sony's proprietary name for the IEEE 1394 bus standard, implemented as FireWire on some computer systems. → 1.138 FIREWIRE

**1.145 internal modem** A modem that is installed inside, or integrated with, a computer. → 1.150 MODEM

**1.146 local area network** (**LAN**) A collection of hardware devices in a small ("local") area—one room, say—linked together via appropriate connections and software. At its simplest, a LAN may be a single computer linked to a printer. → 1.152 NETWORK

**1.147 LocalTalk** Apple's proprietary networking system, which was used prior to the release of the iMac and G3 computers. It used a derivation of telephone-type cables for (generally) low-speed networking.

**1.148 log on** To connect to a network. Usually requires a userame and, generally, a password.

**1.149 mips** Acronym for million instructions per second. Usually used in the context of processor speeds. → 10.078 HERTZ (Hz); 1.415 PROCESSOR (CHIP)

**1.150 modem** Acronym for modulator-demulator. A device that converts digital data to analog for transfer from one computer to another via standard telephone lines. The receiving modem converts it back again. Also used (incorrectly) to describe all-digital IDSN and ADSL terminal adaptors.

**1.151 multiplex(ing)** The simultaneous transmission of many messages concurrently along a single channel.

**1.152 network** Any connection of computers and (usually) peripherals designed to share resources and information. Local area networks (LANs) are networks within (typically) a single building; wide area networks (WANs) spread across multiple sites (for example, company sites).

**1.153 network link** The part of the network that forms the link between your computer and the network itself, such as a telephone line or Ethernet cable.

**1.154 node** (**1**) The name given to any device connected to a network, such as a computer, printer, or server.

**1.155 nodename** Identifies an individual computer on a network or the Internet.

**1.156 null modem cable** A communications link between two computers, over a short distance, without using a modem (null = nonexistent). Sometimes called a crossover cable since the internal wiring connects the output of one to the input of the other.

**1.157 offline** Work done on a computer with access to a network or the Internet but not while actually connected to the network. The opposite of online. → 1.158 ONLINE

**1.158 online** Any activity taking place on a computer or device while it is connected to a network such as the Internet. When the connection is broken the device is described as being offline. → 1.157 OFFLINE

**1.159 packet** A bundle of data—the basic unit transmitted across networks. When data is sent over a network such as the Internet it is broken up into small chunks called packets, which are sent independently of each other.

**1.160 parallel interface** A PC computer connection in which packets of data are transmitted simultaneously in the same direction along a single cable. As distinct from serial interface in which data packets are transmitted sequentially, one at a time. "Average" in terms of data transmission, it can handle data at around 1.5 Mb/sec. Gradually being superseded by USB and FireWire connectors. → 1.178 SERIAL INTERFACE

**1.161 parity bit** An extra bit of data used to verify that the bits received by one communications device match those transmitted by another. → 1.016 BIT

**1.162 peer-to-peer** A network system in which files are spread around different computers, the users of which access them from each other rather than from a central "server."

**1.163 peripheral cable** A cable that connects a peripheral device to a computer. Different cables are required for different connection types, such as SCSI, parallel, serial, ADB, USB and FireWire.

**1.164 port** A socket in a computer or device into which other devices are plugged.

**1.165 port address** The precise "address" (of the

program on the receiving end) to which data is delivered by a remote computer on a network.

**.166 printer port** The socket through which a computer is connected to a printer or, on Macintosh computers, a network or modem. Newer computers (both PC and Macintosh) now tend to offer USB connections to printers.

**.167 protocol** A set of mutual rules that hardware and software must observe in order to communicate with one another.

**.168 resource** A system file that provides information to the central processing unit so that it can communicate with a peripheral device.

**.169 router** An interface between groups of distinct, individual networks. → 1.140 GATEWAY

**.170 RS232** The formal designation of the PC serial connection used in computers and computer-based equipment for data transfer.

**1.171 SCSI bus** The data path which links SCSI devices to a computer. → 1.180 SCSI

**1.172 SCSI chain** Sequential linking of a number of SCSI devices to a computer. Also called a "daisy-chain." → 1.128 DAISY-CHAIN; 1.180 SCSI

**1.173 SCSI device** A device such as a disk drive or scanner that can be attached to a computer by means of a SCSI connection. SCSI devices may be inside the computer ("internal device") or outside ("external device"). Such devices can be for input (such as scanners), storage (disks), or output. → 1.180 SCSI; 1.038 DEVICE

**1.174 SCSI ID (number)** The identifying number or "address" assigned to each SCSI device

attached to a computer. Each number must be unique. → 1.401 DIP SWITCH; 1.172 SCSI CHAIN; 1.173 SCSI DEVICE

**1.175 SCSI port** The point at which the SCSI chain connects to the computer by means of a connecting plug. SCSI ports can be of the 25-pin or 50-pin variety. The devices being connected almost always have 50-pin ports, while some computers (Macintosh, for example) have 25-pin ports. → 1.180 SCSI

**1.176 SCSI terminator** A device for protecting the SCSI bus from "signal echo," which can corrupt data transfer. It is placed at the end of a SCSI chain, although some SCSI devices are self-terminating. → 1.180 SCSI; 1.172 SCSI CHAIN

**1.177 serial** The process of transmitting data sequentially, or consecutively in a sequence, as opposed to simultaneously.

**1.178 serial interface** The connection between computer hardware devices in which data is transmitted sequentially, one bit at a time. → 1.160 PARALLEL INTERFACE

**1.179 serial port** The socket, or port, on a computer, used for the connection of devices which use a serial interface—modems or printers, for example. → 1.178 SERIAL INTERFACE

**1.180 small computer system interface (SCSI)** (pron.: "skuzzy") A computer industry standard for interconnecting peripheral devices such as hard disk drives and scanners.

**1.181 start bit** A single bit used in data communication to indicate the beginning of transmission. → 1.016 BIT; 1.182 STOP BIT

**1.182 stop bit** The data bit which indicates the

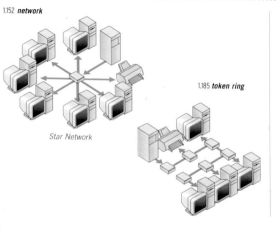

1.152 *network*

1.185 *token ring*

Star Network

1.164 *port*

1.180 *SCSI*

1.136 *Ethernet*

<•—•>

1.187 *USB*

1.138 *FireWire*

1.177 *Serial*

end of one byte in data transmission. → 1.181 START BIT

**1.183 synchronous communication / transmission** High-speed data transmission whereby data is sent in chunks between rigid electronic synchronizing signals.

**1.184 terminal** Any device used to communicate with another computer via a network. Terminals can sometimes be computers themselves; "dumb" terminals merely pass keystrokes (or other inputs) directly to the main, host computer. → 1.152 NETWORK

**1.185 token ring** A method of linking computers in a ring network. Data can only be sent from one to another after a digital code or token is transmitted from one computer to the next. → 1.146 LAN; 7.233 WAN

**1.186 twin processor** The use of two principal processing (CPU) chips in a single computer. Currently employed by Apple with their twin processor G4 computers. → 1.392 CENTRAL PROCESSING UNIT (CPU); 1.406 G4

**1.187 Universal Serial Bus (USB)** A port (socket) for connecting to your computer peripheral devices that can be daisy-chained together. These can include devices such as scanners, printers, keyboards, and hard drives. → 1.179 SERIAL PORT; 1.164 PORT; 1.128 DAISY-CHAIN; 1.092 PERIPHERAL DEVICE

**1.188 upload** To send data from your computer to a distant computer such as a server. The opposite of download. When an e-mail message is sent, it is uploaded to an e-mail server. The recipient then downloads it to his or her computer. → 1.041 DOWNLOAD

**1.189 USB-to-SCSI converter** A connector enabling devices originally built for SCSI operation to be connected to and used with a USB-enabled computer. Generally requires special software drivers for correct operation. These allow users of newer computers to retain and use their earlier devices, although performance tends to be compromised to some degree (the USB data rate is lower than the SCSI data rate). → 1.187 USB

## Software and application terms

**1.190 Adobe Acrobat** An Adobe application for producing documents that can subsequently be viewed on any computer or computing platform that is equipped with the Acrobat Reader software, irrespective of the operating system or font availability. Files

created by Acrobat are called PDF (portable document format) files. Documents can include text, images, and graphics. Fonts not supported by the host computer can be reproduced. → 3.044 PDF

**1.191 Adobe Illustrator** Adobe's vector-based graphics program, with an interface very similar to Photoshop's. Although Illustrator is vector based, it can exchange items with Photoshop. For example, clipping paths created in Photoshop can be transposed to Illustrator to provide an image with transparent areas. → 1.195 ADOBE PHOTOSHOP

**1.192 Adobe ImageReady** Photoshop sibling optimized for the creation of web graphics.

**1.193 Adobe InDesign** A powerful desktop publishing and page-layout program from Adobe, designed as a competitor for the long-established Quark Xpress package. It features an interface similar to that in Photoshop and Illustrator.

**1.194 Adobe PageMaker** A page layout and desktop publishing program from Adobe. Somewhat eclipsed now by Adobe's latest offering, InDesign. → 1.193 ADOBE INDESIGN

**1.195 Adobe Photoshop** Adobe's pixel-based image-editing program, and an industry standard tool.

**1.196 Adobe Premiere** Adobe's video editing program.

**1.197 Adobe Type Manager (ATM)** A utility for managing, displaying, and printing fonts. ATM improves the display (and printing, on non-PostScript printers) of PostScript Type 1 fonts by using the outlines contained within their corresponding printer files, rather than relying on the jagged, inelegant appearance of screen fonts.

**1.198 Apple File Exchange (AFE)** Feature of the Mac OS that enables files created on Windows PCs (or other computers) to be recognized and opened by a corresponding Mac OS application.

**1.199 AppleShare** A standard feature of the Mac OS which allows computers to share files across a network. → 1.152 NETWORK

**1.200 beta test copy** Version of software released to selected users (usually those very fluent in the application)—after initial testing (alpha testing) and prior to commercial release—for testing to eliminate errors ("debugging"). Sometimes called a beta version.

**1.201 C / C++** A family of structured programming languages. The original C version appeared in the early 1970s and was implemented (largely) on UNIX computers. The more versatile C++ appeared a decade later and was adopted by a number of platforms, notably Sun and Apple. ➔ 1.012 PROGRAM

1.**202 code** The instructions in a piece of software that tell the computer what to do. Code can take various forms, from "binary code"—a series of 1s and 0s, which is actually the form all code must take for the computer to understand it—to programming languages and "scripts"—code which is written in a sort of English so that the user can understand it. HTML is a programming code written for web browsers. ➔ 7.151 HTML; 1.395 COMPILER; 1.326 INTERPRETER; 7.109 BROWSER; 1.265 APPLESCRIPT

1.**203 copy-protected** Software that is made in order to prevent its unauthorized use. This is achieved either by software "encryption" (embedding it with a unique serial number) or, in extreme cases—and especially where very expensive software is concerned— protecting it with a hardware "dongle" (a device that must be plugged into your computer in order for the application to work). ➔ 10.059 ENCRYPTION; 1.040 DONGLE

1.**204 cut** A feature that allows you to remove an item from a location in a document, at the same time copying it to the clipboard so that it can be "pasted" elsewhere. As distinct from "copy," which places the item on the clipboard while leaving the original where it is. ➔ 1.297 CLIPBOARD; 1.205 CUT AND PASTE; 1.302 COPY (2)

1.**205 cut and paste** The process of removing an item from a document ("cutting" the item, which places it on the "clipboard") and then placing it elsewhere ("pasting" it), either in the same or a different document. ➔ 1.204 CUT; 1.297 CLIPBOARD; 1.302 COPY (2)

1.**206 data processing** The systematic processing of information, whether it be sorting text or batch processing images.

1.**207 database** Information stored on a computer in a systematic fashion and thus retrievable. This generally means files in which you can store any amount of data in separate but consistent categories (called "fields") for each type of information, such as names, addresses, and telephone numbers. The electronic version of a card index system (each card is called a "record"), databases are constructed with applications called "database managers," which allow you to organize information any way you like. Relational databases allow complex data manipulation between multidimensional arrays of data. ➔ 1.208 DATABASE MANAGER; 1.243 RECORD; 1.214 FIELD

1.**208 database manager** An application for constructing databases, allowing you to define, enter, search, sort, and output information. Database managers can be "flat-file," in which information can be created and accessed only in a single, self-contained database, or "relational," in which information can be shared and exchanged across separate databases. Other database managers contain predefined fields (but are unmodifiable) for a specific purpose, such as in contact managers (electronic address

1.207 *database*

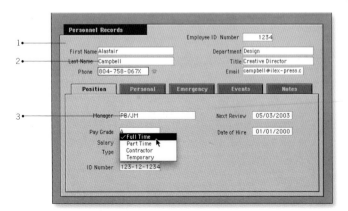

Personnel Records

Employee ID Number 1234

1 • First Name Alastair
2 • Last Name Campbell

Department Design
Title Creative Director

Phone 804-758-067X

Email campbell@ilex-press.c

| Position | Personal | Emergency | Events | Notes |

3 • Manager PB/JM

Pay Grade A
Salary
Type

✓ Full Time
Part Time
Contractor
Temporary

ID Number 123-12-1234

Next Review 05/03/2003

Date of Hire 01/01/2000

1 *Record*
2 *Field*
3 *Data*

books). Database managers are also known as "database engines," "database management systems" (DBMS), or even as a "database." → 1.216 FLAT-FILE DATABASE; 1.244 RELATIONAL DATABASE; 1.207 DATABASE

1.**209 debug(ging)** The process (often long and complex) of hunting out and correcting programming errors in computer software. → 1.023 BUG

1.**210 device independent** Any software that controls the preparation or output of pages or images regardless of the hardware device on which they are prepared or output. PostScript, for example, is a device-independent page description language (software that describes to a printer how the content of a page is to be arranged when it is output).

1.**211 drag-and-drop** A feature of some operating systems and applications that enables you to select an item such as a picture box or passage of text in one location, and move or copy it to another simply by "dragging" it with the mouse button held down and then "dropping" it in the desired location by releasing the mouse button.

1.**212 draw(ing) application** Drawing applications can be defined as those that are object-oriented (they use "vectors" to mathematically define lines and shapes), as distinct from Photoshop (and its compatriates), which use pixels to make images ("bitmapped graphics")—though some applications can combine both methodologies. → 1.231 PAINT(ING) APPLICATION

1.**213 driver / device driver** A small piece of

software that tells a computer how to handle or operate a piece of hardware, such as a printer, scanner, or disk drive. Depending on its function, a driver may be located with the operating system software and therefore loaded at startup, or it may form a "plug-in" to an application (as with some scanner drivers, for example). → 6.060 PLUG-IN

1.**214 field** In documents and dialog boxes, the term generally describing any self-contained area into which data is entered. In some applications, such as databases and spreadsheets, a field generally interacts with another field in the same (or another) record, or with the same field in another record. → 1.207 DATABASE; 1.253 SPREADSHEET; 3.008 DIF

1.**215 firewall** A software security system that protects web sites and networks from unauthorized access. → 1.048 GARDEN WALL

1.**216 flat-file database** A database application (a type of filing system that enables you to organize information such as names and addresses) in which each file—or collection of "records"—is self-contained and cannot exchange information with another file. As distinct from a "relational" database in which information in separate files is interchangeable. → 1.207 DATABASE; 1.208 DATABASE MANAGER; 1.244 RELATIONAL DATABASE; 1.243 RECORD

1.**217 foreground application** When working on a computer, the application that is currently active.

1.**218 freeware** Any piece of software that is declared by its author to be in the public domain and free of copyright restrictions, as

1.212 *draw(ing) application*

1.222 *image-editing application*

distinct from shareware or commercial software. → 1.249 SHAREWARE

1.**219 group** A feature of some graphics applications in which several selected items can be combined so that all can be moved around together, or so that a single command can be applied to all the items in the group. Reverting a group back to individual items is called "ungrouping."

1.**220 high-level language** Any programming language that is based as closely as possible on English rather than machine code. → 1.227 MACHINE CODE

1.**221 image analysis software** Software designed to extract quantitative information from an image. Though image-editing packages emulate some of the techniques and can give some similar results, this is a specialized field designed for studying (say) the texture or characteristics of the subject of an image.

1.**222 image-editing application** A computer application such as Photoshop for manipulating either scanned or user-generated images. Image-editing applications are pixel-based ("bitmapped" as opposed to "vector"), and provide features for preparing images for process color printing (such as color separations), as well as tools for painting and "filters" for applying special effects. Also called an "image-manipulation program" or "paint program" (although the term paint program is usually applied simpler graphics programs with limited image-editing features).

1.**223 insertion point** The point in a document or

dialog box at which the next character or action typed on the keyboard will appear. It is indicated by a blinking vertical line ("text insertion bar") which can be positioned in the appropriate place by using the pointer and clicking.

1.**224 install** To add any item of software to a computer so that it can be used. This is invariably achieved by means of an installer program, which puts files in their appropriate places. → 1.324 INSTALLER

1.**225 Java** A programming language originated by Sun Microsystems for creating small applications ("applets"), which can be downloaded from a web server to a user's computer to add dynamic effects such as animations. → 1.011 APPLET; 7.109 BROWSER

1.**226 launch** To open, or start, a software application. You can do this by (a) double-clicking on the application's icon; (b) highlighting the icon and choosing "Open" from the File menu or "Start;" or (c) use either (a) or (b) to open a document created in that application. Some applications will only permit you to open a document from within the application, i.e. you have to launch the application itself and then use the "Open" command to access the document.

1.**227 machine code** The lowest level of programming code; it is easily understood by the computer and is normally generated directly or indirectly by a computer program. → 1.202 CODE

1.**228 marching ants** Colloquial description for an active marquee. The moving alternate white/black bands look like ants walking

1.219 *group*

1.231 *paint(ing) application*

around the selection. → 2.106 SELECTION MARQUEE/RECTANGLE/BOX; 6.028 SELECTION

1.**229 multiple selected items** The selection of two or more items so that they can be modified or moved as one—for example, move, group, or resize. → 1.219 GROUP

1.**230 optical character recognition (OCR)** A means of inputting copy without "keying" it in. This is achieved with software which, when used with a scanner or "page reader," converts typescript into editable digital text.

1.**231 paint(ing) application** Applications that use bitmaps of pixels to create images rather than the "vectors" that describe lines in drawing applications (called "object-oriented"), although some applications combine both. Photoshop is a painting application. → 10.160 VECTOR

1.**232 Pascal** High-level programming language. → 1.240 PROGRAMMING LANGUAGE

1.**233 paste** A command that places a copied item (which might be text, a graphic, image, or something else) in a destination document. → 1.302 COPY (2); 1.204 CUT; 1.297 CLIPBOARD; 1.205 CUT AND PASTE

1.**234 Perl** A programming language much favored for creating CGI programs and source for some components of Mac OS X. → 7.116 CGI (1)

1.**235 Photoshop Elements** A version of Adobe Photoshop designed to sit between Adobe's entry-level consumer program Photodeluxe and the "full" Photoshop, offering features specifically designed for the amateur digital photographer, such as Back Light, Fill Flash, and Red Eye. Some of Photoshop's prepress

elements have been sacrificed (it does not support CMYK color) and it does not feature a Bézier curve tool, QuickMask, or Layer Masking. Also omitted are the History Brush (although there is still a History palette), the Curves dialog box, and some more advanced features such as Channels and layer "blend if" controls. These shortfalls are made up for by comprehensive help and tutorial support. The interface is similar to that of full-blown Photoshop, but simplified.

1.**236 PostScript** Adobe Systems Inc.'s proprietary "page description language" (PDL) for image output to laser printers and high-resolution imagesetters. → 9.112 PAGE DESCRIPTION LANGUAGE (PDL)

1.**237 PostScript interpreter** The code used by printing devices to understand PostScript instructions. → 1.326 INTERPRETER

1.**238 preferences** A folder that contains the user's preferences for that program. For example, in Photoshop the preferred cursor type is stored here. The preferences are automatically configured each time the program is started. → 2.245 PREFERENCES

1.**239 program defaults** Program settings that were configured at the time of installation. These include screen layouts, palette positions, and colors. However, appearance features can also be modified by the user. Often there is a "Reset Defaults" option that will reset these settings to their original "factory" settings.

1.**240 programming language** Special languages devised for writing computer software. Programming languages are either "high-

1.235 *Photoshop Elements*

level" (based as closely as possible on English), or "machine code," the lowest level (the least like English but the easiest for a computer to understand). Typical languages include BASIC, C++, FORTRAN, and Pascal. → 1.220 HIGH-LEVEL LANGUAGE; 1.227 MACHINE CODE

1.**241 Quark Xpress** Industry standard publishing tool. It provides advanced page layout features in an architecture similar to that of Photoshop, in that it offers users the opportunity to add plug-ins to extend and enhance the basic functionality. Quark Xpress Passport extends the basic Xpress program into a multilanguage publishing tool.

1.**242 QuickTime** Apple's software program and system extension that enables computers running either Windows or a Mac OS to play movie and sound files, particularly over the Internet and in multimedia applications. It provides cut, copy, and paste features for moving images and automatic compression and decompression of image files. → 3.062 CODEC; 3.003 AVI

1.**243 record** An individual entry on one subject—such as a person—in a database, comprising a set of related fields, such as that person's name, address, and telephone number. → 1.207 DATABASE; 1.208 DATABASE MANAGER

1.**244 relational database** A database application in which the information in separate files—completely different "address books," for example—is interchangeable. As distinct from a "flat-file" database in which each file

is self-contained and cannot exchange information with another file. → 1.207 DATABASE; 1.208 DATABASE MANAGER; 1.216 FLAT-FILE DATABASE

1.**245 release version** A software program that is finally ready for general sale; produced after the initial alpha tested version (normally tested in-house) and the more extensively beta tested version (usually tested using large, experienced user groups). → 1.200 BETA TEST COPY

1.**246 search path** The route taken by software when it looks for a file. → 7.198 SEARCH ENGINE

1.**247 segment** A part of an application. Several segments may make up an application; not all of these segments need to be in RAM at the same time. → 1.012 APPLICATION/APPLICATION PROGRAM

1.**248 select(ing)** The choosing of an item, such as a piece of text, graphic symbol, or icon, in order for it to be altered, moved, or manipulated. Any item must be selected, or made active, before its state can be altered in any way. If no part of a document has been selected, but a function such as a spelling check is requested, some applications will check the entire document for spelling. An item is selected by clicking on it, dragging across it, or using a command such as "Select All," depending on the circumstances.

1.**249 shareware** Software that is available through user groups, magazine cover disks, etc., which is usually only paid for by those users who decide to continue using it. Although shareware is not "copy protected"

1.238 *preferences*

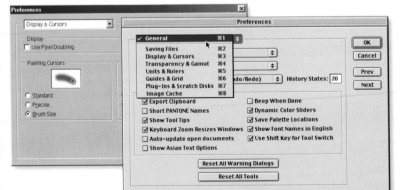

it is nonetheless protected by copyright and a fee is normally payable for using it, unlike "freeware." → 1.218 FREEWARE

**1.250 software** Specially written "pieces" of data, called programs, which make it possible for a computer or any other item of computer-related hardware to perform its tasks. Software comes in the form of the operating system and related files ("extensions"), which make your computer work, utilities for performing specific day-to-day work such as virus-checking and backups, and applications that are used to produce work, whether it be page–layout (for which you may use e.g. Adobe InDesign or Quark XPress), image manipulation (Adobe Photoshop), drawing (Adobe Illustrator or Macromedia FreeHand), or word processing (Microsoft Word). → 1.012 APPLICATION/APPLICATION PROGRAM; 1.051 HARDWARE

**1.251 Software Developers Kit (SDK)** A kit containing information and special software to help programmers write programs for a particular software product.

**1.252 spool / spooler / spooling** Software that intercepts data on its way to another computer or device and temporarily stores it on disk until the target device, such as a printer, is available, thus allowing you to carry on working. As distinct from a "buffer," which is temporary storage in memory. → 1.460 BUFFER

**1.253 spreadsheet** An application that enables you to make complex calculations to almost any user-defined criteria. A spreadsheet places the information being manipulated in a table of rows and columns, and the spaces in the grid, known as "cells," can be moved and mathematically manipulated. Some spreadsheet applications will also generate graphics (three-dimensional ones in some cases) from the data entered into cells. Microsoft Excel and Lotus 1-2-3 are typical commercial examples. → 3.008 DIF

**1.254 syntax checker** A program that checks a programmer's use of a particular programming language against the rules set for that language. → 1.115 SYNTAX

**1.255 terminal emulation** Software that allows your computer to mimic another (remote) computer by acting as a terminal for the other machine—in other words it is as though you are actually working on that remote computer. → 1.184 TERMINAL

**1.256 text editor** Any application, such as a word-processing application, used to enter and edit text and characters only.

**1.257 tool** A feature of most graphics applications, the piece of kit with which you perform specific tasks. A tool is a function represented by an icon which, when selected, is then used to perform the designated task, i.e. you use a brush tool for painting in Photoshop.

**1.258 user-specified defaults** Program defaults that have been specified or modified by the user; as distinct from "factory" defaults, which are those that have been defined at the time of manufacture. Most programs feature a "reset default" that enables them to be reset to the factory settings.

1.257 *tool*

*By clicking on a tool alternative settings (where available) or options are displayed. Similar tool functions in different applications generally use the same icon vernacular.*

1.**259 utility (program)** A program that enhances or supports the way you use your computer generally, as distinct from those programs which enable you to do work specifically ("applications"). Typical utilities are programs for backup, font management, file-finding, disk management, and file recovery, plus plug-ins, screen savers, etc.

1.**260 virus protection utility / program** A utility program designed to at least alert you to the fact that a disk or file is infected and, at best, to eradicate the virus and prevent any other possible infections. There are many such utilities available, both commercial and shareware. → 1.120 VIRUS

1.**261 word processor** A software program used to create, store, retrieve, and edit text, providing features for checking spelling, indexing, sorting, etc. A word processor also describes special computers dedicated to achieving the above. More advanced word processors allow the inclusion of images and graphics to provide limited desktop publishing features. → 1.256 TEXT EDITOR

1.**262 zoom** A feature of some applications that enables you to enlarge a portion of an image, making it easier to see and work with. The Zoom tool in Photoshop is denoted by the spyglass icon on the Toolbar. → 2.114 ZOOM TOOL

## Macintosh Operating System

1.**263 alias** A duplicate file icon on Mac OS computers. Because it is a copy, but not of the file itself, an alias occupies very little space. It is used as a means of convenient access to a file, which may be buried deep in the file hierarchy or reside on a different, networked computer. On the Windows OS the shortcut feature has a similar action. → 1.152 NETWORK; 1.286 SHORTCUT

1.**264 Apple menu** A menu item on a Macintosh computer, identified by the Apple logo, which is available in all applications and where, among other things, information on memory usage and open applications can be gathered. The advent of Mac OS X sees the functions of the Apple menu divested to other components of the new interface.

1.**265 AppleScript** The scripting feature built into the Mac OS that allows the user to write scripts that will automate common tasks. Many applications support AppleScript, enabling scripts to perform automatic operations within those programs. Analogous to macros. → 1.067 MACRO

1.**266 Aqua** The interface used for Mac OS X. The screen layout follows much of the traditional Mac interface "rules" but adds improved graphics (thanks to Quartz), a "Dock" for placing frequently-used applications and a more fluid appearance. → 1.277 QUARTZ; 1.270 DOCK; 1.275 OS X

1.**267 Classic (environment)** An operating environment within Mac OS X that emulates an OS 9 environment. Enables applications not specifically engineered for OS X to be used on an OS X computer. Photoshop versions up to and including 6.0 must operate in the Classic environment.

1.**268 Command key** Macintosh key sometimes called the "Apple key" or "Clover key" (because of the symbols printed on it). It is normally pressed in conjunction with another key to activate additional commands or perform keyboard shortcuts. → 2.026 KEYBOARD SHORTCUT

1.**269 Darwin** The core OS of Apple's OS X operating system. The Darwin component provides features such as preemptive multitasking and memory protection in order that the principal components (known as Carbon, POSIX, and Cocoa) are best placed to take advantage of them.

1.**270 Dock** Feature of the Mac OS X interface. The Dock sits at the bottom of the screen and holds icons that correspond to all folders, applications, documents, and more that the user can access (or might like to access) speedily. It is scalable (including an option to be hidden) to enable the workspace to be maximized.

1.**271 Finder** On Macintosh computers, one of the three fundamental components (the others are the System file and the hardware ROM chips) which provide the desktop, file, and disk management, and the facility to launch and use other applications.

1.**272 Mac OS** The operating system used on Apple Computer's "Macintosh" computers, that provides the underlying "graphical user interface" (GUI) on which all the applications and files depend. Unlike other operating systems, such as Microsoft's "DOS" and "Windows," which are entirely software-based, the Mac OS is part software and part "firmware" (software built into a hardware

"ROM" chip on the Mac's motherboard). It can thus provide a consistent interface with standard control mechanisms, such as dialog boxes and windows, which allows all software written for the Macintosh to have the same look and feel. Mac OS X introduces new features and a UNIX core. → 1.322 GUI; 1.336 MS-DOS; 1.288 WINDOWS; 1.475 ROM

1.**273 Mach 3.0** More correctly called the Mach 3.0 kernel, this is the latest version of an open-source programming kernel that has been in intensive development for some years. It is used in the Mac OS X operating system to provide processor "control" for the computer, handling memory protection, processor scheduling, and processor availability. → 1.275 OS X

1.**274 OpenDoc** Mac OS feature that allows you to work on different types of data within a single document by using several applications to do so.

1.**275 OS X** Version ten (X) of the Macintosh operating system; it combines UNIX-based underpinnings with new graphics technologies like Quartz to deliver a potent environment. With robust features (such as memory protection and fully integrated web resources) it offers a stable and powerful platform but does need a reasonably well-specified Mac to exploit it. Not totally backward compatible, Mac OS X runs software designed for earlier versions (including OS 9) in a "shell" environment called "Classic." → 1.269 DARWIN

1.**276 PrintMonitor** Part of the Mac OS up to OS 9, PrintMonitor is a print spooling application

that enables "background" printing, allowing you to print while you carry on working. → 1.252 SPOOL/SPOOLER/SPOOLING

1.**277 Quartz** This is a 2D graphics system based on the portable document format (PDF) designed for dynamic (real-time) rendering of graphics, antialiasing, and construction of PostScript graphics at the highest possible resolution quality. Used in Mac OS X, including the Aqua interface. → 3.044 PDF; 1.266 AQUA

1.**278 QuickDraw** The part of the Mac OS that performs all display operations on your screen. It is also responsible for outputting text and graphics to non-PostScript printers. → 1.236 POSTSCRIPT

1.**279 QuickTime VR** QuickTime "virtual reality." An Apple extension that provides features for the creation and playback of 3D objects and panoramic scenes. → 1.242 QUICKTIME

1.**280 ResEdit** An Apple-supplied application for editing resources (icons, sounds, menus, etc.), used for modifying any Macintosh file or software program (system or otherwise). → 1.168 RESOURCE; 3.094 RESOURCE FORK

1.**281 system folder** A folder in Mac OS systems containing all the files, including system and finder files, necessary fused to runng system. → 1.339 OPERATING SYSTEM (OS)

1.**282 zapping the PRAM** The term that describes the resetting of the parameter RAM (PRAM) on a Macintosh computer to its "factory" settings. You do this by holding down the Option+Command+P+R keys while restarting the computer. Date and time settings are not affected. → 1.470 PARAMETER RAM (PRAM)

1.272 *Mac OS*

1 *Apple Menu*
2 *Finder window*
3 *Desktop*
4 *Dock*

## Windows operating system

**1.283 control panel** (1) Appearing as a conventional Windows window and accessed from the Start menu. Contains icons that link you with applications that manage the computer's hardware and software, such as network settings, printer settings, and fonts.

**1.284 My Computer** (**window and icon**) Click on the My Computer icon to access the My Computer window. This uses icons to indicate available hard drives, disk drives, and network resources.

**1.285 Recycle bin** Drag-and-drop items no longer required into this bin. Items are not deleted from the computer until you action the "Empty Recycle Bin" command.

**1.286 shortcut** A feature of Windows (95 onward) that allows the creation of "dummy" icons that can be placed in various locations (usually on the desktop). Clicking on the shortcut icon provides the same action as clicking on the original icon. A useful way to open frequently used applications that might be deeply nested in other folders. Many installers give the option of creating shortcuts. → 1.263 ALIAS

**1.287 Start menu** The Windows system menu used to launch programs, help and access control panels, and to shut down the computer. Analogous to the Apple menu in Mac OS.

**1.288 Windows** The PC operating system devised by Microsoft that uses a graphical user interface (GUI) in a similar way to the Macintosh OS. Using either special software or hardware, Windows can be run on a Macintosh computer, but the Mac OS cannot be used on PCs designed to run Windows. Windows has appeared in several versions, but Windows 3 was the first to be widely available. Windows 95 brought a more Mac-like appearance to the interface and has since been updated to include workstation variants (NT, 2000) and consumer editions, including Windows 98. → 1.339 OPERATING SYSTEM (OS)

**1.289 Windows key** Key found on some Windows computers that provides a shortcut to the Start menu. Indicated by the Windows logo.

**1.290 Windows XP** Windows version originally known by the project name "Whistler," and short for "Experience." It features a simplified interface and closer, improved media handling facilities. It is also designed for multiple users on shared computers. It echos elements of Mac OS X→ 1.288 WINDOWS

**1.291 WinSock** Windows operating system software, used to connect PCs to the Internet. → 1.288 WINDOWS; 7.158 INTERNET

## General commands and terms

**1.292 A / UX** A version of the AT&T UNIX operating system that can be used (exceptionally) on Macintosh computers. → 1.339 OPERATING SYSTEM

**1.293 Basic Input / Output System** (**BIOS**) The code, usually residing on a chip placed on the motherboard of a computer, that handles basic hardware input and output operations, such as interactions with a keyboard or hard disk drive.

1.288 **Windows**

1 Desktop
2 Window
3 Taskbar
4 Start menu button

**1.294 cancel / abort** The button in dialog boxes that allows you to cancel the action which invoked the box.

**1.295 checkbox** A button in a graphical user interface, such as Windows or Mac OS. Normally comprises a small square. Clicking within the square causes a tick (check mark) to appear, indicating that the corresponding command has been selected.

**1.296 clean install** The process of installing completely new operating system software. A clean install will create new system software components rather than updating existing ones. If you perform a clean install all the other components of your system, which may have been loaded when you installed your applications and utility software, will have to be reinstalled or copied separately—a time-consuming business. However, a clean install is sometimes necessary to "flush out" unnecessary or corrupt files that cannot be removed by any other means. → 1.339 OPERATING SYSTEM

**1.297 clipboard** The place in the memory of a computer where text or picture items are temporarily stored when they are copied (or cut). The item on the clipboard is positioned in an appropriate place when "Paste" is selected from the menu. Each process of copying or cutting deletes the previous item from the clipboard.

**1.298 closed file** A "hidden" file that does not have an access path, thus preventing you from reading from or writing to it.

**1.299 command** An instruction to a computer, given by the operator, either by way of the

mouse when selecting a menu item for example, or by the keyboard. → 1.432 MOUSE

**1.300 command-line interface** Interface used prior to graphical user interfaces where explicit commands were enter as text adjacent to a "prompt" character. → 1.322 GRAPHICAL USER INTERFACE (GUI)

**1.301 control panel (2)** A small application within the Mac OS and Windows operating system that enables you to configure system software or to customize various aspects of your computer, such as time, date, speaker volume, etc.

**1.302 copy (2)** The facility in virtually all computer software to copy a selected item, which places it on the "clipboard" so that it can be "pasted" elsewhere. As distinct from "cut," which deletes the item while at the same time copying it. → 1.297 CLIPBOARD; 1.233 PASTE; 1.204 CUT; 1.205 CUT AND PASTE

**1.303 cross-platform** The term applied to software, multimedia titles, or anything else (such as floppy disks) that will work on more than one computer platform—that is, those which run on different operating systems, such as the Macintosh OS or Microsoft Windows. → 1.339 OPERATING SYSTEM

**1.304 cursor** The name for the blinking marker that indicates the current working position in a document; for example, the point in a line of text at which the next character will appear when you strike a key on the keyboard. The cursor may be represented by a small vertical line or block and is not to be confused with the "pointer"—the marker indicating the current position of the mouse.

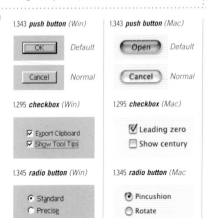

1.343 **push button** (Win)          1.343 **push button** (Mac)

OK        *Default*          Open        *Default*

Cancel    *Normal*          Cancel      *Normal*

1.295 **checkbox** (Win)          1.295 **checkbox** (Mac)

☑ Export Clipboard                ☑ Leading zero
☑ Show Tool Tips                  ☐ Show century

1.345 **radio button** (Win)          1.345 **radio button** (Mac

⦿ Standard                        ⦿ Pincushion
○ Precise                         ○ Rotate

1.301 **control panel** (Win)

**1.305 deselect** To deactivate an active item, such as a picture box or highlighted text, usually by clicking outside or away from the item. In Photoshop a specific menu item allows selections to be deselected.

**1.306 desktop** The general environment of a graphical user interface (GUI), imitating, as far as is practical, a real desk, with folders, files, and even a trashcan for throwing things away. → 1.322 GRAPHICAL USER INTERFACE (GUI)

**1.307 dimmed command** The condition of an item in a menu or dialog box when it is disabled or unavailable for use. The disabled item is displayed as gray or in a paler color than its active counterpart, and is thus "dimmed." Also known as a "grayed command."

**1.308 dimmed icon** The condition of an icon that indicates a file or folder is open or that a disk is unmounted (not available, as in an ejected disk). Also known as a "grayed icon" or "ghosted icon." Similarly, dimmed or "grayed out" menu items are unavailable or unavailable with regard to the current action. → 1.055 ICON

**1.309 double-click** The action of clicking the mouse button twice in rapid succession. Double-clicking while the pointer is positioned in an appropriate place is a short-cut to performing functions such as opening documents or highlighting words in text. → 1.432 MOUSE

**1.310 drag** Carrying out an action by holding down the mouse button while you move the mouse, thus moving the pointer onscreen, then releasing the mouse button to complete the action. Dragging is used to perform such tasks as selecting and moving items, selecting pull-down menu commands or text, and, in some applications, creating items with an appropriate tool selected.

**1.311 drop-down menu** The menu that appears when you click on a title in the menu bar along the top of your screen. Also called "pop-down menu" or "pull-down menu." → 1.333 MENU TITLE; 1.301 MENU BAR

**1.312 Edit menu (1)** A standard menu (in the Mac OS, one of the three standard menus alongside the "Apple" and File menus), containing commands for such actions as cut, copy, and paste. → 3.080 FILE MENU

**1.313 Enter key** On keyboards, the key that confirms an entry or command or may force a carriage return. On some computer systems the Enter key duplicates much of the function of the Return key. In some applications it may also have a specific function. → 1.346 RETURN KEY

**1.314 Esc(ape) key** A keyboard key, the function of which depends on the operating system or application you are using, but generally used to cancel something you are doing.

**1.315 event-handling mechanism** A facility, built into the operating system software, which allows other software programs to respond to circumstances or commands as they occur. → 1.339 OPERATING SYSTEM (OS)

**1.316 Exit** syn. Quit (PC) Command issued to leave an application. Usually found at the foot of the File menu.

**1.317 extension** A file that adds functions to a computer or application. Operating system extensions include such things as hardware "drivers," which control devices like printers and monitors, while application extensions (usually called "plug-ins") can include any kind of enhancement, from mundane file-handling operations (such as importing and exporting documents) to more exciting special effects. → 6.060 PLUG-IN; 1.213 DRIVER/DEVICE DRIVER

**1.318 extension / init conflict** A problem caused by some extensions being incompatible with other extensions, system files, or applications, and which may cause your computer to crash or behave erratically. There are several utilities available which test and resolve extension problems. → 1.317 EXTENSION; 1.319 EXTENSION/INIT MANAGER

**1.319 extension / init manager** Utility software that enables you to manage extensions, for example, to turn off the ones you don't need (extensions use up memory) or to test them for incompatibilities.

**1.320 firmware** Any permanent software incorporated into a hardware chip (usually a "ROM" chip). On Macintosh computers part of the operating system is built into a hardware ROM chip. → 1.475 ROM

**1.321 forward delete key** A key found on some keyboards that deletes characters to the right of the text insertion point rather than the left, as with the standard delete key.

**1.322 graphical user interface (GUI)** The feature of some computer operating systems, such as the Mac OS and Windows, that allows you to interact with the computer by means of pointing at graphic symbols (icons) with a mouse rather than by typing coded commands. Also known as a "WIMP" or "pointing interface." → 1.325 INTERFACE; 1.300 COMMAND-LINE INTERFACE; 1.306 DESKTOP

1.**323 help** A feature of operating systems that provides online explanations and advice. Some software packages use application-specific help systems. Others, including Photoshop versions up to 5.5, use system (Mac or Windows) help routines. Photoshop 6 uses a web browser to deliver help.

1.**324 installer** Program that enables you to load software onto your hard disk. Installer programs also put the application support files in their appropriate places, creating folders for them and putting files, if necessary, into your system folder. Installers are also used to install updates to programs. → 1.224 INSTALL

1.**325 interface** The physical relationship between human beings, systems, and machines—in other words, the point of interaction or connection. The involvement of humans is called a "human interface" or "user interface." → 1.300 COMMAND-LINE INTERFACE; 1.322 GRAPHICAL USER INTERFACE (GUI)

1.**326 interpreter** Software that converts program code into machine language piece by piece; as distinct from a "compiler," which converts a program in its entirety. → 1.202 CODE; 1.394 COMPILER

1.**327 key(board) combination** → 2.026 KEYBOARD SHORTCUT

1.**328 keyboard character** Any character generated by pressing a key (or combination of keys) on the keyboard. → 1.431 KEYBOARD; 2.026 KEYBOARD SHORTCUT

1.**329 Linux** Operating system derived from UNIX that can be run on a variety of platforms including PCs and Macs. It is "open sourced" meaning that any user can purchase or download a copy and undertake their own customization or changes, notionally for the benefit of the whole Linux community. Several user interfaces have been developed (making it appear less like UNIX and more like a Mac or Windows operating system) and some "end-user" software has been developed. Though gaining ground rapidly it is gathering particular strength with users of Internet servers.

1.**330 menu** List of commands from which a user makes a selection (normally applied to graphical user interfaces). Both Windows and the Mac OS feature drop-down menus in which clicking on a header word drops down a list of commands or features relevant to that header. Pop-up, pull-out, and contextual menus also feature in both operating systems.

1.**331 menu bar** The horizontal panel across the top of a computer screen containing the titles of available menus. → 1.330 MENU

1.**332 menu indicator** Symbols within a menu that expand the range of options. An ellipsis (…) following an item means that selecting it will display a dialog box before the command can be executed; a check-mark indicates that a command is already active; a right-pointing triangle points to a submenu; and a downward-pointing triangle indicates that there's more on the menu (indicators may vary slightly according to operating system). → 1.330 MENU

---

1.322 *graphical user interface* (*GUI*)

The graphic display of the contents and commands on a computer, sometimes called a 'WIMPs' interface because of its key elements.

1 *Window*
2 *Icon*
3 *Menu*
4 *Pointer*

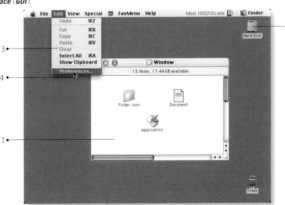

1.**333 menu title** The title of a menu as displayed in the menu bar. → 1.331 MENU BAR

1.**334 message box** Information box that appears in Windows, Mac OS, and other graphical user interfaces to advise on a condition, such as an alert or the need to save a document before continuing. → 1.008 ALERT BOX

1.**335 modifier key** Key that when pressed (and usually held) modifies the actions of other keys. Keys that perform such modification (not necessarily under all circumstances) include the Control, Alt, and Fn keys on Windows keyboards, and Control, Option (Apple key), and Fn keys on Mac OS keyboards. The Shift key is also sometimes considered a modifier key.

1.**336 MS-DOS** Acronym for Microsoft disk operating system, the operating system used on Intel-based personal computers (PCs). MS-DOS (or just plain "DOS") also provides the skeleton on which Microsoft's "Windows" operating system hangs. → 1.300 COMMAND-LINE INTERFACE; 1.339 OPERATING SYSTEM (OS)

1.**337 multithreaded** A feature of operating systems in which they (or the applications that run on them) divide into smaller "subtasks", each of which runs in parallel and independently but ultimately combine to deliver the intended outcome. → 1.078 MULTITASKING

1.**338 Open** (**1**) A standard operating system command that reveals the contents of a selected file or folder or launches an application. → 1.226 LAUNCH

1.**339 operating system** (**OS**) The software (and in some cases "firmware") that provides the environment within which all other software and its user operate. The major operating systems are Microsoft's "DOS" and "Windows", Apple's "Mac OS", and AT&T's "UNIX", the last three of which all use "GUIs" (graphical user interfaces). → 1.320 FIRMWARE

1.**340 option** Any keyboard key, button, checkbox, menu, or command that allows alternative choices. On keyboards, this is the "Option" (Macintosh) and "Alt" (Windows) keys which, when used in conjunction with another key, provide a special character or a shortcut to menu commands.

1.**341 plug and play** The marketing description of computer or hardware devices that do not require complicated "setting up"—in other words, you just plug them in and start playing them. Macintosh computers have always featured plug and play though it did not arrive in the Windows world until Windows 95, and was not then always effective! → 1.066 MACINTOSH

1.**342 pop-up menu** A menu in a dialog box or palette that "pops up" when you click on it. Pop-up menus usually appear as a rectangle with a drop shadow and a downward- or sideways–pointing arrow.

1.**343 push button** A button in a dialogue box which, when clicked, invokes the command specified on the button.

1.**344 Quit** The command by which you "shut down" an application, as distinct from closing a document within the application, in which

1.311 *drop-down menu*

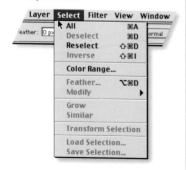

1.342 *pop-up menu*

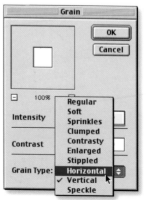

case the document disappears but the application remains open.

1.**345 radio button** A button in a graphical user interface, such as Windows or Mac OS. Comprises a small circle containing another circle. Clicking on the center selects the button and causes that circle to darken. Named after the push buttons in old car radios. → 1.295 CHECKBOX

1.**346 Return key** The key on a computer keyboard that performs operations similar to a typewriter "carriage return" key in that it moves the text insertion point to the beginning of the next line, usually creating a new paragraph as it does so. In many applications and dialog boxes, it also duplicates the actions of the Enter key, for example confirming a command. → 1.313 ENTER KEY

1.**347 Save dialog box** A box that appears onscreen the first time a document is saved, requiring the user to supply the name with which it should be saved and the location. → 2.250 SAVE

1.**348 scroll arrow** An arrow which, when clicked on, moves the contents of a window up, down or sideways.

1.**349 scroll bar** The bar at the side and, usually, the bottom of a window within which the scroll box operates and which indicates if there are parts of the document hidden from view. → 1.351 SCROLLING

1.**350 scroll box** A box sitting within the scroll bar of a window that can be moved up and down to access different parts of the open document. The position of the scroll box in the bar indicates position in relation to the size of the entire document. → 1.351 SCROLLING

1.**351 scrolling** The "sliding" of an application's window contents either horizontally or vertically (or both) to enable hidden parts to be viewed.

1.**352 Shift key** The modifier key used to generate upper case and other characters on a keyboard.

1.**353 shift-click(ing)** The process of holding down the shift key while clicking on several items or passages of text on the screen, thus making multiple selections.

1.**354 title bar** The bar at the top of the open image document displaying the name of that document, usually accompanied by the display magnification and image mode. In the Windows and Mac operating systems the bar at the top of any open window that contains its name is known as the title bar. The window can be moved around the desktop by dragging this bar. → 1.301 MENU BAR

1.**355 toggle** Those buttons, menus, and checkboxes that switch between off and on each time you select or click on them.

1.**356 TWAIN** Acronym for technology without an interesting name. Cross-platform driver interface used particularly for acquiring images from scanners.

1.**357 UNIX** An advanced and stable operating system that was developed by AT&T and was devised to be multitasking and portable from one machine to another. UNIX is used widely on web servers and also underpins the latest Macintosh operating system

1.360 *window*

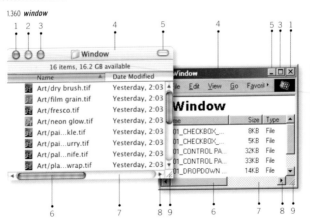

Mac OS X (far left)
Windows (left)

1 *Close box*
2 *Add to Dock*
3 *Zoom/maximize*
4 *Title bar*
5 *Collapse/minimize*
6 *Scroll bar*
7 *Scroll box*
8 *Scroll arrows*
9 *Resize box*

(Mac OS X). → 1.339 OPERATING SYSTEM (OS); 1.292 A/UX

**1.358 what you see is what you get (WYSIWYG)** (pron.: "wizzywig") The display of a document onscreen exactly as it appears when it is printed. All major computer operating systems now offer WYSIWYG displays.

**1.359 WIMP** abb.: windows, icon, mouse (or menu), and pointer. An acronym for the constituent parts of a computer graphical user interface. → 1.322 GUI

**1.360 window** Part of the 'graphical user interface' (GUI) of a computer, a window is an area of a computer screen that displays the contents of disk, folder, or document. A window can be resized and is scrollable if the contents are too large to fit within it. → 1.322 GUI

**1.361 wristwatch / hourglass pointer** On your computer, the shape the pointer icon assumes to indicate that a process is underway but not yet complete. By default the Windows operating system provides an hourglass, and the Mac OS a wristwatch, but third-party applications may provide alternatives.

**1.362 X Window System** One of several GUIs (graphical user interfaces) used on UNIX computers, to provide a more "friendly" interface for the user. Conceptually similar to Windows and the Mac OS interface. → 1.322 GUI; 1.357 UNIX

**1.363 zoom box** The box at the right of some window title bars that, when clicked, expands or reduces the visible area of the window. → 1.354 TITLE BAR

## Monitors

**1.364 CCD pitch, CCD element pitch** The linear distance between the center points of two adjacent picture elements in a CCD array or screen. → 8.208 CHARGE-COUPLED DEVICE (CCD)

**1.365 cathode ray tube (CRT)** The picture tube of a monitor or television, so named because "cathode rays" (later known as electrons) were seen to be emitted from a cathode valve at the neck of the tube and attracted to the "anode" surface of the screen.

**1.366 convergence** A term used with CRT-based color monitors, referring to the adjustment of the three RGB beams so they come together in the right place in all parts of the screen. → 4.055 RGB; 1.375 MONITOR; 1.365 CRT

**1.367 degauss(ing)** The technique of removing, or neutralizing, any magnetic field that may have built up over time in a color monitor and which will distort the fidelity of color display both linearly across the whole screen and selectively (usually along edges and in corners). Since most modern monitors perform a degauss automatically, this process is usually only necessary on older monitors.

**1.368 dot / stripe pitch** The distance between the dots (or in the case of some monitors, including Sony's Trinitron, stripes) that comprise a monitor screen. → 1.095 PIXEL; 10.139 RESOLUTION

**1.369 flat screen / panel display** A flat panel computer display that uses technologies such as liquid crystal or gas plasma to generate the image rather than a bulky cathode ray tube (CRT).

**1.370 flicker** Rapid variations in brightness due to a light source (usually a computer monitor or a fluorescent tube) flashing at high speed. Though our persistance of vision tends to even out variations, some change can be detected at lower frequencies, particularly when the source is viewed up close or in peripheral vision.

**1.371 gas plasma display** A computer display panel comprising a large matrix of tiny glass cells, each filled with a combination of gases. The simple structure means that gas plasma displays can be made in large sizes, typically ranging from 30 to 50 inches diagonally, and enable viewing from most angles compared with the more restricted angle of view typical of LCD displays.

**1.372 interlacing (1)** A technique employed by cathode ray tube and television engineers to build an image. The odd numbered rows of the image are displayed first as one "field" followed by the even numbered rows. Together they build the full image.

**1.373 liquid crystal display (LCD)** A digital display technology commonly seen on calculators, clocks, and computer displays, particularly on portables and laptops. Liquid crystal display monitors are easier on the eye than cathode ray tube monitors (CRTs) but are still slightly behind the CRT in terms of absolute color fidelity.

**1.374 Melzoic** A development of 100-Hz CRT technology that limits digital artifacts, particularly in moving images, and makes viewing the image more restful. Also known as third-generation 100-Hz technology.

**1.375 monitor** The unit comprising your computer screen. Monitors display images in color, grayscale or monochrome, and are available in a variety of sizes (measured diagonally) ranging from 9 in. (229 mm) to 21 in. (534 mm) or more. Although most monitors use cathode ray tubes, some contain liquid crystal displays ("LCDs")—particularly portables and laptops—and, more recently, "gas plasma" (large matrices of tiny, gas-filled glass cells). Monitors are also called "screens," "displays," "VDUs" (video display units), and "VDTs" (video display terminals).
→ 1.366 CONVERGENCE; 1.365 CRT; 1.371 GAS PLASMA DISPLAY; 1.373 LCD

**1.376 mono(chrome) / monochromatic (1)** A computer monitor, now only used in specialized applications, which displays pixels as either black or white, rather than in shades of gray as "grayscale" monitors do.
→ 1.375 MONITOR

**1.377 multiple screens / multiscreen** Two or more monitors attached to a single computer, used for presentations or to increase the workspace.

**1.378 phosphor** The coating on the inside surface of cathode ray tubes, which glows momentarily when struck by a bombardment of electrons, creating a brief image. → 1.365 CATHODE RAY TUBE (CRT)

**1.379 pincushion** The tendency of a monitor image to curve in along its vertical sides. The opposite effect (where the edges tend to bulge out) is known as ballooning or barrel distortion.

**1.380 portrait monitor** A monitor in which the screen is in an upright format, as distinct from the more usual landscape format. Conventionally used for page layouts and text-based work (many are monochrome/grayscale rather than color). → 1.375 MONITOR

**1.381 radiation shield / screen** A wire mesh or glass filter that fits over a monitor to reduce the level of radiation being emitted. Can be incorporated into an antiglare filter.

**1.382 refresh rate** The frequency at which a screen image, or "frame" (a single pass of an electron beam that "rakes" the screen from top to bottom) is redrawn. It is measured in hertz (Hz), and a refresh rate of 72 Hz means that the image is "refreshed" 72 times every second. A screen with a slow refresh rate is liable to produce an undesirable flicker.

**1.383 screen capture** A "snapshot" of part or all of a monitor display. Also called a "screen shot," "screen grab," or "screen dump." PC screens can be grabbed using the PrtScr key; on Mac computers press Shift-Apple-3 together (a successful screen grab is announced by a camera shutter noise!).

**1.384 screen resolution** → 10.139 RESOLUTION

**1.385 screen saver / blanker** A means of dimming the screen image or replacing it with a randomly changing pattern after a preset time of inactivity in order to preserve the phosphor coating on the monitor. Newer monitors tend to be more resistant to image "burn in," and these days screen savers are more commonly employed for aesthetic or security reasons.

**1.386 SuperVGA (SVGA)** A video display standard that supports 256 colors or more in a variety of resolutions. → 1.375 MONITOR

**1.387 Trinitron** A cathode ray tube produced by Sony and used extensively by Apple for its monitors. Uses an aperture grille of slots (rather than the more conventional dots) to build the image. Trinitron tubes produce pictures where vertical lines are linear, although there is still curvature in horizontal planes. Trinitron tubes tend to be deeper than conventional models.

**1.388 two-page display (TPD)** Term used mainly in the graphics, image editing, and DTP world to describe a 21-in. monitor. It is capable of showing two 8x11 imch pages side by side, or a 11x16 format image in landscape format.

**1.389 Video Graphics Array (VGA)** A basic video display standard for PC monitors. → 1.375 MONITOR; 1.386 SuperVGA

## CPUs and associated hardware

**1.390 accelerator board / card** An ancillary circuit board added to a computer (often as an optional extra) to improve certain computer operations. Typical operations include complex mathematical functions or improving onscreen rendering of graphics. Boards added with the specific task of speeding graphics operations are known as graphics accelerators. → 1.392 CENTRAL PROCESSING UNIT (CPU); 1.403 EXPANSION BOARD/CARD

**1.391 add-on board** → 1.403 expansion board/card

**1.392 central processing unit (CPU)** The computational and management center of the computer. In most desktop computers the CPU is a single-chip microprocessor; it performs the principal computational calculations and governs the operation of other components. → 1.415 PROCESSOR (CHIP); 1.397 COPROCESSOR

**1.393 chip** → 1.415 processor (chip)

**1.394 circuit board** An insulating baseboard (usually epoxy or phenolic resin) upon which electronic circuits are built. Basic circuit boards use simple interconnecting cables or ribbons between the electronic components mounted on the board, more sophisticated ones use printed or etched tracks (hence "printed circuit board").

**1.395 compiler** Software that converts high-level programming code ("source" code), such as that written in C++, into low-level machine code ("object" code)—a language that hardware will understand. This is necessary because although programming code for writing applications, for example, is in a language that the user can understand, a machine only understands binary code—on or off, 1s and 0s, etc. For example, if you were to instruct your computer to add two numbers in binary code it would look something like: 1101 0011 0001 0011 1110, while a high-level language would allow you to write "add 1 to 2." → COMPUTER LANGUAGE; 10.011 BINARY; 1.201 C/C++; 1.326 INTERPRETER

**1.396 complex instruction set computing (CISC)** A type of microprocessor used in some earlier computers. → 1.415 MICROPROCESSOR; 1.417 RISC

**1.397 coprocessor** A secondary microprocessor chip that can sit alongside your computer's main processing unit (CPU) and carry out specific specialized functions, e.g. speeding up graphics display or handling data-intensive tasks such as maths calculations. A coprocessor may sometimes be described by its specific function, for example "floating-point" ("FPU") or "math coprocessor," both of which carry out maths calculations. Increasingly the functions of coprocessors are incorporated into the main CPU chip. → 1.392 CENTRAL PROCESSING UNIT (CPU)

**1.398 daughterboard** A circuit board that plugs into another board, such as the "motherboard" (the board containing the main circuitry and processors of a computer). → 1.410 MOTHERBOARD; 1.394 CIRCUIT BOARD

**1.399 desktop computer** Those personal computers which not only perform all the necessary functions of desktop publishing, but will also fit on a real desktop. Originally named to distinguish them from the more substantial (room-sized) mainframe machines. → 1.036 DESKTOP PUBLISHING (DTP)

**1.400 digital video interactive (DVI)** A computer chip developed by Intel that compresses and decompresses video images.

**1.401 DIP switch** Small switches on hardware devices that are used to select an operating mode, such as giving the device a unique identity number when connected to others. → 1.174 SCSI ID (NUMBER)

**1.402 dumb terminal** A display device and keyboard that does not possess any computing power on its own, but that is networked to a server on which it relies for intelligent processing. → 1.184 TERMINAL; 7.215 TELNET

**1.403 expansion board / card** A circuit board added to a computer that allows you to extend its capabilities—an accelerator card, for example. → 1.394 CIRCUIT BOARD; 1.390 ACCELERATOR BOARD/CARD

**1.404 expansion slot** The place in a computer where additional circuit boards can be plugged in. → 1.394 CIRCUIT BOARD; 1.403 EXPANSION BOARD/CARD

**1.405 G3** Version of the PowerPC processor produced by the Apple/IBM/Motorola consortium and used in Apple computers. A RISC processor, it can run at speeds of up to 500 MHz. Note that PowerPC RISC speeds do not relate directly to Pentium (or equivalent processor) speeds. → 1.417 RISC

**1.406 G4** More powerful version of the G3 PowerPC processor.

**1.407 graphics accelerator** An additional computer circuit board used to provide additional functionality and performance in the execution of graphics commands. → 1.390 ACCELERATOR BOARD/CARD

**1.408 integrated circuit** The electronic circuit embedded in a microchip.

**1.409 MMX** Commercial name for an enhancement to the Pentium series of PC computer chips that provided enhanced multimedia capabilities.

1.**410 motherboard** The principal circuit board in a computer, holding the CPU, memory chips, connectors for "daughterboards" and other components. → 1.394 CIRCUIT BOARD

1.**411 multiprocessor** Computer architecture that uses more than one central processing unit. Actions are divided among two or more chips. Found only on powerful computers.

1.**412 NuBus** The "bus architecture" found mostly in older Macintosh computers that provides "slots" for adding circuit boards such as video cards and accelerator cards. → 1.394 CIRCUIT BOARD

1.**413 Pentium** Name of the processor series produced by Intel for use in personal computers and following on from the 80486 series (the name was coined when Intel discovered that the logical name—586—was already used elsewhere).

1.**414 peripheral component interconnect** (**PCI**) A high-performance, 32-bit or 64-bit "bus" for connecting external devices to a computer.

1.**415 processor** (**chip**) A silicon "chip," containing millions of micro "switches" that respond to binary electrical pulses, which performs specific functions in a computer, such as the "central processor" (CPU) and memory (RAM). Also known as a "microprocessor" or "microchip." → 1.392 CPU; 1.397 COPROCESSOR

1.**416 processor direct slot** (**PDS**) An expansion slot that connects to the CPU directly rather than indirectly through a bus.

1.**417 reduced instruction set computing** (**RISC**) A microprocessor that is capable of providing high-speed processing while requiring only a limited number of instructions. As distinct from a "complex instruction set computing" (CISC) processor, which requires more instructions and is therefore slower. RISC processors of a given clock speed are nominally faster than CISC processors of an equivalent quoted clock speed. → 1.415 MICROPROCESSOR

1.**418 video card** A plug-in board that provides dedicated control for an external monitor.

## Input devices

1.**419 card reader** Any device capable of reading—and generally also writing to—a data card (such as a PC card, SmartMedia, or CompactFlash card) and found, for example, on digital cameras. Also the name for devices connected to computers to download information stored on these cards. → 1.093 PC CARD; 1.552 SMARTMEDIA; 1.500 COMPACTFLASH

1.**420 charge-injection device** (**CID**) Specialized imaging chip that, unlike a CCD, retains a charge in each pixel cell, which can be read out by injecting an "interrogation charge." Although it reduces some of the artifacts created by CCD chips, its complexity and high current drain limit its widespread use. → 8.208 CCD

1.**421 desktop scanner** A small, (usually) flatbed device for scanning images and text that will often form part of a desktop system. Although such scanners are becoming increasingly sophisticated and capable, the quality of image that they generate does not yet match that produced by a high-

1.421 *desktop scanner*          1.424 *desktop drum scanner*          1.426 *film scanner*

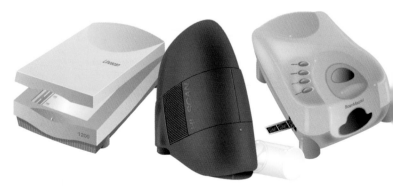

end "drum" scanner. → 1.438 SCANNER; 1.424 DRUM SCANNER

**.422 digitizer** Any hardware device such as a scanner or camera that converts drawn or photographed images into binary code so that you can work with them on your computer. The term is generally used more specifically with reference to digitizing tablets. → 1.423 DIGITIZING TABLET/PAD

**.423 digitizing tablet / pad** A hardware device consisting of a flat, rectangular pad that allows you to input images into your computer by drawing on it with a stylus (a penlike instrument) as though you were working on paper. Also called a "graphics tablet/pad." → 1.439 STYLUS

**1.424 desktop drum scanner** A scanner used for high-grade reprographic work. Original artwork (transparencies, negatives, or prints) is fixed to the outside of a drum that encloses (usually) a halogen light source. The drum rotates at high speed (up to 1000 rpm) while a recording head moves across the surface of the drum scanning the original. The principle benefits of drum scanners over flatbed types are higher resolution and better dynamic range. → 1.438 SCANNER

**1.425 Dvorak keyboard** A keyboard layout on which the more frequently typed keys are positioned most comfortably in relationship to your dominant typing fingers. An alternative layout to the familiar and widely-used 'QWERTY' arrangement found on typewriters and computer keyboards. → 1.100 QWERTY

**1.426 film scanner** A scanner designed to scan 35-mm to medium format transparencies and negatives. → 1.438 SCANNER

**1.427 frame grabber** Peripheral device that can "grab" a frame or image from an analog source (for example a television or analog video) and convert it to a digital format for storage or manipulation.

**1.428 front-end system** The collection of hardware devices such as keyboards and scanners on which data is input. So-called to distinguish it from the collection of devices on which data is output, such as imagesetters and printers.

**1.429 function keys** A set of keys on some keyboards that can be assigned specific functions to carry out a sequence of mouse and keyboard actions, such as those defined by a "macro" program. Not to be confused

with Fkeys, which execute default commands. → 1.045 FKEY

**1.430 input device** Any item of hardware specifically designed for, or capable of, entering data into a computer—a keyboard or scanner, for example. → 1.038 DEVICE

**1.431 keyboard** A device for entering data (characters, numerics, or functions) into a computer.

**1.432 mouse** The small, handheld, mechanical device that you manipulate to position the pointer on your monitor.

**1.433 mouse mat / pad** A small pad designed to enable the smooth motion of a mouse interface. Not essential for all mice. Newer optical mice (i.e. those that use reflected light patterns rather than a trackerball to determine motion) don't require one, though some older optical mice need a special gridded mat.

**1.434 numeric keypad** A cluster of number keys (normally) situated to the right on most keyboards. Sometimes available as a separate keyboard.

**1.435 puck** The rather more complex "mouse" used in CAD (computer-aided design) and graphics systems that provides precise measurement input functions and relative positional features in addition to conventional mouse features. → 1.439 STYLUS; 1.423 DIGITIZING TABLET/PAD

**1.436 scan(ning)** An electronic process that converts an image into digital form by sequential exposure to a moving light beam such as a laser. The scanned image can then be manipulated by a computer or output to separated film. → 1.424 DRUM SCANNER; 1.421 DESKTOP SCANNER; 10.100 LASER

**1.437 scan resolution** The resolution at which an original transparency, negative, or flat artwork is scanned by a scanner. Generally quoted in pixels per inch (ppi) or lines per inch (lpi)

**1.438 scanner** Electronic device that uses a sequentially moving light beam to convert artwork or photographs into digital form so that they can be manipulated by a computer or output to separated film. A scanner can be a simple flatbed type, used on the desktop for positioning pictures only, or a sophisticated reprographic device ("drum scanner") used for high-quality color separation. Handheld scanners are now rarely found; these devices are drawn over the surface of a page of text or graphics and the underlying document is read by the scanner head as it passes overhead.

These rarely have the quality or accuracy needed for imaging work. → 1.421 DESKTOP SCANNER; 1.424 DRUM SCANNER

1.**439 stylus** The penlike pointing device used with digitizing tablets, replacing the mouse. An increasing number of styli are pressure sensitive and this feature can be exploited with Photoshop. With many selection, darkroom and painting tools you can specify size (with greater pressure relating to a wider stroke), color (where light pressure applies the background color, heavy pressure applies the foreground color, and medium pressure applies a blend) and opacity/ pressure/exposure. In the last case, the pressure applied is proportional to the effect. Note that a plug-in was needed to use these features with Photoshop versions prior to 5. → 1.423 → DIGITIZING TABLET

1.**440 trackball** A device which replaces the mouse, actually resembling an upturned mouse—i.e. with the mouse ball on top rather than underneath. You move the pointer by manipulating the ball. The device remains stationary, thus occupying less desk space than the conventional mouse.

1.**441 trackpad** A device found on portable computers that replaces a mouse. The pad is sensitive to finger movements, which control the position of the cursor onscreen.

## Output devices

1.**442 bubblejet printer** A type of inkjet printer in which minute quantities of liquid ink (measured in picoliters) are heated to boiling point, creating bubbles that eject the ink. → 1.446 INKJET PRINTER

1.**443 DeskJet** A range of printers produced by Hewlett Packard.

1.**444 dot matrix printer** Impact printer that uses a matrix of pins (usually nine or twenty-four) to strike alphanumeric and shape characters through a ribbon. Although not suitable for photographic applications, they are nonetheless useful for general (and economic) text printing applications.

1.**445 film recorder** An output device for creating photographic film images from digital data. A laser or LED light source is used to draw the image on the film. These devices were once in widespread use when high-quality transparencies were demanded by reprographic houses for page layouts. They are now scarce as many reprographic houses have turned to all-digital techniques.

1.**446 inkjet printer** A printing device that creates an image by spraying tiny jets of ink onto a paper surface at high speed. → 1.442 BUBBLEJET PRINTER

1.**447 laser printer** A printer that uses a laser as part of the mechanical process of printing onto paper. A laser is used to alter the electrostatic properties of a metallized drum which, consequently, attracts toner powder. This is then fused (by heat) to the paper page. LED page printers achieve a similar result using light-emitting diodes rather than a laser. Color laser printers can provide virtual photographic quality, albeit at a high price. → 10.100 LASER

1.432 *mouse*

1.440 *trackball*

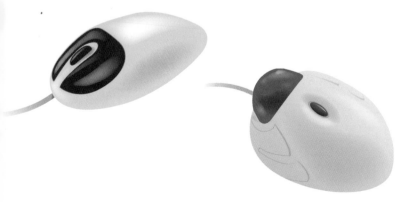

**1.448 output** Any data or information extracted from a computer, by whatever means, but typically via a monitor, printer, or storage device.

**1.449 output device** Any hardware device capable of producing or displaying computer data in a visible form, such as a monitor, printer, plotter, imagesetter, etc.

**1.450 phase change printer** Inkjet printer that uses solid inks, rather than liquid ones. Inks are phase-changed (melted) and sprayed onto the paper where they resolidify, almost instantly.

**1.451 PostScript printer** Any printing device that uses the Adobe-licensed "PostScript" page description language (PDL). → 1.236 POSTSCRIPT; 9.112 PAGE DESCRIPTION LANGUAGE (PDL)

**1.452 print buffer** A hardware device where items are stored ("queued") while waiting for a printer to become available, thus allowing you to continue working. As distinct from a print spooler. → 1.460 BUFFER; 1.252 SPOOL/SPOOLER/SPOOLING

**1.453 printer** An output device that produces a hard copy of your onscreen work. This can be text or graphics/imagery. Certain printers are more appropriate for certain outputs. For high-quality graphics and images photorealistic or photo quality printers are required. → 1.092 PERIPHERAL DEVICE ; 1.449 OUTPUT DEVICE; 1.446 INKJET PRINTER; 1.442 BUBBLEJET PRINTER; 1.447 LASER PRINTER

**1.454 Stylus, Stylus Photo** Range of inkjet printers produced by Epson. Those with the Photo appelation are particularly well suited to photorealistic reproduction.

**1.455 target printer** The device that a document is sent to for printing. → 1.117 TARGET

**1.456 thermal printer** A device that uses a heat-sensitive paper to produce an image. It is most commonly found in older models of fax machines.

## Memory terms

**1.457 application heap / memory** The portion of the computer's memory (RAM) reserved for use by an application when it is launched or opened. It is separate from the memory reserved for other applications or for the computer's operating system. → OPERATING SYSTEM (OS); 1.339 APPLICATION MEMORY PARTITION/SIZE; 1.474 RAM

**1.458 application memory partition / size** The amount of memory (RAM), measured in megabytes, reserved by an application when it is being used. The allocation is normally automatic although allocations can sometimes be altered (increased) manually. → 1.457 APPLICATION HEAP/MEMORY; 1.474 RANDOM ACCESS MEMORY (RAM)

**1.459 backside cache** A dedicated chip for temporary storage of frequently accessed data. "Backside" means that it is connected directly to the main CPU of a computer, thus bypassing the speed límitations of the data transfer "bus" (the path along which data travels). → 1.461 CACHE; 1.392 CPU

**1.460 buffer** An area of computer memory set aside for the storage or processing of data while it is in transit. The buffer can either be in RAM or on a hard disk, and within your computer the buffer is called the "cache." Buffers are commonly used by output devices such as modems and printers. A print buffer, for example, stores print data until the printer is ready to action that data. → 1.461 CACHE; 1.474 RANDOM ACCESS MEMORY (RAM); 1.252 SPOOL/SPOOLER/SPOOLING

**1.461 cache** A small area of memory (RAM)—or a separate hardware chip—set aside for the temporary storage of frequently accessed data. Because data access from RAM is somewhat faster than from disk some computer operations—accessing font information, for example—can be speeded up using predictive techniques (the computer "guesses" the information that will be requested next). Disk caches are areas of the hard disk reserved for caching activities. → 1.461 RANDOM ACCESS MEMORY (RAM); 1.460 BUFFER; 1.459 BACKSIDE CACHE

**1.462 DIP SIMM** A "high profile" (taller) SIMM chip. → 1.477 SIMM

**1.463 dual inline memory module (DIMM)** A standard type of computer memory ("RAM") chip. → 1.461 RAM; 1.468 MEMORY; 1.477 SIMM

**1.464 dual inline package (DIP)** The particular way in which some chips are mounted—with two parallel rows of pins—so that they can be plugged into a computer circuit board. → 1.394 CIRCUIT BOARD

**1.465 dynamic RAM (DRAM)** pron. "dee-ram." RAM (random access memory) that is only active while supplied by an electric current, and is thus lost when power is turned off. Generally referred to simply as "RAM." The more expensive "static RAM" ("SRAM") does not lose its memory in the absence of power. DRAM comes in the form of chips which plug into the motherboard of your computer. → 1.461 RAM

1.**466 extended data output** (**EDO**) A RAM chip with particularly fast access time. → 1.474 RAM

1.**467 main memory** A term used to describe installed memory (RAM) to distinguish it from "virtual memory." → 1.461 RAM; 1.480 VIRTUAL MEMORY

1.**468 memory** The part of the computer where information is electronically stored. Includes dynamic RAM, the volatile "random access" memory that is emptied when a computer is switched off (data needs to be stored on media such as a hard disk for future retrieval), and ROM, the stable "read-only" memory that contains unchanging data, typically the basic startup and initialization functions of some computers (such as Macintoshes). "Memory" should not be confused with storage, even though both are described in terms of megabytes. → 1.461 RAM; 1.475 ROM

1.**469 parameter RAM** (**PRAM**) In Macintosh computers, an area of memory—stored in a chip—that maintains basic settings such as time and date, even when it is switched off (unlike the memory provided by RAM, which is lost when the computer is switched off). The PRAM chip is provided with a continuous power supply from its own lithium battery.

1.**470 PRAM chip** The hardware chip that stores parameter RAM. → 1.470 PARAMETER RAM (PRAM); 1.282 ZAPPING THE PRAM

1.**471 programmable ROM** (**PROM**) A type of memory chip that can be programmed to perform specific functions, using a hardware device known as a PROM programmer. PROM chips can only be programmed once. → 1.475 ROM

1.**472 memory (protected)** An advanced memory management technique that gives a unique address for each application running. Each application effectively has its own memory space and will not interfere with any other application. Should one application crash it is very unlikely that any other processes will be affected.

1.**473 RAM cache** A piece of RAM that stores the most recent actions you have carried out, so that if you need them again they do not need

to be retrieved from disk. → 1.461 CACHE

1.**474 random access memory** (**RAM**) The "working space" made available by the computer, into which some or all of an application's code is loaded and remembered while you work with it. However, an item is memorized in RAM only for as long as your computer is switched on, or until you "save" it to disk. The amount of memory is important, since not only do some graphics applications require substantial amounts of memory to operate, some specific tasks may demand even more. Operating system and application extensions also add to the demand on memory. → 1.465 DYNAMIC RAM (DRAM)

1.**475 read-only memory** (**ROM**) Memory that can be read from but not written to. As distinct from RAM (random access memory), in which data can be written to memory but is lost when power to the computer is switched off. → 1.474 RAM

1.**476 scratch** (**space / disk**) Disk space which, not needed for normal data storage, has been set aside as "virtual memory" for temporary data storage by an application, typically image-editing applications. → 1.480 VIRTUAL MEMORY

1.**477 single inline memory module** (**SIMM**) A computer chip that provides RAM. → 1.462 DIP SIMM; 1.463 DIMM; 1.474 RAM

1.**478 swap file** A file used to temporarily hold the contents of memory in a PC to free memory for other actions. Photoshop typically creates large swap files. The process allows relatively large files to be opened with even small amounts of RAM. The process of "swapping" can take a considerable time and hence the use of swap files should not be seen as an alternative for providing a sufficient level of RAM. → 1.480 VIRTUAL MEMORY

1.**479 video RAM** (**VRAM**) Specialized RAM (random access memory) dedicated to the support of the video display/monitor. → 1.474 RAM

1.**480 virtual memory** A technique of making memory (RAM) seem larger than it really is by using other means of storing data elsewhere, such as on a hard disk. This means that you can work with as much memory as you have disk space, but the tradeoff for this luxury is speed—virtual memory is only as fast as the data transfer speed of the disk. Also called "scratch space" in some applications. → 10.162 VIRTUAL

## Backup terms

1.**481 archive** Any file or collection of files that has been backed up for storage or compressed to free up disk space. → 1.483 BACKUP, ARCHIVAL

1.**482 backup** General name for the items generated as the result of backing up, or copying, the files on your hard disk. A backup is used to restore damaged, lost, or archived files to your hard disk. Different regimes can be employed (either alone or together) to ensure data safety. Such regimes include archival, global, incremental, same-disk, and mirror-image backups. → 1.483 BACKUP, ARCHIVAL; 1.484 BACKUP, GLOBAL/BASELINE; 1.485 BACKUP, INCREMENTAL; 1.486 BACKUP, MIRROR-IMAGE; 1.487 BACKUP, SAME-DISK; 1.788 BACKUP SET

1.**483 backup, archival** A backup routine that specifically copies files on your hard disk without overwriting, or replacing, previously backed up versions of those files. Consequently, archival backups just keep growing, but provide the bonus of allowing a user to recall any historical information. → 1.482 BACKUP

1.**484 backup, global / baseline** A backup routine in which the contents of your hard disk are duplicated, creating a "snapshot" of your disk at one moment in time. Global backups usually form the first copy, or backup "set," of your hard disk, and from then on backups to that set are either "archival" or "incremental." → 1.483 BACKUP, ARCHIVAL; 1.485 BACKUP, INCREMENTAL; 1.488 BACKUP SET; 1.482 BACKUP

1.**485 backup, incremental** A copy to a backup set of only those files on your hard disk that have been modified since the last time you backed up the disk. With some backup software an incremental backup may replace previously backed up versions of newly modified files, so if you want to keep earlier versions you should create an archival backup. → 1.483 BACKUP, ARCHIVAL; 1.488 BACKUP SET; 1.482 BACKUP

1.**486 backup, mirror-image** An exact copy of one hard disk to another, replacing any data which may previously have been stored on the target disk. → 1.482 BACKUP

1.**487 backup, same-disk** A copy of files made to the disk on which the originals reside. As a general backup strategy same-disk backups are not advisable, and should only be used, for example, to keep temporary copies of the file you are working on as a precaution against data corruption. Disk failure will render both original and same-disk backups unreadable. → 1.482 BACKUP

1.**488 backup set** Disks, tapes, files, etc., that form the backed-up copy of your hard disk. Also called a "storage set." → 1.482 BACKUP

1.**489 restore** To copy backed-up files to disk from an archive if the originals are damaged or have been deleted.

## Storage devices and terms

1.**490 Bernoulli drive** A removable disk system that employs the Bernoulli principle. When a flexible magnetic disk is spun at high speeds the air flow creates pressure differentials that cause the disk to rise toward the read/write head. In the event of component or power failure the disk tends to fall away from the head, reducing the risk of damage. Zip disks and drives feature Bernoulli principles.

1.**491 cartridge, removable** Storage medium protected by a plastic casing so that it can be transported from one drive to another. Generally describes tape mechanisms, but can also be applied to optical or magnetic disk media. → 1.517 FLOPPY DISK

1.**492 Clik! disk** Small memory storage disk from Iomega designed for use in portable devices (such as digital cameras) and with a capacity of 40 Mb. Now called a PocketZip disk. → 1.565 ZIP DISK; 1.524 JAZ DISK; 1.523 IOMEGA; 1.493 CLIK! DRIVE

1.**493 Clik! drive** Drive that accepts Iomega's Clik! disks. These drives are sufficiently compact to be incorporated into digital cameras and PC cards and are available as external devices. Now called a PocketZip. → 1.492 CLIK! DISK; 1.093 PC CARD

1.**494 compact disc (CD)** A digital storage technology developed by Philips and Sony Corporation. Data is stored on a compact disc by means of tiny pits burned into the disc's surface; the size of a pit determines whether it is read as a 0 or a 1. → 1.495 CD-I; 1.496 CD-ROM; 1.498 CD-R

1.**495 compact disc interactive (CD-I)** A compact disc technology similar to CD-ROM and originally intended for the consumer electronics market. Developed by Philips, CD-I discs require a special player but can be viewed on a regular television set. CD-I technology has been supplanted by the widespread acceptance of CD-ROM technology in both the consumer and business markets, and also by the introduction of the very capacious DVD (digital versatile disc). → 1.496 CD-ROM; 1.505 DVD; 10.076 GREEN BOOK

**1.496 compact disc read-only memory (CD-ROM)** A CD technology developed for the storage and distribution of digital data for use on computers. Data is stored by means of tiny pits—the size of which determines whether they are read as a 0 or a 1—burned into an encapsulated layer and read by a laser that distinguishes the pits from the "lands" (the spaces between the pits). CD-ROMs are based on audio CD technology, and are 12 cm (5 in.) in diameter and come in two capacities: 74 minutes in duration (CD capacity is calibrated by the time it takes to record a whole disc), giving a data capacity of around 650 Mb; or 63 minutes, giving a data capacity of 550 Mb. The exact capacity can vary from one manufacturer to another. → 1.494 CD; 1.495 CD-I; 1.498 CD-R; 10.167 YELLOW BOOK; 8.003 BURN

**1.497 compact disc read-only memory extended architecture (CD-ROM / XA)** An extended version of the original CD-ROM standard that enhances the real-time playback capability of time-based data. CD-ROM/XA is similar to CD-I technology but is intended for use with computer CD-ROM drives rather than with special players. A CD-ROM/XA drive will also read CD-ROM and CD-I discs. → 1.496 CD-ROM; 1.495 CD-I

**1.498 compact disc recordable (CD-R)** Specially-made CDs which can record data by means of a laser that burns microscopic holes ("pits") into a thin recording layer. CD-Rs can be read by standard CD-ROM players, but are rather more fragile than mass-replicated CDs. → 1.496 CD-ROM; 1.562 WORM; 10.118 ORANGE BOOK; 1.494 CD; 8.003 BURN

**1.499 compact disc rewritable (CD-RW)** A recordable CD onto which data can be written over and over again, much like magnetic media. Also called an "EO" (erasable optical) disc. → 1.498 CD-R; 1.562 WORM; 1.494 CD; 1.514 EO

**1.500 CompactFlash** Small memory storage card, resembling a small PC card. Can be slotted into an adaptor card that, in turn, can be slotted in a PC (PCMCIA) card slot for downloading of images. Nikon and Canon tend to prefer the CompactFlash card for their cameras. → 1.093 PCMCIA CARD; 1.552 SMARTMEDIA

**1.501 constant angular velocity (CAV)** Playback mode for certain optical disks (e.g. LaserDisc, LaserVision).

**1.502 constant linear velocity (CLV)** Playback mode for certain optical discs (e.g. LaserVision, LaserDisc).

**1.503 defragment(ing)** The technique of joining together pieces of "fragmented" files—those which due to a shortage of contiguous storage space on the disk have been split into smaller pieces—so that they are easier for the drive heads to access, thus speeding up disk operations. The process is also known as "optimizing." → 1.535 OPTIMIZE/OPTIMIZING

**1.504 digital audio tape (DAT)** A magnetic medium used to store large amounts of data. Used for either backing up or archiving data, DAT tapes are "linear"—that is, they run from beginning to end—and thus cannot be used for primary storage like a hard disk, because the data cannot be accessed at random.

**1.505 digital versatile disc (DVD)** A high-capacity (up to 17.08 gigabytes (GB) of data) storage disc similar to a CD-ROM, on to which data is "written" by means of tiny pits burned into the disc's surface by a laser, but which uses a shorter wavelength laser so that the pits can be closer together. There are four capacities of DVD, some of which are double-sided while others have two layers of information on each side: DVD5 (which holds 4.7 GB of data), DVD9 (8.5 GB), DVD10 (9.4 GB), and DVD18 (17.08 GB), as well as several different types: DVD-Video, DVD-ROM, DVD-Audio, DVD-R (recordable), and DVD-RAM (rewritable). All DVD drives can generally read all four capacities, although not necessarily all types of DVD, as well as "old-fashioned" CD-ROMs. → 1.496 CD-ROM; 1.507 DVD-ROM; 1.509 DVD-VIDEO; 1.508 DVD-R; 1.506 DVD-RAM

**1.506 digital versatile disc random access memory (DVD-RAM)** A DVD which is rewritable like a CD-RW but is more capacious. → 1.499 CD-RW; 1.505 DVD; 1.507 DVD-ROM; 1.509 DVD-VIDEO; 1.508 DVD-R

1.**507 digital versatile disc read-only memory** (**DVD-ROM**) A high-capacity version of a CD-ROM, holding up to 17 GB of data. → 1.496 CD-ROM; 1.505 DVD; 1.509 DVD-VIDEO; 1.508 DVD-R; 1.506 DVD-RAM

1.**508 digital versatile disc recordable** (**DVD-R**) A high-capacity storage media which, in much the same way as a CD-R, enables you to write your own DVDs. → 1.498 CD-R; 1.507 DVD-ROM; 1.505 DVD; 1.509 DVD-VIDEO; 1.506 DVD-RAM

1.**509 digital versatile disc video** (**DVD-Video**) A high capacity DVD used for storing feature-length movies, playing back via set-top boxes plugged into a TV. The DVD players contain an MPEG decoder that enables playback features—a choice of camera angles, for example—in a variety of formats such as wide-screen or HDTV (high-definition TV). → 1.505 DVD; 1.507 DVD-ROM; 1.508 DVD-R; 1.506 DVD-RAM; 10.114 MPEG

1.**510 disk** A circular platter with a magnetic surface on which computer data is stored. Data is written to and read from the disk by a mechanism called a disk drive. Disks may be rigid ("hard disk") or flexible ("floppy disk"), and may reside on a disk drive installed inside your computer ("internal disk drive"), in a device connected to your computer ("external disk drive"), or in a cartridge that can be transported between disk drives ("removable disk"). A disk drive may contain several "platters," but is referred to in the singular—"disk." Not to be confused with "disc," which is much the same thing, but uses optical rather than magnetic techniques

to store data. There is also a third type of disc, which combines both techniques and is called a "magneto-optical disc" (MO). → 1.529 MAGNETO-OPTICAL DISC (MO/MOD)

1.**511 disk crash** A colloquialism describing the operating failure of a hard disk drive, preventing you from accessing data. This may be brought about by corruption of the disk's "format" (the way information is arranged on the disk), dirt or dust on the disk's surface, or failure of a mechanical part in the drive. If the former, repairs can sometimes be made with a disk maintenance utility, but in the latter case repair is unlikely and may result in complete loss of all your data. You should always regard a disk crash as being inevitable—not a question of "if" but "when"—and back up your data regularly. → 1.520 FORMATTING

1.**512 disk / disc drive** Often referred to simply as a "drive," this is a hardware device which writes data to, or reads it from, a disk (or disc). A disk drive may contain several "platters" housed in a sealed unit (sometimes called a hard drive to distinguish it from other kinds), or it may be a device that reads disks (or discs) which are inserted into it. It may be installed inside your computer (internal disk drive) or it may be a remote device connected to your computer (external disk drive). → 1.510 DISK

1.**513 drive head** The part of any kind of disk drive that extracts (reads) data from, and deposits (writes) data to, a disk or tape, for example. In hard drives, one read/write head is positioned above each side of every disk

1.510 *hard disk*

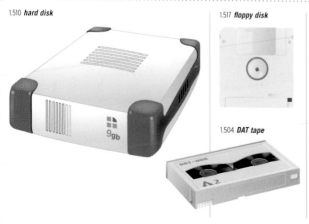

1.517 *floppy disk*

1.534 *optical disc/media*

1.504 *DAT tape*

1.565 *zip disk*

platter (a hard drive may consist of several platters). These move on rails over the surface of the platter, which rotates at high speed. → 1.512 DISK/DISC DRIVE

1.**514 erasable optical (EO) media** Storage media that can be written to as well as read from, such as "CD-RW" (compact disc rewritable) media. → 1.499 CD-RW

1.**515 external (disk) drive** Any disk drive connected to a computer that does not reside inside the computer's case. → 1.044 EXTERNAL DEVICE; 1.512 DISK/DISC DRIVE

1.**516 floppy** Colloquial name for a floppy disk. Term originates from description of early 8-in and 5.25-in disks which were housed in flexible plastic envelopes. → 1.517 FLOPPY DISK

1.**517 floppy disk** A flexible circular platter coated with a magnetic medium and housed in a plastic case, on which computer data is stored. Floppy disks are typically 3.5-in in diameter and may be single-sided (400 K capacity, now more-or-less obsolete), double-sided (800 K, also obsolete), or high density ("FDHD"—floppy disk, high density, 1.4 MB). Also called "diskettes," floppy disks are becoming less viable as a storage medium and will eventually disappear as modern computers are increasingly being built without floppy disk drives. → 1.512 DISK/DISC DRIVE

1.**518 floppy (disk) drive** A hardware device for reading and writing data to and from floppy disks. Although internal floppy disk drives are standard on most computers built to date, the low storage capacity of floppy disks makes them less viable as a storage medium and they will eventually disappear as computers are increasingly being built without floppy disk drives. → 1.517 FLOPPY DISK

1.**519 floptical** A contraction of "floppy" and "optical." A floptical is a "magneto-optical" (MO) disc of the same size as a common 3.5-in "floppy" disk, but which contains much more data—up to 230 MB compared with 1.4 MB on a floppy. → 1.529 MAGNETO-OPTICAL DISC (MO/MOD)

1.**520 formatting** The process of preparing a new disk so that it can be used with a computer for organizing and storing data. When a disk is formatted, sectors, tracks, and empty directories are created. Any disk can be reformatted, generally with the loss of all data upon it. → 3.089 INITIALIZE; 1.511 DISK CRASH

1.**521 head crash** The failure of a disk drive, sometimes caused by one of its read/write heads coming into contact with, and damaging, the hard disk surface. → 1.544 READ/WRITE HEAD

1.**522 interleave ratio** The ratio between the numbers and the order of track sectors on a disk. Sectors which are numbered consecutively have a ratio of 1:1, while a ratio of 3:1 means that the numbers run consecutively only in every third sector. This indicates how many times a disk needs to rotate so that all data in a single track is read; a computer with a slow data transfer rate requires a disk to spin more often so that it has time to absorb all of the data in a track, thus a 3:1 interleave ratio requires a disk to rotate three times because it only reads every third sector. The fastest ratio is 1:1 because all the data in a track will be read in a single revolution of the disk. Also called "sector interleave factor." → 1.131 DATA TRANSFER RATE

1.**523 Iomega** Creator and manufacturer of the popular Zip, Jaz, and Clik! (now PocketZip) disks and drives.

1.**524 Jaz disk** A removable disk from Iomega, available with a storage capacity of up to 2 Gb. Not compatible with Zip disks or drives. → 1.525 JAZ DRIVE; 1.565 ZIP DISK; 1.566 ZIP DRIVE

1.**525 Jaz drive** Iomega drive that supports the 1 Gb or 2 Gb Jaz disks. Usually provided as an external device connected to the computer via a SCSI connector. → 1.524 JAZ DISK

1.**526 locked disk** A removable or floppy disk that is write-protected and thus can only be read from.

1.**527 logical volume** A volume such as a partition created by software; as distinct from a "physical volume" such as a disk. → 1.537 PARTITION(ING)

1.**528 magnetic media / storage** Any computer data storage system which uses a magnetic medium, such as disk, tape or card, to store information. → 1.510 DISK

1.**529 magneto-optical disc (MO / MOD)** A rewritable storage medium that combines the technologies of a laser and an electromagnet for writing and reading data, the result being that data cannot be corrupted by stray magnetic fields. → 1.510 DISK; 1.519 FLOPTICAL

1.**530 master directory block** The area of a computer disk that contains the disk directory (the catalog of files), which is put into RAM when you start or insert the disk. → 3.075 DIRECTORY

**1.531 media (hardware)** A plural term now accepted as a singular to describe the actual item on which digital data is stored, such as a floppy disk, hard disk, CD-ROM, etc., as distinct from the devices in which they are used. → 1.510 DISK

**1.532 memory allocation** The allocation of memory to specific tasks, thus enabling system software, application software, utilities, and hardware to operate side by side. → 1.457 APPLICATION HEAP/MEMORY

**1.533 Microdrive / IBM Microdrive** Miniature hard disk produced by IBM for large scale storage in digital cameras and other portable devices. Based on the dimensions of a CompactFlash Type II card (and compatible with these) it offers capacities of 170MB, 340MB, 512MB, and 1GB

**1.534 optical disc / media** Generic term for media that store digitized data by means of minute pits in the surface of a disc. The size of the pit detemines whether it indicates the binary digit 1 or 0, and the pits are "read" by an optical pickup using a laser which is reflected off a shiny metallic layer on the disc's surface. Optical discs are widely used for audio and video recording and for computer data storage, and are capable of holding huge amounts of data. Commonly called CDs (compact discs) or DVDs (digital versatile discs), optical discs are more resilient than magnetic media and thus provide more secure data storage.

**1.535 optimize / optimizing** The technique of speeding up disk operations by using special "utility" software to shuffle files around and join together those which, due to a shortage of contiguous storage space on the disk, have become "fragmented" (split into smaller pieces). This also creates contiguous areas of unused storage space on your drive, thus allowing files to be written to disk faster when you save them. → 1.503 DEFRAGMENT(ING)

**1.536 parked** The state of a disk drive's read/write heads when they are at rest, important if the drive or cartridge is to be moved without damage to the disk.

**1.537 partition(ing)** The division of a hard disk into smaller volumes, each of which behaves as if it were a separate disk. There are two kinds of partitions: "real partitions" (sometimes called "SCSI partitions") in which you divide the disk up during formatting, and "file partitions" (also called "disk images"), which are large files created on an existing disk drive. → 3.077 DISK IMAGE

**1.538 PhotoCD** A proprietary, cross-platform technology developed by Kodak for scanning and storing photographs on CD-ROM. PhotoCD files can be opened and edited with most image-editing applications. → 1.540 PICTURE CD

**1.539 PhotoCD Portfolio** A multimedia-capable derivation of the PhotoCD format originally designed for presentations using dedicated PhotoCD players as well as computer-based applications. Can store up to 680 images of low-to-medium resolution or up to one hour of sound, or a mix of both. → 1.538 PHOTOCD

1.535 *optimize/optimizing*

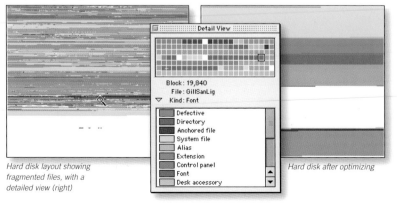

Hard disk layout showing fragmented files, with a detailed view (right)

Detail View

Block : 19,840
File : GillSanLig
▽ Kind : Font

Defective
Directory
Anchored file
System file
Alias
Extension
Control panel
Font
Desk accessory

Hard disk after optimizing

1.**540 PictureCD** CD-based image storage format devised by Kodak and Intel. Designed as an expedient and cost-effective alternative to PhotoCDs, PictureCDs are produced at the time a film is processed. In addition to being produced as conventional prints, images are recorded in JPEG format onto CD, so that a reasonable quality 8x11 in. print can be produced. Additional features provided on the CD include basic image-editing software, and viewing, e-mailing, and printing applications. This additional content varies according to the PictureCD release version, which is denoted by volume and issue numbers. Original PictureCDs provided only Windows-based additional content, although images can be opened on any platform.

1.**541 Pro PhotoCD** "Professional" version of Kodak's PhotoCD technology that includes the high-resolution 64base files, yielding a file size of 72 MB per image, along with the smaller conventional image sizes. 64base files are capable of much greater enlargement and, subject to the quality of the originals, are capable of supporting much more detail. → 1.538 PhotoCD

1.**542 RAID** Acronym for redundant array of independent disks. A set of hard disks normally mounted in a single enclosure. Critical data is written to more than one disk at a time, thus improving read/write performance and reducing the risk of data loss following a single disk failure.

1.**543 RAM disk** A feature of some operating systems or utility software in which a part of the RAM can be temporarily "tricked" into thinking that it is a disk drive. Because the process of retrieving data from RAM is so much faster than from disk, operations performed by items—such as applications or documents—stored in a RAM "disk" will speed up. Critical data should never be commited to a RAM disk because the "disk" will disappear when the computer is switched off. → 1.474 RAM

1.**544 read / write head** The part of a disk drive that "reads" data from, and "writes" data to, a disk. One read/write head is positioned above each side of every platter in a disk drive, and there may be several platters in a drive. These heads move, on rails, over the surface of the platter, which rotates at speed. → 1.512 DISK/DISC DRIVE

1.**545 removable media** Hard disks or optical discs that can be ejected from their hardware, thus making it easier to transport large amounts of data between computers that are not networked, and back-up data.

1.**546 removable media drive** A drive for media (tape or disks) that can be removed from the drive (as compared with a fixed hard-disk drive).

1.**547 SCSI partition** → 1.537 partition(ing)

1.**548 sector** A segment of a track on a disk, and the smallest contiguous space in which data can be stored, usually allowing space for 512 consecutive bytes.

1.**549 seek time** The time it takes for a disk head to move from whatever track it is on to whatever track you tell it to read next. → 1.001 ACCESS TIME

1.**550 session** A term used to describe the recording of data onto a recordable CD. Unlike other media, most CDs need a continuous feed of data that is recorded at a constant rate. The process of continuous recording is known as a session.

1.**551 shared disk** Any hard disk attached to a networked computer which other computers on the network can access. → 1.152 NETWORK

1.**552 SmartMedia** Small memory storage card used mainly in digital cameras and some MP3 music players. Favored by, among others, Fuji. → 1.093 PCMCIA CARD; 1.500 CompactFlash

1.**553 storage** The preservation of data (on disk, tape, etc.) so that it can be accessed at a future date, as distinct from "memory" where data is in transit.

1.**554 Syquest** Proprietary name for disk drives and removable disks made by the Syquest Corporation. Now largely superseded by Zip disks/drives and similar.

1.**555 system disk** A disk containing all the operating system files necessary to start up the computer and carry out processing operations.

1.**556 tape drive** A device used for copying data from a primary storage device, such as a hard disk, for backup archiving purposes. A tape drive uses magnetic tape housed in removable cartridges. Tape drives are not used for primary storage because the data is stored on them "sequentially" (in a linear form, from end to end), and cannot be accessed at random, as it can on disks.

1.**557 track** The concentric "rings" circumscribing a "platter" in a hard disk drive, on which data is stored. Each track is divided into "sectors," which aid the accessibility of the data. → 1.548 SECTOR

1.**558 unmount** To remove a volume (disk) from the desktop by disconnecting or ejecting it. → 1.510 DISK

1.**559 verification, verify** A term used to describe the process of testing the integrity of data or the data blocks on a disk drive by repeatedly writing and reading data to the disk. → 1.034 DATA

1.**560 volume** A device or a partition where data is stored—usually a disk or tape, or a part thereof.

1.**561 volume bitmap** A record of the used blocks (represented by an "on" bit) and unused blocks (off) on a volume.

1.**562 write-once read-many (WORM)** Large capacity storage media such as CD-recordable (CD-R) discs that can be written to only once and cannot be erased. → 1.498 CD-R

1.**563 write-protect** To protect a computer disk from erasure (accidental or otherwise) or from contamination by viruses, by preventing any data from being written to it or deleted from it, although the contents can still be read. Some removable media

is equipped with a small tab which, when moved to reveal a hole, write-protects the disk. Sliding it back again to fill in the hole "write-enables" the disk so that data can be added or deleted.

1.**564 write / writing head** The part of a disk drive that retrieves (reads) data from, and deposits (writes) data to, a disk. One read/write head is positioned above each side of every disk platter (a hard drive may consist of several platters). These move, on rails, across the surface of the platter while the platter rotates at speed. → 1.512 DISK/DISC DRIVE

1.**565 Zip disk** A 3.5-inch removable disk, devised by Iomega, that has a storage capacity of 100 Mb or 250 Mb. It has become a standard for the exchange of large image files. Although Zip disks are the same size as floppies (albeit a little thicker) the disks and drives cannot be interchanged. → 1.524 JAZ DISK; 1.566 ZIP DRIVE; 1.523 IOMEGA

1.**566 Zip drive** Iomega's drive that supports their 100- and 250-Mb floppy-sized Zip disks. Zip drives are available as external and internal devices. Note that 100-Mb disks can be read by 250-Mb drives, but 250-Mb disks are not compatible with the smaller drive.

## Photoshop interface

2.**001 Auto-Update option** Select the Auto-Update option (in Photoshop and ImageReady) to automatically save changes to a document when you save the document in a jumped-to application. This ensures that the application that originally created the document displays the latest version.

2.**002 background color** (1) The color that appears when part of an image is erased. This color is indicated in the lower part of the Toolbar, partially covered by the foreground color. Clicking on the double arrowhead icon adjacent to the colors will reverse the background and foreground colors. → 2.106 FOREGROUND COLOR

2.**003 bounding border/box** A border frame, complete with adjustment handles, that appears around an object or selection to allow resizing or distortion, such as in Transform. → 2.287 TRANSFORM

2.**004 brush creation** You can add brushes to or delete them from the standard array offered. To add a brush click on the empty area in the brushes palette outside the brush squares, or alternatively select New Brush

from the Brushes palette menu. In either case you can then use the New Brush dialog box to formulate your new brush. Results are shown in the preview box. After completion, your new brush is added to the brushes palette for future use.

2.**005 canvas** The term canvas is used in Photoshop to describe the editable image area. → 2.055 WORKING CANVAS

2.**006 clipboard purge** A large image, or image element, stored on the clipboard can hog a considerable amount of memory, limiting that available for Photoshop processing tasks. To restore that memory, clear the contents of the clipboard. From the Edit menu select Purge > Clipboard. Note that there is no undo for this command.

2.**007 color samplers** An alternative color selection device to the eyedropper tool. Using the Color Sampler tool (found on the Eyedropper pull-out menu) you can place up to four color read-out markers on an image.

2.**008 context menus** These appear in Photoshop as pop-up menus activated by a right mouse click (Windows) or Control-click (Mac OS).

2.**009 Current tool** Status bar option. Displays the name of the currently active tool.

2.018 *Gamma control panel*

2.023 *Hints*

**010 Display** Action of showing Photoshop palette. All open palettes may be displayed or hidden using the tab key.

**011 Efficiency** Status bar option. Efficiency displays an approximation of Photoshop operations using RAM (rather than scratch disk space), as a percentage. Below 100% efficiency scratch disk space is being used and thus performance is compromised.

**012 ellipse** An oval shape that corresponds to the oblique view of a circular plane. One option for the Marquee tool. → 2.090 MARQUEE TOOL

**013 export module** Module that permits the exporting of data (such as a path created in Photoshop) to another application (such as Illustrator).

**014 Feather** (**1**) Enabling the Feather option blurs the edges of selections. This helps blend these selections when they are pasted into different backgrounds, giving less of a "cut out" effect. → 2.333 FEATHER (2)

**015 floating palette** A description of any of the Photoshop palettes (because they all float!). This enables them to be placed anywhere on the desktop that is convenient to the user. → 2.166 PALETTE

**016 foreground color** The "active" color that will be used by default when a painting tool is selected. The current foreground color is shown in the Toolbar, along with the background color. The foreground color may be selected or changed from the Color Picker or the Eyedropper tool or from within the Color palette → 2.002 BACKGROUND COLOR (1)

2.**017 frame selection** A selection made by a marquee (either rectangular or elliptical) that comprises only a frame, i.e. the central area and the area outside the frame are unselected. Created by first making the major selection (the outside of the frame) and then deselecting the central area using Alt-drag (Windows) or Option-drag (Mac OS).

2.**018 Gamma control panel** Mac OS control panel provided in Photoshop prior to version 5 to assist in the calibration of monitors. Version 5 onward features the replacement Adobe Gamma control panel.

2.**019 Gradient Editor** This permits the creations of new gradients to be used by the Gradient tool, or the editing of existing gradient. To use the editor choose a gradient, select the Gradient Options palette and click on Edit. The Gradient Editor will be displayed. From here you can create new gradients, duplicate existing ones (for editing, without disturbing the original) or remove unwanted gradients. → 2.082 GRADIENT TOOL

2.**020 grid** The Photoshop grid appears as nonprinting lines (or, alternatively, dots) and can be used for accurate alignment and positioning of image elements. To turn the grid on or off select Show/Hide Grid from the View menu. → 2.021 GUIDES

2.**021 guides** Lines that appear to float over the entire image space but do not print. Unlike the similar grid, guide lines can be manually positioned vertically or horizontally across any part of the image. → 2.020 GRID

2.**022 Hide** Action of hiding a Photoshop palette. → 2.10 DISPLAY

.019 *Gradient Editor*

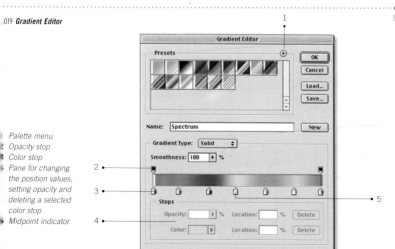

Palette menu
Opacity stop
Color stop
Pane for changing the position values, setting opacity and deleting a selected color stop
Midpoint indicator

2.**023 Hints** Photoshop Elements feature. Hints provide context sensitive advice in the form of a palette. The hints are usually pertinent to the tool or action in progress. The more extensive Recipes give extended help for achieving particular effects. → 2.035 RECIPES

2.**024 histogram** A graphic representation of image data in the form of solid vertical or horizontal bars. Used to graph the number of pixels at each brightness level in a digital image, thus giving a rapid idea of the tonal range of the image so that you can tell if there is enough detail to make corrections.

2.**025 History** Photoshop feature that enables you to selectively undo any of up to ninety-nine previous stages of an image editing session. Each of these stages is referred to as a state. Using the History Brush tool you can selectively restore areas of an image to a chosen previous state, either by filling a selection with a previous state or by erasing the current state to reveal a previous one.

2.**026 keyboard shortcut** A keystroke (or more often a combination of keystrokes) that invokes a Photoshop function normally selected via the mouse and menus. For example, the "L" key will make the currently displayed lasso option active; "W" will activate the magic wand. See the keyboard shortcut table for a complete list of commands.

2.**027 Layer Clipping Path** Photoshop 6 feature. A vector-based mask (the feature was originally to be called Vector Mask), this is drawn with the Pen tool but works with a layer mask to create a smooth-edged outline that renders

everything within as visible and everything outside as hidden.

2.**028 menu command** A command given to the computer from a list of choices available within a menu, as distinct from a command made via the keyboard ("keyboard command").

2.**029 noncontiguous selection** Selections of nonadjacent area with a common parameter (for example, areas of equal tone, or color).

2.**030 Olé No Moire** Special image provided with Mac OS versions of Photoshop. Centered on a Carmen Miranda-esque lady, the image provides a full-color image along with proof printing elements that can be used to test color fidelity and printer settings (among other things). The image includes a black overprint color bar, registration marks, progressive color bar, crop marks, gradient tint bar, and star target. Windows users should use the Testpict.jpg file.

2.**031 Photoshop interface** Both the Mac OS and Windows versions of Photoshop comply with the respective regimes with regard to menu placement and operating system functionality. Hence the fundamental menus and operation of windows and other elements are consistent with other applications. The Photoshop interface is characterized by the Toolbar (to which minor changes have been applied with successive Photoshop versions) and the floating palettes. The ImageReady interface is similar to that of Photoshop (and is even closer with Photoshop 6/ImageReady 3) but includes minor differences reflecting the differing nature of these products.

2.007 *color samplers*

2.034 *Quick Start Window*

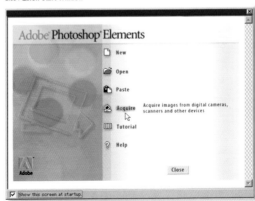

2.**032 Precise cursor** Preferences file setting. Changes the cursor from the default shape (which generally matches that of the tool) to a precise cross-hair graticule. Essential for determining the exact start point for the tool action. A second option, Brush Size cursor, displays a cursor the size (and shape) of selected brush.

2.**033 Quick Start Window** Window that opens on launch of Photoshop Elements (unless the "Show Screen at startup" box is unchecked). Permits easy selection from the options of "Create a new image," "Open an image file," Paste from clipboard, Acquire (from a scanner or camera), Tutorial, and Help. If the screen does not appear at startup (or the user wishes to display it at any other time), it can be shown by selecting Window menu > Quick Start.

2.**034 Quick Start** Photoshop Elements command that displays the Quick Start Window at any time.

2.**035 Recipes** Feature of Photoshop Elements that gives directions, as in a conventional recipe, for performing certain tasks such as red-eye removal or cleaning up an image.

2.**036 Rulers** Rulers can be optionally made to appear along the top and left edge of the active window by choosing Show Rulers from the View menu. The current cursor position is indicated by dash marks on each ruler.

2.**037 Scratch Disk** Photoshop is a RAM-memory hungry program. If your computer lacks sufficient RAM to perform a specific task it will invoke a scratch disk, a virtual memory system (or, more correctly, a virtual RAM system) wherein a portion of an allocated disk is assigned as "surrogate RAM." It will use this scratch disk in lieu of real RAM. Although it might seem an ideal solution (hard disk megabytes are cheaper than their RAM equivalent), this method is time-consuming and inefficient. For best performance select your fastest hard disk (if you have more than one) or create a dedicated partition for use as the scratch disk. But there really is no substitute for physical RAM.

2.**038 Shortcuts Bar** Photoshop Elements interface feature. The Shortcuts bar is displayed between the menu bar and the tool options bar. It provides conventional shortcuts to file save, print, save for web, and others. An extension of the shortcuts bar comprises a palette well similar to that of Photoshop 6, but extended to accommodate the additional palettes offered in Photoshop Elements.

2.**039 shrink/expand** The size of a palette can be changed by dragging on its corner to enlarge or reduce its size and make more options visible or reduce it to a convenient size for the workspace.

2.**040 signal strength meter** Enables the robustness of a digital watermark created using the Digimarc process to be evaluated. Digital watermarks are designed to withstand copying and transmission of images, but the more robust the encoding the greater the degradation of the image. The signal strength meter (accessed by selecting Digimarc > Read Watermark from the Filter

2.035 *Recipes*

2.041 *Slice tool*

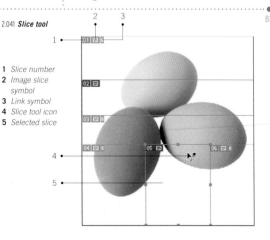

1 *Slice number*
2 *Image slice symbol*
3 *Link symbol*
4 *Slice tool icon*
5 *Selected slice*

menu) is shown as a bar along the bottom edge of the image. Note that this feature will only provide a reading for images to which you have added a watermark.

2.**041 Slice tool** (**1**) The Slice tool first appeared in Photoshop in version 6. It enables complex graphics and imagery to be created from and within a single document. A slice is a distinct rectangular area of an image that is assigned as a cell in an HTML table in the corresponding HTML file for that image. When slices are created using ImageReady, further slices are created automatically such that the entire image is assigned to cells in the HTML table. Slices drawn in an image are known as user-slices. Auto-generated slices created by ImageReady are auto-slices. Every file contains one auto-slice, by default. → 7.082 SLICES

2.**042 Snapshot** Command that saves a copy of the image (in its current edit state) to the list of snapshots shown at the top of the History palette. You can later work with a copy of the image in that edit state by clicking on the appropriate snapshot. This is a temporary storage facility; snapshots are lost when the image is closed.

2.**043 standard cursor** Preferences setting that is the default setting for Photoshop cursors. Normally mimics the shape of the corresponding tool icon.

2.**044 status bar** The status bar is shown at the base of the active window (Mac OS) or at the base of the Photoshop window (Windows). It is always visible on Macintosh computers but can be toggled on or off with Windows computers: choose Hide/Show Status Bar from the Window menu. Depending on the operating system, the status bar displays the zoom percentage, document sizes, scratch sizes (RAM currently accessible to Photoshop), efficiency (percentage of that RAM that is currently being used), timing and short comments relating to the current tool or command. Pressing and holding the status bar will show an image thumbnail. Option-press (MacOS) or Alt-press (Windows) on the status bar to display resolution and dimension information. → 2.114 ZOOM TOOL

2.**045 Styles** (**1**) A set of layer effects that can be saved and applied to a chosen layer or image. Styles can be used to create button effects, textures, image effects or text

effects. Suites of predefined styles are included in Photoshop 6 and can be selected from the Styles palette. → 5.021 LAYER EFFECTS; 5.026 LAYERS

2.**046 text box** A box in which to enter and edit text. Accessed via the Type tool.

2.**047 threshold** A determining value for a pixel. Setting a threshold level for a particular function causes those pixels either above or below that level (depending on the conditions) to be affected by the result of the function.

2.**048 Timing** Status bar option. Measure of the time, in seconds, taken to perform the last operation.

2.**049 Tool Options bar** Photoshop 6 feature. Comprises a strip (34 pixels deep) across the monitor immediately below the menu bar (default setting). Provides essential information and controls for the selected tools, in the manner of the corresponding Tools palette in earlier versions of Photoshop. The Options bar can be moved by dragging the title bar on the left edge When selection tools are selected the Options bar features new buttons enabling Boolean operations to be carried out on the selection, including adding to, removing from, and intersecting with the selection. The Options bar also includes an area to dock palettes. This area, however, is only available when the Options bar is docked at the top or bottom of the screen and when the screen resolution is 800 x 600 pixels or greater.

2.**050 Toolbox, Tool Palette** The main feature of the Photoshop workspace that holds the main tools and controls and, by default, appears down the left-hand edge of the workspace. Also known as the Toolbar. The Toolbox is divided into several areas (although the exact makeup does vary according to version). Uppermost are the Selection tools, including the Lasso, Magic Wand, and Marquee. Next come the Painting tools (such as Airbrush and Paintbrush, Rubber Stamp tool and Brushes). Darkroom (Dodge/Burn, Sponge) and Text tools come next, followed by the Navigation and Utility tools. Additions to Photoshop 6 mean that the Toolbox features some new tools, while others have been repositioned. The Tool Options bar (which replaces earlier tools palettes) changes according to the selected tool. Principal changes are: The addition of a

## 2.049 **Tool Options bar**

Brush size        Blending mode        Brush dynamics        Palette well

## 2.050 **Toolbox**

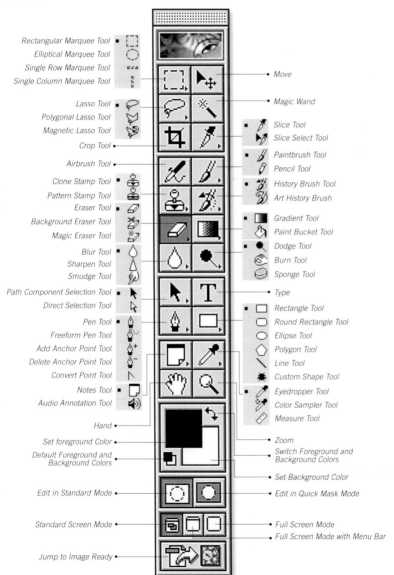

Rectangular Marquee Tool
Elliptical Marquee Tool
Single Row Marquee Tool
Single Column Marquee Tool

Lasso Tool
Polygonal Lasso Tool
Magnetic Lasso Tool
Crop Tool

Airbrush Tool

Clone Stamp Tool
Pattern Stamp Tool
Eraser Tool
Background Eraser Tool
Magic Eraser Tool

Blur Tool
Sharpen Tool
Smudge Tool

Path Component Selection Tool
Direct Selection Tool

Pen Tool
Freeform Pen Tool
Add Anchor Point Tool
Delete Anchor Point Tool
Convert Point Tool

Notes Tool
Audio Annotation Tool

Hand

Set foreground Color
Default Foreground and
Background Colors

Edit in Standard Mode

Standard Screen Mode

Jump to Image Ready

Move

Magic Wand

Slice Tool
Slice Select Tool

Paintbrush Tool
Pencil Tool

History Brush Tool
Art History Brush

Gradient Tool
Paint Bucket Tool

Dodge Tool
Burn Tool
Sponge Tool

Type

Rectangle Tool
Round Rectangle Tool
Ellipse Tool
Polygon Tool
Line Tool
Custom Shape Tool

Eyedropper Tool
Color Sampler Tool
Measure Tool

Zoom

Switch Foreground and
Background Colors

Set Background Color

Edit in Quick Mask Mode

Full Screen Mode
Full Screen Mode with Menu Bar

85

Slices tool (with options of Slice tool and Slice Select tool), as previously featured only in ImageReady; Pull-out menu options now feature the name of the tool options, as well as the icon and shortcut; Paintbrush and Pencil share a menu position; Bucket and Gradient tools share a menu position; Shape and Notes tools have been added, each with their own menu position. → 1.257 TOOL

2.051 Toolbox (Photoshop Elements) The toolbox for Photoshop Elements features the conventional tools (in an array similar to that of Photoshop 6) and the foreground/background color selector. It does not feature a quickmask mode selector, "jump to" button, or alternative display option buttons.

2.052 Warp Text Photoshop 6 feature. Enhanced text feature that enables text to be warped as if being entered along a curved path. A range of warp styles are provided which can be changed later. Further options enable precise control over the perspective of the text and also enable the orientation to be altered.

2.053 watermark Because digital images are, by their nature, easy to copy it is worthwhile considering adding some protection to avoid seeing your treasured images exploited by someone else. In Photoshop you can add a Digimarc watermark to your image. As it is stored as digital noise in the image it is not immediately apparent but can survive most image edits—it can even be traced when an image is printed and rescanned.
→ 6.069 DIGIMARC

2.054 watermarks When images are opened

Photoshop will automatically scan them for watermarks using a special plug-in, the Digimarc Detect Watermark. If an appropriate watermark is found by the plug-in, Photoshop will display a copyright symbol in the image's title bar and enter information in the Copyright & URL fields of the File Info dialog box.

2.055 working canvas The working canvas (or work canvas) describes the current working document. Work space can be added or removed from the working canvas using the Canvas Size command (Image menu > Canvas size). → 2.005 CANVAS

## Main menus

2.056 Edit menu (2) Fundamental menu featuring generic Edit menu items (Undo, Cut, Copy, Paste, etc.) and Photoshop-specific items (Fill, Stroke, Transform/Free Transform, Define Pattern, and Purge).

2.057 Filter menu Photoshop's image manipulation filters are grouped in this menu, which normally has three subsections. Filters that comprise the basic Photoshop suite are grouped in the center section, under headings such as Artistic, Distort, and Texture. Plug-ins—additional filters provided by third parties—appear in the bottom section. The top section shows the last selected filter (for reapplication) and the Fade Last Filter command. The latter allows the last used filter to be applied in varying strengths ranging from zero to full (normal application).

2.052 *Warp Text*

1 *Plain text*
2 *Arch*
3 *Arc*
4 *Fish*
5 *Flag*
6 *Bulge*

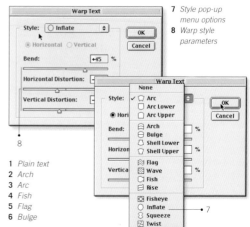

7 *Style pop-up menu options*
8 *Warp style parameters*

2.**058 Help menu** The place for the user to go to for help and assistance. In addition to the listed help topics, the help menu also gives specific help on color management, exporting of transparent images, and image resizing. Help is offered using the Windows or Mac OS help browser in versions up to and including 5.5, and via a web browser from version 6.0.

2.**059 Image menu** Menu group that provides fundamental image functions including Mode (for image mode selection), Adjust (for basic color/contrast/brightness control), Canvas Size (for adding areas to or removing them from the workspace), and Image Size (for modifying an image's file resolution, dimensions, or size).

2.**060 Layer menu** The menu dedicated specifically to layer manipulations. Options allow you to create, delete, or duplicate layers, link, group, and arrange layers, and flatten an image.

2.**061 Select menu** You can control and make selections from this menu. The primary options allow you to Select All (the entire image or layer), to Deselect (have nothing selected), Reselect (restore the last selection), and Select Inverse (swap selected and unselected areas). Further commands can be used to allow you to smooth, enlarge or decrease selections, feather selection edges (to make montages more convincing), and save selections from channels. The Color Range command permits the creation of a selection based solely on color parameters.

2.**062 View menu** The view menu commands are principally concerned with the look of imagery within the Photoshop interface. Using New View permits the display of the image being worked on in a second window. This allows you, among other things, to zoom in on the detail in one window while monitoring the full image in the second. Gamut Warning displays those colors in the image that will not print using a conventional four-color process. Hide/Show options are provided for Edges, Paths, Rulers, Guides, and Grids

2.**063 Window menu** Principally devoted to the showing or hiding of palettes and the status bar. The conventional Window menu function of providing selection between open windows is also provided.

## Tools

2.**064 3D Transform tools** Set of tools that appears in the 3D Transform dialog box. The set comprises the regular Selection, Hand, and Zoom tools, along with selected path tools (Add, Delete, and Convert Anchor points) and some transform-specific tools (Cube, Sphere, and Cylinder). The Pan Camera and Trackball tools can be used to view the object being worked on. → 6.113 3D TRANSFORM FILTER

2.**065 Airbrush tool** Painting tool that simulates the behavior and effect of a mechanical airbrush. The airbrush applies gradual tones where the edges of the stroke path are increasingly more diffuse. The speed of application and the final density can be controlled using the airbrush tool controls.

2.**066 Aligned, Clone Aligned** Rubber stamp option. With Aligned selected the cloning point and painting point move in parallel. Don't check this box if you want to clone repeatedly from the same source point.

2.**067 Angular Gradient** Gradient tool option which shades in a counterclockwise direction around the start point. → 2.082 GRADIENT TOOL

2.**068 Background Eraser tool** → 2.078 Eraser tool

2.**069 Burn tool** Tool that simulates the tool used in hand-enlarging to intensify part of an image by giving it more exposure.

2.**070 clone** The process of duplicating pixels in an image in order to replace defective ones, or of adding to an image by duplicating parts of that—or another—image. Usually referred to as the Rubber Stamp tool in Photoshop. → 2.104 RUBBER STAMP TOOL

2.**071 Crop (in Perspective)** Photoshop 6 feature. An enhancement of the Crop tool that enables objects to be cropped and displayed using perspective controls. For example, a painting on a wall photographed obliquely (and with receding horizontals) can be cropped and displayed rectilinearly.

2.**072 Crop tool** The Crop tool permits the trimming of superfluous or unwanted elements from the edges of an image. This tool is one of the options in the marquee box of the Toolbar. The Crop tool features a marquee that is dragged over the portion of the image that is to be kept; double clicking within the selected area applies the crop.

Images may also be cropped by dragging with a conventional marquee and then selecting Crop from the Image menu.

2.**073 Default Colors icon** Part of the Foreground/Background Color selector on the Toolbar. Selecting this icon reverts the foreground to black and the background to white → 2.080 FOREGROUND/BACKGROUND COLOR SELECTOR

2.**074 Diamond Gradient** Gradient tool type which is similar to the Radial Gradient. The gradient is defined by drawing a line from the center of the diamond to one of the corners. The gradient is defined as a diamond pattern based on this axis of the diamond. → 2.082 GRADIENT TOOL

2.**075 drag-copy** Move function. Use the move tool to move a copy of a selection to a new location. Hold down the Alt or Option key before and while dragging the selection to the new location. Release the mouse button then the Alt or Option key at the new position. Press Alt-arrow or Option-arrow to move the selection by one pixel increments.

2.**076 Edge Contrast** Option in the Lasso and Magnetic Pen Options palettes. Ranges between 0 and 100 and determines the amount of contrast needed between objects for an edge to be recognized. Use higher levels of edge contrast in higher contrast images.

2.**077 Elliptical Marquee tool** The marquee option is accessed by double-clicking on the Marquee icon in the Toolbar. It allows the selection of elliptical shapes, including circles. The marquee options palette allows you to set the amount of feathering (used to soften the edges of the selection), a fixed size, or a constrained aspect ratio (useful for defining circles and ellipses of particular sections of images). → 2.150 MARQUEE OPTIONS PALETTE

2.**078 Eraser tool** Toolbar tool group. Includes three options (depending on the version of Photoshop being used) which are selectable from the pull-out menu: Eraser, Background Eraser, and Magic Eraser. Using the Eraser you can erase pixels from a layer to reveal the underlying layer or the background. On the background or on a layer with the Preserve Transparency option enabled erased pixels will change to the background color. The Background Eraser tool is used to erase pixels on a layer to transparency; tolerance and sampling options can be adjusted using the Background Eraser Options palette. The Magic Eraser erases all similar pixels in a layer to transparency, after clicking on a representative sample point. Use the tolerance setting in the Magic Eraser Options palette to determine the range of pixels that will be erased. A low tolerance will remove pixels in the layer with a color value close to the selected one; a higher tolerance will erase pixels with a greater range of color values.

2.**079 Eyedropper tool** Toolbar tool. Conventionally used to select the foreground or background color. The eyedropper is normally accurate to within one pixel, which can sometimes be too precise; this sample size can be increased to an average of a 3 x 3

2.069 *Burn tool*

*before*

*after*

2.072 *Crop tool*

pixel or 5 x 5 pixel array by selecting Sample Size in Eyedropper Options.

2.**080 Foreground/Background Color selector** Part of the main Toolbar. Shows foreground and background colors. These can be reversed using the Switch Colors icon (arrowed line) or restored to default values by clicking on the black/white icon.

2.**081 Grabber hand/tool** The tool that enables you to either reposition a picture inside its box or move a page around in its window. In later versions of Photoshop you can use the hand tool while another tool is active: Hold down the spacebar when you drag the image.

2.**082 Gradient tool** Tool permitting the creation of a gradual blend between two or more colors within a selection. The Gradient pull-out menu in the Toolbar permits the selection of one of five gradient types: Linear, Reflected, Radial, Diamond, and Angular. A selection of gradient presets are provided, but you can also use the Gradient Editor to create your own gradients. NB: The Gradient tool cannot be used for images in either the Bitmap or Indexed Color modes. → 2.088 LINEAR GRADIENT; 2.102 RADIAL GRADIENT; 2.067 ANGULAR GRADIENT; 2.103 REFLECTED GRADIENT; 2.074 DIAMOND GRADIENT; 2.019 GRADIENT EDITOR

2.**083 Hand tool** Editing or manipulating small elements within an image often involves zooming in to a specific region. You can move the image relative to the viewable window area using the Hand tool. This is often quicker than zooming out and then

zooming in on a new area. You can use the Hand tool while working with another tool: Just hold down the spacebar and drag the image.

2.**084 History Brush tool** This tool, to be found in the more recent versions of Photoshop, lets you paint over a mistake in an image using an earlier selected state from the History palette. Pixels from that earlier state will overwrite the current ones. Note that an image that has been resized in any direction cannot be edited using the history brush as the process depends on direct correspondence between pixel positions. It is impossible to make such correlations between resized images.

2.**085 Impressionist Brush tool** Brush introduced with Photoshop Elements that enables painting with stylized strokes. Impressionist painting styles can be simulated by varying the tool controls (style, size, and fidelity).

2.**086 Lasso** The freehand selection tool indicated by a lasso in the Toolbar. Later versions of Photoshop also feature a Magnetic Lasso that can identify the edges nearest to the selection path (aiding accurate selection of discrete objects) and a Polygon Lasso that allows straight-edged selections to be made. To draw a straight line using the Polygon Lasso, place the cursor point at the end of the first line and click. Place the cursor at the end of the next line and click again to select the second segment.

2.**087 Line tool** The Line tool draws straight lines in the foreground color. Double-click on the Line tool to display its Options palette. The

89

2.082 *Gradient tool*

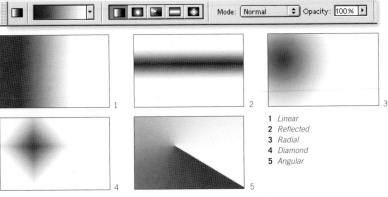

1 *Linear*
2 *Reflected*
3 *Radial*
4 *Diamond*
5 *Angular*

lines can be constrained to multiples of 45° by holding down the shift key when dragging the line.

2.**088 Linear Gradient** Gradient tool type. Shades uniformly along a line drawn across the selection. The start point is colored in the first color (or foreground, in a foreground to background gradient) and the end point in the last color (or background). A gentle gradient is achieved by drawing a long line over the selection (which can extend beyond the selection at either extreme); a harsher gradient will result from drawing a short line within the selection. → 2.082 GRADIENT TOOL

2.**089 Magic Wand tool** This is the selection tool shown in the Toolbar as a magician's wand. You can use this to select image areas of the same brightness and color level. By setting a tolerance value in the Magic Wand options palette you can limit the selection to those pixels with brightness and color levels very close to the selected one (low tolerance level) or, by setting a higher value, to a much broader range of levels. Selection can also be made in an individual color channel. → 5.036 CHANNELS

2.**090 Marquee tool** The marquee tool is one of the principal selection tools and so can be found at the prime position on the Toolbar. It provides an easy way to make rectangular, elliptical, single column, or single row selections of the image being worked on. The marquee selections are user-determined positional selections, in that, unlike the Lasso or Magic Wand tools, there is no interaction with the image itself. The marquee toolset also features the Crop tool. → 2.150 MARQUEE OPTIONS PALETTE

2.**091 Measure tool** Toolbar tool. Measures the distance between any two points in the working image. Results are shown in the Info palette. All measurements are shown in the measurement units currently set (those shown on the rulers, if displayed).

2.**092 Move tool** Allows a selection or layer to be dragged to a new position. → 6.028 SELECTION; 5.026 LAYERS

2.**093 Notes tool** Photoshop 6 feature. Offering two options, Notes and Audio Annotation, this feature, launched in Photoshop 6 enables notes and audio to be added anywhere on an image canvas. Either notes or audio annotations can be added "live" by selecting the appropriate tool and positioning on the canvas, or exisiting text or audio can be appended.

2.**094 Paint Bucket tool** The Paint Bucket tool floods selected pixels with the foreground color, and also colors adjacent pixels that are similar (determined by setting a Tolerance level in the Options palette) in color value. NB: The Paint Bucket tool will not work with images in Bitmap color mode.

2.**095 Paintbrush tool** Along with the Airbrush tool and the Pencil tool, used to apply color directly to an image layer or to the background. Shown in the Toolbar as an artist's sable brush. Creates soft strokes of color nominally in the foreground color. The size and texture depends on the brush type selected from the Brushes palette. Use the Paintbrush Options palette to fine-tune the

2.084 *History Brush tool*

before

after

2.086 *Magnetic Lasso*

paintbrush performance. → 2.084 HISTORY BRUSH TOOL; 2.119 BRUSHES OPTION PALETTE; 2.165 PAINTBRUSH OPTIONS PALETTE

2.**096 painting tools** Set of tools used for painting pixels onto the current image. Comprises the Paintbrush (soft strokes), Airbrush (emulating traditional airbrushes and aerosols), and the hard-edged Pencil.

2.**097 Pattern Stamp** Clone tool option. Makes a selection into a pattern tile. Make a rectangular selection using the marquee. Select Define Pattern from the Edit menu to define this as the pattern to be stamped. Choose the Pattern Stamp tool from the Toolbar (from the Clone tool pull-out menu) and click the Aligned box in the options palette.

2.**098 Pen tool** Shown in the Toolbar by a fountain pen nib, the Pen toolset comprises up to three variants (depending on version) that can be used to create a path, which, in turn, can be used to create a selection. The basic Pen tool is used to draw around an intended selection, adding anchor points that are connected to make the path. You can add as many or as few anchor points as required to draw the path; simple, basic shapes will require few anchor points, while more complex selections will need more. Closed paths are completed by clicking on the original starting point. Open paths (for example a straight line) are completed by clicking in the Pen tool icon in the toolbar. The Magnetic Pen uses the same technique as the Magnetic Lasso: It identifies the "edge" closest to the track being described by the user and snaps the path to it. Anchor points are automatically added as the path progresses and can be added, removed, or moved later. The Freeform pen provides a means of drawing a freeform path. Use this to draw paths when the selection outline is not critical or you are confident of your drawing abilities. Again, anchor points are added along the path automatically. Additional options on the pull-out menu include the Add/Delete Point tools, Direct Selection tool (selects points on a path), and Convert Point tool (converts corner points into curve points and vice versa). → 5.055 PATH (2)

2.**099 Polygon Lasso** One of the Lasso tool options, selected from the Lasso pull-out menu. Unlike the conventional lasso, which permits freehand selections, the Polygon Lasso makes it easy to select rectilinear objects. The polygon is defined by clicking on corner (or turn) points, and "closed" by clicking on the start point.

2.**100 Quick Mask** Toolbar tool. Provides a quick method of creating a mask around a selection. You can increase or decrease the mask by using any of the painting tools or the eraser respectively.

2.**101 radial fill** An option of the Gradient fill tool that provides a fill comprising a pattern of concentric circles of graduated tints. Shades begin with the foreground color (if selected) from the starting point and change through to the background color at the end point. → 2.082 GRADIENT TOOL

2.**102 Radial Gradient** Gradient tool type. Shades along a radius line in a circular manner. The start point of the line is the "origin" and is colored in the first, or start, color, while the end point defines the circumference and is colored with the end color. → 2.082 GRADIENT TOOL

2.**103 Reflected Gradient** Gradient tool type. Produces a symmetrical pattern of linear gradients to either side of the start point. The effect is one of a "ridge" or "furrow." → 2.082 GRADIENT TOOL

2.**104 Rubber Stamp tool** Sometimes called the cloning tool (on account of its action), the Rubber Stamp tool is often considered by newcomers to be the fundamental tool in as much as it provides the image-editing principal of "removing unwanted image elements." Latest Photoshop versions feature two such tools, the basic tool and the Pattern Stamp. The basic tool is used as a brush (and shares the common Brushes palette for brush type selection) but "paints" with image elements drawn from another part of the image, or a separate image. Choose the point you wish to use as the origination point for painting and Alt-click or Option-click on it. Now move to the image element you wish to cover or remove and click the mouse to paint on the pixels from the origination point. When you click and drag the selection point can be set to move also, thus providing an exact copy of the original area. Careful use of the opacity setting in the Rubber Stamp Options palette can provide more subtle results and further options. → 2.097 PATTERN STAMP; 2.182 RUBBER STAMP OPTIONS PALETTE

2.**105 screen display mode** The screen display mode ia a toolbar feature. Indicated at or near the base of the Toolbar (depending on version) by a row of three buttons. The first, standard screen mode (default), displays your image, menus, and tools on the conventional desktop (along with any other open windows and the desktop image itself). The second button, full screen mode with menus, shows only the Photoshop environment against a plain gray background. The final button, full screen mode, dispenses with the menus, displaying only the tools, palettes, and image.

2.**106 selection marquee/rectangle/box** A dotted line that forms a rectangle, oval or array. The line is drawn by means of the Marquee tool, and becomes a marquee. → 2.090 MARQUEE TOOL

2.**107 Shape tool** Photoshop 6 feature. Shares much of its algorithmic detailing with the Layer Clipping Path feature. Provides an array of basic shapes (ranging from circles and rectangles through to stars, polygons, and freeforms) that can be drawn over artwork in their own layers. Their shape and outline is determined by a clipping path that enables them to be edited using the Pen tool.

2.**108 Smudge tool** Tool simulating the dragging of a finger through wet, viscous paint. Color is drawn from the first point of contact and dragged through with the "finger." Smudging can be used to give motion effects by drawing parallel smudges to one side of an object.

2.**109 Sponge tool** A toning tool, the sponge can be used to introduce subtle changes to the color saturation of an image area. It can be set to increase or decrease color saturation or, in grayscale mode, move tone toward or away from the mid-gray level.

2.**110 Switch Colors icon** Icon in the Foreground/Background Color selector on the Toolbar that reverses background and foreground colors.

2.**111 transformation tool** The generic name given to tools that change the location or appearance of an item, by scaling, reflection, or a three-dimensional transformation.

2.**112 Type Mask tool** The Type Mask tool and Vertical Type Mask tool let you produce selection borders in the outline of text type characters. Type selections will appear in the active layer from where they can be moved, filled, stroked, or copied in the same manner as any other selection.

2.**113 Type tool** The Type tool pull-out menu has four options: conventional type, vertical type, type mask, and vertical type mask. In recent versions of Photoshop each piece of text automatically creates a new layer (Type layer) for itself. Select the appropriate text tool, place the cursor where you wish to place the text and click. The Type tool dialog box will appear. As you type your text in the text window it will also appear in the active window. Select OK once text entry is complete. You can then fine tune the placement of the text using the Move tool. → 2.112 TYPE MASK TOOL; 2.211 TYPE TOOL DIALOG BOX

2.117 *arrowheads*

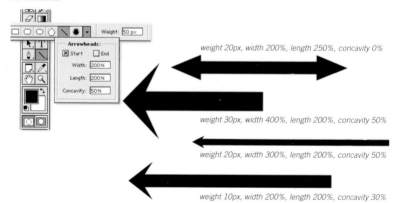

weight 20px, width 200%, length 250%, concavity 0%

weight 30px, width 400%, length 200%, concavity 50%

weight 20px, width 300%, length 200%, concavity 50%

weight 10px, width 200%, length 200%, concavity 30%

2.**114 Zoom tool** Indicated by a magnifying glass in the Toolbar, the Zoom tool will enlarge or reduce an area of the current active window. Sometimes called a "reduction tool" or "reduction glass." Place the Zoom tool over the part of the image you wish to enlarge and press the mouse (or the return key). Press and hold the Alt or Option key and press return to zoom out. The zoom percentage is shown in the window's title bar at all times. The same percentage is also shown in the status bar; you can enter a specific zoom setting here. Press return to effect the zoom. The notional 100% view of the document is based on monitor and image resolution rather than actual linear dimensions. → 2.044 STATUS BAR

## Palettes and associated features

2.**115 Actions palette** Photoshop actions are rather like scripts, macros, and wizards, in that they are semiautomated routines that perform tasks likely to be repeated. The Actions palette is displayed by choosing Show Actions from the Window menu; it permits the editing of an existing action (for example, turning on or off a particular stage in the action) and the creation ("recording") of a new one. → 5.062 ACTIONS

2.**116 Airbrush Options palette** Palette that provides a range of adjustments to the airbrush tool. Parameters that can be adjusted include pressure (from 0 to 100%) and degree of fade (and whether the fade is to transparent or to the background color).

A painting mode (or blending mode) can also be optionally specified. → 2.065 AIRBRUSH TOOL; 4.086 BLENDING MODE

2.**117 arrowheads** Line tool Options palette feature. Allows arrowheads to be added to the start or end (or both) of a line. Pressing the Shape button allows you to define the width, length, and concavity of the arrowhead. → 2.147 LINE TOOL OPTIONS PALETTE

2.**118 Brush Options** Brushes palette pull-out option to define diameter, hardness, angle, roundness and spacing of the brush.

2.**119 Brushes Option palette** Palette for the selection of brush type. The default set comprises a selection of conventional circular brushes of differing diameters and with hard or soft edges. Random "spray" brushes are available in later versions of Photoshop. Double clicking on any brush brings up the Brush Options palette where new brushes may be created. New and modified brushes will then be indicated in the main palette window.

2.**120 Button mode** Selected from the Actions palette pull-out menu. Button mode alters the display of actions from a list of commands applied to buttons. Selecting Button mode again returns the display to a list. → 5.062 ACTIONS

2.**121 Channels palette** Lets you manage, create, and delete the channels within an image. All channels are shown, headed by the composite (RGB, CMYK, or Lab, as appropriate) followed by, in order, the color channels, spot color channels, and alpha channels.

2.121 *Channels palette*

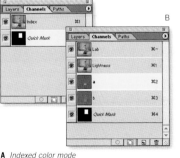

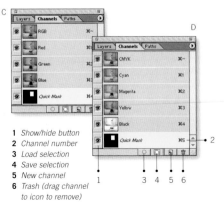

**A** *Indexed color mode*
**B** *Lab color mode*
**C** *RGB color mode*
**D** *CMYK color mode*

1 *Show/hide button*
2 *Channel number*
3 *Load selection*
4 *Save selection*
5 *New channel*
6 *Trash (drag channel to icon to remove)*

2.**122 Character palette** Photoshop 6 feature. Provides options for formatting characters, including selection of font, font size, aspect ratio, kerning, and font style. Like the Paragraph palette, this feature is also available in ImageReady 3.0. Note that some formatting options may also be presented in the Tool Options bar.

2.**123 CMYK sliders** Color palette adjustments option. Selected from the pull-out menu, this option provides sliding adjusters for cyan, magenta, yellow, and black. By appropriate setting, foreground colors can be selected.

2.**124 CMYK Spectrum** Color palette spectrum option. Selects a CMYK spectrum to be displayed in the Color palette Color Bar. → 2.125 COLOR BAR

2.**125 Color Bar** Component appearing at the bottom of the Color palette. All colors are displayed as a spectrum (the form this takes will depend on the color mode selected) and a foreground color can be directly selected. Can also aid in fine tuning a foreground color in association with the color sliders.

2.**126 Color palette** Displays the color values for the current selection of foreground and background colors. Sliders enable the colors to be changed (edited) based on different color models. These models can be selected from the pop-out menu. A color bar enables foreground and background colors to be selected directly.

2.**127 Color/Swatches/Brushes** Palette group. Click on the tabs to select the Color, Swatches, or Brushes Option palettes. →

2.126 COLOR palette; 2.187 SWATCHES palette; 2.119 BRUSHES OPTION palette

2.**128 Current Colors** Color palette spectrum option. Displays a gradient between the current foreground and background colors in the Color palette Color Bar. → 2.125 COLOR BAR

2.**129 Define Brush** (**1**) Brushes palette pull-out option. Use Define Brush to create a custom brush shape from an image selection. Your custom brush can be up to 1,000 pixels by 1,000 pixels in extent.

2.**130 Delete Brush** Brushes palette pull-out option. Lets you delete the currently selected brush.

2.**131 Delete Channel** (**1**) Channels palette pull-out option. Permits a selected channel to be deleted. Note that Photoshop does not ask for confirmation when you use this deletion method. If you would like to be prompted before the channel is deleted, use the following method: Select the channel; click on the Trash icon at the bottom of the palette; click Yes when the Delete Channel? query appears.

2.**132 Delete Layer** (**2**) Layers palette pull-out option. Deletes the currently selected layer. → 2.347 DELETE LAYER (1)

2.**133 Duplicate Channel** It is the channels palette pull-out option that creates a duplicate channel. You can give this new channel your preferred name and choose a destination or, by selecting New, copy the channel to a new image. You can also invert the channel as you duplicate it by clicking in the Invert box.

2.140 *History palette*

1  *Sourcepoint for history brush*
2  *Snapshot thumbnail*
3  *History state slider*
4  *Create new document from current state button*
5  *Create new snapshot button*
6  *Trash icon*
7  *History options*

2.**134 Duplicate Layer** (**1**) Layers palette pull-out option. Duplicates the current active layer.

2.**135 Eye icon** Layers and Channels palette feature. Indicates that the layer or channel is currently visible in the working image. Click on the icon to toggle visibility on and off.

2.**136 Flatten Image** (**Layers palette**) Layers palette pull-out option. Enables the working image to be flattened. Has the same effect as the Flatten Image command in the Layers menu. Note that layer (and other) information is lost when an image is flattened. The command Flatten Image in File > Save a Copy will save a flattened copy but retain the image information in the original. → 2.352 FLATTEN IMAGE; 2.229 FLATTEN IMAGE (SAVE A COPY)

2.**137 Gradient Options palette** Options palette for the Gradient tool. Allows setting of color blending mode, opacity, gradient type, and selection of the Gradient Editor for creating your own gradient.

2.**138 Grayscale Ramp** Color palette spectrum option. Selects a grayscale ramp for display in the Color palette Color Bar. → 2.125 COLOR BAR

2.**139 Grayscale slider** Color palette adjustments option. Selected from the pull-out menu, the Grayscale Slider replaces the color sliders with a grayscale ramp and slider. Moving the slider alters the foreground color between black and white.

2.**140 History palette** Use this to selectively undo one or more of your previous image-editing steps. Every time you perform an edit, no matter how small, the operation is listed here. You can delete states or even return to a previous state. The palette displays History states in chronological order, the most recent being at the bottom of the list.

2.**141 History/Actions** Palette group. Tabs permit selection of the History or Actions palette. → 2.115 ACTIONS PALETTE; 2.140 HISTORY PALETTE

2.**142 HSB sliders** Color palette adjustments option. Selected from the pull-out menu, this option provides sliding adjusters for hue, saturation, and brightness, allowing a foreground color to be created from these parameters.

2.**143 Info palette** Displays a breakdown of the pixel currently under the pointer along with readouts for up to four color samplers. Positional and relative position data is also displayed.

2.**144 Lab sliders** Color palette adjustments option. Selected from the pull-out menu, this option provides sliding adjusters for luminance (L), green-to-red (a), and blue-to-yellow (b). By appropriate setting, foreground colors can be selected.

2.**145 Layer Options** (**1**) Layers palette pull-out option. Use this to rename a layer, set an opacity and set blending modes and conditions.

2.**146 Layers/Channels/Paths** Palette group. Select a tab to choose the Layers, Channels, or Paths palette. → 5.027 LAYERS PALETTE; 2.121 CHANNELS PALETTE; 5.056 PATHS PALETTE

2.**147 Line tool Options palette** Activated by double-clicking on the Line tool in the Toolbar. Use this palette to set a blending mode, opacity for the line and a weight (thickness). You can also add an arrowhead to the start or end (or both) of the line by clicking in the appropriate boxes. If you do select either of the arrowhead options an Arrowhead Shape dialog box will open, allowing you to define the exact size and shape of the arrowhead. → 4.086 BLENDING MODE; 2.117 ARROWHEADS

2.**148 Load Brushes** Brushes palette pull-out option. Enables a set of brushes stored in a file to be added to your current set.

2.**149 Load Swatches** Swatches palette option. Appends swatches to the current set. Additional swatch sets are stored in the Photoshop application folder for a range of specific uses: For example, there are web-safe colors, Pantone colors, and Trumatch colors.

2.**150 Marquee Options palette** Palette displayed when the marquee tool is selected. Provides options for setting the amount of feathering (the width of a soft edge to a selection, measured in pixels) and the style. The style can be Normal (a free format option, allowing the marquee to be drawn at will), Constrained Aspect Ratio (maintaining a fixed width-to-height ratio only), or Fixed Size. If Constrained Aspect Ratio is selected, width and height ratios can be entered in the appropriate boxes. The default is 1 and 1. Select Fixed Size and you will be prompted to enter the width and height required, this time measured in pixels.

2.**151 Merge Channels** Channels palette pull-out option. Merges grayscale images into a single image.

2.**152 Merge Linked** (**1**) Layers palette pull-out option. Enables linked layers to be merged into a single layer. This operation works like Flatten Layers but for the selected linked group.

2.**153 Merge Spot Channel** Channels palette pull-out option that merges spot channels. Merging spot channels enables the printing of a proof of that spot color image immediately.

2.**154 Merge Visible** (**1**) Layers palette pull-out option. Merges all layers that are currently visible.

2.**155 Navigator palette** Palette characterized by a thumbnail view of the active image. The area of the image displayed in the main image window is shown by a frame. Use the Zoom slider at the base of the palette to adjust the image view size. You can also use the Zoom In or Zoom Out buttons on either side of the slider to rescale the image.

2.**156 Navigator/Info/Options** Palette group. Tabs at the top select the Navigator, Info, or Options palettes. → 2.155 NAVIGATOR PALETTE; 2.143 INFO PALETTE; 2.164 OPTIONS PALETTE

2.**157 New Adjustment Layer** Layers palette pull-out option. Creates a new adjustment layer.

2.**158 New Brush** Brushes palette pull-out option. Lets you create a new brush for use with the painting tools. The New Brush dialog shows the current brush tip; adjustments to the parameters will be indicated. Any new brushes you save will be appended to the existing list.

2.**159 New Channel** Channels palette pull-out option. Creates a new alpha channel in the working image. You can also create a new channel by clicking on the New Channel button at the base of the palette.

2.**160 New Layer** Layers palette pull-out option. Creates a new layer in the working document.

2.**161 New Spot Channel** Channels palette pull-out option. Creates a new spot channel.

2.**162 Opacity option** An option that appears in the Options palettes of several tools, layers, and masks. In painting tools, selecting an opacity of 100% will provide total coverage of the underlying pixels; 0% would be totally transparent. Similarly in Layer options a layer opacity of 100% makes that layer totally opaque. Opacity corresponds to Pressure in some tool's Option palettes and in earlier versions of Photoshop.

2.**163 Opacity slider** Slider control provided in options palettes to select the degree of opacity. When the control is slid to the right it gives 100% opacity, and to the left 0%. Click on the right arrowhead next to the percentage symbol to reveal the slider. → 2.162 OPACITY (OPTION); 2.173 PRESSURE

2.**164 Options palette** Virtually every tool has its own Options palette, revealed by selecting first the tool and then Show Options from the Window menu. Parameters such as modes and opacity are common to most tools; others, such as Finger Painting on the Smudge tool palette, are unique to a particular tool.

2.**165 Paintbrush Options palette** When using the Paintbrush tool, a brush type is selected from the Brushes floating palette. In the

2.169 *Palette well*

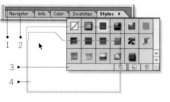

| | |
|---|---|
| 1 Palette well | 10 Add space (before/ after)paragraph |
| 2 'Docked' palettes | 11 Font |
| 3 Selected palette | 12 Font style |
| 4 Palette dragged from well | 13 Font size |
| 5 Text alignment button | 14 Set kerning |
| 6 Justify last (left, centre, right) | 15 Set leading |
| | 16 Set tracking |
| 7 Justify all | 17 Vertical scale |
| 8 Indent left/right margins | 18 Set baseline shift |
| 9 Indent first line | 19 Horizontal scale |
| | 20 Font color |

2.170 *Paragraph palette*

2.122 *Character palette*

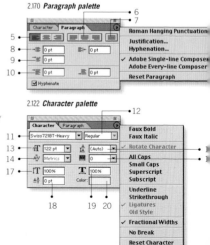

Paintbrush Options palette details of the appearance of the brush strokes can be set. Variables include the general settings Blending Mode and Opacity, Fade (defining how the edges of the brushstroke fade), and how that fade occurs (to transparent or to the background color). → 2.119 BRUSHES OPTION PALETTE

2.**166 palette** A window, often "floating" (movable), that contains features such as tools, measurements, or other functions. Palettes can be hidden or revealed as required, generally using the Window menu along with the Show/Hide commands.

2.**167 Palette Options** (**1**) Option provided from the Info palette. Click on the arrowhead at the top left of the palette and select Palette Options. The Info Options dialog box will open and provide selections for First Color Readout (whether to display actual color or a specific mode), Second Color Readout (providing the option of a subsidiary display), and options for displaying the mouse coordinates.

2.**168 Palette Options** (**2**) Palette pull-out option. Enables modest customization of certain palette displays (for example by selection of thumbnail sizes).

2.**169 Palette well** Photoshop 6 feature. Feature of the Tool Options bar (also new to Photoshop 6). Palettes can be "dropped" into the well to clear the desktop workspace. Clicking on a palette in the well opens that palette allowing changes to be made to the parameters of that palette. Afterward the palette disappears back into the well.

2.**170 Paragraph palette** Photoshop 6 feature. Photoshop treats any text with a carriage return at the end of a line as a paragraph. Using the Paragraph palette you can set options with regard to such paragraphs including alignment and justification, indentation and spacing between lines. Note that when using point text each line will be regarded as a separate paragraph. With box text paragraphs may be multilined.

2.**171 pop-up slider** The pop-up slider is an adjustment tool provided in some Photoshop palettes. It comprises a drag strip with an arrowhead; clicking and dragging on the arrowhead adjusts the parameter (normally between 0 and 100%). Usually provided with an input box where the percentage value may be entered directly.

2.**172 Preserve Transparency box** A feature of the Layers palette. Selecting Preserve Transparency restricts any painting or editing to those parts of that layer that already contain pixels. An object in an otherwise transparent layer can thus have its color balance altered, be recolored, or have a filter applied without compromising the remainder of the layer.

2.**173 Pressure** Pressure is given as a parameter in some painting tool options palettes. You can set a percentage figure on the palette to determine the strength of the painting tool applied. Normally 100% is required for full (opaque) coverage. Equivalent to the Opacity settings found in some palettes. → 2.162 OPACITY OPTION

2.**174 Replace Brushes** Brushes palette pull-out option. Replaces the current brush set with those stored in a file.

2.**175 Replace Swatches** Swatches palette option. Replaces the currently displayed swatches with those held in a Photoshop swatches file. → 2.149 LOAD SWATCHES

2.**176 Reset All Tools** Tool Options palette option. Resets all tools to their default settings.

2.**177 Reset Brushes** Brushes palette pull-out option. Resets your brush palette to the default set. Use this to return to the default or to append the default set to the current set.

2.**178 Reset Swatches** Swatches palette option. Returns the color swatches in the Swatches palette to their default status, removing any custom colors added by the user.

2.**179 Reset Tool** Tool Options palette option. Returns the current tool to its default settings.

2.**180 RGB sliders** Color palette adjustments option. When selected from the pull-out menu the RGB sliders let you create a foreground color by mixing different amounts of red, green, and blue.

2.**181 RGB Spectrum** Color palette spectrum option. Selects an RGB spectrum to be displayed in the Color palette Color Bar. → 9.039 COLOR BAR

2.**182 Rubber Stamp Options palette** Permits selection of a blending mode and opacity. Click in the Use All Layers check box to clone image elements based on all underlying layers.

2.**183 Save Brushes** Brushes palette pull-out option. Saves the current brush set to a file.

**2.184 Save Swatches** Swatches palette option. Saves the currently displayed swatches to a file. The current set might include default colors, an additionally loaded set, and user-defined colors. The saved set can later be loaded or used to replace the displayed set.
→ 2.149 LOAD SWATCHES

**2.185 Split Channels** Channels palette pull-out option. Splits the channels in the image into separate images. Your original image will be closed and replaced with the individual images in their own grayscale windows.

**2.186 Styles palette** (**1**) Photoshop 6 palette that displays currently available styles. Styles can be drag and dropped onto an image from this palette. A pull-out menu lets you add, change, remove, and edit styles or style sets.

**2.187 Swatches palette** Palette that enables the selection of foreground or background colors from predefined color swatches. You can add frequently used colors to make selection easier, and delete those that are used rarely. You can also save custom sets as files for later use.

**2.188 Tolerance** Options palette option. The range of pixels within which a specific tool operates. Specifies, for example, the range of colors the Magic Wand selects, or the range of colors the Paint Bucket tool floods.

**2.189 Use All Layers** Painting tools palette option. Permits sampling, cloning or blur/sharpening based on sampled data from all visible layers rather than the default condition of only the active layer. In most circumstances (except when using the Rubber Stamp tool) it is advisable to keep Use All Layers selected.

**2.190 Web Color sliders** Color palette adjustments option. Selected from the pull-out menu, this option provides sliding adjusters for only those colors that comprise the web palette. By appropriate setting, foreground colors suitable for web use can be selected.

**2.191 Wet Edges** "Wet edges" can be created using the painting tools palette option. It creates a watercolor effect when painting with the paintbrush. Emulating the effect of surface tension, color becomes subdued in the main stroke and bolder at the edge. This option is also available with the Eraser tool in some Photoshop versions. Selecting Wet Edges results in the erased effect building up along the edge of the brush stroke.

**2.192 Zoom In button** Navigator palette feature. Zooms in on the main image based on the position of the marker in the proxy image.

**2.193 Zoom Out button** Navigator palette feature. Zooms out on the main image based on the position of the marker in the proxy image.

## Dialog boxes

**2.194 Auto Kern** Type tool dialog box option. Kerning is normally automatic, but by unchecking this box manual adjustments may be made. → 10.188 KERNING

**2.195 Fill dialog box** Dialog box for the Fill tool. To display the Fill dialog box press Shift+Delete (Mac) or Shift+Backspace (Windows). Permits the selection of the fill color and the setting of any blending parameters.

2.185 *Split channels*

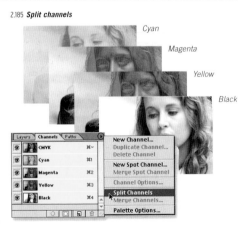

Cyan

Magenta

Yellow

Black

2.191 *Wet edges*

On

Off

**2.196 Frequency** Lasso and Magnetic Pen Options palettes option. Ranging from 0 to 100, it determines how often fastening points are placed as the selection is made. Use a high frequency (which creates a greater number of points) to select irregular objects.

**2.197 Fuzziness** A feature in the dialog box of the Color Range command that alters the range of colors selected. Its function is similar to the Tolerance option offered by some selection tools and the Paint Bucket tool.

**2.198 gradient bar** Part of the Curves dialog box, shown as a graduated bar beneath the main curve window. Clicking on the gradient bar reverses the curves configured in the curve window. → 2.302 CURVES

**2.199 Gradient Editor dialog box** Photoshop 6 feature. Enables a new gradient to be created or an existing one modified. Furthermore, new intermediate colors can be added to existing gradients to create multicolor blends.

**2.200 Indexed Color dialog box** Dialog box for setting parameters for Indexed Color mode. → 2.312 INDEXED COLOR

**2.201 JPEG Options dialog box** When saving an image file as a JPEG format this dialog permits the selection of image options. The Quality setting allows a range from low quality (but small file) through to high quality (but correspondingly large). Different versions of Photoshop have different representations of the Quality control. Versions 5 and 5.5 use a sliding quality scale with settings between 1 (low quality, small

file) and 12 (high quality, large file). Next a Format Option can be selected. Choose the default Baseline ("Standard") setting to minimize data loss during the compression (JPEG is a "lossy" compression method); the Baseline Optimized option to preserve as much image quality as possible during compression; and Progressive to produce a progressive JPEG file. (When a progressive JPEG is displayed, say on a web browser, it will appear first as a crude graphic then, with further passes, will increase in resolution.) → 3.028 JPEG

**2.202 Layer Styles dialog** Photoshop 6 feature. Enhanced dialog box that includes the options and parameters that were set in the Layer Options dialog box in earlier versions.

**2.203 monitor control dialog** Windows dialog box provided in Photoshop (prior to version 5) to assist in monitor calibration and setting. In more recent releases it has been replaced by the Adobe Gamma control panel. → 4.105 ADOBE GAMMA CONTROL PANEL

**2.204 New dialog box** Dialog box displayed when New is selected from the File menu. The box provides you with the opportunity to create a new blank workspace or canvas. Enter a name for the new document, a width and height (which may be specified in centimeters, inches, points, pixels, picas, columns or rows) and a resolution. You can then use the Contents box to define whether the document has a white background, adopts the current background color, or is transparent.

2.201 *JPEG Options dialog box*

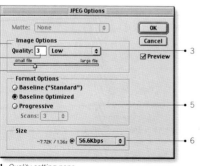

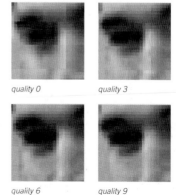

quality 0

quality 3

quality 6

quality 9

**1** Quality setting pane
**2** Quality level setting (numeric, 0 to 12)
**3** Quality level setting (from 'low' to 'maximum')
**4** Quality level slider (small file to large file)
**5** Format options pane
**6** File size (shows approx. download time for selected modem speed)

**2.205 Offset filter dialog box** The Offset filter (accessed through the Filter menu under Other > Offset) moves selected pixels by a predetermined amount, leaving a "hole" at the position of the original selection. The degree of offset and the fill for the undefined areas can be set in the Offset filter dialog box.

**2.206 Open dialog box** Dialog box that opens when Open is selected from the File menu. It allows you to select and open an existing file via the file navigation system.

**2.207 Page Setup (1)** A dialog box accessed from the File menu that enables you to select various options for printing, such as paper size, enlargement or reduction, paper orientation, inversion, etc. The available options depend on the printer you are using. Exact layout tends to vary according to the printer currently available.

**2.208 Profile Mismatch** A dialog box that appears when you attempt to create a profile for legacy files. The box opens automatically when you open a file whose embedded profile does not match the current RGB Setup space.

**2.209 Rasterize Generic EPS Format** Dialog box for opening EPS, PDF, or Illustrator files. Illustrator, EPS, and PDF images are vector based; they need to be converted into pixels for use in Photoshop.

**2.210 Save As dialog** Dialog box for defining the name (and location) of a copy of the current image document. Unlike the Save command (which saves all changes to the current file) Save As permits a copy of the image to be saved at its current stage of development, allowing further work to be done on the original image.

**2.211 Type tool dialog box** Selecting the Type tool and clicking on the text placement point in the active window will display the Type tool dialog box. You can select font and style (regular, bold, italic, or underline), size, color, kerning (which can be set to auto), and justification, as well as the degree of antialiasing within this dialog box.

### File menu commands

**2.212 Anti Aliased PICT** Mac-OS-only menu option, accessed through File > Import. It enables antialiased PICT files (sometimes called object-orientated PICT files) to be imported. Such files are typically created by the now-rare MacDraw and also by Canvas. This module requires that the whole PICT file is held in memory; it may not function if the application's available memory is insufficient. You can also use the conventional Open command to open these files as PICT files but without antialiasing. You can change the size of the file and its dimensions from the Anti Aliased PICT dialog box.

**2.213 Automate** File menu feature permitting easy performance of automated tasks for creating contact sheets, batch conversion of file formats, and more.

**2.214 Batch** File > Automate menu option that enables an action to be played on a group of files. For example, you can import a series of images from a digital camera and perform certain image edits on all of them automatically. Batch processing can also be applied to a folder, in which case batch commands will be applied to all files. (It's a good idea to have all files in the folder at the same level and to direct the edited files to a new location, e.g. "Processed Files.")

**2.215 Caption** An option on the File menu under File Info. If you want to add a caption to your image (which will remain with that image) enter it here. Captions can be attached to images stored in any file format in the Mac OS, but only to images in TIFF, JPEG, EPS and PDF formats for Windows. → 2.227 FILE INFO

**2.216 Categories** Option on the File > File Info menu. A category is a three-character code used by Associated Press to define the content of an image file. → 2.227 FILE INFO

**2.217 Close** File menu item for closing the current working document. A Save prompt will be issued if changes have been made since the previous save.

**2.218 CMYK Setup** File > Color Settings menu option. If you intend to edit CMYK files for print purposes you'll need to enter CMYK Setup information for the best results. Use the CMYK dialog box to set the CMYK color space. You can use ICC profiles, color separation tables or the characteristics of the ink and paper that will form your eventual output. → 4.112 COLOR SPACE

**2.219 Color Settings (1)** File menu command. Use to set up RGB, CMYK, Grayscale, or Profile color.

**0 Conditional Mode Change** File > Automate menu option. Automated command for changing the color mode of an image document to the mode you select, based on the original mode.

**1 Contact Sheet** File > Automate menu option. Produces a "contact sheet" of image thumbnails from image files in a folder. The display sequence is normally alphabetical, based on the image names. All image files to be contact printed must be closed before this command is initiated.

**2 Copyright & URL** File > File Info option. Dialog box providing options to add file information such as the URL for the image and a copyright notice. Click on Mark as Copyrighted to add the copyright symbol. This display is automatically updated if a Digimarc watermark is detected in the image. → 2.227 FILE INFO; 6.069 DIGIMARC

**3 Credits** File > File Info option, allowing you to enter the credit for the copyright of the image. In the File Info dialog you can enter Credit, Image Source, and Byline information in this space. → 2.227 FILE INFO

**4 Exclude Alpha Channels** Option in the Save a Copy dialog box. Saves a copy of the current working image but discards alpha channel information. This information does, however, remain intact in the working image.

**5 Exclude Non-Image Data** Option in the Save a Copy dialog box. Saves a copy of the working image but does not save any non-image data (including any annotations).

**6 Export** File menu command permitting the export of an image in a nonstandard format such as GIF89a, or the export of paths created in Photoshop to Adobe Illustrator. → 5.055 PATH (2)

**7 File Info** File menu command. File Info allows you to annotate an image with text information such as a caption, headline, image source, and copyright. You can also append useful keywords that would help with database searching for image types later. Data entered here conforms to the International Press Telecommunications Council (IPTC) standards for the transmission of text and images. → 10.093 IPTC

**28 Fit Image** File > Automate menu option. The current working image is fitted to the width and height specified (subject to maintaining its aspect ratio). It changes only the physical dimensions; resolution is unaffected.

**2.229 Flatten Image** (**Save a Copy**) Option on the Save a Copy dialog box. Enables a multilayer image copy to be flattened when saved. Multilayer images consume considerably more memory space; a flattened image is more space efficient. → 2.352 FLATTEN IMAGE

**2.230 GIF89a Export** File > Export menu option. Enables an RGB or indexed color image to be saved to GIF89a format. You can assign background transparency to the image. → 3.020 GIF89A

**2.231 Grayscale Setup** File > Color Settings menu option. The Grayscale Setup command opens the Grayscale Setup dialog. To edit grayscale images you'll need to choose a grayscale behavior setting: RGB or Black Ink. Choose RGB if you intend to use the images on screen (for example on the Web). Choose Black Ink if your image will ultimately be printed. The Black Ink setting makes appropriate adjustment for dot gain.

**2.232 Import** File menu command enabling the import of an image file from (say) a TWAIN device (scanner, camera) or specialized acquisition plug-in.

**2.233 Jump to** File menu command offering a shortcut to another application. The default installation of Photoshop 6, for example, provides a jump to Adobe ImageReady 3.0 here. The same feature is available from the Toolbar in later versions of Photoshop and ImageReady.

**2.234 Keywords** Option on the File > File Info menu. Selected words pertinent to the image can be entered in this box and subsequently used to identify the image when searched by appropriate image databases. → 2.227 FILE INFO

**2.235 Multi-Page PDF to PSD** File > Automate menu option. Converts each page of an Adobe Acrobat PDF (portable document format) document into separate Photoshop files. The Convert Multi-Page PDF to PSD dialog box prompts you for the name of the PDF file, a page range, output resolution, and a destination for the resulting Photoshop PSD files.

**2.236 New** (1) File menu item for the creation of a new (blank) canvas. Selecting New will open the New dialog box. → 2.204 NEW DIALOG BOX

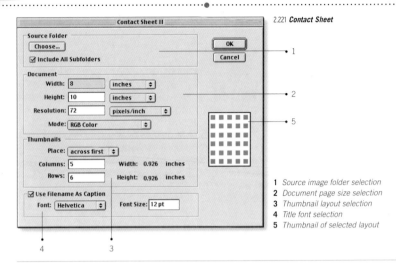

2.221 *Contact Sheet*

1 Source image folder selection
2 Document page size selection
3 Thumbnail layout selection
4 Title font selection
5 Thumbnail of selected layout

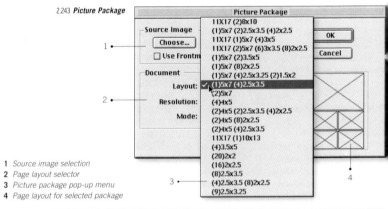

2.243 *Picture Package*

1 Source image selection
2 Page layout selector
3 Picture package pop-up menu
4 Page layout for selected package

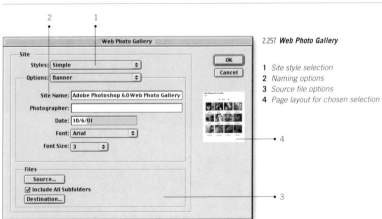

2.257 *Web Photo Gallery*

1 Site style selection
2 Naming options
3 Source file options
4 Page layout for chosen selection

**2.237 Open** (**2**) File menu command to open an existing image file.

**2.238 Open Recent** Photoshop 6 File menu command. Lists the most recently opened document and opens them when selected.

**2.239 Origin** Option on the File > File Info menu. Space is provided in the File Info dialog box to provide supplemental information, usually historical and locational. Click on the Today box to add the current date to the Date Created box. → 2.227 FILE INFO

**2.240 Page Setup** (**2**) File menu item. Like the similar feature in most applications, it is used to define page printing criteria. Options and screen layout depend on the printer currently connected and selected.

**2.241 Paths to Illustrator** File > Export menu option. Enables Photoshop paths to be exported as Adobe Illustrator files and consequently used with Illustrator artwork.

**2.242 PICT Resource** (**1**) File > Import menu option (Mac OS only). Lets you open PICT resource files created in another application. A PICT resource is a PICT file that is contained within a Mac OS's file resource fork. Typical examples are splash screens (graphics that appear when a program starts) and Scrapbook contents.

**2.243 Picture Package** File > Automate menu option. Enables an image to be printed several times on a single page. The Picture Package dialog box prompts you for a source image (click on Use Frontmost Document to use your working image) and a layout. The pull-down menu features a range of layouts that are displayed as a graphic.

**2.244 Place** File menu command used to import files created in vector-based applications such as Adobe Illustrator. Place literally places an Illustrator, Acrobat PDF, or encapsulated PostScript file (EPS) on a new layer in a Photoshop image.

**2.245 Preferences** File menu command. Selecting Preferences opens the Preferences dialog box from where you can adjust Photoshop's performance to more closely meet your needs. The dialog box features eight options: General: Select your preferred color picker and interpolation technique; Saving Files: Choose whether image previews are saved, icons are created, and file extensions are added; Displays & Cursors: Choose between the standard, graphic cursors, precise (cross-hair) cursors, and brush-sized cursors; Units & Rulers: Define your preferred units for rulers and columns; Guides & Grids: Choose color and styles for the grids and guides; Transparency & Gamut: Select a pattern to indicate transparent areas and a color to mark out-of-gamut colors when Gamut Warning is selected; Plug-ins & Scratch Disks: Choose an optional alternative directory for Photoshop to scan for plug-ins. Also choose up to four disks (or locations) for Photoshop to use as scratch disks. For best performance specify a fast hard disk, but on no account specify removable media; Image Cache: Increase the number of cache levels to speed up work on larger image files (requires sufficient RAM).

**2.246 Print** File menu command. Used to print the current active document.

**2.247 Profile Setup** File > Color Settings menu option. Select Profile Setup for the Profile Setup dialog box. This is where you can determine how Photoshop will handle files imported with color spaces other than those of the current working space.

**2.248 Revert** File menu command, useful for correcting mistakes. Revert will reverse all the image editing changes made since the image was last saved. → 2.288 UNDO; 5.072 HISTORY BRUSH

**2.249 RGB Setup** File > Color Settings menu option. The RGB Setup dialog offers you a range of RGB working color spaces to choose from. The default is sRGB. Although this has much to commend it, it is disliked by many (especially those working in the print industry) because it clips some of the CMYK gamut. sRGB is a good option if you intend to output images for the Web, but otherwise ColorMatch RGB or SMPTE-240M are better options. Ensure the Display Using Monitor Compensation box is checked to enable Photoshop to compensate for the characteristics of your monitor. → 4.112 COLOR SPACE; 4.120 sRGB

**2.250 Save** File menu command. Use to save changes to the working document.

**2.251 Save a Copy** File menu command (before version). Provides a means of creating a copy of an open working file but leaving the open file unchanged so you can continue working on it. When you save a copy you can perform actions such as flattening multilayer images and nonimage data.

2.**252 Save As** File menu command. Saves a copy of the working document under a new filename. Opens the Save As dialog box. The original file remains, under the original filename, but only contains those changes made up to the previous save. You can also use Save As to save the file in a different format.

2.**253 Save for Web** File menu command. Choose Save for Web to select a compression file format and other optimization appropriate to Web applications of the image. Corresponds to the Optimize feature in ImageReady.

2.**254 TWAIN_32 Source** Windows-specific command on the File > Import menu. The Mac equivalent is "TWAIN Acquire." TWAIN—technology without an interesting name (!)—is a cross-platform interface standard for acquiring images and graphics from most scanners and a number of digital cameras and other imaging peripherals. Photoshop for Windows supports the latest TWAIN_32 standard; if your TWAIN device has the earlier Windows 3.1 compatible version you'll need to upgrade.

2.**255 TWAIN Acquire** Mac-specific option on the File > Import menu. The equivalent of the Windows "TWAIN_32 Source" option. → 2.254 TWAIN_32 SOURCE

2.**256 TWAIN Select** Option on the File > Import menu. Use this to select a particular TWAIN device if more than one is resident. → 2.254 TWAIN_32 SOURCE

2.**257 Web Photo Gallery** File > Automate menu option. Enables images to be exported as a gallery website. Your images are accompanied by thumbnails (which can be small, medium, or large in size). Image sizes, number of images, and web site details are entered in the Web Photo Gallery dialog box.

## Edit menu commands

2.**258 Again** (**Transform menu**) Edit > Transform menu item. Repeats a transformation with duplicate data. → 2.287 TRANSFORM

2.**259 Clear** (**1**) Edit menu item. Deletes (entirely) the current selection. → 2.263 CUT

2.**260 Color Settings** (**2**) Photoshop 6 Edit menu item that enables customized color settings to be used. Select Color Settings and, from the dialog box, use a preset color management configuration to provide the basis of your customization. Color settings can then be altered, for example to achieve the color profile specified by an external bureau that may ultimately print your imagery.

2.**261 Copy** (**command**) Edit menu item. Copies the current selection to the clipboard.

2.**262 Copy Merged** Edit menu item. Copies a merged version of all the currently visible layers in the current selection.

2.**263 Cut** Edit menu item that cuts a selection and sends it to the clipboard. From the Edit menu choose Clear (or press delete) to remove a selection entirely.

2.**264 Define Brush** (**2**) Photoshop 6 feature that enables a customized brush to be created and reserved for future use.

2.276 *Perspective*

2.280 *Rotate*

2.285 *Skew*

2.**265 Define Custom Shape** Photoshop 6 feature that enables a shape which has been created using a combination of other shape tools to be defined and named. It will then be available for selection from the shape list in the Options bar.

2.**266 Define Pattern** (**1**) Edit menu item. Permits the selection of an image area for use with the Edit>Fill command. If this pattern is smaller than the fill area the defined pattern will be repeated as image tiles within the Fill selection. Defined patterns can be saved for later use.

2.**267 Define Pattern** (**2**) Photoshop 6 feature that enables a selected rectangular image region (which may be an entire image, or part thereof) to be saved for later use in fills and otherwise.

2.**268 Distort** Edit > Transform menu item. Pulls or pushes any handles to distort the image at will; use Alt-drag (Windows) or Option-drag (Mac OS) to make any distortion symmetrical.

2.**269 Fill** Edit menu item. Fills the current selection with a color selected via the Fill dialog. The "color" can also be a pattern that has been selected using the Define Pattern command. A blending mode and opacity level can be selected. → 2.66/7 DEFINE PATTERN

2.**270 Flip Horizontal** Edit > Transform menu item. Flips the image selection about a vertical axis, transposing left and right.

2.**271 Flip Vertical** Edit > Transform menu item. Flips the image selection vertically about a horizontal axis, transposing top and bottom.

2.**272 Free Transform** Edit menu item. Enables the free transformation of an image, layer, path, or selection. Transformation is achieved by pulling, pushing, or rotating the selection handles.

2.**273 Numeric** Edit > Transform menu option. Enables transforms such as scale, rotate, skew, or move to be enacted on a layer path or selection using precise numerical data rather than freehand pulling or pushing of selection handles.

2.**274 Paste** Edit menu item. Pastes the clipboard contents into the current document.

2.**275 Paste Into** Edit menu item. Use Paste Into to paste a cut or copied clipboard selection into another selection (which may be in the original or a different image). The process pastes the source selection into a new layer while the destination selection border becomes a layer mask.

2.**276 Perspective** Edit > Transform menu item. Allows the creation of perspective effects in an otherwise rectilinear image, or the correction of perspective effects in an image with such artifacts. The most common use is to remove converging verticals in buildings when the original image was taken with a conventional lens (relatively) up close.

2.**277 Preset Manager** Photoshop 6 Edit menu feature. Use the Preset Manager to create, delete, load, or save sets of brushes, gradients, styles, patterns, color swatches or contours. The Preset Manager enables changes to be made to the Photoshop interface presets (including resetting to the defaults) but will not delete any items from

---

2.287 *Transform*

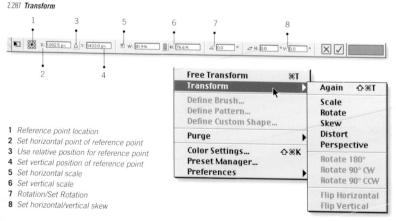

1  Reference point location
2  Set horizontal point of reference point
3  Use relative position for reference point
4  Set vertical position of reference point
5  Set horizontal scale
6  Set vertical scale
7  Rotation/Set Rotation
8  Set horizontal/vertical skew

the computer's hard disk. New brushes (or other items) need to be saved using the Preset Manager if they are intended for future use and you wish to incorporate them into existing sets.

**2.278 Print Options** Photoshop 6 feature. Provides page preview features (long overdue in Photoshop) along with the opportunity to reposition the intended print area. Print can be rescaled in the window for a better fit within the print boundaries.

**2.279 Purge** Edit menu item. Clears memory hogging data held in Photoshop buffers or RAM including Undo, Clipboard, Histories, Pattern or All.

**2.280 Rotate** Edit > Transform menu item. Rotates a selection about central point.

**2.281 Rotate 180°** Edit > Transform menu item. Rotates the entire image through 180°.

**2.282 Rotate 90° CCW** Edit > Transform menu item. Rotates image 90° counterclockwise.

**2.283 Rotate 90° CW** Edit > Transform menu item. Rotates entire image 90° clockwise.

**2.284 Scale** Edit > Transform menu item. Transforms the scale of the current selection. You can adjust height or width independently or maintain the aspect ratio.

**2.285 Skew** Edit > Transform menu item. Skews an image selection; pulling or pushing a side handle will skew the selection along the current vertical or horizontal axis.

**2.286 Stroke** Edit menu command. Provides a method of painting a border around a selection (or layer). A dialog box permits selection of a stroke width (in pixels) and location: inside, outside, or centered on the

selection line. The stroke can also be blended. To prevent it from extending into any transparent areas in the layer, click on the Preserve Transparency box.

**2.287 Transform** Edit menu item. Provides a set of tools to distort an image including rotations, horizontal and vertical flips, and perspective control.

**2.288 Undo** Edit menu item that undoes the last action performed on the image. For example, when a filter is applied, it can be removed by using Undo. The Undo command can undo the last command and no more. → 2.248 REVERT; 5.062 ACTIONS

## Image menu commands

**2.289 8Bits / Channel** Accessed through the Image menu under Mode. RGB, CMYK, and grayscale images generally contain eight bits of data per channel. RGB images, which use three channels, thus have an overall bit depth of 24 (3 x 8), while CMYK images have a bit depth of 32 (4 x 8). Images can also have sixteen bits of data per channel, giving somewhat greater overall depth and finer color detail. Unfortunately 16-bit-per-channel image files are substantially larger than their 8-bit-per-channel equivalents. The 8Bits/Channel command converts larger files down to eight bits per channel, and the16Bits/Channel command converts 8-bit-per-channel files up to the larger size.

**2.290 Adjust** Image menu item. Provides access to image adjustment features such as Hue/Saturation, Color Balance, and Levels.

2.304 *Duotone*     3   4

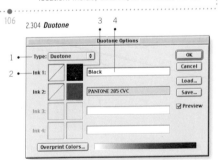

*Monotone*

*Duotone*

*Tritone*

*Quadtone*

1 *Selection (Monotone/Duotone/Tritone/Quadtone*
2 *Ink curve (click to modify)*
3 *Ink color (click on square to select)*
4 *Color name*

2.**291 Apply Image** image menu command. Blends the layer and channel of a source image with the layer and channel of the current active image. → 2.296 CALCULATIONS

2.**292 Auto Contrast** Image > Adjust menu item. New to Photoshop 5.5, Auto Contrast adjusts the shadows and highlights in an image by mapping the darkest and lightest pixels to black and white respectively. Highlights are thus rendered lighter and shadows darker. Like Auto Levels, this command is effective in images that display an average range of values. Distributions that are skewed in any way can lead to unpredictable (and unsatisfactory) results. → 2.293 AUTO LEVELS

2.**293 Auto Levels** Image > Adjust menu item. This command automatically sets the optimum levels by defining the lightest and darkest pixels in each channel as white and black (0 and 255) and spreading the intermediate levels proportionately. Effective use of this function depends on a "typical" or average distribution of values in the image. It is less successful with images with a less even distribution. Using either Levels or Curves leads to more precise results, but effective use of these demands a moderate level of experience. The Auto buttons in the Levels and Curves dialog boxes perform the same actions on the image.

2.**294 Bitmap** Image > Mode menu item which sets the image mode to Bitmap. In this mode two color values (black and white) are used to represent all the pixels in an image. Bitmapped images are sometimes referred to as one-bit images because they have a bit depth of 1. An image must be in Grayscale mode before it can be converted to Bitmap. → 1.018 BIT DEPTH

2.**295 Brightness/Contrast** Image > Adjust menu item. Select this to set Brightness and Contrast levels in the Brightness/Contrast dialog box.

2.**296 Calculations** Image menu item that lets you blend two channels (from one or two source images) and apply the combined result to a new channel or selection in the active image. → 2.291 APPLY IMAGE

2.**297 Canvas Size** The Canvas Size command can be selected from the Image menu. It adds new workspace or removes existing workspace. The Canvas Size dialog box features a canvas icon. In the default state the dark, central square represents the current canvas. The arrows indicate that new workspace will be added to each edge of the canvas. Click in a different square if you wish to constrain the addition of new workspace to particular areas. Define the extent of the new canvas size by entering the new width or height (acceptable parameters are inches, centimeters, points, picas, pixels, and percentages). Dimensions larger or smaller than the current values are permitted.

2.**298 Channel Mixer** Image > Adjust menu item. Enables a color channel to be modified using a mix of the current color channels. Useful for creating graphic color effects and grayscale images based on uneven contributions from color channels (emulating the effect of color filters in black-and-white photography).

2.**299 CMYK Color** Image > Mode menu item. You should convert your image to CMYK mode prior to printing it on a color printer, or prior to the production of color separations. The only exception is with a Level 2 Postscript filter where the final conversion should be to Lab color mode.

2.**300 Color Balance** Image > Adjust menu item. Enables color casts to be adjusted and under- or oversaturated colors to be corrected. Adjustments can be made to the image shadows, midtones, or highlights. The dialog box provides three sliders. Move a slider toward any color you want more of.

2.**301 Color Table** Image > Mode menu command. The Color Table dialog displays the color table (the colors available) for Indexed Color images. A pop-up menu gives the option of four predefined color sets and provides for the creation of a custom set. Select the Black Body set to create a color table based on the colors that result when a black body radiator is heated. Colors range from black to red to orange, yellow and white. Select Grayscale for a range of grays between (and including) black and white. Select Spectrum for the conventional spectral range. Select System for the standard Mac OS or Windows (as appropriate) color palette. For specific purposes you may want to alter one of these palettes to include (or exclude) colors.

2.**302 Curves** Image > Adjust menu item. Use this command to access the Curves dialog box. Here you can alter the tonal range of an image at any point in the 255-point scale.

107

For example, by suppressing the lower values and raising the higher ones (to describe a subtle Roman Ogive or Ogee) a flat image can be given more "punch."

2.**303 Desaturate** Image > Adjust menu item. Removes all color value information from an image resulting in a grayscale image. Note that the image remains in the original mode; for example, desaturating an RGB color image will produce an RGB color image with only black, white, and grays.

2.**304 Duotone** Image > Mode menu item. Duotone mode permits the creation of both two-color duotones, three-color tritones, and four-color quadtones. These are grayscale images printed with two, three, or four color inks respectively. The term duotone is used to describe all three types.

2.**305 Duplicate** Image menu item. Duplicate lets you copy an entire image (including channels, layers, and layer masks) into memory. A dialog box will request a name for the duplicate image. Select Merged Layers Only to duplicate the image without layers. Holding down the Option key (Mac OS) or Alt key (Windows) when choosing Duplicate creates a duplicate with the original file name appended with "copy."

2.**306 Equalize** Image > Adjust menu item. Acts on the brightness values of pixels in an image. The brightest and darkest values in an image are assigned to white and black and the intermediate pixels are distributed as evenly as feasible between them. A typical use can be in "lightening" a dark PictureCD image or scanned image. → 1.540 PICTURECD

2.**307 Extract;** Photoshop 5.5 command that makes the selection of difficult foreground subjects from backgrounds much easier. A sophisticated development of the "magnetic" lasso-type tools, Extract makes the selection of intricate detail (such as foliage and hair) simple. The Extract dialog box (which is unique among Photoshop offerings) enables you to define the edge of your subject using a highlighter pen tool. Next you define the interior of the selection and can preview the extraction. Extraction parameters can be varied and the process repeated until a satisfactory preview achieved. When the extraction is performed the background is erased leaving only the foreground subject.

2.**308 Grayscale** Image > Mode menu item. Each pixel has a brightness value between 0 (black) and 255 (white). There is no color information. If a color image is stored as a grayscale image color information is irretrievably discarded.

2.**309 Histogram** Image menu item. Select Histogram to display the histogram for the current active image. The Photoshop histogram displays the number of pixels at a specific brightness level in an image enabling the user to determine whether the image holds enough information to enable effective corrections to be applied. The x-axis is scaled in color values from the darkest (0) to the brightest (255). The y-axis is a measure of the number of pixels. The histogram is also useful as a "quick look" tool for the tonal range in the image. A good image has good "levels" at all points along

2.309 *Histogram*

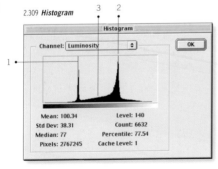

1 *Shadows*
2 *Midtones*
3 *Highlights*

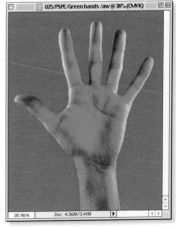

the histogram. Hold down the Alt key (Windows) or Option key (Mac OS) when selecting Histogram if your image includes spot channels and alpha channels and you wish to include pixel data from these. If part of an image is selected, the histogram will represent that selection. → 2.024 HISTOGRAM

2.**310 Hue / Saturation** Image > Adjust menu item. Select it to open the Hue/Saturation dialog box. This box features sliders for Hue, Saturation, and Lightness. Adjustments to hue are cyclical based on the color wheel (the extreme left end of the slider is an adjacent hue to that at the extreme right) and shift the each of the individual hues in the image through 360° of the color wheel. You can alter the saturation of color though from -100 (no color) to +100 (totally saturated). Clicking on the Colorize box will reduce the image to a single tone that can be precisely adjusted using the Hue control. Useful for creating "toned" (e.g. sepia toned) prints.

2.**311 Image Size** Image menu item. There will be occasions when you need to change the size of your image, whether in terms of the linear dimensions, the resolution or both. Selecting the Image Size command will open the Image Size dialog box. Here you can set your new measurements and resolution. If the Constrain Proportions box is checked you need alter only one dimension; the other will automatically be calculated. Uncheck this box if you wish to alter the proportions. → 2.297 CANVAS SIZE

2.**312 Indexed Color** Image > Mode menu item.

Indexed Color mode uses no more than 256 colors and one channel. Conversion to Indexed Color can create some graphic arts type effects, but the mode finds more general use in web graphics. In particular the GIF89a file format can only be created by exporting from an Indexed Color image. Note that only limited editing facilities are available in this mode; you'll need to remain in, or convert to, RGB to perform certain edits.

2.**313 Invert** Image > Adjust submenu command. Use the Invert command to make an image (or a layer, or image background) look like a photographic negative. Monochrome images will have each pixel replaced with one of the opposite brightness value; in color images the color value is also replaced by its opposite.

2.**314 Lab Color** Image > Mode menu item. Originally designed as a mode that provided consistency between display and printing devices. It uses three channels, one representing lightness, the second colors green through to red, and the third colors blue to yellow. Some operating systems work best with Lab mode images.

2.**315 Levels** Image > Adjust menu item. Opens the Levels dialog box featuring the histogram and the output levels grayscale gradient. Use this to make manual correction to the image based on the RGB histogram or individual channels. → 2.309 HISTOGRAM

2.**316 Liquify** Photoshop 6 feature. An image distortion "filter" or filter set that allows a series of tools to be used to alter the

2.310 *Hue/Saturation*

1 Drop down menu for color selection
2 Hue, Saturation and Lightness sliders
3 Reference color bar (does not change)
4 Adjusted color bar

*Normal*

*Hue + 90*

*Saturation +70*

*Lightness +70*

2.319 **Posterize** – *normal*

**Posterize** – *6*

**Posterize** – *3*

2.325 **Threshold**—*original*

2.325 **Threshold**—*Level 80*

2.325 **Threshold**—*Level 120*

2.313 **Invert**—*before*

2.313 **Inverted**

2.313 **Invert**—*before*

2.313 **Inverted**

charateristics and linearity of an image. Distorting tools include Twist, Bloat, and Pucker, the last giving a pinched, pincushion effect. Reconstruction modes are provided to undo or alter the effect of the distorting tools. The three modes of reconstruction are known as Amplitwist, Affine, and Displace. A Warp Mesh is drawn over the surface of the image to enable distortions to be easily seen and monitored. Image areas can also be masked at any point (prior to distorting, prior to reconstruction, or otherwise) to prevent the tools from taking effect in those areas. In Liquify this masking (and the consequential unmasking) is known as freezing and thawing. Liquify is a command in the Image menu.

2.**317 Mode** Image menu item. Allows images to be converted from one mode to another. Available options are Bitmap, Grayscale, Duotone, Indexed Color, RGB Color, CMYK Color, LAB Color, and Multichannel. You can also alter the bits per channel between eight and sixteen.

2.**318 Multichannel** Image > Mode menu item. Comprises multiple 256-level grayscale channels. Useful in specialized printing regimes such as conversion of duotones to Scitex CT format. Multichannel mode can also be used to assemble channels from several images (or several image edits) before converting the result to a color mode.

2.**319 Posterize** Image > Adjust menu item. Creates an image with large flat areas of color. Specify a number of levels in the dialog box. Modest numbers (4 to 8) work best. Setting four levels in an RGB image will result in four tonal levels for each of the three color channels—twelve in all.

2.**320 Profile to Profile** Image > Mode menu item. Converts the color space of the working image to that defined in the RGB Setup, CMYK Setup, or Grayscale Setup dialog boxes.

2.**321 Replace Color** Image > Adjust menu item. Helps create a mask based on precise image colors. Unlike other masks this does not create a selection and will disappear when the command is completed. Use this to change the hue, saturation, and lightness values of an element in the image. Masking and color transforms are all handled in the Replace Color dialog box.

2.**322 RGB Color** Image > Mode menu item. RGB Color is the most commonly used mode. Only in RGB Color are all Photoshop's tool options and filters accessible and usable.

2.**323 Rotate Canvas** image menu item. Permits the canvas to be rotated through 90° (either clockwise or counterclockwise, 180°, or an arbitrary amount. You can also flip the canvas along a horizontal or vertical axis.

2.**324 Selective Color** Image > Adjust menu item. Selecting it causes the Selective Color dialog box to appear. This enables you to make color adjustments to match the characteristics of process colors for additive and subtractive colors in an image. As well as its corrective use, this dialog box can also be used to create powerful graphic images by removing or inverting colors.

2.**325 Threshold** Image > Adjust menu item. Creates a high-contrast "lith film" effect from grayscale or color images. The dialog box asks for a threshold level. Any levels below will be represented as black, those above as white.

2.**326 Trap** Image menu item. A trap is a slight overlap between colors that ensures that any slight misalignment of color plates when printing will not reveal an obvious white gap (on white paper). In Photoshop a trap can be created for CMYK images by choosing Trap from the Image menu. This reveals the Trap dialog box where a width (trapping value) can be specified. This value would normally be provided by a print shop and provides a measure for how far colors are permitted to overlap. Photoshop uses the standard trapping rules. → 9.021 TRAP; 9.125 TRAPPING

2.**327 Trim** Photoshop 6 feature. Crop-type command. Use Trim in preference to Crop to discard a border around an image based on transparency or edge color.

2.**328 Variations** Image > Adjust menu item. Select Variations to open the Variations dialog box. Perhaps the most visual of the color adjustment features, Variations illustrates your current image as a thumbnail surrounded by others that are identical except for having a slightly different color balance. These are denoted appropriately by, for example, More Red, More Blue, etc. Another part of the display shows thumbnails lighter and darker than the original. By clicking on the appropriate icon, that color (or brightness) value is applied to the image. You can make multiple applications and a comparative pair of thumbnails, Original and Current Pick, lets you monitor your progress.

## Select menu commands

**2.329 All** Select menu item. Selects the whole of the current active image.

**2.330 Color Range** Select menu item. Permits the selection of a color, or color range, from an existing selection (or the whole image). Using the Color Range dialog colors can be sampled for selection. You can set the Fuzziness control to determine the range of colors sampled.

**2.331 Defringe** This command, accessed from the Select menu under Matting > Defringe, helps reduce the prominence of any join seams where objects are pasted onto one layer from another, or from another image. Colors at the edge of the selection are colored along with those pixels adjacent, to a specified pixel radius.

**2.332 Deselect** Select menu item. Deselects any currently selected image areas, irrespective of the original selection method.

**2.333 Feather (2)** Select menu item. Softens the edge of a selection to give a better transition between it and the surrounding pixels. A feather radius (in pixels) can be entered in the Feather dialog box. Although this feature can make for a better blend between objects, it can also lead to a loss of definition at the boundary which may be critical in some instances.

**2.334 Grow** Select menu item. Expands a selection to include further areas of similar color. This might typically be used following a selection with the Magic Wand tool. A selection can be enlarged in a contiguous manner based on the current tolerance setting for the Magic Wand. → 2.340 SIMILAR

**2.335 Inverse** Select menu item. Allows selected and unselected elements of an image to be reversed. Useful, for example, for selecting a border area of an image. Select the main image area using the marquee. That area is now the selected one. Choose Inverse from the Select menu and the border becomes the selection, while the main image area is deselected.

**2.336 Load Selection** Select menu item. Permits the loading of a selection (or an alpha channel) into an image. → 5.036 CHANNELS; 5.035 ALPHA CHANNEL

**2.337 Modify** Select menu item. Expands or contracts a selection by a specified number of pixels. Use this if your selection includes a boundary you wish to exclude (by contracting the selection), for example, if you have drawn freehand with a lasso and not been able to keep entirely to the object boundaries. You can also smooth a boundary (to remove unsteady selection) and place a border of specified width around the selection.

**2.338 Reselect** Select menu item. Restores the previous selection prior to a Deselect command.

**2.339 Save Selection** Select menu item. Saves a selection to a new or existing channel.

2.333 *Feather*

Feather radius 20

Feather radius 40

Feather radius 60

Feather radius 100

Choosing Save Selection opens a dialog box that enables you to define a destination document and channel.

2.**340 Similar** Select menu item. Allows the selection of noncontiguous areas of color based on (say) the tolerance setting of the Magic Wand tool if that has been used to make the original selection. → 2.334 GROW

2.**341 Smooth** The Smooth command adds or removes pixels from a selection within a specified radius. Useful when using e.g. the Magic Wand to absorb small unselected areas in a scene

2.**342 Transform Selection** Select menu item. Permits a selection to be transformed. Handles appear around the selection to enable an image to be flipped, rotated, skewed, or rescaled. Note that the transformation applies only to the selection marquee; it does not rescale the object originally selected.

## Layer menu commands

2.**343 Add / Remove Layer Mask** Layer menu item. From the Layer menu select Add Layer Mask > Reveal All to create a mask that reveals the entire layer; or Add Layer Mask > Hide All to create a mask that hides the entire layer. Remove the mask by selecting Remove Layer Mask. → 6.040 MASK

2.**344 Adjustment Options** Layer menu item which is available only when an adjustment layer is active. Opens the Levels dialog, permitting changes to be made via the controls therein. → 5.003 ADJUSTMENT LAYER

2.**345 Align Linked** Layer menu item that aligns a linked group of layers. Submenu selections include Vertical Center, which aligns the vertically central pixel in the linked layers to the corresponding one on the active layer, and Bottom, which aligns the bottom pixel on the linked layers to that on the active layer.

2.**346 Arrange** Layer menu item that allows individual layers within a layer stack to be moved relative to other layers. Includes the commands Bring to Front (brings layer to top of stack), Bring Forward (moves layer up one level in a stack), Send Backward (moves layer down one level in the stack), and Send to Back (pushes layer to bottom of the stack). Actions can be monitored using the Layers palette.

2.**347 Delete Layer** (1) Layer menu item that deletes the selected layer. The command can be undone using Edit > Undo Delete Layer. → 2.132 DELETE LAYER (2)

2.**348 Disable Layer Mask** Layer menu item. Disables the function of the layer mask; the disable function is indicated on the Layers palette by a red cross.

2.**349 Distribute Linked** Layer menu item. You can use this command to distribute linked layers according to the options in the sub menu: Top, Vertical Center, Bottom, Horizontal Center, Right, and Left. For example, choose Top and the linked layers will be evenly spaced, starting from the top pixel of each layer. However, it works only on layers whose pixels have an opacity of more than 50%.

2.**348** *Disable Layer Mask*

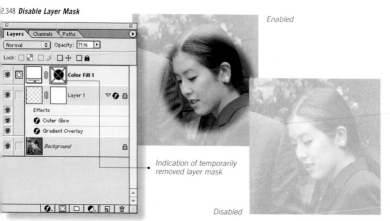

*Enabled*

*Indication of temporarily removed layer mask*

*Disabled*

113

2.**350 Duplicate Layer** (**2**) Layer menu item. Duplicates a selected layer in an image. You'll be prompted for a name (the default is [layer name] copy) and can optionally provide a destination for the layer.

2.**351 Effects** (**1**) Layer menu item. Layer-based effects such as drop shadows, bevels, and glows can be created via the Effects submenu. → 5.021 LAYER EFFECTS; 6.063 DROP SHADOW (2); 5.005 BEVEL AND EMBOSS

2.**352 Flatten Image** Layer menu item. Flattens all visible layers into the background. This process results in the loss of hidden layers and layer information. It is normally done when all image editing on the individual layers is complete. A flattened file is smaller (often much smaller) than the original. Some color modes do not support layers; hence converting between modes can result in automatic flattening.

2.**353 Group Linked** Layer menu item that groups linked layers together; they can be released using the Ungroup command.

2.**354 Layer Options** (**2**) Layer menu item. Opens the Layer Options dialog box, where you can rename the layer, alter the opacity, and choose a blending mode. You can also blend this layer subject to it, or the underlying layer, conforming to certain criteria which you can set.

2.**355 layer style** Photoshop 6 term. Synonymous with layer effects in earlier versions of Photoshop. Numerical limits for styles have been removed (and hence allow more extensive effects limited only by system memory). New effects that join Contract,

Expand, Scratches, Emboss, and others include contours, bevels, and noise. Selectable from the Layer menu. → 5.201 LAYER EFFECTS; 2.202 LAYER STYLES DIALOG

2.**356 Lock Image Pixels** Photoshop 6 feature. Previous versions of Photoshop enabled layer transparency to be locked. Version 6 also enables the image pixels to be locked: A layer can be moved or transformed but no painting actions can be performed on it. A complementary feature, Lock Position, permits painting on the layer but does not allow transformations or movement.

2.**357 Matting** Layer menu item. Helps edit edge "fringe" pixels that can result when an antialiased selection is pasted into another image. Three options are available from the submenu: Defringe replaces edge pixels with the color of nearby pixels. "Valid" nearby pixels are those not containing background color. Remove Black Matte can be used when an antialiased selection is taken from against a black background. Remove White Matte works in the same way, but with a white background. Typical use of this last case would be the situation where black text is lifted from a white page and placed, say, on a green background. The antialiasing technique would result in some gray pixels, particularly around curves in the font. Selecting Remove White Matte would remove these errant pixels.

2.**358 Merge Linked** (**2**) Layer menu item. Merges linked layers together.

2.**359 Merge Visible** (**2**) Layer menu item. Merges all layers that are currently visible.

2.351 *Effects*

2.366 *Gamut Warning*

*Unchecked*

*Checked, with out of gamut colors displayed as green*

Layers may be set to visible or invisible in order to create a merge group.

2.**360 New** (**2**) Layer menu item. Creates a new layer in the current image. Options offered include new background layer, new adjustment layer, and creation of a layer via a cut or copy. → 5.003 ADJUSTMENT LAYER

2.**361 Type** Layer menu item that only acts on Type layers. When you add text to an image, using the Type tool, it is placed in its own Type layer. Via the Type command you can change the type layout from horizontal to vertical and choose to render the layer.

2.**362 Ungroup** Layer menu item. Makes layers grouped with the Group Linked command separately editable again.

## View menu commands

2.**363 Actual Pixels** View menu item. Displays an image at 100% scale.

2.**364 Clear Guides** View menu item. Removes all guides in the currently selected window. If you have more than one guide but only want to remove selected ones, use the move tool to drag the appropriate guides from the window.

2.**365 Fit on Screen** View menu item. Adjusts the scale of the view and the window to fit the monitor. Double clicking on the hand tool has the same effect.

2.**366 Gamut Warning** View menu item. The gamut is a representation of the actual colors a color printing system can print or the colors a display system (a monitor, for example) can display. Each color model has a restricted range of colors in its gamut compared with the human eye. The Gamut Warning marks all those colors in an image that are out of gamut and, consequently, will not be displayed or printed correctly. You can choose a different color to indicate out-of-gamut colors from Edit> Preferences > Transparency & Gamut. → 4.016 COLOR GAMUT

2.**367 Lock Guides** View menu item. Positionally locks all guides on the selected image.

2.**368 New View** View menu item. Allows the opening of multiple views of the same image. Edits to either view are incorporated into that image.

2.**369 Preview** View menu item. You can use Preview to preview CMYK colors in an RGB image. This is a preview-only mode; no changes are made to the image. You can also preview the image as it would appear in Macintosh RGB, Windows RGB,ß and Uncompensated RGB color fields.

2.**370 Print Size** View menu item. Onscreen image is adjusted to display image at approximate printed size.

2.**371 Show/Hide Edges** View menu item. Shows or hides the selection marquee. In either condition the selection remains active. If you are unsure whether the selection is still active, click on the Select menu. Nearly all the commands should be active.

2.**372 Show/Hide Grid** View menu item. The grid is a fixed, nonprinting series of vertical and horizontal lines (or, optionally, dots) that aid symmetrical compositions. Show/Hide Grid toggles the grid on and off.

2.355 *layer style*

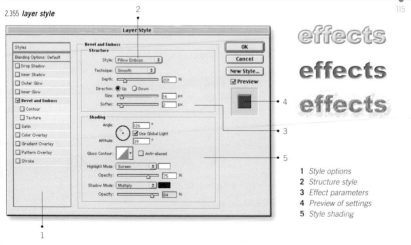

1 *Style options*
2 *Structure style*
3 *Effect parameters*
4 *Preview of settings*
5 *Style shading*

115

2.**373 Show/Hide Guides** View menu item. Toggles guides on or off. To remove guides permanently select Clear Guides from the View menu.

2.**374 Show/Hide Path** View menu item. Shows or hides a path. If you are working with multiple paths in an image, you'll need to select the appropriate path from the Paths palette before selecting Hide Path. Selecting Show Path will show all paths in an image.

2.**375 Show/Hide Rulers** View menu item. Toggles on or off the rulers that appear on the top and left sides of an image window. When shown, each ruler will indicate the respective cursor position on its axis.

2.**376 Snap to Grid** View menu item. Turns on (or off, if already selected) the "snapping" of objects to the nearest gridlines. → 2.020 GRID

2.**377 Snap to Guides** View menu item. Guides are individual nonprinting index lines that can be placed parallel to either ruler axis to aid layout and composition. With Snap to Guides active a tool or selection will snap to a guide if brought within eight pixels of it.

2.**378 Zoom In/Zoom Out** View menu item. Zooms in (or out) on the image, enlarging (or diminishing) the entire image (unlike the Zoom tool, which enlarges or reduces within the existing image window).

## Window menu commands

2.**379 Show/Hide Actions** Window menu item. Shows or hides the Actions palette.

2.**380 Show/Hide Brushes** Window menu item. Shows or hides the Brushes palette.

2.**381 Show/Hide Channels** Window menu item. Shows or hides the Channels palette.

2.**382 Show/Hide Character** Photoshop 6 feature. Shows or hides the Character palette.

2.**383 Show/Hide Color** Window menu item. Shows or hides the Color palette.

2.**384 Show/Hide History** Window menu item. Shows or hides the History palette.

2.**385 Show/Hide Info** Window menu item. Shows or hides the Info palette. → 2.143 INFO PALETTE

2.**386 Show/Hide Layers** Window menu item. Shows or hides the Layers palette.

2.**387 Show/Hide Navigator** Window menu item. Shows or hides the Photoshop Navigator palette. → 2.155 NAVIGATOR PALETTE

2.**388 Show/Hide Options** Window menu item. Shows or hides the Options palette for the currently selected tool.

2.**389 Show/Hide Paragraph** Photoshop 6 feature. Shows or hides the Paragraph palette.

2.**390 Show/Hide Paths** Window menu item. Shows or hides the Paths palette.

2.**391 Show/Hide Styles** (**1**) Shows or hides the Styles palette.

2.**392 Show/Hide Swatches** Window menu item. Shows or hides the palette containing the color swatches.

2.**393 Show/Hide Tools** Window menu item. Toggles the Toolbar on and off.

## Help menu commands

2.**394 Export Transparent Image** An assistant (or wizard) that helps with the export of an image in accordance with the user's requirements for the final image. From the Help menu choose Export Transparent Image. Subsequent screens prompt you for details such as the intended use of the image.

2.**395 Online Help** A range of options (depending on Photoshop version) including, online registration of product, direct access to the Adobe web site, downloadable "value added" features, top issues.

2.**396 Resize Image assistant** An assistant (or wizard) that helps resize an image in accordance with the user's requirements for the final image. It is accessed from the Help menu under Resize Image. Subsequent screens prompt you for details such as the intended use of the image (i.e. print or screen), intended size, halftone screens, and quality.

2.**397 Top Issues** Photoshop 6 Help feature. Provides a link to Adobe's web site, which details any pertinent issues relating to the operation of Photoshop.

# FILE MANAGEMENT

## File formats

3.**001 animated GIF** A GIF file composed of multiple images, which simulates an animation when displayed in a web browser. → 3.021 GIF

3.**002 ASCII** Acronym for the American Standard Code for Information Interchange, a code which assigns a number to the 256 letters, numbers, and symbols (including carriage returns and tabs), which can be typed on a keyboard. ASCII is the cross-platform, computer-industry-standard, text-only file format. → 1.303 CROSS-PLATFORM

3.**003 Audio Video Interleave (AVI)** The AVI format is normally used only in Windows environments, where it is the standard format for audio and video data. ImageReady can create (and edit) files in this format. → 1.242 QUICKTIME; 3.062 CODEC

3.**004 binary file** A file in which data is described in binary code rather than text. Binary files typically hold pictures, sounds, or a complete application program. → 10.011 BINARY; 3.005 BINHEX

3.**005 BinHex** An acronym for binary to hexadecimal, a file format that converts binary files to ASCII text, usually for transmission via e-mail. This is the safest way of sending document files—particularly to and from Macintosh computers—since some computer systems along the e-mail route may only accept standard ASCII text characters. Some e-mail software may encode and decode BinHex files automatically, but otherwise it must be done manually, usually with a file compression utility. → 10.011 BINARY; 3.002 ASCII; 7.125 E-MAIL

3.**006 BMP** Standard Windows image format, concatenated from "bitmap". It supports bitmap, RGB, indexed color, and grayscale color modes but does not recognize alpha channels. Bit depths can be specified when saving for Windows or OS/2 operating systems.

3.**007 CompuServe GIF** Little-used "full" name for Graphic Interchange Format files; named after CompuServe who developed it for use in their Internet service. → 2.021 GIF

3.**008 Data Interchange Format (DIF)** A file format used by database and spreadsheet applications for exporting records. DIF files preserve field names but not formatting. → 3.015 FILE FORMAT; 1.207 DATABASE; 1.253 SPREADSHEET; 1.213 FIELD; 1.520 FORMATTING

3.001 *animated GIF*—animation from ImageReady

1 *Original (start) image*
2 *Final (end image)*
3 *Tweened images* → 7.043 TWEEN

3.**009 Encapsulated PostScript (EPS)** A standard graphics file format used primarily for storing "object-oriented" or vector graphics files (a vector is a tiny database giving information about both the magnitude and direction of a line or shape) that are generated by drawing applications such as Adobe Illustrator and Macromedia FreeHand. An EPS file usually has two parts: one containing the PostScript code, which tells the printer how to print the image; the other an onscreen preview that can be in PICT, TIFF, or JPEG format. Although used mainly for storing vector-based graphics, the EPS format is also widely used to store bitmapped images, particularly those used for desktop color separation ("DCS"); these EPS files are encoded as either "ASCII" (a text-based0 description of an image) or "binary" (which uses numbers rather than text to store data). Bitmapped EPS files to be printed from a Windows-based system use ASCII encoding, while those to be printed on the Mac OS are usually saved with binary encoding, although not all printing software supports binary EPS files. Photoshop EPS supports bitmap, Lab, CMYK, RGB, indexed color, duotone, and grayscale color modes and also clipping paths (but not alpha channels). → 3.002 ASCII; 10.011 BINARY; 10.160 VECTOR; DCS

3.**010 EPS PICT Preview Format** Available only on Mac OS systems, this, like the EPS TIFF Preview format, lets you open files that create previews but are not supported by Photoshop. Once opened a preview file can be edited, but normally only at low resolution.

3.**011 EPS TIFF Preview Format** Appearing as an option in the Open (and Open As) dialog box, this "preview" format enables you to open files that create previews but are not supported by Photoshop. Once opened a preview file can be edited, but normally only at low resolution.

3.**012 Exchangeable Image Format (EXIF)** A file format used in many Fujifilm digital cameras.

3.**013 file** A collection of data that is stored as an individual item on a disk. A file can be a document, a folder, an application, or a resource. → 3.015 FILE FORMAT

3.**014 file extension** The abbreviated suffix at the end of a filename that describes either its type (such as EPS or JPG) or origin (the application which created it, such as PSD for Photoshop). A file extension usually comprises three letters (although Macintosh and UNIX systems may use more) and is separated from the filename by a full point.

3.**015 file format** The way a program arranges data that so that it can be stored or displayed on a computer. A file format may be used by a particular application or by many different software programs. To help you work on a job that requires several applications, or to work with other people who may be using different applications to yours, file formats tend to be standardized. Common file formats include TIFF and JPEG for bitmapped image files, EPS for object-oriented image files, and ASCII for text files. → 3.055 TIFF, 3.028 TIF; 3.009 JPEG; 3.002 EPS; ASCII

3.**016 file type** In the Mac OS, the four-letter code assigned to every file when it is created

3.015 *file format*

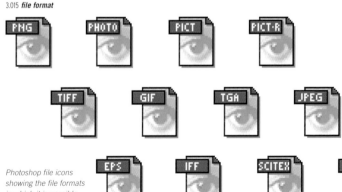

*Photoshop file icons showing the file formats in which it is possible to save Photoshop files.*

to identify its kind or format, such as "APPL" for an application, "TEXT" for text files, and so on. Special software such as ResEdit is generally required to identify the file type. → 3.013 FILE

**3.017 Filmstrip** A Macintosh file format created from PICT files and used, for example, to create high-speed animated buttons in multimedia presentations. Normally created by Adobe Premiere, these files can be opened in Photoshop but if some image edits are then performed (such as resize, resample, remove alpha channels, or change color mode) they cannot be stored back in Filmstrip format.

**3.018 FlashPix (FPX)** File format designed by Kodak, Microsoft, HP and Live Picture for the "consumer" market. FPX represents a multiresolution format that stores image data as a series of arrays, where each array represents a unique spatial resolution. This involves little actual image resizing when the user selects a different image size and/or resolution combination. The drawback is an increased file size (about a third more than an equivalent TIFF file), but much less RAM is needed for viewing (about one fifth of that for the TIFF) and edits can be performed more rapidly. The format formed the basis of the Flashpix CD, a consumer version of PhotoCD launched in 1996 but superseded by PictureCD. → 1.538 PHOTOCD; 1.540 PICTURECD

**3.019 GIF87a** A bitmapped graphics format originally devised by CompuServe, an Internet service provider (now part of AOL), and sometimes (although rarely) referred to as "CompuServe GIF". This original specification (GIF87a) was superseded by GIF89a which permits (among other refinements) transparent backgrounds. → 3.021 GIF

**3.020 GIF89a** Version (so-named because it was introduced in 1989) of the GIF file format that allows image transparency in web pages. Images can also be rendered progressively, in the same manner as progressive JPEG files. GIF89a also permits multiple images to be stored for replay as an animation (the result is known as an animated GIF). → 3.021 GIF; 3.058 TRANSPARENT GIF; 3.001 ANIMATED GIF

**3.021 Graphics Interchange Format (GIF)** A graphics file format designed principally for the delivery of raster images over the Internet. A GIF image uses eight-bit color and can thus contain up to 256 colors (including a transparent one). File size is dependent on the number of colors used in the actual image and also on the degree of compression invoked (using the LZW compression method). The GIF format is supported by most browsers and can be used for creating animated images. → 3.068 LZW COMPRESSION; 3.001 ANIMATED GIF; 3.025 INTERLACED GIF; 3.058 TRANSPARENT GIF

**3.022 High Sierra standard** Data format for CD-ROMs. The High Sierra standard specifies the layout of the data in tracks and sectors on the disc. Adopted by the International Organization for Standardization as ISO 9660, it lays down certain requirements for the reading of CD-ROMs on different computer platforms.

**3.023 image file** Any digital file in which a graphic image such as a photograph is stored, as distinct from other data such as a text file, database file, 3D file, etc. Image files can be saved in a variety of formats, depending upon the application they were created with, but typical formats include TIFF, GIF, JPEG, PICT, BMP, EPS, etc. Confusingly, the data format in which some images are stored is actually text—for example EPS graphics are saved in "ASCII" (text) format—but the file is still an image file. → 3.009 EPS; 3.002 ASCII

**3.024 Interchange File Format (IFF)** A file format used to transfer files to and from Commodore Amiga systems.

**3.025 interlaced GIF** A GIF89a format image in which the image reveals increasing detail as it downloads to a web page. Similar to the progressive JPEG format. → 3.021 GIF; 3.058 TRANSPARENT GIF

**3.026 IPE** Image Pac Extension. The 64base component of a Pro PhotoCD (as distinct from the consumer level PhotoCD). → 1.538 PHOTOCD; 3.060 BASE RESOLUTION

**3.027 IVUE** File format devised by Live Picture Inc. for their functional interpolating transformation system (FITS). Image edits are stored as mathematical expressions in a FITS file and the original image data is stored in an IVUE file. Finally a new output file, based on the IVUE file, is created with the FITS modifications. The big benefit is that the computer handles only data relevant to the section of the image being edited, rather than the whole image, thus saving time and resources.

3.**028 Joint Photographic Experts Group (JPEG)** An ISO group that defines compression standards for bitmapped color images. JPEG gives its name to a "lossy" (meaning some data may be lost) compressed file format in which the degree of compression from high compression/low quality to low compression/high quality can be defined by the user, thus making the format doubly suitable for images that are to be used either for print reproduction or for transmitting across networks such as the Internet (for viewing in web browsers, for example). → 3.021 GIF; 3.064 FILE COMPRESSION; 3.015 FILE FORMAT; 3.067 LOSSY COMPRESSION

3.**029 JPEG2000** New image compression standard developed with the Joint Photographic Experts Group (part of ISO). It uses Wavelet technology to improve upon the existing standard and offers improved compression that accommodates higher resolutions and richer content. Other enchancements include greater error resilience to enable successful transmission in "noisy" environments (such as the Internet). For the user, the best feature of this revision is the ability for the recipient of an image to determine what bit depth and what resolution the final decompressed image should have. It therefore adds a whole new level of flexibility to image compression. → 3.028 JPEG

3.**030 JPEG File Interchange Format (JFIF)** A standard for JPEG compressions that ensures that JPEG files can be viewed across applications and platforms. → 3.028 JPEG

3.**031 MacBinary** A file format that allows Macintosh files to be transferred via modem or shared with non-Mac computers by ensuring that all component parts such as the resource and data forks remain together. → 3.094 RESOURCE FORK; 3.074 DATA FORK

3.**032 native file format** A file format for exclusive use by the application in which the files were created, although some applications may be able to read files created in another's native format.

3.**033 PCX** PC-based file format supporting bitmap, RGB, indexed color, and grayscale color modes. Bit depth can be 1, 4, 8, or 24.

3.**034 Photo JPEG (codec)** A QuickTime compression setting ("codec") generally used for still photographic images. Useful for movies with a slow frame rate, such as slide shows or web movies. → 1.242 QUICKTIME; 3.062 CODEC

3.**035 Photoshop 2.0** Mac OS only, this is the default file format generated by Photoshop 2. This version of Photoshop does not support some of the features fundamental to Photoshop images today. In particular layers are not supported, hence any images opened or saved in this format are flattened and the layer information is discarded.

3.**036 Photoshop DCS 1.0** File format comprising four separate (CMYK) PostScript files (desktop color separations) and a fifth composite "master" channel. → 3.009 EPS

3.**037 Photoshop DCS 2.0** DCS file format that additionally supports (and retains) a single alpha channel and multiple spot channels. Color channel information can be stored as multiple files (as in Photoshop DCS 1.0) or as a single, more compact file. → 3.036 PHOTOSHOP DCS 1.0

3.**038 Photoshop format** The default file format for images and graphics created in Photoshop. Only the Photoshop format (denoted where appropriate with the .PSD extension) will support all the Photoshop image modes (RGB, CMYK, bitmap, grayscale, duotone, indexed color, Lab, and multichannel) along with other image features such as layers (including adjustment, type, and effects layers), alpha and spot channels, and image guides. Note that newer versions of Photoshop include features not found in earlier versions; hence editing or saving an image in an earlier version will result in those features being discarded.

3.**039 PICS animation** A Macintosh animation format that uses PICT images to create a sequence. → 3.040 PICT

3.**040 PICT** Acronym for picture. A standard file format for storing bitmapped and object-oriented images on Macintosh computers. Originally the PICT format only supported eight colors, but a newer version, PICT2, supports 32-bit color. When saving a PICT file in Photoshop you'll be prompted to choose 16-bit or 32-bit resolution and, in the Mac OS (with QuickTime installed), one of four JPEG compression options. → 3.041 PICT RESOURCE (2)

3.**041 PICT Resource (2)** A Mac OS-only file format. This is a PICT file that is contained

3.036 **Photoshop DCS 1.0**

Long Melford.C

Long Melford.M

Long Melford.Y

Long Melford.K

Long Melford.eps

*DCS 1 files comprise five files—a single low-resolution composite file (left) for placing in a layout plus four high-resolution files, one each for cyan, magenta, yellow, and black separations.*

---

3.037 **Photoshop DCS 2.0**

*The DCS 2 format allows you to save spot colors with the image, which you can choose to save as a single file or as multiple files.*

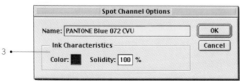

1

1  *Original image with type*
2  *Spot channel for type*
3  *Spot channel options palette*

within the Mac OS file resource fork. This is where images used, say, in the scrapbook and application splash screens are stored. If you wish to create a Mac OS splash screen (to appear as the Mac OS loads extensions) it needs to be a PICT Resource.

3.**042 PICT2** Extension of the PICT file format used with 32-bit color images. → 3.040 PICT

3.**043 PIXAR** File format for image file exchange with PIXAR image computers. These are used for high-end graphics and (particularly) three-dimensional graphics, rendering, and animation.

3.**044 Portable Document Format (PDF)** A cross-platform format that allows complex, multifeatured documents to be created, retaining all text and picture formatting, then viewed and printed on any computer that has an appropriate "reader" installed, such as Adobe Acrobat Reader. Generic PDF files, created using Adobe Acrobat or Adobe Illustrator, can contain multiple pages and images. These are rasterized when opened in Photoshop, which opens each page of a multipage document as a single file. Photoshop PDF files (created using Save As) contain just one image and support bitmap, RGB, CMYK, indexed color, grayscale, and Lab modes. Images can only be saved in Photoshop PDF format from Photoshop.

3.**045 Portable Network Graphics (PNG)** A file format for images used on the Web which provides 10–30% "lossless" compression, and supports variable transparency through "alpha channels", cross-platform control of image brightness and interlacing. Originally created as an alternative to the patented GIF file format. PNG supports 24-bit images and background images with "smooth-edged" transparency. Grayscale and RGB color modes with a single alpha channel are permitted, along with an indexed-color mode with no alpha channel. There are two "flavors": PNG-8 and PNG-24. PNG-8 uses 8-bit color and should be used for those images originated as such. PNG-24 uses 24-bit color and is able to retain full color and brightness in an image. Though file sizes are larger than PNG-8 or JPEG, PNG-24 supports multilevel transparency, offering up to 255 levels of transparency. Note that some (an ever-decreasing number) of web browsers will not recognize this format.

3.**046 PostScript printer description (PPD)** A file that defines the characteristics of individual PostScript printers.

3.**047 progressive JPEG** A digital image format used for displaying JPEG images on web pages. The image is displayed in progressively increasing resolutions as the data is downloaded to the browser. Sometimes called "proJPEG". → 3.028 JPEG; 3.025 INTERLACED GIF; 7.157 INTERLACING (2)

3.**048 QuickTime Movie** A cross-platform format for audio/video data. ImageReady animations can be saved as QuickTime Movie format files (QuickTime movies) and existing QuickTime movies can be edited and optimized.

3.**049 Raster Image File Format (RIFF)** A seldom-used proprietary file format (devised by Letraset) for storing images.

3.**050 raw** A digital file format that saves image data for transferring between applications and computer platforms. It comprises a data stream that defines the color information in the file and supports RGB, CMYK, and grayscale color modes with alpha channels, and multichannel, indexed color, Lab, and duotone modes without.

3.**051 Rich Text Format (RTF)** A Microsoft file format for transferring formatted text documents. It is an intermediate format between plain ASCII text and sophisticated word processing formats. RTF can be used to transfer most basic and intermediate level word processing documents between platforms and applications even if the host application does not recognize the format of the creating application.

3.**052 Scitex CT** Scitex Continuous Tone format files are generated by Scitex computers and used for high-end image processing. Files saved in Photoshop in the Scitex CT format will need additional utilities to enable them to migrate to the Scitex platform but these are not part of the standard Photoshop suite. While Scitex CT format does not support alpha channels it does support RGB, CMYK, and grayscale color modes. You will find files of this type generally used with high-quality reprographics (such as glossy magazine covers) rather than mainstream image editing.

3.**053 self-extracting archive (SEA)** Extension applied to Macintosh files that have been compressed using Aladdin System's Stuffit.

Files automatically unpack when loaded to the computer (from, usually, an Internet transfer or CDROM). → 3.064 FILE COMPRESSION

3.**054 SIT** The suffix of files which have been compressed using Stuffit, a file compression utility. → 3.064 FILE COMPRESSION

3.**055 Tagged Image File Format (TIFF, TIF)** A standard and popular graphics file format originally developed by Aldus (now merged with Adobe) and Microsoft, used for scanned, high-resolution, bitmapped images and for color separations. The TIF format can be used for black-and-white, grayscale, and color images that have been generated on different computer platforms.

3.**056 Targa** A digital image format for 24-bit image files, commonly used by computer systems in the MS-DOS environment which contain the "Truevision" video board.

3.**057 text file** A file containing only ASCII text bits, with no formatting, which can be "read" on any operating system. Unusually, image or graphics information can be sent as a text file that is converted by an application on a host computer. → 3.002 ASCII

3.**058 transparent GIF** A feature of the "GIF89a" file format that supports transparency and lets you place a nonrectangular image on the background of a web page. → 3.021 GIF; 3.025 INTERLACED GIF; 3.020 GIF89A

## File compressions

3.**059 Animation (codec)** A "lossless" compression setting ('codec') used by QuickTime which will work with all bit depths. Since it is very sensitive to picture changes the Animation codec is most useful for creating sequences in images that were rendered digitally. → 1.242 QUICKTIME; 10.097 KEY FRAME; 10.004 ANIMATION; 1.018 BIT DEPTH; 3.062 CODEC

3.**060 base resolution** The fundamental resolution of a PhotoCD. The 512 x 768 pixel resolution corresponds to that of US and Japanese NTSC standard televisions. The full range of resolutions presented on a PhotoCD represents fractions or multiples of the base. These are (depending on the type of PhotoCD) base/16, base/4, 4base, 16base, and 64base. The last is typically found only on Pro PhotoCDs. → 1.538 PHOTOCD; 1.541 PRO PHOTOCD

3.**061 CCITT encoding** abb.: Comité Consultatif International Téléphonique et Télégraphique. A lossless compression technique used for black-and-white images. This compression is supported by EPS and PDF file formats.

3.**062 codec** Acronym for compressor/decompressor, the technique used to rapidly compress and decompress sequences of images, such as those used for QuickTime and AVI movies. → 1.242 QUICKTIME; 3.003 AVI

3.**063 Component Video (codec)** A QuickTime "codec" (compression setting) which generates a 2:1 compression and, being limited to 16-bit color depth, is best suited for archiving movies. → 3.062 CODEC; 1.242 QUICKTIME

3.**064 file compression** The technique of rearranging data so that it either occupies less space on disk or transfers faster between devices or along communication lines. Different kinds of compression techniques are employed for different kinds of data—applications, for example, must not lose any data when compressed, while photographic images and movies can tolerate a certain amount of data loss. Compression methods that do not result in data loss are referred to as "lossless", while methods in which some data is lost are described as "lossy". Movies and animations employ compression techniques known as "codecs" (compression/decompression). There are many proprietary utilities for compressing data, while typical compression formats for images are LZW (lossless), JPEG, and GIF (both lossy), the last two being commonly used for files transmitted across the Internet. → 1.242 QUICKTIME; 3.062 CODEC; 3.068 LZW COMPRESSION; 3.028 JPEG; 3.021 GIF; 3.070 RLE

3.**065 Graphics (codec)** A QuickTime compression codec for use with still images with limited color depth. Also called "Apple Graphics." → 1.242 QUICKTIME; 3.062 CODEC

3.**066 lossless compression** File compression techniques that can reduce the file size without reducing or compromising image quality. Typical examples are RLE, LZW, and CCITT. → 3.068 LZW COMPRESSION; 3.061 CCITT ENCODING; 3.070 RLE

3.**067 lossy compression** Methods of file compression in which some data may be irretrievably lost during compression (as distinct from "lossless" compression). JPEG is a lossy compression format. → 3.066 LOSSLESS COMPRESSION; 3.028 JPEG

**3.068 LZW compression** The so-called Lempel–Ziv–Welch compression, a widely supported "lossless" compression method for bitmapped images, giving a compression ratio of 2:1 or more depending on the range of colors in an image (an image with large areas of flat color will yield higher compression ratios). LZW uses repeating strings of data in the compression of character streams into code streams; this is the basis of the compression used in GIF files. → 3.064 FILE COMPRESSION; 3.021 GIF

**3.069 None (codec)** A QuickTime compression codec meaning no compression. → 1.242 QUICKTIME; 3.062 CODEC

**3.070 Run Length Encoding (RLE)** Run Length Encoding is a Photoshop-supported, lossless compression technique that can be used with both Photoshop and TIFF format files.

**3.071 Video (codec)** A QuickTime full-motion, video compression codec. Although Video features fast compression it suffers from inferior quality and is limited to 16-bit color depth. Also called "Apple Video." → 3.062 CODEC; 1.242 QUICKTIME

**3.072 visually lossless compression** Image compression technique used with Kodak PhotoCD systems that exploits physiological differences between perception of color and detail. Some color information is discarded while detail is retained; with a greater acuity to detail this loss does not appear as image degradation. → 1.538 PHOTOCD

**3.073 zip (file)** File, or directory, compression procedure that compacts information for more effective transmission, e.g. by e-mail. Not only does the procedure reduce the size of the file being transmitted, it also makes the file more stable and less liable to corruption.

## File handling

**3.074 data fork** Part of a document file in the Mac OS containing user-created data, text, or graphics (as distinct from the "resource fork", which contains resources such as icons and sounds). A document file may consist only of a data fork or it may contain a resource fork as well, while an application always has a resource fork and may also have a data fork. → 3.094 RESOURCE FORK

**3.075 directory** A catalog of the filenames and other "inferior" directories (i.e. those of a lower hierarchical level) stored on a disk. In Macintosh operating systems (and in strict Windows terminology) directories are known as folders and are denoted with a file icon metaphor.

**3.076 directory structure** The underlying hierarchical structure of all the files on a hard disk. → 3.075 DIRECTORY

**3.077 disk image** A single file that represents an entire volume such as a floppy disk, hard disk, or CD-ROM and which, when opened ("mounted"), can be used as though it were a separate disk. Disk images are typically used for making copies of "installer" disks and also for creating partitions for recording data to CD-Rs. Also called "software partitions," or "file partitions." Not to be confused with an image file, which is a picture file stored on disk. → 3.023 IMAGE FILE; 1.537 PARTITION(ING)

**3.078 file allocation table (FAT)** A method used by computer operating systems to keep track of files stored on a hard disk.

**3.079 file conversion software** Software designed to enable files of one format to be opened in another or on another platform entirely. Commercial products include Debabilizer and Dataviz Conversions Plus.

**3.080 File menu** One of three standard menus appearing in the menu bar of Photoshop and most other applications, where you invoke commands which allow you to create, open, save, print and close files, and quit the application. → 3.013 FILE

**3.081 file recovery** The process of resurrecting a file after you have deleted it or when it has become corrupted. The data comprising a file remains on a disk even if the file has been deleted—only its name is in fact erased (from the invisible directory which keeps track of all the files on a disk). Until the space the data occupies is used by the computer for something else, it is sometimes possible to recover it with the aid of one of the many utilities available for recovering deleted files. Recovering files that have become corrupted is rather more difficult and, although some applications offer features for recovering corrupted files, there is no better safeguard than making very regular backup copies of your files as you work on them (many applications provide features for automating backup copies).

**3.082 filename** The name given to a file. Macintosh filenames can be up to 31 characters long, while Windows filenames can be up to 255 characters, although it is safer (especially if files are to be transferred between computers) to use the DOS naming convention of "8.3" (eight characters followed by a three-character suffix—all capitals). Windows filenames cannot contain: / \ | : * ? " $$$. When naming Macintosh files it is best to avoid: • : / \ since these have been known to interfere with some program functions.

**3.083 folder** The pictorial representation of a directory, and a place provided by computer operating systems where you can organize your documents, applications and other folders (when one folder is inside another, it is said to be "nested"). Folders form the basis for the organization of all data on your computer. → 3.075 DIRECTORY

**3.084 folder bar** In many file dialog boxes (such as Open and Save), the bar that sits above the scrolling list that, when clicked on, reveals a list of the folder hierarchy. → 3.083 FOLDER

**3.085 fragment(ed)** The state of files stored on a hard disk when, over time, they become split into noncontiguous chunks, leaving only small areas of free space into which new data can be written. The consequence of this is that new files are divided into smaller pieces so that they will fit onto the disk, thus

both the disk and the files on it are said to be "fragmented." The result can be a dramatic increase in the time it takes to access data, since any files being accessed may be spread over several areas of the disk. Many applications are available which "defragment" disks by rearranging the files contiguously. → 1.535 OPTIMIZE/OPTIMIZING; DEFRAGMENT(ING)

**3.086 hierarchical file system (HFS)** The method used by the Mac OS to organize and store files and folders so that they can be accessed by any program. Files are organized inside folders which may, in turn, be inside other folders, thus creating a hierarchy.

**3.087 hierarchical menu** A menu containing items which, when selected, generate their own menus, called "submenus." The presence of a submenu is normally indicated by a triangular symbol to the right of the menu item. → 3.086 HIERARCHICAL FILE SYSTEM (HFS)

**3.088 hierarchical structure** The technique of arranging files (or information) in a graded, structured order, which establishes priorities and therefore helps the user find a path that leads them to what they want. Used extensively in networking and databases and in file management. → 3.086 HIERARCHICAL FILE SYSTEM (HFS)

**3.089 initialize** To clear the directory on a disk and create a new one so that new data can be stored. When a hard disk is initialized its directory is emptied of file information, but the data itself remains (although it is

3.085 *fragment(ed)*—see also optimize on page 72

*Graphical representation of a hard disk. Different colors indicate files, free space, "fixed" files, and applications.*

invisible) until it has been written over by the new files. When a floppy disk is initialized the disk is formatted at the same time, and therefore any files that have been stored on it are deleted along with the directory. → 1.520 FORMATTING

**3.090 invisible file** Any file that is not visible but nonetheless exists. Examples of invisible files include files such as a directory file or icon file. Files can, for security reasons, for example, be made invisible using a suitable utility program, although such files may still appear in directory dialog boxes. It is common practice to make the support files of multimedia applications invisible.

**3.091 legacy files** Files created in, and worked on, in a previous version of an application. Some of the features in newer versions are not supported. In Photoshop 5 and later the term specifically applies to files created without embedded profiles. → 2.208 PROFILE MISMATCH

**3.092 nested folder** A folder that is placed inside another folder.

**3.093 OpenGL** Short for Open Graphics Library, OpenGL is a set of standard programming tools originated by Silicon Graphics Inc. for use on their workstations but now available for many platforms. The Mac OS in particular makes use of OpenGL for special effects, gaming and some 3D application software packages.

**3.094 resource fork** On computers running the Mac OS, the part of a file that contains resources such as icons and sounds (on Macintosh computers there are two parts,

called "forks", to every file unless the file only contains data). Distinct from the "data fork", which contains user-created data such as text or graphics files. Resources contained in the resource fork of a file can be modified with resource editors such as "ResEdit". → 3.074 DATA FORK; 1.280 RESEDIT

**3.095 root directory / level** The first level at which files and folders are placed, represented by the window which appears when you double-click on (open) a disk icon

**3.096 subdirectory** Any directory that is secondary to the principal, or "root", directory. → 3.095 ROOT DIRECTORY/LEVEL

**3.097 temp file** A temporary file, usually used by the application or operating system that created it.

**3.098 toolbox** The part of the Mac OS written into the ROM chip that enables software developers to take advantage of the Mac OS interface, handling such things as dialog boxes, windows, fonts, mouse, keyboards, and so on.

**3.099 transparent** Term used to describe any software or hardware item that operates without interaction on the part of the person using the computer—apart from its initial installation.

**3.100 uudecode** Acronym for UNIX to UNIX decode—a method of encoding and decoding binary data, such as that used by graphics files, so that they may be transferred more effectively over the Internet in ASCII format between computers running the UNIX operating system. → 3.002 ASCII; 1.357 UNIX

3.095 *root directory (1)*
3.096 *subdirectory (2)*
3.092 *nested folder (3)*

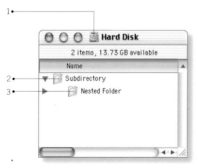

3.087 *hierarchical menu* •

# COLOR MANAGEMENT

## General terms

**4.001 16-bit color** A facility in some image-editing applications, such as Photoshop, which allows you to work on images in 16-bit-per-channel mode rather than in 8-bit mode. RGB images usually use three 8-bit channels (totaling 24 bits), while CMYK images use four 8-bit channels (totaling 32 bits). A 16-bit-per-channel image provides finer control over color but, because an RGB image then totals 48 bits (16 x 3) and a CMYK image totals 64 bits (16 x 4), the resulting file sizes are considerably larger than for 8-bit-per-channel images. → 1.018 BIT DEPTH

**4.002 additive colors** The color model describing the primary colors of transmitted light: red, green and blue (RGB). Additive colors can be mixed to form all other colors in photographic reproduction and computer display monitors. → 4.018 COLOR MODEL; 4.063 SUBTRACTIVE COLORS; 4.055 RGB

**4.003 background color (2)** A color or tint that has been applied to the background of any item, such as a page, text box, or illustration.

**4.004 cast** Undesirable predominance of one color in an image. For example, photographs taken on daylight film under tungsten lighting might have an orange cast due to that light source. Though many of Photoshop's features can help eradicate unwanted casts (or introduce deliberate ones) adjusting the color balance (by selecting Adjust > Color Balance from the Image menu) is the most flexible option. → 2.300 COLOR BALANCE

**4.005 chroma** The intensity, or "quality," of a color, defined by hue and degree of saturation. → 4.037 HUE

**4.006 chrominance (c)** In video, the component of a signal carrying the color information (as opposed to the luminance signal carrying brightness information). → 4.005 CHROMA

**4.007 CIE** abb.: Commission Internationale de l'Eclairage. An international organization that defined a visual color model that forms the basis for colorimetric measurements of color. → 4.079 CIE L\*A\*B\* COLOR SPACE

**4.008 CMY** Cyan, magenta, and yellow—the primary colors of the "subtractive" color model, created when you subtract red, green, or blue from white light. In other words, if an object reflects green and blue light but absorbs, or subtracts, red, it will appear to you as cyan. Cyan, magenta, and yellow are the basic printing process colors. → 4.009 CMYK; 4.055 RGB; 4.018 COLOR MODEL; 4.063 SUBTRACTIVE COLORS

**4.009 CMYK** Initial letters for the four colors cyan, magenta, yellow, and black (black is represented by the letter "K," for "key" plate)—the four printing process colors based on the subtractive color model. In color reproduction most of the colors are achieved by cyan, magenta, and yellow, the theory being that when all three are combined they produce black. However, this is rarely achievable and would be undesirable since too much ink would be used, causing problems with drying time, etc. For this reason black is used to add density to darker areas, while to compensate smaller amounts of the other colors are used (this also has cost benefits since black ink is cheaper than the colored inks). The degree of color that is "removed" is calculated by a technique known as "undercolor removal" (UCR). → 4.008 CMY; 4.055 RGB; 9.046 UCR; 4.018 COLOR MODEL

**4.010 Color Swatches** Photoshop palette showing an array of colors. The preset array can be modified (by means of either addition or deletion) in order to provide a palette of colors to be used with painting tools when required.

**4.011 ColorSync** A color management system designed to provide color consistency and conversion options. ColorSync converts the colors used in one application or device so that they can be accurately reproduced on another (ColorSync-compatible) one. ColorSync works by embedding a ColorSync profile in an image file when it is saved in TIFF, JPEG, or PICT format. When that image is printed, ColorSync compares the characteristics of the display monitor with those of the printer and, if appropriate, alters the image color to match that displayed on the monitor. → 4.111 COLOR MANAGEMENT SYSTEM (CMS)

4.**012 color** The visual interpretation of the various wavelengths of reflected or refracted light.

4.**013 color cast** A bias in a color image that can be either intentional or undesirable. If the former, it is usually made at a proof correction stage to enhance the color of an image; if the latter, the cast could be due to any number of causes and may have occurred, for example, when the image was photographed, scanned, manipulated on computer, output, proofed, or printed.

4.**014 color depth** The number of bits required to define the color of each pixel. For example, only one bit is required to display a black-and-white image (it is either on or off), while an 8-bit image can display either 256 greys or 256 colors, and a 24-bit image can display 16.7 million colors—eight bits each for red, green, and blue (256 x 256 x 256). → 1.016 BIT

4.**015 color difference signals** In the YCC color model (which forms the basis of the PhotoCD system) there are three channels: the luminance (Y) channel and two chrominance (CC) channels. The chrominance channels, representing red minus luminance and blue minus luminance, are usually described as the color difference signals. → 1.538 PHOTOCD

4.**016 color gamut** Gamut, or "color space," describes the full range of colors achievable by any single device on the reproduction chain. Although the visible spectrum contains many millions of colors, not all of them are achievable by all devices and, even if the color gamuts for different devices overlap, they will never match exactly—the 16.7 million colors which can, for example, be displayed on a monitor cannot be printed on a commercial four-color press. For this reason, various "color management systems" (CMS) have been devised to maintain the consistency of color gamuts across various devices. → 4.111 COLOR MANAGEMENT SYSTEM (CMS); 4.110 COLOR MANAGEMENT MODULE (CMM)

4.**017 color lookup table (CLUT)** A preset table of colors (to a maximum of 256) that the operating system uses when in 8-bit mode. CLUTS are also attached to individual images saved in 8-bit "indexed" mode— that is, when an application converts a 24- bit image (one with millions of colors) to 8-bit it draws up a table ("index") of up to 256 (the total number of colors depends on where the image will be viewed—Mac, Windows or the Web, for example) of the most frequently used colors in the image. If a color in the original image does not

4.009 **CMYK**

Cyan     Magenta     Yellow     Black

4.055 **RGB**

Red     Green     Blue

appear in the table, the application chooses the closest one or simulates it by "dithering" available colors in the table. → 2.312 INDEXED COLOR; 6.007 DITHER(ING); 1.339 OPERATING SYSTEM (OS)

4.**018 color model** The method of defining or modifying color. Although there are many proprietary color models, such as PANTONE, FOCOLTONE, TRUMATCH, TOYO, and DIC, the two generic models are those based on the way light is transmitted—the "additive" and "subtractive" color models. The additive color model is used, for example, in computer monitors, which transmit varying proportions of red, green and blue (RGB) light which we interpret as different colors. By combining the varying intensities of RGB light we can simulate the range of colors found in nature and, when 100% values of all three are combined, we perceive white, while if there is no light we see nothing or, rather, black. The subtractive color model is based on the absorption (i.e. subtraction) and reflection of light; for example, consider the printing inks cyan, magenta, and yellow—if you subtract 100% values of either red, green or blue from white light, you create cyan, magenta, or yellow. This is the CMYK model. Photoshop principally uses the RGB, CMYK, and hue, saturation, brightness (HSB) models. → 4.055 RGB; 4.009 CMYK; 4.002 ADDITIVE COLORS; 4.063 SUBTRACTIVE COLORS; 4.082 HSB; 4.008 CMY

4.**019 color picker (1)** A book of printed color samples that are carefully defined and graded and from which you can select spot colors. Color pickers generally conform to a color model, such as PANTONE, so that you can be confident that the color you choose will be faithfully reproduced by the printer. As distinct from a "color chart," which is generally used to select colors made up from process color inks. → 9.081 COLOR CHART; 4.021 COLOR SWATCH; 4.018 COLOR MODEL

4.**020 color picker (2)** A color model when displayed on a computer monitor. Photoshop has its own default color picker (most computers and operating systems and color regimes offer alternate pickers) that appears by default when you double-click on the foreground or background colors on the Toolbar. → 4.018 COLOR MODEL

4.**021 color swatch** A sample of a specific color, taken from a color chart, color picker or some other printed example, and used as a guide for specification or reproduction of spot colors or process tints. Existing swatches appear in Photoshop's Color Swatches palette, and new swatches can be added to this palette. → 9.081 COLOR CHART; 4.019 COLOR PICKER (1)

4.**022 color table** A predefined table (or list) of colors used to determine a specific color model, e.g. for converting an image to CMYK. A color lookup table, or "CLUT," also describes the palette of colors used to display an image. → 4.110 COLOR MANAGEMENT MODULE (CMM); 4.116 ICC PROFILE; 4.017 CLUT; 4.018 COLOR MODEL; 4.009 CMYK

4.**023 color value** The tonal value of a color when related to a light-to-dark scale of pure grays. → 4.039/40 LIGHTNESS

4.013 *color cast*

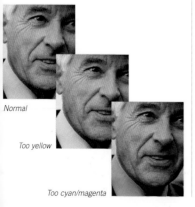

Normal

Too yellow

Too cyan/magenta

4.018 *color model*

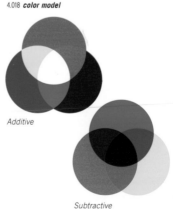

Additive

Subtractive

4.**024 color wheel** The complete spectrum of visible colors represented as a circular diagram and used as the basis of some color pickers. → 4.019 COLOR PICKER (1); 4.020 COLOR PICKER (2)

4.**025 complementary colors** Two colors directly opposite each other on a color wheel, which, when combined, form white or black depending on the color model (subtractive or additive). → 4.002 ADDITIVE COLORS; 4.063 SUBTRACTIVE COLORS; 4.018 COLOR MODEL; 4.024 COLOR WHEEL

4.**026 continuous tone image** Photographic or graphic image in which color (or shades of gray) varies continuously as a series of gradients, rather than as discontinuous "blocks" as represented by (say) magazine pictures. Continuous tone images cannot be directly handled by a computer or displayed on a computer monitor; they must first be digitized.

4.**027 cool colors** A relative (and subjective) term used to describe colors with a blue or green bias. → 4.073 WARM COLORS

4.**028 cyan (c)** With magenta and yellow, one of the three subtractive primaries, and one of the three process colors used in four-color printing. Sometimes referred to as "process blue."

4.**029 desaturate** To reduce the strength or purity of color in an image, thus making it grayer. The Photoshop Desaturate command (Image > Adjust > Desaturate) removes color from an image, leaving a monochrome result but retaining the original image mode. The Sponge tool (on the Toolbar) also has saturate and desaturate options that respectively increase or decrease the color in areas of the image treated by the sponge "brush." → 4.056 SATURATION; 2.109 SPONGE TOOL

4.**030 desaturated color** Color that contains a greater amount of gray in proportion to the hue. → 4.029 DESATURATE; 4.056 SATURATION

4.**031 device-independent color** Color produced from a color managment system that can be accurately reproduced on any device or computer platform. The L*a*b model is an example of a model designed to deliver device-independent color. → 4.079 CIE L*A*B* COLOR SPACE

4.**032 embedded profiles** Profiles (generally ICC profiles) indicating the correct color space embedded in an image file. → 4.116 ICC PROFILE

4.**033 gray** Any neutral tone in the range between black and white, with no added color.

4.**034 gray balance** The appropriate levels of yellow, magenta, and cyan that produce a neutral gray.

4.**035 green** One of the three additive primary colors, the other two being red and blue. → 4.002 ADDITIVE COLORS

4.**036 hexachrome** A printing process based upon six inks rather than the conventional four inks of the CMYK process. True Hexachrome (capital "H") adds orange and green inks to CMYK. Other six-ink systems often go by the name of hexachrome but should properly be called six-color systems. These usually add pale magenta and pale yellow to offer improved skin tones.

4.016 *color gamut*

**1** *Visible spectrum*
**2** *RGB monitor*
**3** *CMYK process*

4.024 *color wheel*

4.025 *complementary colors*

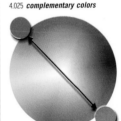

**4.037 hue** Pure spectral color that distinguishes one color from another. Red is a different hue from blue, and although light red and dark red may contain varying amounts of white or black, they may be the same hue. → 4.005 CHROMA; 4.056 SATURATION

**4.038 International Color Consortium (ICC)** An organization responsible for defining cross-application color standards. → 4.111 COLOR MANAGEMENT SYSTEM (CMS)

**4.039 lightness (1)** One component of the L*a*b color model, also known as the luminance component.

**4.040 lightness (2)** The tonal measure of a color relative to a scale running from black to white. Also called "brightness" or "value." → 4.082 HUE, SATURATION, BRIGHTNESS (HSB)

**4.041 lookup table** → 4.017 COLOR LOOKUP TABLE (CLUT)

**4.042 luminance (y)** The strength of a grayscale video signal.

**4.043 magenta (m)** With cyan and yellow, one of the three subtractive primaries, and one of the three process colors used in four-color printing. Sometimes called "process red."

**4.044 MESECAM** Middle Eastern SECAM. Television standard used in parts of the Middle East. → 4.057 SECAM

**4.045 MIRED** Acronym for micro reciprocal degree which is a method of expressing color temperature as an alternative to degrees Kelvin. A MIRED is worked out at one million divided by the Kelvin value of the light source. MIRED values tend to be used in color temperature meters. → 10.020 COLOR TEMPERATURE

**4.046 NTSC** The US National Television Standards Committee. Responsible for defining and monitoring television standards in the United States. The analog NTSC standard is 525 line, 30 frames per second. The NTSC (1953) color space has been defined for images intended for broadcast on NTSC systems.

**4.047 NTSC (1953)** Color space model based on the television and video standard used mainly in the United States and Japan (which uses 525 lines and displays images at 30 frames per second). It would typically be used only if an image is primarily intended for broadcast in NTSC format.

**4.048 PANTONE** The proprietary trademark for Pantone Inc.'s system of color standards, control, and quality requirements, in which each color bears a description of its formulation (in percentages) for subsequent printing. The PANTONE MATCHING SYSTEM (PMS) is used throughout the world so that colors specified by any designer can be matched exactly by any printer.

**4.049 pastel shades** Lighter shades of color, created by the addition of various quantities of white.

**4.050 phase alternation by line (PAL)** A western European (except France) color television standard which uses 625 lines and displays images at 25 frames per second. → 4.046 NTSC; 4.057 SECAM

**4.051 pixel depth** The number of shades that a single pixel can display, determined by the number of bits used to display the pixel. One bit equals a single color (black), so four bits

4.029 *desaturate*

*Original*

*Desaturated color*

4.082 *hue, saturation, brightness*
4.037 *hue*
4.040 *lightness*

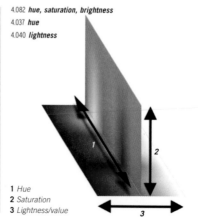

**1** Hue
**2** Saturation
**3** Lightness/value

(any permutation of four 1s and 0s, such as 0011 or 1001) produce 16 shades, and so on up to 32 bits (although actually only 24 are available, the other 8 being reserved for functions such as masking), which produce 16.7 million colors.

**4.052 primary colors** Pure colors from which, theoretically (but not in practice), all other colors can be mixed. In printing they are the "subtractive" pigment primaries: cyan, magenta, and yellow. The primary colors of light, or the "additive" primaries, are red, green, and blue. → 4.002 ADDITIVE COLORS; 4.063 SUBTRACTIVE COLORS

**4.053 profile** The color (and, generally contrast) characteristics of a device or process that is used by a color management system to achieve faithful color reproduction. In Photoshop the most common profile is the ICC profile, which is a cross-application standard. → 4.116 ICC PROFILE

**4.054 red** One of the three additive primary colors, the other two being green and blue. → 4.002 ADDITIVE COLORS

**4.055 RGB** Initial letters of the colors red, green, and blue. The primary colors of the "additive" color model. → 4.002 ADDITIVE COLORS

**4.056 saturation** The variation in color of the same tonal brightness from none (gray) through pastel shades (low saturation) to pure color with no gray (high saturation, or "fully saturated"). Also called "purity" or "chroma." → 4.082 HSB

**4.057 SECAM** Système Electronique pour Couleur avec Mémoire, a color television standard used in France, eastern Europe, Russia, and the Middle East (where it is called "MESECAM"), which uses 625 lines and displays images at 25 frames per second. → 4.046 NTSC; 4.050 PAL

**4.058 separation table** When you create artwork that is to be printed at a print store, you'll first create an RGB to CMYK conversion and receive color proofs showing the parameters for the color separations from the store. You can save the conversion information in color separation tables so that any future work undertaken with that print store can be appropriately calibrated. From the File menu select Color Settings > CMYK Setup and click on the Tables button.

**4.059 sepia** A brown color and also a monochrome print in which the normal shades of gray appear as shades of brown. Due originally to the effects of ageing and oxidation on a print, the tone can be simulated chemically using sepia toners, and in Photoshop by altering the hue of a colorized image. → 8.049 SEPIA TONING

**4.060 SMPTE** Society of Motion Picture and Television Engineers (SMPTE)

**4.061 Society of Motion Picture and Television Engineers (SMPTE)** A US organization that defines broadcast standards such as HDTV (high-definition television) and which has been responsible for certain colors spaces, including SMPTE-240M and SMPTE-c. → 4.060 SMPTE-240M; SMPTE-c

**4.062 spectrum** The series of colors, not all visible, which result when normal white light is dispersed into its component parts by

4.049 *pastel shades*

4.056 *saturation*

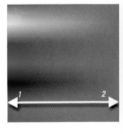

**1** Fully saturated
**2** Desaturated

refraction through a prism. The region between red and violet, which is visible to the human eye, is termed the "visible spectrum".

4.**063 subtractive colors** The color model describing the primary colors of reflected light: cyan, magenta, and yellow (CMY). The subtractive colors, plus black, form the basis for printed process colors (CMYK). → 4.018 COLOR MODEL; 4.002 ADDITIVE COLORS

4.**064 swatch** A color sample.

4.**065 tertiary color** The resulting color when two secondary colors (mixtures of two primary colors) are mixed.

4.**066 tint** A shade produced by adding white to a solid color.

4.**067 tonal range** The range of tone values within an image. Within Photoshop the tonal range is most easily seen from the histogram. An image with a full tonal range has pixels ranged across all areas of the histogram; identification of variations in the distribution enables tonal corrections to be applied.

4.**068 tonal reproduction** A measure of the tones reproduced (in a print, or on a monitor) compared with those present in the source image.

4.**069 tonal value/tone value** The relative densities of tones in an image.

4.**070 TOYO** A system of specifying spot colors, mainly used in Japan.

4.**071 trichromatic** Comprising three colors.

4.**072 twenty-four-bit / 24–bit color** The allocation of 24 bits of memory to each pixel, giving a possible screen display of 16.7 million colors (a row of 24 bits can be written in 16.7 million different combinations of 0s

and 1s). Twenty-four bits are required for CMYK separations—8 bits for each of red, green, and blue. → 4.014 COLOR DEPTH

4.**073 warm colors** Any color with a hue veering toward red or yellow, as distinct from cool colors which veer toward blue or green. → 4.027 COOL COLORS

4.**074 white balance** Light sources providing notionally "white" light often have unequal levels of red, green, or blue, resulting in a color cast. Almost all video cameras and many digital cameras feature a "white balance" setting that enables these to be neutralized, either by reference to a neutral gray surface or against presets (precalibrated settings for tungsten lighting, overcast sky, fluorescent lighting, etc.).

4.**075 white light** The color of light that results from red, blue, and green being combined in equal proportions. → 4.002 ADDITIVE COLORS

4.**076 white point (monitor)** White point is the color measure of white light when the intensities of the red, green, and blue components are equal. With gamma and phoshors, one of three monitor setup parameters. Normally it should be left to the default value of 6500K, which represents "typical" cool daylight. Alternate settings can be made and viewed "live".

4.**077 YCC** Color model that forms the basis of the PhotoCD system. → 4.015 COLOR DIFFERENCE SIGNALS; 1.538 PHOTOCD

4.**078 yellow (y)** With cyan and magenta, one of the three subtractive primaries, and one of the three process colors used in four-color printing. Sometimes called "process yellow."

4.059 *sepia*

4.062 *spectrum*

## Color modes

4.**079 CIE L\*a\*b\* color space** A three-dimensional color model based on the system devised by CIE for measuring color. L\*a\*b\* color is designed to maintain consistent color regardless of the device used to create or output the image, such as a scanner, monitor, or printer; L\*a\*b\* color consists of a luminance or lightness component (L) and two chromatic components: a (green to red) and b (blue to yellow). Lab color (without the asterisks) is the internal color model used by Adobe Photoshop when converting from one color mode to another, and "Lab mode" is useful for working with Kodak PhotoCD images. ➔ 4.007 CIE

4.**080 color modes** A color mode determines which color model will be used to display (and print) images. Modes are based on the common models (such as RGB, HSB, CMYK, and CIE L\*a\*b) but additional modes are provided for specialized applications, and include duotones, bitmap, grayscale, multichannel, and indexed color.

4.**081 grayscale (image)** The rendering of an image in a range of grays from white to black. In a digital image and on a monitor this usually means that an image is rendered with 8 bits assigned to each pixel, giving a maximum of 256 levels of gray. Monochrome monitors (rarely used nowadays) can only display black pixels, so grays are achieved by varying the number and positioning of black pixels using a technique called "dithering." ➔ 6.007 DITHER(ING); 1.016 BIT; 1.042 EIGHT-BIT/8-BIT

4.**082 hue, saturation, brightness (HSB)** A color model based upon the light transmitted in an image or in your monitor, hue being the spectral color (the actual pigment color), saturation the intensity of the color pigment (without black or white added), and brightness the strength of luminance from light to dark (the amount of black or white present). Also called "HSL" (hue, saturation, lightness) and "HLV" (hue, lightness, value), but "HSB" (hue, saturation, brightness) is the Photoshop preferred term. ➔ 4.056 SATURATION; 4.037 HUE

4.**083 indexed color** An image "mode" with a maximum of 256 colors which is used to reduce the file size of RGB images so that they can be used, for example, in multimedia presentations or on web pages. This is achieved by using an indexed table of colors (a color lookup table, or CLUT) to which the colors in an image are matched; if a color in the image does not appear in the table, the application selects the nearest color or simulates it by arranging the available colors in a pattern called "dithering." In Photoshop indexed color mode can be set from the Image menu by selecting Image > Mode > Indexed Color. Specific settings for the mode can be made using the Indexed Color dialog box. ➔ 4.017 CLUT; 6.007 DITHER(ING); 1.042 EIGHT-BIT

4.**084 Multichannel mode** Specialized color mode. Images created in (or converted to) Multichannel mode contain multiple channels of up to 256 levels of gray. A

4.083 *indexed color*

*The image above was created using the CLUT index table. The original colors have been matched or simulated by dithering.*

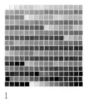

1

2

3

4

*Color tables*
**1** *Mac*
**2** *Web*
**3** *Windows*
**4** *CLUT colors/adaptive*

typical use is to assemble channels from different original images to create an image that will ultimately be converted to a color mode. Note that when an RGB color mode image is changed to Multichannel mode the red, green, and blue channels are changed to cyan, magenta, and yellow.

## Blending modes

4.085 **Behind** Blending mode. Only the transparent parts of a layer are modified; existing base-color pixels are not affected. The nature of this mode means it will work only on a layer with the Preserve Transparency option turned off. Often described as similar to painting on the back of a sheet of acetate. ➔ 4.086 BLENDING MODE

4.086 **blending mode** The blending mode is a feature of the Photoshop Options and Layers palettes (and appears in some dialog boxes) and defines how image pixels are changed when a painting or editing tool is applied. There are 18 blending modes: Normal, Behind, Clear, Dissolve, Multiply, Screen, Soft Light, Hard Light, Color Dodge, Color Burn, Darken, Lighten, Difference, Exclusion, Overlay, Saturation, Color, and Luminosity. Blending modes enact changes on the original pixels in an image (sometimes called the base layer) by means of an applied blend color. This produces a resultant color based on the original color and on the nature of the blend.

4.087 **Clear** (**2**) Blending mode. Applicable only to multilayer images with the Preserve Transparency option turned off. Using the Fill or Stroke commands, line tool, or paint bucket tool each base color pixel is made transparent by the application of the blend color. ➔ 4.086 BLENDING MODE

4.088 **Color** Blending mode. The luminance levels of the base color are combined with the hue and saturation of the blend color to produce a "tinted" result. By preserving gray levels in the image a monochrome image can be colored and color images can be tinted. ➔ 4.086 BLENDING MODE

4.089 **Color Burn** Blending mode. Use a dark paint to darken the base color or a light color to tint the base color. Using white produces no effect. ➔ 4.086 BLENDING MODE

4.090 **Color Dodge** Blending mode. A light paint over a base color produces a lightening effect, while a darker color produces only a tint in the base color. Black has no effect at all. ➔ 4.086 BLENDING MODE

4.091 **Darken** Blending mode. Compares color information in base and blend paint layers. Colors in the base that are lighter than the paint color are changed, but darker colors are not; hence the paint color chosen should be darker than the base colors that you wish to change. ➔ 4.086 BLENDING MODE

4.092 **Difference** Blending mode. Ostensibly creates a "negative" effect by subtracting the paint blend color from the base color or the base color from the paint blend color, depending on which has the greatest brightness level. Use white as a paint color to invert the base color (black does not have any effect). ➔ 4.086 BLENDING MODE

4.088 *blending mode—Color*

4.088 *blending mode—Color*

4.090 *Color Dodge*

4.090 *Color Dodge*

4.089 *Color Burn*

4.089 *Color Burn*

4.091 *Darken*

4.091 *Darken*

4.092 *Difference*

4.092 *Difference*

4.093 *Dissolve*

4.093 *Dissolve*

4.094 *Exclusion*

4.094 *Exclusion*

4.095 *Hard Light*

4.095 *Hard Light*

137

4.104 *Soft Light*

4.104 *Soft Light*

4.096 *Hue*

4.096 Hue

4.097 *Lighten*

4.097 *Lighten*

4.098 *Luminosity*

4.098 *Luminosity*

138

4.099 *Multiply*

4.099 *Multiply*

4.100 *Normal*

4.100 *Normal*

4.101 *Overlay*

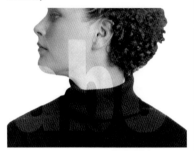

4.101 *Overlay*

4.102 *Saturation*

4.102 *Saturation*

4.103 *Screen*

4.103 *Screen*

4.**093 Dissolve** Blending mode. Creates a "video" dissolve effect proportional to the pressure (or opacity) set. Each pixel is edited or painted to give a resulting color that is then used to randomly replace base or blend colors. → 4.086 BLENDING MODE

4.**094 Exclusion** Blending mode. Similar to the Difference mode but with lower contrast. Base color is converted to a gray when the paint color is dark and inverted when light. → 4.686 BLENDING MODE; 4.092 DIFFERENCE

4.**095 Hard Light** Blending mode. Creates an effect similar to directing a bright light at the subject. Base color is lightened if the paint color is light, and darkened if the paint color is dark. Contrast tends to be emphasized and highlights exaggerated. → 4.086 BLENDING MODE

4.**096 Hue** Blending mode. The hue of the blend color is applied to the luminance and saturation values of the base color, producing a potentially strongly colorized result. → 4.086 BLENDING MODE

4.**097 Lighten** Blending mode. Achieves an overall lightening effect by lightening base colors that are darker than the paint color while leaving lighter base colors unchanged. → 4.086 BLENDING MODE

4.**098 Luminosity** Blending mode. Luminosity values in the base color are replaced with the corresponding luminosity value from the paint color. The hue and saturation remain unchanged. → 4.086 BLENDING MODE

4.**099 Multiply** Blending mode. Useful tool for creating or enhancing shadow effects. A dark paint color multiplies (i.e. darkens) the lighter parts of the base color to create a darker blend. A light paint imparts a gentler, but similar, effect. → 4.086 BLENDING MODE

4.**100 Normal** Blending mode. The default mode, which is called Threshold in bitmap or indexed color mode images. Every pixel is edited to create a resultant mixed color. → 4.086 BLENDING MODE

4.**101 Overlay** Blending mode. Retains black and white in their original forms but darkens dark areas and lightens light areas. The base color is mixed with the blend color but retains the luminosity values of the original image. → 4.086 BLENDING MODE

4.**102 Saturation** Blending mode. An image combining the luminance and hue of the original base color with the saturation value of the blend color. There is no change in areas with zero saturation (i.e. those with shades of gray). → 4.086 BLENDING MODE

4.**103 Screen** Blending mode. Use a light paint (or blend layer) to remove or reduce the darkest parts of the base color, producing a bleached effect. A darker paint color will still have a bleaching effect, but to a much reduced degree. → 4.086 BLENDING MODE

4.**104 Soft Light** Blending mode. A light paint or layer color lightens the base color, a dark one darkens the base color. Luminosity values in the base are preserved. If the blend paint or layer is lighter than 50% gray the image is lightened in the same manner as would result from photographic dodging. Blends darker than 50% produce a burned effect. The overall effect is one of a gentle (soft!) lighting effect. → 4.086 BLENDING MODE

## Color management terms

44.**105 Adobe Gamma control panel** A control panel that leads you through the accurate calibration of your monitor. It replaces the Gamma control panel (Mac OS) and monitor control dialog (Windows) on Photoshop 5. The calibration process involves adjusting the contrast, brightness, gamma, color balance, and white point of your monitor. Additional adjustments to the color-conversion settings ensure that an image is displayed consistently on any monitor.

4.**106 Apple RGB** Color space that was the default in Photoshop, used in the desktop printing industry, it was on the Macintosh's near-ubiquitous 13-in Trinitron monitor.

4.**107 CIE RGB** Color space with a wide gamut but a poor handling of cyan and blue. Capable of handling 16-bit color channels. → 4.112 COLOR SPACE; 4.018 COLOR MODEL

4.**108 Color Settings** (**3**) Photoshop 6 offers an easy way to select one of several color-management settings using this feature on the Edit menu using the pull-down menu. Color Management Off means only minimal color-management settings. This emulates applications that do not support color management. Use this for presentations on a computer display or for video. Emulate Photoshop 4: Uses the basic color workflow used in Photoshop 4 and earlier. U.S. Prepress Defaults: Color management follows the requirements in the US market. Europe Prepress Defaults: Color

4.108 *Color settings (3)*

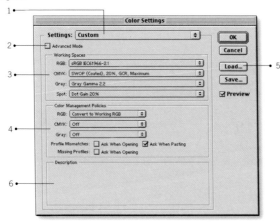

1 *Color settings drop down menu*
2 *Advanced mode (when checked opens panes for Color Conversion options and Advanced Controls)*
3 *Drop down menus for RGB, CMYK, Gray, and Spot profiles*
4 *Color management policies: can be off, Preserve Embedded Profiles or Convert to Working (RGB, CMYK, or Gray)*
5 *Load/Save options for custom settings*
6 *Help/description panel*

4.108 *Color settings (3) (custom CMYK)*

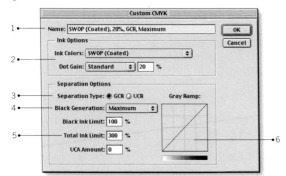

141

1 *Custom settings name*
2 *Ink options*
3 *Separation type (select between Grayscale Component Removal and Under Color Replacement)*
   → 9.042 GRAYSCALE COMPONENT REPLACEMENT
   → 9.046 UNDERCOLOR REMOVAL
4 *Black generation (amount of black that appears on the black film—"Medium" is default; "Maximum" puts all black on the black film)*
5 *Ink limits*
6 *Grayscale ramp*

management follows the requirements in the European market. Japan Prepress Defaults: Color management follows the requirements in the Japanese/Pacific market. Web Graphics Defaults: Color management follows the requirements for publication on the World Wide Web. ColorSync Workflow (Mac OS only): Uses the ColorSync 3.0 color-management system and profiles selected from the ColorSync control panel. Note that Windows systems will not recognize this, and neither will systems using earlier versions of ColorSync.

4.**109 Colormatch RGB** A color space defined by monitor manufacturer Radius for their PressView monitors, once heavily used in prepress environments. Mainly features an expanded RGB gamut. → 4.112 COLOR SPACE

4.**110 color management module** (**CMM**) A profile for managing colors across different platforms. CMMs conform to a color management system (CMS) such as the International Color Consortium (ICC). CMMs interpret ICC profiles, which describe the RGB and CMYK color spaces. Standard ICC profiles are installed by ICC-compliant applications such as Adobe Photoshop, but you can create your own. The selected profile is embedded in the image so that it is used by other devices in the production process. You may find a variety of CMMs on your computer: those built-in to ICC-compliant applications (the best if you are unsure); Kodak's Digital Science Color Management System (mainly for the Kodak PhotoCD format); or CMMs specified by the operating system, such as Apple's ColorSync and Microsoft's ICM. → 4.116 ICC PROFILE; 4.111 COLOR MANAGEMENT SYSTEM (CMS); 4.055 RGB; 4.009 CMYK

4.**111 color management system** (**CMS**) A method which provides accuracy and consistency of color across all devices in the reproduction—scanners, monitors, printers, imagesetters, and so on. Most CMSs are defined by the International Color Consortium (ICC), Kodak's Digital Science Color Management System, Apple's ColorSync, and Microsoft's ICM. → 4.038 ICC; 4.016 COLOR GAMUT; 4.110 COLOR MANAGEMENT MODULE (CMM)

4.**112 color space** Three-dimensional version of a color model, illustrating all variations possible. → 4.020 COLOR PICKER (2); 4.018 COLOR MODEL

4.**113 custom color space** A color space in which the user is free to set the control parameters,

such as gamma, white point, and phosphor levels. Usually only required by the advanced user and those with particular requirements in their color space. Unpredictable results can occur when used by the inexperienced! → 4.112 COLOR SPACE

4.**114 Digital Science CMS** A color management system devised by Kodak and automatically installed when you choose to install the Kodak PhotoCD acquire plug-in. → 4.111 COLOR MANAGEMENT SYSTEM (CMS)

4.**115 FOCOLTONE** A color matching system in which all of the colors can be created by printing the specified process color percentages. → 4.000 PROCESS COLOR

4.**116 ICC profile** Color management system from the ICC (International Color Consortium). The ICC profile is a color space designed for cross-platform and cross-application use and hence can produce consistent results. It can also be used for color management in hardware devices. A CMM (color managment module) is invoked by Photoshop to interpret the ICC profile (either RGB or CMYK) in current use. This then becomes part of the image and is available for other systems and devices to enable them to ensure correct color output.

4.**117 Monitor RGB** ICC profile for a specific monitor (usually your computer's own). This color space is therefore not device independent. → 4.116 ICC PROFILE

4.**118 SMPTE-240M** RGB color space designed for high-definition television (HDTV). Features a large gamut and is suitable for prepress and where high quality is required. Wide Gamut RGB offers an even wider gamut. → 4.122 WIDE GAMUT RGB;

4.**119 SMPTE-c** Color space. More recent than SMPTE-240M, but with a limited gamut. Used in specialized applications, such as in images for North American NTSC television.

4.**120 sRGB** A color space used by Hewlett Packard and Microsoft as an Internet standard. Based on the characteristics of an "average" PC monitor, it is the Photoshop default but has a restricted gamut. → 4.112 COLOR SPACE; 4.018 COLOR MODEL

4.**121 TRUMATCH** A system of color matching used for specifying process colors.

4.**122 Wide Gamut RGB** A color space that uses wavelengths of red, green, and blue to yield a wide gamut, but stops many colors from being reproduced in print or on screen.

## Layers

**5.001 Add Layer Mask** Layer menu item that adds a layer mask to an image. Layer masks are transparent layers that confer visibility onto areas within an image. A range of special effects can be applied to an image by making changes to the layer mask. A layer mask will be shown as a thumbnail in the Layers palette to the right of the layer in which it is placed.

**5.002 Add Layer Mask icon** Layers palette feature. Click on this icon (a rectangle with a circle) to create a layer mask for the currently selected layer.

**5.003 adjustment layer** An adjustment layer is a specialized layer that has the same features as a conventional layer (opacity, blending modes), and can be manipulated in the same way (rearranged, made visible and invisible, duplicated, and deleted), but enacts its effects upon all those layers below it in the image "stack." Adjustment layers allow you to apply effects (which can involve changes in levels, brightness/contrast, color balance, and even posterization) to an image without actually changing any of its pixels. It

can be thought of as a "magic filter" whose effect is removed when the filter is removed (or made invisible). By selecting Merge Down (from the Layers menu or Layers palette) the adjustment layer can be permanently applied. Adjustment layers cannot be merged with other adjustment layers—because they contain instructional information, rather than pixel data, there is nothing physical to merge. → 5.026 LAYERS

**5.004 adjustment layer icon** Layers palette feature. Indicates that the named layer is an adjustment layer.

**5.005 Bevel and Emboss** Layer effect accessed from the Layer menu by selecting Effects > Bevel and Emboss. It adds a range of highlight, shadow, and form features to the contents of a layer and is typically used to add depth or "substance" to text and to increase the apparent separation of text from an underlying image.

**5.006 clipping group** A layer clipping group comprises a group of two or more layers, with the bottom-most layer acting as a mask. If the base layer is a selection shape (say an ellipse), the next layer a transparent texture (such as craquelure), and the top layer a

**2    5.019 *Gradient Map***

*An adjustment layer (2) that maps a color gradient (4) to the grayscale levels in an image (a), even if it is in color, producing a colorized effect (3).*

143

pattern, the clipping group including all three would deliver a textured pattern in the shape of an ellipse.

5.**007 Colorfill** Photoshop 6 feature. Adjustment layer that fills a layer with a solid color of variable opacity and which may be changed.

5.**008 Color Overlay** New layer style, first appearing in Photoshop 6. Fills a layer with a single color (varied using a slider and modulated using a blend mode).

5.**009 Create New Layer icon** Layers palette feature. Click on this icon, which is at the base of the Layers palette, to create a new layer. The new layer is placed immediately above the currently selected layer.

5.**010 Create New Set icon (layers)** Photoshop 6 feature. Click on this icon (which resembles a folder) to create a new set of layers.

5.**011 Current Layer** Layers palette feature. Denoted (usually) by a blue background, the current layer is the one to which edits and commands will be applied.

5.**012 Delete Current Layer icon** Layers palette feature. Click on this icon to delete the currently selected layer (you'll be asked to confirm your decision). Alternatively drag your selected layer to the icon and it will be deleted immediately.

5.**013 Delete Selection** Make a selection then press delete (or backspace or choose Clear from the Edit menu). If you delete a selection from a layer that section of the layer becomes transparent; if you make a deletion from the background the selected area will be filled with the currently selected background color.

5.**014 Drop Shadow** (**1**) Layer effect accessed by selecting Effects > Drop Shadow from the Layer menu. It creates a shadow of the objects in the selected layer that falls on the underlying layer(s). → 6.063 DROP SHADOW (2)

5.**015 Flatten** Layers menu option. Flattens a multilayered image into one comprising only a background layer. Flattening the image discards layer information, so no alterations can be made to layers once an image has been flattened.

5.**016 Glow** (**Inner and Outer**) Layer effect accessed by selecting Effects > Inner [Outer] Glow from the Layer menu. It adds a glow to the contents of a layer that appears to develop from the inner or outer edges of objects, respectively.

5.**017 Gradient Adjustment** Photoshop 6 feature. Enables the characteristics of a gradient to be altered. The gradient's scale, shape, and type can all be adjusted.

5.**018 Gradient Fill** Photoshop 6 feature. Adjustment layer that fills a layer with a selected gradient.

5.**019 Gradient Map** Photoshop 6 feature. Adjustment layer that colorizes the underlying image using the original grayscale values. The effect is similar, but not identical, to that obtained by altering the curve in the Curves dialog box.

5.**020 Inner Shadow** Layer effect accessed by selecting Effects > Inner Shadow from the Layer menu. It adds a shadow effect to the inside edge of a selected layer's contents, giving the impression of a concave or depressed region.

144

5.021 *layer effects*

*A feature for applying shadow, glow, bevel, emboss, pattern and stroke styles to an image, either individually (below) or combined (right).*

1

2

3

4

1  5.016 *Outer Glow*
2  5.016 *Inner Glow*
3  5.020 *Inner Shadow*
4  5.014 *Drop Shadow*

**5.021 layer effects** Layer effects are a series of effects, such as Drop Shadow, Inner Glow, Emboss and Bevel which are enacted on the contents of individual layers.

**5.022 layer mask** A control feature that determines how much of the layer to which it is linked will appear in the overall image. Changes applied to the layer mask can create effects in the layer but without changing the pixels of that layer. The mask can be applied to the layer (to make the changes permanent) or removed, along with any changes.

**5.023 Layer menu commands (Photoshop 6)** The Layer menu of Photoshop 6 includes several new commands based on the modifications to layers in this version. Changes include unlimited numbers of layers and the ability to create layer groupings. New commands include:
Layer Style (equivalent to Effects in previous versions);
New Fill Layer (create a new Fill Layer);
Change Layer Content and Layer Content Options;
Type (type controls, including aliasing options and Convert to Shape option);
Rasterize (changes nonpixel elements into pixel-based data);
Add Clipping Path;
Lock All Layers in Set.

**5.024 Layer Opacity input box** Feature of the Layers palette, which allows you to enter a percentage figure for the layer opacity or use the pop-out slider to observe the effect on the image in real time.

**5.025 layer visibility** Image layers can be made selectively visible or invisible using the 'eye' icon in the Layers palette. Click on this to toggle between the two states. If an image is printed, layers that are not visible at the time will not be printed, but they can be made visible, and printed, later. → 5.026 LAYERS; 5.026 LAYERS PALETTE

**5.026 layers** Compositional facility in Photoshop (introduced in version 3) that enables an image to be composed on a layer of transparent overlays. Rather in the method that is used by a cartoon animator, an opaque background is overlaid with the transparent "cells" (layers) upon which pixels can be painted or copied. Layers can be reordered, blended, and have their transparency altered. Effects can be applied to individual layers (or to groups of layers) without affecting all layers. A layer option, Preserve Transparency, ensures that transparent areas are not affected when paint or effects are applied. → 5.022 LAYER MASK; 5.025 LAYER VISIBILITY

**5.027 Layers palette** Floating palette that displays current image layers sequentially from the foreground (uppermost layer) through to the background (lowermost layer). You can also add new layers, delete layers, add layer masks, and control layer visibility from this palette.

**5.028 link icon** Layers palette feature. Shown as a short iconic chain, the link icon indicates layers that are linked together.

**5.029 linked layers** Any two or more image layers can be linked so that their contents

---

5.027 **Layers palette**

1  Blending mode
2  Prevents painting on transparent part of the image
3  Link icon
4  Add a layer style
5  Add layer mask
6  Create a new set
7  Create new fill or adjustment layer
8  Create a new layer
9  Trash
10  Background layer
11  Locks all
12  Select opacity of selected layer

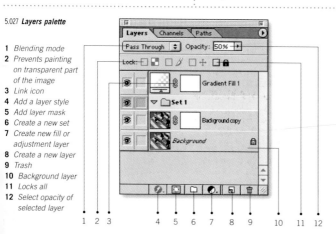

can be moved together and certain tasks (transformations, alignments, merges and the creation of clipping groups) can be applied to the linked set. Layers are linked by selecting the first layer in the group then selecting additional layers by clicking in the column to the left of the layer name. The link icon will appear.

**5.030 locking layers** Photoshop 6 feature. Linked sets of layers can be locked in Photoshop 6 in order to prevent some properties from being altered. Layer locks are indicated by a solid lock icon when all properties have been locked against changes and by an outline lock when only certain properties (layer masks and transparency) are locked. Locked layers can be moved within the stack of layers but they cannot be deleted. Selected layers can be locked using the Lock All Layers in Set option on the Layers menu (or the same command in the Layers palette menu) or by clicking the lock icon on the Layers palette.

**5.031 opacity** The degree of transparency that each layer of an image has in relation to the layer beneath. → 5.026 LAYERS

**5.032 Pattern Fill** Photoshop 6 feature. Creates an adjustment layer based on a selected pattern.

**5.033 restack** The action of reordering layers in an image. In the Layers palette select the layer you wish to move then click and drag it to the new location.

**5.034 Stroke Effect (style)** New style introduced in Photoshop 6. Adds a smooth stroke up to 250 pixels in width to a selected layer.

## Channels

**5.035 alpha channel** A specific channel where information regarding the transparency of a pixel is kept. In image files this is a separate channel—additional to the three RGB or four CMYK channels—where "masks" are stored, simulating the physical material used in platemaking, which is used to shield parts of a plate from light. → 6.040 MASK; 4.009 CMYK; 4.055 RGB

**5.036 channels** Each image manipulated in Photoshop comprises at least one and usually (for color images) three colored overlays called channels. Each color channel contains a monochrome representation of the parts of the image that include that color. For an RGB image, for example, channels containing the red, green, and blue color images are combined to produce a full-color image. Individual channels can be manipulated in much the same way as a complete image. Special additional channels perform specific tasks. Grayscale channels that save selections for masking are known as alpha channels. Spot color channels are used to provide separate channels for specific spot colors (premixed inks used either in addition to or in place of CMYK inks) that will ultimately be printed using a separate color separation plate. Each channel type is indicated on the Channels palette.

**5.037 Create New Channel icon** Channels palette feature. Creates a new alpha channel and appends it to the bottom of the Channels palette listing.

5.036 *channels*

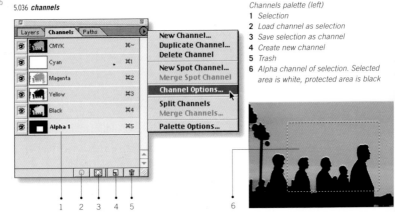

*Channels palette (left)*
1  *Selection*
2  *Load channel as selection*
3  *Save selection as channel*
4  *Create new channel*
5  *Trash*
6  *Alpha channel of selection. Selected area is white, protected area is black*

5.**038 Delete Current Channel icon** Channels palette feature. Deletes the currently selected channel. Alternatively, channels can be dragged to this icon for deletion.

5.**039 Load Channel as Selection icon** Channels palette feature. Loads a selected previously saved alpha channel as an image selection.

5.**040 Save Selection as Channel icon** Channels palette feature. Saves the current selection as a new channel (invariably an alpha channel) in the current image, using only the current option settings.

5.**041 spot channel** A special channel that contains the channel information for elements in an image to be represented by a spot color. Spot colors are specially mixed colors that are normally printed in addition to (or instead of) the conventional CMYK colors. Using a spot color can also be an inexpensive way to print that color in artwork (a brochure, for example) without resorting to full-color printing.

## Paths

5.**042 Bézier curve** A curved line between two Bézier control points (BCP). Each point is a tiny database, or "vector," which stores information about the line, such as its thickness, color, length, and direction. Complex shapes can be applied to the curve by manipulating "handles" which are dragged out from the control points. → 10.160 VECTOR

5.**043 clipping path** A Bézier outline that defines which areas of an image should be considered transparent or "clipped." This lets you isolate the foreground object and is particularly useful when images are to be placed on top of a tint background in a page layout, for example. Clipping paths are generally created in an image-editing application such as Photoshop and are embedded into the image file when you save it in EPS format. → 5.042 BÉZIER CURVE

5.**044 Clipping Path** (**command**) Paths palette pull-out option. Saves a path as a clipping path, for use in another application such as Adobe Illustrator. → 5.043 CLIPPING PATH

5.**045 Delete Current Path icon** Paths palette feature. Deletes the currently selected path. Paths can also be dragged to this icon, and they will automatically be deleted.

5.**046 Delete Path** Paths palette pull-out option. Deletes the currently selected path (can be undone using the Undo command from the menu bar).

5.**047 Duplicate Path** Paths palette pull-out option. Creates a duplicate path from the currently selected path.

5.**048 Fill Path** Paths palette pull-out option. Fills path with the current foreground color.

5.**049 Fill Path icon** Paths palette feature. Fills current path with the foreground color. → 5.045 FILL PATH

5.**050 Load Path as Selection icon** Paths palette feature. Converts the currently selected path to a selection.

5.**051 Make Selection** Paths palette pull-out option that converts a closed path to a selection. The same command can be enacted by clicking on the Make Selection icon at the base of the Paths palette.

5.042 *Bézier curve*

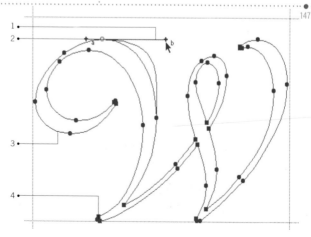

1 Direction line
2 Direction point
3 Curved segment
4 Corner point

5.**052 Make Work Path** Paths palette pull-out option that converts a selection (made with a selection tool) into a path. Any feathering applied to the selection is removed. The selection shape can sometimes be modified, depending on the selection shape and complexity. A work path can also be created by selecting the Make Work Path icon at the base of the palette.

5.**053 New Path** Paths palette pull-out option. Creates a new path in the currently active document. Note that New Path will not appear if a path selected in the window has not been saved.

5.**054 New Path / Create New Path icon** Paths palette feature that creates a new path; once the icon has been selected you can begin drawing your path, with the path being saved automatically.

5.**055 path** (**2**) A line curve or shape drawn using Photoshop's Pen tool. Paths typically comprise anchor points linked by curved (or straight) line segments. The anchor points can be repositioned to alter a path if required. Each anchor features a direction line (Bézier line) and (normally) a pair of direction points. These can be pulled and moved to smoothly reshape the curve. Closed paths can be converted into selections and vice versa. → 5.042 BÉZIER CURVE; 5.060 WORK PATH

5.**056 Paths palette** Floating palette that displays current paths and permits certain path manipulations. Icons enable paths to be created from selections, deleted, loaded from selection, filled with a foreground color, or stroked.

5.**057 Stroke Path** Paths palette pull-out option. Strokes a path using the selected painting or editing tool. A tool and a brush must be specified before selecting Stroke Path. → 2.286 STROKE

5.**058 Stroke Path icon** Paths palette feature. Alternative to the Stroke Path command for stroking a path using the selected painting or editing tool. A tool and a brush must be specified first. → 5.057 STROKE PATH

5.**059 Turn Off Path** Paths palette pull-out option. Deselects and hides the current path(s). Click on the Path icon to reselect.

5.**060 work path** Path created (initially) from an image selection or using the Pen tool. In the latter case the path appears as a temporary work path until saved. → 5.052 MAKE WORK PATH

## Actions and history

5.**061 Action Options** Actions palette feature. Opens the Action Options dialog box when an action is highlighted. Permits the action to be (re)named, assigned to a function key, and appended to a set (if action sets are configured).

5.**062 Actions** Photoshop-specific macros, or scripts, that apply series of predefined commands to an image. Photoshop has a number of preconfigured actions (including creating a sepia toned print, a vignette, and frames) but also provides a "recorder" that enables you to save often-used sequences of commands as your own action, to be applied to future images. An action can be displayed

5.056 *Paths palette*

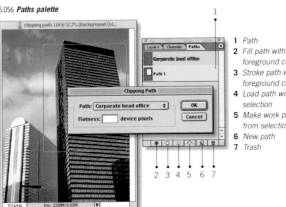

1 Path
2 Fill path with foreground color
3 Stroke path with foreground color
4 Load path with selection
5 Make work path from selection
6 New path
7 Trash

in the Actions palette either as the series of commands (which is editable) or as a one-touch button. Use the Batch command to apply actions to multiple images. → 2.214 BATCH

5.**063 Actions command toggle icon** Actions palette feature which toggles action command on and off. Appears as a tick box adjacent to the action command.

5.**064 Clear Actions** Actions palette feature. Permanently deletes all actions.

5.**065 Clear History** History palette feature. Permanently clears the history for the current image.

5.**066 Create New Document icon** History palette feature. Uses the selected state as the basis for a new image document.

5.**067 Create New icon** Actions palette feature. Click on this to create a new action.

5.**068 Create New Set icon (actions)** Actions palette feature. Click on this icon to create a new set of actions.

5.**069 Create New Snapshot icon** History palette feature. Creates a new snapshot from the currently selected state. Note that you can have a new snapshot created at the start of every editing session by clicking on the Automatically Create First Snapshot button in the History Options dialog box.

5.**070 Delete Current icon** Actions palette feature. Deletes the currently selected action.

5.**071 Delete Current State** History palette feature. Deletes the currently selected state from the History. Note that with the History palette in linear mode all subsequent states are automatically deleted when you click back to an earlier state; in nonlinear mode subsequent states are neither dimmed nor deleted.

5.**072 History Brush** Brush tool that can be used to paint over the current edit-state image with pixels from a previous state of that image taken from the History palette. Note that this tool cannot be used on an image that has been resized or rescaled. → 2.084 HISTORY BRUSH TOOL

5.**073 History Options** Selected from the pull-out menu on the History palette, the History Options dialog box lets you specify the maximum number of history states, switch between linear and nonlinear views and enable the automatic creation of a snapshot at the start of an editing session.

5.**074 History palette, linear mode** A history palette feature. This feature is enabled and disabled using the Allow Non-Linear History box found on the History Options dialog box. When the palette is in linear mode any history states will be deleted when you click on an earlier state. Note that you may switch between linear and other modes at any point in an edit.

5.**075 History palette, nonlinear mode** History palette feature. This feature is enabled/disabled via the Allow Non-Linear History box in the History Options dialog box. When the palette is in nonlinear mode subsequent history states are retained when an earlier state is selected (compare this with linear mode, when these are deleted). Note that you may switch between modes at any point in an edit.

---

5.062 *Actions*

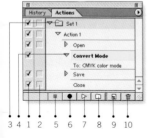

3  4   1  2   5   6   7   8   9  10

| | | |
|---|---|---|
| **1** Toggle item on/off | **6** | Begin recording |
| **2** Toggle dialog on/off | **7** | Play selection |
| **3** Actions set | **8** | Create new set |
| **4** Individual actions | **9** | Create new action |
| **5** Stop play/recording of actions | **10** | Trash |

5.073 *History options*

1  *Set source for history brush*
2  *History state slider*

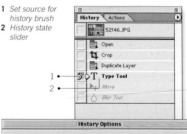

5.**076 Insert Menu Item** Actions palette feature. Inserts a menu command, which can be selected from the menu listing or typed in to the Insert Menu Item dialog box.

5.**077 Insert Path** Actions palette feature. It enables you to record a path that will be included as part of an action. This path is recreated as part of the action every time it is replayed.

5.**078 Insert Stop** Actions palette feature. Lets you insert a stop point (e.g. for a manual intervention) in an action.

5.**079 Load Actions** Actions palette feature. Loads a saved set of actions.

5.**080 Maximum History States** A history option that determines the number of history steps that are recorded in an edit. If you exceed this maximum number the earlier steps are removed sequentially to accommodate the latest steps. The greater the number of states, the larger the amount of memory required.

5.**081 modal control** Modal controls can be inserted into actions to pause a command and display the corresponding dialog box (to change/add settings). Pressing return or enter will let the action proceed with the new values. With no modal control applied the action will be run using the values in the dialog box that were specified when the action was first recorded.

5.**082 New Action** Actions palette feature. Click on this icon or select the option from the pull-out menu to begin creating a new action.

5.**083 New Set** Actions palette feature that creates a new set of actions. Actions can be grouped into sets to aid in organization.

5.**084 Play** Actions palette feature. Click on this button (or select the option from the pull-out menu) to play the currently selected

action. "Stops" can be built in to halt the playback at a point where some manual intervention is required; to resume playback click Play again.

5.**085 Play Button icon** Actions palette feature. Click on this button to start playing the currently selected action.

5.**086 Playback Options** Actions palette feature. Opens a dialog box that enables you to control the performance of an action by selecting the "Accelerated," "Step by Step," or "Pause for" options.

5.**087 Record Again** Actions palette feature. Lets you rerecord an existing action.

5.**088 Record Button icon** Actions palette feature. Click on this button to start recording a new action.

5.**089 Replace Actions** Actions palette feature. Replaces the current actions with the default set.

5.**090 Reset Actions** Actions palette feature that resets action list to the default set. By clicking on Append, the default actions set is appended to the current set. Replace will replace the current set with the default set.

5.**091 Save Actions** Actions palette feature. Saves the current actions as a set for reuse later.

5.**092 Start Recording** Actions palette feature. Click on this button (or select the option from the pull-out menu) to start compiling a new action. All editing actions will be recorded until Stop Recording is selected.

5.**093 state** Stage of an image manipulation as recorded in the History palette. → 2.025 HISTORY

5.**094 Step Forward / Step Backward** History palette feature. Selected from the History palette command menu, these options let you move through current history states.

5.**095 Stop Button icon** Actions palette feature. Stops recording an action.

# IMAGE MANIPULATION

## General terms

**6.001 aliasing** The jagged appearance of bitmapped images or (especially) fonts occurring either when the resolution is insufficient or when they are enlarged. This effect is caused by the square pixels making up the image becoming visible to the eye. Sometimes called "jaggies," "staircasing," or "stairstepping."

**6.002 antialiasing** A technique of optically eliminating the jagged appearance of bitmapped images or text reproduced on low-resolution devices such as monitors. This is achieved by blending the color at the edges of the object with the background color by averaging the density of the range of pixels involved. Antialiasing is also sometimes used to filter texture maps, such as those used in 3D applications, to prevent moiré patterns. → 6.001 ALIASING; 1.019 BITMAP; 1.020 BITMAPPED GRAPHIC; 10.169 BITMAPPED FONT; 10.112 MOIRÉ

**6.003 area process** The action of image processing groups of pixels rather than individual pixels. Most image editing involves area processing.

**6.004 background (1)** The base layer in a Photoshop image.

**6.005 brightness** Defined by Photoshop as "the relative lightness or darkness of the color, usually measured as a percentage from 0% (black) to 100% (white)."

**6.006 destination image** An image to which elements of a source image are to be copied. Conventionally in Photoshop both images are opened and displayed on the desktop. A destination image may have more than one corresponding source image. → 6.030 SOURCE IMAGE

**6.007 dither(ing)** A technique of "interpolation" that calculates the average value of adjacent pixels. This technique is used either to add extra pixels to an image—to smooth an edge, for example, as in antialiasing—or to reduce the number of colors or grays in an image by replacing them with average values, which conform to a predetermined palette of colors. For example, dithering is used when an image containing millions of colors is converted ("resampled") to a fixed palette ("index") of, say, 256 colors. A color monitor operating in eight-bit color mode (256 colors) will automatically create a

6.002 *antialiasing*

crisp

strong

smooth

dithered pattern of pixels. Dithering is also used by some printing devices to simulate colors or tones. → 6.002 ANTIALIASING; 4.017 CLUT; 4.026 CONTINUOUS TONE IMAGE; 6.039 INTERPOLATION; 4.083 INDEXED COLOR; 6.045 RESAMPLE

6.**008 downsampling** The reduction in resolution of (usually) a digital image. Samples (measures of pixel characteristics) are made over groups of pixels which are then merged to comprise the pixels of the smaller image.

6.**009 downsize** The reduction in size of an image usually by reducing the resolution by downsampling. → 6.008 DOWNSAMPLING

6.**010 dynamic effects** Term for image manipulations that involve changes to the entire image, such as flipping and reversing, resizing, distortions, and warps.

6.**011 edge enhancement** General term for techniques that enhance detail (mostly edges) to give the perceived effect of greater focus or detail. → 6.094 SHARPEN FILTERS

6.**012 gamma** A measure of contrast in a digital image, photographic film or paper, or processing technique. → 6.038 → GAMMA CORRECTION

6.**013 ghosting** To decrease the tonal values in the background of an image so that the main subject stands out more clearly. Also known as "fadeback."

6.**014 Illustrator import** Vector-based images (or selections) can be imported from applications such as Adobe Illustrator. When imported an image becomes bitmapped and is rendered at the nominal resolution of the Photoshop image into which it is being pasted. Clearly better rendering will occur with higher resolution Photoshop images. Paths can also be imported from Illustrator, and will appear on a new layer.

6.**015 image assembly** The process of creating an image from a series of image elements, usually comprising a background and overlaying image layers. → 5.026 LAYERS

6.**016 input resolution** The degree of definition with which an image is "captured," or recorded, and which determines the final quality of output. Final output quality depends on three aspects of input: the scan resolution, the size of the original image as compared with its final size (in which case the resolution of the scanning device itself may also be significant), and the resolution of the output device. → 9.111 OUTPUT RESOLUTION

6.**017 joiner** Image composed of two or more images with common elements. Most commonly used in panoramic photography where separate views of the panorama are digitally combined by identifying and blending common features at adjacent edges.

6.**018 low-pass filter** In image editing, the type of data filter used to blur image detail or smooth away fine blemishes by reducing the intensity or levels of high-frequency information in the image.

6.**019 mesh warp** In some applications, the facility to distort an image by means of dragging "handles" at the intersections of the lines of a grid ("mesh") placed over the image. Also called "rubber sheeting."

6.007 *dither(ing)*

1  *original grayscale*

2  *1-bit no dithering*

3  *1-bit, diffusion dithered*

4  *8-bit color, diffusion dithered*

5  *8-bit color, pattern dithered*

6  *8-bit color, noise dithered*

Photoshop 6's Liquify command works on similar principles.

6.**020 montage** An assembly of several images, forming a single original. A montage of photographs is called a "photomontage." → 10.019 COLLAGE

6.**021 object** A term that describes an image layer in some image-editing applications, including Corel's PhotoPaint.

6.**022 overscan** A technique for acquiring more color (or gray) at the scanning stage than will be required for creating an output. Rather than discarding the extra information it is then used to optimize shadow or highlight detail.

6.**023 Paste as Pixels** When an object is copied into Photoshop from a vector-based package such as Adobe Illustrator, the Paste dialog box opens. It provides the option to paste the object as either a pixel group or a path.

6.**024 peaking** A method of digitally sharpening images by using a filter that increases the difference in density where two tonal areas meet. Interpreted in Photoshop through the Sharpen Edges filter and also implemented in the Unsharp Mask technique. → 8.053 UNSHARP MASKING (USM); 6.092 SHARPEN EDGES FILTER

6.**025 Photoshop filters** In Photoshop, filters offer image enhancement and manipulation functions, including those of traditional photographic filters. Photoshop provides a collection of filters grouped according to their type and their image enhancement ability. Hence there are filter collections such as "Artistic" (emulating painting and drawing

techniques), "Sketch" (pencil/crayon effects), and "Stylize" (more extreme), along with "corrective" types (blur and sharpen). Photoshop also accepts plug-in filters produced by third parties. → 6.060 PLUG-IN

6.**026 pixel-based editing** Generalized term for image editing based on performing changes (manipulations or painting) to individual pixels or groups of pixels. This is distinguished from the vector-based editing that underpins some drawing and design packages such as Adobe Illustrator. Photoshop is substantially a pixel-based image editor, although new features in Photoshop 6 add vector-based editing functionality.

6.**027 pixelation / pixelization** An image that has been broken up into square blocks resembling pixels, giving it a "digitized" look. Can be done for deliberate creative results. → 6.001 ALIASING

6.**028 selection** Any image, or part of an image, that is selected for editing. A selection might be determined by physical location or by parameters relating to its pixels (brightness, color value). Selections are made using the selection tools (such as the Marquee, Lasso or Magic Wand) or, for example, with color range selection commands.

6.**029 smoothing** The refinement of bitmapped images and text by a technique called "antialiasing" (adding pixels of an "inbetween" tone). Smoothing is also used in some drawing and 3D applications, where it is applied to a path to smooth a line, or to "polygons" to tweak resolution in the final render. → 6.002 ANTIALIASING

6.019 *mesh warp—liquify*

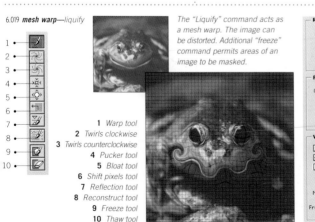

The "Liquify" command acts as a mesh warp. The image can be distorted. Additional "freeze" command permits areas of an image to be masked.

1 *Warp tool*
2 *Twirls clockwise*
3 *Twirls counterclockwise*
4 *Pucker tool*
5 *Bloat tool*
6 *Shift pixels tool*
7 *Reflection tool*
8 *Reconstruct tool*
9 *Freeze tool*
10 *Thaw tool*

6.**030 source image** An image from which image elements, selections, or pixels are to be copied, usually to a destination image. → 6.006 DESTINATION IMAGE

6.**031 spatial frequency** The brightness value in a digital image. Major changes between adjacent or near-adjacent pixels correspond to a high spatial frequency, gentle changes give low spatial frequencies. Band pass filters can remove or reduce (attenuate) selected spatial frequencies. Using a low pass filter, for example, smooths away fine detail and forms the basis for Blur and Dust & Scratches type filters.

6.**032 white point** Point on a histogram denoting where those pixels that define white are. Though nominally at the extreme end of the histogram, the white point should normally be moved to the position of the first "white" pixels.

### Image adjustment

6.**033 bicubic interpolation** When an image is resampled (for example to change its size or resolution), and new pixels are created, Photoshop uses interpolation to determine the color values for these newcomers. It does this by judging the colors of the neighboring pixels and applying an interpolation algorithm. Bicubic interpolation gives the highest quality result, with the best tonal gradations. The penalty is that it is the slowest method. Use bicubic interpolation when quality is paramount and bilinear or nearest neighbor when speed is more important.

6.**034 descreen** Filter, usually part of a scanner's software or image acquire software, that reduces or removes dot screen artifacts in images scanned from books, magazines, or newspapers.

6.**035 displacement map** An image used with filters such as Displace to determine the level and position of distortion to be applied. Sample displacement maps are included with Photoshop (usually, depending on version and platform, in the plug-ins folder).

6.**036 equalize / equalization** The process of digitally enhancing an image by increasing its tonal range.

6.**037 error diffusion** In digital scanning, the enhancement of an image by averaging the difference between adjacent pixels. In graphics applications this technique is more commonly referred to as antialiasing, and uses a technique known as interpolation. → 6.002 ANTIALIASING; 6.039 INTERPOLATION; 6.045 RESAMPLE

6.**038 gamma correction** Modification of the midtones of an image by compressing or expanding the range, thus altering contrast. Also known as "tone correction." → 6.012 GAMMA

6.**039 interpolation** A computer calculation used to estimate unknown values which fall between known values. This process is used, for example, to redefine pixels in bitmapped images after they have been modified in some way, such as when an image is resized (called "resampling"), rotated, or if color corrections have been made. In such cases the program makes

6.033 *bicubic interpolation*

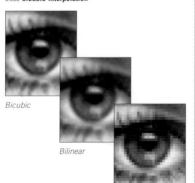

Bicubic

Bilinear

Nearest neighbor

6.036 *equalize/equalization*

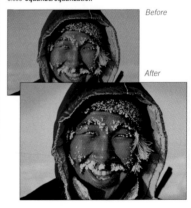

Before

After

estimates from the known values of other pixels lying in the same or similar ranges. Interpolation is also used by some scanning and image-manipulation software to enhance the resolution of images that have been scanned at low resolution. The insertion of animation values between two keyframes of a movie sequence also involves interpolation. Some applications allow you to choose an interpolation method—Photoshop, for example, offers "Nearest Neighbor" for fast but imprecise results that may produce jagged effects, "Bilinear" for medium-quality results, and "Bicubic" for smooth and precise results, but with slower performance. → 6.045 RESAMPLE; 9.090 DESCREEN(ING); 6.007 DITHER(ING)

6.**040 mask** Originally a material used to protect all or part of an image or page in photomechanical reproduction, photography, illustration, or layout. Photoshop provides a masking feature that enables you to apply a mask to all or selected parts of an image. Such masks are stored in an "alpha channel" and simulate the physical material used in platemaking which is used to shield parts of a plate from light. → 5.035 ALPHA CHANNEL

6.**041 masking** Blocking out an area of an image with simulated opaque material to prevent editing actions or to allow for modifications such as adjusting the values of color and tone. → 6.040 MASK

6.**042 midtones / middletones** The range of tonal values in an image anywhere between the darkest and lightest, usually referring to those approximately halfway.

6.**043 morphing** Image manipulating technique that enables one image object to "evolve" seamlessly into another that is often quite different. The effect is achieved by mapping points between the before and after objects and animating the positional changes.

6.**044 optical resolution** Actual resolution achievable by a scanner. The greater the optical resolution, the better the image quality. Though lower than interpolated resolution, optical resolution captures the greatest amount of image data. → 6.039 INTERPOLATION

6.**045 resample** Altering an image by modifying pixels to either increase or decrease its resolution. Increasing the number of pixels is called "resampling up," while reducing the number is called "resampling down" or "downsampling." → 6.007 DITHER(ING); 6.039 INTERPOLATION

6.**046 reverse(d) image** An image that has been reversed, either horizontally or vertically, so that what was on the left of the image is now on the right, or what was at the top is now at the bottom, as in a mirror–image.

6.**047 scale / scaling** The process of working out the degree of enlargement or reduction required to bring an image to its correct reproduction size.

## Plug-ins

6.**048 acquire module** → 6.060 plug-in

6.**049 Alien Skin** Manufacturer of Photoshop plug-ins sets. The first offering, "Black Box," was followed by Eye Candy, Eye Candy 4000,

6.041 *masking*

Original

Quick mask applied

Background modified

and Xenofex. Alien Skin filters have characteristic interfaces and feature extensive controls including the useful "Random Seed" that virtually ensures uniqueness in the application of many of the filters.

6.**050 Andromeda** Creator of Photoshop plug-in filter sets, generally quite extreme in nature, such as Mezzo Line-Screen (transforms images to black and white mezzo line art), Rainbow (spectral effects), and Velocity (multiple ghosting, highlight smears, and fade-out effects).

6.**051 Carve** Photoshop plug-in from Alien Skin's Eye Candy set. Gives a chiseled appearance to image details.

6.**052 Cutout** Photoshop plug-in from Alien Skin's Eye Candy. Makes a selection into a "hole" complete with appropriate shadow effects. The hole adopts the background color.

6.**053 Extensis** Creator of image filter and other Photoshop plug-ins. Principal products include the intelligent enhancement tool Intellihance/Intellihance Pro and PhotoTools and PhotoBars, which add extra functionality to the Photoshop interface. → 6.055 INTELLIHANCE; 6.058 PHOTOBARS; 6.059 PHOTOTOOLS

6.**054 HSB Noise** Photoshop plug-in from Alien Skin's Eye Candy. Naturalizes surfaces by introducing random variations in the hue, saturation, and brightness.

6.**055 Intellihance** A Photoshop plug-in from Extensis that permits rapid but comprehensive analysis of images for color correction and effects filtering. Previews

enable you to compare an original image with up to twenty-four surrogates with slightly different image characteristics. A souped-up version of Photoshop's own Variations command with valuable extra functionality. → 6.053 EXTENSIS; 2.328 VARIATIONS

6.**056 Kai's Power Tools** (**KPT**) Kai's power tools are a set of Photoshop plug-in effects filters, originally created by Kai Krauss for Metacreations. Characterized by unique, organic dialog box interfaces (similar to Kai's PhotoSoap), filters that range from the subtle to the bizarre, with a number of the most recent offerings (KPT5 and KPT6) relying on fractal algorithms for effect generation. → 6.060 PLUG-IN; 10.066 FRACTALS

6.**057 Paint Alchemy** Set of Photoshop plug-ins from software house Xaos. Predominantly concentrates on converting Photoshop images into painterly effects with tools such as Colored Pencil, Impressionist, and Pastel. Many of the effects are quite unique and offer a significant level of control.

6.**058 PhotoBars** Photoshop (pre Version 6) plug-in from Extensis that delivers customizable toolbars and buttons that can make Photoshop tasks simpler. Buttons offer predefined and user-definable features. → 6.053 EXTENSIS

6.**059 PhotoTools** Set of plug-ins from Extensis enabling many additional filter effects to be added to the Photoshop host portfolio. Effects like PhotoTexture permit infinitely variable textures to be created; others enable special effects for images and web graphics. → 6.053 EXTENSIS

6.055 *Intellihance Pro*

*Modified images*
1 *Quick enhance*
2 *Last applied*

*Extensis Intellihance Pro interface. In this option, the original image (left section) is compared with "QuickEnhance"* *(an automated adjustment) and the last applied enhancement (right). Settings can be adjusted using the dialog boxes.*

6.**060 plug-in** Small software module designed to integrate with a larger application. The plug-in blends seamlessly with the host, delivering new or enhanced functionality. Plug-ins are common in image-editing and page-layout applications for such things as special-effect filters. They are also common in web browsers. Many third-parties now provide filter plug-ins for Photoshop (additional filter sets that appear in the filter menu), and many manufacturers of scanners provide acquire plug-ins to aid in image acquisition.
→ 7.139 HELPER APPLICATION; 1.317 EXTENSION

6.**061 Squizz** Plug-in filter set that provides tools for advanced image distortions. Filters include Silly Putty and Bézier Grid Mapping, and complex morphing techniques are also possible. Useful subsidiary tools allow unlimited undos.

6.**062 Xaos Tools** Manufacturer of the popular Photoshop plug-in filter set, Paint Alchemy.
→ 6.057 PAINT ALCHEMY

## Effects

6.**063 Drop Shadow** (**2**) One of Photoshop's layer effects. It has the result of creating a shadow behind a selected object in a layer. The angle of the shadow, its thickness, color and density can all be adjusted from the corresponding dialog box. → 5.021 LAYER EFFECTS

6.**064 duotone** A monochromatic image combining two halftones with different tonal ranges made from the same original, so that when printed in different tones of the same color (usually black, thus sometimes described as a "double-black duotone"), a wider tonal range is reproduced than is possible with a single color. Special effects can be achieved by using the same technique and printing with different colored inks. The term is sometimes used erroneously to describe a "duplex halftone," or "false duotone" (a duplicate halftone printed in two colors).

6.**065 Effects (2)** In Photoshop Elements, the term Effects has been used to describe effects achieved through the preprogrammed automatic sequencing of program functions, layer styles, and filters. A range of effects are shown on the Effects palette and can be dragged and dropped onto a selected image. Effects are similar to Styles in later Photoshop versions and ImageReady.

6.**066 monotone** Reproduction in a single color, without tonal variation.

6.**067 solarize / solarization** An effect involving the "simplification" of color differences. Subtle changes in color become flat tones, or are replaced by different colors. Photoshop features a Solarize filter, one of the Stylize group. → 8.020 POSTERIZE

6.**068 tritone** A halftone image that is printed using three colors. Typically a black-and-white image is enhanced by the addition of two colors; for example, process yellow and magenta when added to black will produce a sepia-colored image. Photoshop considers tritones (and four-color quadtones) to be variations on duotones.
→ 6.064 DUOTONE

6.056 *KPT Goo*

1  *Brush parameters and selection*
2  *Image preview*
3  *Cancel*
4  *Apply*
5  *Animation preview*
6  *Help*

## Filters menu commands

6.**069 Digimarc** Filter menu item. Enables a Digimarc watermark to be incorporated into your image. → 10.025 COPYRIGHT; 6.060 PLUG-IN

6.**070 Fade [filter name]** Filter menu item. Enables the last chosen filter to be applied to the selected image at a chosen "strength" between zero and full. Full strength corresponds to the normal application of that filter. In Photoshop 6 the Fade command has more extensive use and appears in the Edit menu.

## Filters: Artistic

6.**071 Artistic filters** Accessed through the Filter menu under Artistic. A group of filters that apply specific "traditional" paint effects, or effects appropriate to "artistic" applications. Filters such as Dry Brush, Watercolor, and Palette Knife are some of the traditional effects, while Cutout, for example, provides collagelike effects for artistic compositions.

6.**072 Colored Pencil filter** Accessed through the Filter menu under Artistic > Colored Pencil. Redraws the image using a solid background color and a pencil-like texture for the image elements. Small details and edges are emphasized using light crosshatching.

6.**073 Cutout filter** Accessed through the Filter menu under Artistic > Cutout. Converts the image to a "paper collage." Contrast is increased and color values flattened to produced images that appear to have been built from layers of colored paper.

6.**074 Dry Brush filter** Accessed through the Filter menu under Artistic > Dry Brush. Uses the dry brush technique (where a loaded brush has most of the paint removed before being brushed firmly on the canvas) to give an effect of paint drawn over the surface. Though color variation tends to be reduced by blending, additional brush texture is added.

6.**075 Film Grain filter** Accessed through the Filter menu under Artistic > Film Grain. Restores characteristics to an image that the film manufacturers have struggled long and hard to remove! An even, specular pattern is laid over the dark and midtones and a similar saturated pattern is laid over the lighter areas. Used subtly, this filter is excellent at removing "image banding" (stepwise changes in color gradients) and can also conceal "joins" in image montages.

6.**076 Fresco filter** Accessed through the Filter menu under Artistic > Fresco. Applies large "sloppy" paint dabs based on the underlying color. Works best with bold simple images which become "informal" bold graphics.

6.**077 Neon Glow filter** Accessed through the Filter menu under Artistic > Neon Glow. Applies amorphous glows to, and around, objects. User-selectable glow colors are provided.

6.**078 Paint Daubs filter** Accessed through the Filter menu under Artistic > Paint Daubs. Produces a daubed paint effect using brush sizes that range from 1 to 50 pixels, and types that include simple, light rough, light dark, wide sharp, wide blurry, and sparkle(!).

6.065 *Photoshop Elements Effects palette*

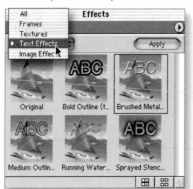

6.067 *solarize/solarization—see examples on page 167–*

Before

After

6.**079 Palette Knife filter** Accessed through the Filter menu under Artistic > Palette Knife. Simulates painting with a fine, narrow palette knife. Paint is applied thinly so that the canvas texture is partially revealed.

6.**080 Plastic Wrap filter** Accessed through the Filter menu under Artistic > Plastic Wrap. Gives the appearance of a three-dimensional image vacuum-packed in shiny plastic, emphasizing surface features.

6.**081 Poster Edges filter** Accessed through the Filter menu under Artistic > Poster Edges. Posterizes the image then describes image edges with black lines.

6.**082 Rough Pastels filter** Accessed through the Filter menu under Artistic > Rough Pastels. Builds the image from broad strokes of colored pastels, allowing a degree of underlying texture to appear through, especially in the darker areas.

6.**083 Smudge Stick filter** Accessed through the Filter menu under Artistic > Smudge Stick. Uses short diagonal strokes to smudge the darker parts of the image. Lighter areas become brighter but tend to lose definition.

6.**084 Sponge filter** Accessed through the Filter menu under Artistic > Sponge. Not to be confused with the saturate/desaturate Sponge tool, the Sponge filter creates a textured image that appears to have been painted with dabs from a natural sponge.

6.**085 Underpainting filter** Accessed through the Filter menu under Artistic > Underpainting. Gives the effect of an image painted on both surfaces of textured glass. The textured image is seen through the translucent top "flat" image.

6.**086 Watercolor filter** Accessed through the Filter menu under Artistic > Watercolor. Translates the image to a "watery" watercolor painted onto lightly textured cartridge paper. The edges of colored areas increase in saturation to simulate wet edges.

## Filters: Sharpen and Blur

6.**087 Blur filter** Accessed through the Filter menu under Blur > Blur. The conventional blur is designed to detect noise around color transitions and remove it. It does this by detecting pixels close to boundaries and averaging their values, effectively eliminating noise and random color variations. Blur More applies the effect more strongly.

6.**088 Blur More filter** Accessed through the Filter menu under Blur > Blur More. An extreme form of the Blur filter, which creates an effect up to four times stronger than the normal "Blur." → 6.087 BLUR FILTER

6.**089 Gaussian Blur filter** Accessed through the Filter menu under Blur > Gaussian Blur. Gaussian Blur applies a weighted average (based on the bell-shaped curve of the Gaussian distribution) when identifying and softening boundaries. It also introduces low-frequency detail and a mild "mistiness" to the image which is ideal for covering (blending out) discrete image information, such as noise and artifacts. A useful tool for applying variable degrees of blur.

6.**090 Motion Blur filter** Accessed through the Filter menu under Blur > Motion Blur. Simulating a time-exposure of a moving object, or poor panning technique, Motion Blur creates a linear blur (implying movement) at any angle. The degree of blur can be altered between arbitrary levels of 1 through to 999.

6.**091 Radial Blur filter** Accessed through the Filter menu under Blur > Radial Blur. Creates either Spin or Zoom blurs. The Spin option blurs around a central axis: the central point remains sharp while points around are blurred to concentric arcs (the degree of rotation can be specified). The Zoom option simulates a time exposure during which the zoom control is operated. The central point of the blur again remains sharp but points around are drawn into radial lines, which increase in length with distance from the image center.

6.**092 Sharpen Edges filter** Accessed through the Filter menu under Sharpen > Sharpen Edges. This variation of the Sharpen filters determines "edge points" where there are major changes in color values, and sharpens them. Edges are thus sharpened but the remaining regions of the image are left in an unsharpened state. Similar to the Unsharp Mask filter, but less controllable. → 6.097 UNSHARP MASK FILTER

6.**093 Sharpen filter** Accessed through the Filter menu under Sharpen > Sharpen. Improves apparent focus in a selection. By emphasizing changes in pixel values, color, and tone transitions become narrower and sharper.

6.**094 Sharpen filters** Accessed through the Filter menu under Sharpen. Filter group that creates increased sharpness in the image. Although they appear to focus blurred objects, the effects are subjective or synthetic in that detail present in the original scene but not recorded due to poor focusing cannot be restored. This group includes Sharpen, Sharpen More, Sharpen Edges, and Unsharp Mask.

6.**095 Sharpen More filter** Accessed through the Filter menu under Sharpen > Sharpen More. Applies a focusing-type effect more strongly than the Sharpen filter. It accentuates boundaries by making transitions more marked and narrower in effect, sharpening two to four times more strongly than the Sharpen filter. → 6.093 SHARPEN FILTER

6.**096 Smart Blur filter** Accessed through the Filter menu under Blur > Smart Blur. A totally controllable blurring tool. By setting a blur radius (a pixel distance for pixels to be included in the blur), a threshold level (below which pixel values will not be blurred) and a blur quality, customized blurs become possible.

6.**097 Unsharp Mask filter** Accessed through the Filter menu under Sharpen > Unsharp Mask. One of the most potent filters, Unsharp Mask can sharpen edges whose definition has been softened by, say, scanning, resampling or resizing. Differing adjacent pixels are identified and the contrast between them increased. The Unsharp Mask uses three control parameters: Amount, Radius, and Threshold. Amount determines the amount of contrast added to boundary (edge) pixels; Radius describes the number of pixels

adjacent to that boundary that are affected by the sharpening; and Threshold sets a minimum value for pixel contrast below which the filter will have no effect. It is a powerful filter, but it is easy to overdo its effects. → 8.053 UNSHARP MASKING (USM)

## Filters: Brush Strokes

6.**098 Accented Edges filter** Accessed through the Filter menu under Brush Strokes > Accented Edges. Adds emphasis to the edges in an image. Set the Edge Brightness control to a high level (40–50) and the emphasis is like a light pastel; a low value (under 10) produces an India-ink-like outline.

6.**099 Angled Strokes filter** Accessed through the Filter menu under Brush Stroke > Angled Strokes. Adds a painted texture comprising diagonal strokes. Image areas lighter than 50% gray are painted with strokes in one direction, darker areas are painted in the opposite direction.

6.**100 Brush Strokes filters** Accessed through the Filter menu under Brush Strokes. A set of filters that can make an image emulate brush-and-ink stroke effects. Textured strokes feature prominently in the filter set, which includes effects such as Accented Edges, Crosshatch, and Ink Outlines.

6.**101 Crosshatch filter** Accessed through the Filter menu under Brush Stroke > Crosshatch. Adds a texture to edges simulating colored pencil hatching. The details of the original image are retained

6.097 *Unsharp Mask filter*

*Applied with the Amount, Radius, and Theshold values as indicated*

0,0,0

250,1,0

250,3,0

350,1,25

making this a good choice for detailed and exceptionally small images.

**6.102 Dark Strokes filter** Accessed through the Filter menu under Brush Stroke > Dark Strokes. Paints short, tightly packed strokes in dark image areas and longer, white strokes across lighter image areas.

**6.103 Ink Outlines filter** Accessed through the Filter menu under Brush Stroke > Ink Outlines. Simulates pen-and-ink drawing styles and techniques, repainting the entire image.

**6.104 Spatter filter** Accessed through the Filter menu under Brush Strokes > Spatter. Simulates a mouth-blown airbrush with poor aerosol dispersal. Effects can vary from a mildly grainy finish through to abstract (an irregular pointilism effect).

**6.105 Sprayed Strokes filter** Accessed through the Filter menu under Brush Strokes > Sprayed Strokes. Converts the image using angled sprayed strokes in a limited palette of colors based on the dominant colors in the palette.

**6.106 Sumi-e filter** Accessed through the Filter menu under Brush Strokes > Sumi-e. Replicates the Japanese technique of using a fully loaded chisel-tipped brush on rice paper. Delivers deep blacks with soft edges.

## Filters: Distort

**6.107 Diffuse Glow filter** Accessed through the Filter menu under Distort > Diffuse Glow. Adds a softer-like diffusion filter to the image. The effect is created by adding transparent white noise across the image, with the intensity being brighter at the image (or selection) center.

**6.108 Displace filter** Accessed through the Filter menu under Distort > Displace. It displaces (distorts) an image according to the characteristics of a displacement map image. → 6.035 DISPLACEMENT MAP

**6.109 Distort filters** Accessed through the Filter menu under Distort. Image filter set that performs geometric distortions to an image. Adobe warns that these filters can be very memory intensive!

**6.110 Glass filter** Accessed through the Filter menu under Distort > Glass. Simulates different glass types placed over the image. Preset glass types are provided, but custom "glasses" can be created and saved.

**6.111 Ocean Ripple filter** Accessed through the Filter menu under Distort > Ocean Ripple. Creates an "underwater" look by placing random ripple effects across the image.

**6.112 Pinch filter** Accessed through the Filter menu under Distort > Pinch. Squeezes or pulls an image. A squeeze of 100% pinches a selection towards its geometric center; a squeeze (pull) of -100% balloons the selection outward.

**6.113 Polar Coordinates filter** Accessed through the Filter menu under Distort > Polar Coordinates. Converts an image's coordinates from conventional x–y axis rectangular to polar, and vice versa. The rectangular-to-polar conversion produces cylindrical anamorphoses—images that make no obvious logical sense until a mirrored cylinder is placed over the center, when the image is displayed in conventional form again.

**6.114 Ripple filter** Accessed through the Filter menu under Distort > Ripple. Simulates random pondlike ripples. The Wave filter provides similar results but with more control. → 6.118 WAVE FILTER

**6.115 Shear filter** Accessed through the Filter menu under Distort > Shear. Creates a distortion along the path of a curved line that can be pulled or dragged using the dialog box.

**6.116 Spherize filter** Accessed through the Filter menu under Distort > Spherize. Wraps the image over a curved surface that can be spherical (concave or convex) or cylindrical (horizontal or vertical).

**6.117 Twirl filter** Accessed through the Filter menu under Distort > Twirl. Twists a selection about a central axis. The selection edges are fixed, so the result is an image that coils progressively more tightly around its center.

**6.118 Wave filter** Accessed through the Filter menu under Distort > Wave. A customizable version of the Ripple filter. The number of wave generators can be specified, as can wavelength and wave height. Waves can be conventionally sinusoidal, triangular, or square.

**6.119 Zigzag filter** Accessed through the Filter menu under Distort > Zigzag. Produces radial distortions in the manner of pebble-in-the-pond ripples but with more flexibility, control and customization options.

## Filters: Noise

6.**120 Add Noise filter** Accessed through the Filter menu under Noise > Add Noise. Adds random discrete pixels to the image, simulating levels of broadband noise or film grain. Gentle use of this filter can reduce the appearance of bands in large areas of color gradients and reduce the impact of image edits (such as image collages and intense areas of manipulation). The default setting delivers panchromatic noise. Click on the Monochromatic button to base the noise on underlying tonal values, Uniform for a random pattern and Gaussian for a result (based on Gaussian statistics) that is often more speckled.

6.**121 Despeckle filter** Accessed through the Filter menu under Noise > Déspeckle. A useful filter that removes noise and unwanted fine detail but preserves the main image details. Edge detection techniques determine the fundamental image edges (i.e. the important ones where major color changes occur) and blurs the rest of the image.

6.**122 Dust & Scratches filter** Accessed through the Filter menu under Noise > Dust & Scratches. Reduces the overall noise level in an image. Fine dust particles and scratches reproduced in the image are regarded as noise and can be eliminated by appropriate setting of the Radius and Threshold parameters. Care should be taken using this filter: Removal of larger dust and scratch artifacts may soften the whole image (genuine image elements are also "smoothed" away).

6.**123 Median filter** Accessed through the Filter menu under Noise > Median. Blends pixel brightness values to reduce the noise level in an image. Pixels that differ markedly from surrounding ones are discarded and replaced with those of median value (based on the value of pixels in the environs). There are two principal uses for this filter. First, it can reduce motion artifacts from handheld images taken at long exposures. Second, it can help remove compression artifacts from areas of similar tone. Flesh tones respond particularly well.

6.**124 Noise filters** Accessed through the Filter menu under Noise. Filter group for adding or removing noise (and noiselike) artifacts from an image. Includes the Add Noise, Despeckle, Dust & Scratches, and Median filters.

## Filters: Pixelate

6.**125 Color Halftone filter** Accessed through the Filter menu under Pixelate > Color Halftone. Creates the effect of a printer's halftone screen on each channel of the image. The image is broken down into rectangles, then for each channel the rectangle is replaced with a circle (with a radius proportional to the luminosity value of the rectangle). → 9.053 HALFTONE (1)

6.**126 Crystallize filter** Accessed through the Filter menu under Pixelate > Crystallize. Breaks the image into "crystals" (polygons of solid color). The hue and luminosity of each polygon is based on the averaged values of the pixels in the space occupied by the polygon.

6.**127 Facet filter** Accessed through the Filter menu under Pixelate > Facet. Creates blocks of continuous color from groups of pixels. The size and shape of the irregular blocks are determined by the underlying tone and brightness levels. Delivers a result that can look hand-painted.

6.**128 Fragment filter** Accessed through the Filter menu under Pixelate > Fragment. Offsets four copies of the image, with the pixels in each copy averaged. Can simulate rapid vibration effects.

6.**129 Mezzotint filter** Accessed through the Filter menu under Pixelate > Mezzotint. Produces an image built from fully saturated colored dots. These "dots" can be large, medium, or fine, or can be short or long strokes.

6.**130 Mosaic filter** Accessed through the Filter menu under Pixelate > Mosaic. Recreates square tile mosaics by creating new square "pixels" of solid color representing the average of the underlying pixels. The size of the mosaic tiles can be adjusted between 2 and 200 pixels.

6.**131 Pixelate filters** Accessed through the Filter menu under Pixelate. The Pixelate filter group exaggerates pixellation (and pixelation-like effects) by grouping pixels into larger units of similar color values. The group includes Color Halftone, Crystallize, Facet, Fragment, Mezzotint, Mozaic, and Pointillize.

6.**132 Pointillize filter** Accessed through the Filter menu under Pixelate > Pointillize. Creates an effect similar to that of a pointillist painting. The image is broken into random dots (of adjustable diameter) based on the color of the underlying pixels. Gaps between the dots are filled with the background color.

## Filters: Render

6.**133 3D Transform filter** Accessed through the Filter menu under Render > 3D Transform. Converts a flat image into a cube, sphere, or cylinder by mapping the conventional rectangular coordinates of points in the image to the corresponding coordinates of the three-dimensional body.

6.**134 Clouds filter** Accessed through the Filter menu under Render > Clouds. Creates a cloudscape using random values between those of the foreground and background colors. Care is therefore needed in selecting sensible colors in order to create a realistic effect. When aiming to create a realistic sky background and foreground colors are completely interchangeable.

6.**135 Difference Clouds filter** Accessed through the Filter menu under Render > Difference Clouds. Like the "Clouds" filter, Difference Clouds creates cloudscapes using random color values between those of the foreground and background colors. It then blends these "clouds" with the underlying image using the same technique as the Difference blending mode. → 6.134 CLOUDS FILTER; 4.086 BLENDING MODE; 4.092 DIFFERENCE

6.**136 Lens Flare filter** Accessed through the Filter menu under Render > Lens Flare. Introduces (controllable) lens flare into images that (through good practice on the part of the photographer) previously had none.

6.**137 Lighting Effects filter** Accessed through the Filter menu under Render > Lighting Effects. Uses four sets of light properties, three light types, and seventeen styles to produce endless variations of lighting effects. "Bump Maps" (texture grayscale files) can be linked to the image to create contour-line three-dimensional effects.

6.**138 Render filters** Accessed through the Filter menu under Render. Filters from the Render group can be used to create cloud effects, refraction patterns, and even three-dimensional transformations. The group includes 3D Transform, Clouds, Difference Clouds, Lens Flare, Lighting Effects, and Texture Fill.

6.**139 Texture Fill filter** Accessed through the Filter menu under Render > Texture Fill. Fills the selection with texture provided from a separate grayscale texture file. Using this filter automatically prompts you to locate the required texture file.

## Filters: Sketch

6.**140 Bas Relief filter** Accessed through the Filter menu under Sketch > Bas Relief. Creates texture from image elements resulting in an image that appears to be carved into linoleum material and lit semiobliquely to emphasize the texture. The foreground color is applied to dark areas of the image and the background color to lighter parts.

6.**141 Chalk & Charcoal filter** Accessed through the Filter menu under Sketch > Chalk & Charcoal. Reduces an image to a bold graphic form. With black as the foreground color and white as the background color, highlight areas are replaced with diagonal chalk strokes, shadows are textured charcoal-black and midtones are represented by a midgray ground. Different foreground and background colors can be substituted for black and white for unusual effects.

6.**142 Charcoal filter** Accessed through the Filter menu under Sketch > Charcoal. Delivers results similar to the Chalk & Charcoal but with only "charcoal" as the drawing medium. Edges are clearly defined while midtones comprise short diagonal strokes. Charcoal thickness, level of detail, and light/dark balance can be adjusted. Like Chalk & Charcoal this filter delivers authentic results with black as the foreground color and white as the background, but any other colors can be used.

6.**143 Chrome filter** Accessed through the Filter menu under Sketch > Chrome. A chrome filter converts the image into a polished metal molding. Image highlights become raised bright areas while shadows become "valleys." By altering the Detail and Smoothness controls effects ranging from mild undulations to a finely detailed representation of the original image are possible. Chrome tends to flatten contrast in the image and often the contrast will need boosting after application of this filter.

6.144 **Conté Crayon filter** Accessed through the Filter menu under Sketch > Conté Crayon. This filter uses foreground and background colors in a manner that simulates a dense-textured conté crayon. For an accurate conté crayon effect set the foreground color (which is applied to the darker areas of the image) to black or deep brown. A Texture control allows you to select the base texture (brick, burlap, painters' canvas, or stone) on which the conté crayon image will be drawn.

6.145 **Graphic Pen filter** Accessed through the Filter menu under Sketch > Graphic Pen. Simulates the use of a graphic or technical drawing pen with fine, parallel ink strokes picking out the original image. Stroke length, light/dark balance, and light direction may be manipulated for best effect.

6.146 **Halftone Pattern filter** Accessed through the Filter menu under Sketch > Halftone Pattern. Converts the image to a grayscale halftone screened image, which resembles a newspaper image. An optional Line setting simulates a black-and-white television picture (with prominent scan lines) while the Circle setting overlays the image with concentric rings.

6.147 **Note Paper filter** Accessed through the Filter menu under Sketch > Note Paper. Images are reduced in tone such that they become layers in a piece of handmade paper. The effect is similar to that of the Emboss filter but the use of texture makes for a more interesting end result.

6.148 **Photocopy filter** Accessed through the Filter menu under Sketch > Photocopy. Creates the effect of an old (not photorealistic) monochrome photocopy. Dark areas are defined by their edges with a sharp fall-off to white (or the background color), while some areas of tone change become emphasized.

6.149 **Plaster filter** Accessed through the Filter menu under Sketch > Plaster. Creates an embossed effect (rather like the Note Paper filter but stronger and with different textures) with the result colored using the foreground and background colors.

6.150 **Reticulation filter** Accessed through the Filter menu under Sketch > Reticulation. Reproduces the crazed "crackle" finish that can result from exposing film emulsion to processing chemicals at

extremes of temperature. The expansion and uneven shrinking of the emulsion is reproduced in the grayscale version of the original image.

6.151 **Sketch filters** Accessed through the Filter menu under Sketch. Conceptually similar to the Artistic filter group, Sketch filters comprise a somewhat eclectic group of filters, some of which give the effect of sketching media while others impart new textures to selections. They include filters such as Bas Relief, which creates three-dimensional effects. The Sketch filters comprise Bas Relief, Chalk & Charcoal, Charcoal, Chrome, Conté Crayon, Graphic Pen, Halftone Screen, Note Paper, Photocopy, Plaster, Reticulation, Stamp, Torn Edges, and Water Paper.

6.152 **Stamp filter** Accessed through the Filter menu under Sketch > Stamp. Converts the image to a black-and-white-only (or foreground and background color only) graphic that resembles a decorators woodcut or linocut stamp.

6.153 **Torn Edges filter** Accessed through the Filter menu under Sketch > Torn Edges. Reduces the image to foreground and background tones only. Image elements are represented as roughly torn pieces of paper.

6.154 **Water Paper filter** Accessed through the Filter menu under Sketch > Water Paper. Reduces the image to a "patchwork" of paint daubs that are laid on damp paper. Gentle bleeding occurs along the paper grain to give a soft effect rather like a slightly blurred tapestry.

## Filters: Stylize

6.155 **Diffuse filter** Accessed through the Filter menu under Stylize > Diffuse. Defocuses an image by moving pixels either randomly or according to their color values; Lighten Only replaces darker pixels with lighter ones, Darken Only replaces lighter pixels with darker.

6.156 **Emboss filter** Accessed through the Filter menu under Stylize > Emboss. Identifies principal edges and raises or depresses the enclosed selection. The fill color becomes gray and the edges colored. The embossing angle can be changed through 360° and the surface of the emboss altered between a depression and a raised platform. Use the Fade command after applying Emboss to return some of the color and detail to the image.

6.**157 Extrude filter** Accessed through the Filter menu under Stylize > Extrude. Creates a three-dimensional effect of the image being extruded through a grille; image elements become square prisms or pyramids, "bursting" from the image center.

6.**158 Find Edges filter** Accessed through the Filter menu under Stylize > Find Edges. Identifies and emphasizes edges in an image. → 6.163 TRACE CONTOUR FILTER.

6.**159 Glowing Edges filter** Accessed through the Filter menu under Stylize > Glowing Edges. Identifies image edges and adds a bright glow to them. The glow width, edge brightness, and smoothness can be adjusted from the dialog box.

6.**160 Solarize filter** Accessed through the Filter menu under Stylize > Solarize. Another emulation of a traditional photographic technique by a Photoshop filter. The image and its negative are combined, simulating a semireversal process due to exposure of film to light during processing.

6.**161 Stylize filters** Accessed through the Filter menu under Stylize. Filters in this group turn images into bold graphical forms, and include Diffuse, Emboss, Extrude, Find Edges, Glowing Edges, Solarize, Tiles, Trace Contour, and Wind.

6.**162 Tiles filter** Accessed through the Filter menu under Stylize > Tiles. The image is broken into tiles, each of which is then moved slightly (and randomly) from its original position. The space between the tiles can be filled with foreground or background colors, with the original image, or with its inverse.

6.**163 Trace Contour filter** The trace contour filter is accessed through the Filter menu under Stylize > Trace Contour. Analyzes changes in brightness and draws thin lines for each color channel. The result is a polychromatic contour map.

6.**164 Wind filter** Accessed through the Filter menu under Stylize > Wind. Draws out the left or the right edges of an image as short, randomized horizontal lines to suggest stylized wind. The Blast option provides a stronger effect, and Stagger offsets the wind slightly.

## Filters: Texture

6.**165 Craquelure filter** Accessed through the Filter menu under Texture > Craquelure. Creates an effect rather like blown polystyrene wallpaper, with fine, rounded cracks echoing the principal features of the image. The spacing, depth, and brightness of the cracks can be adjusted.

6.**166 Grain filter** Accessed through the Filter menu under Texture > Grain. A straightforward filter for adding texture in the form of fine or medium film grain, stippling, horizontal and vertical lines, and more.

6.**167 Mosaic Tiles filter** Accessed through the Filter menu under Texture > Mosaic Tiles. Breaks the image into rough square tiles with depressions between them. By reducing the brightness of the cracks, dirty groutwork can be simulated. Don't confuse this with the Mosaic filter, which breaks the image into enlarged single-colored pixel tiles, with no gaps between them. → 6.130 MOSAIC FILTER

6.**168 Patchwork filter** Accessed through the Filter menu under Texture > Patchwork. Creates an effect more like needlepoint embroidery or tapestry than patchwork. The image is broken into small squares, each of which adopts the most prominent color of the underlying pixels. The squares are given curved edges and are raised or lowered randomly to simulate highlights and shadows.

6.**169 Stained Glass filter** Accessed through the Filter menu under Texture > Stained Glass. Converts the image to a series of cells that take their color from the predominant color of the pixels that are enclosed. Each cell is then outlined in "lead" using the foreground color. A particularly memory-intensive filter!

6.**170 Texture filters** Accessed through the Filter menu under Texture. Filter group for applying texture effects to images. Comprises Craquelure, Grain, Mosaic Tiles, Patchwork, Stained Glass, and the freeform Texturizer.

6.**171 Texturizer filter** Accessed through the Filter menu under Texture > Texturizer. Applies one of four standard textures (stone, burlap, brick, or canvas) at a variable scale and relief. You can also load your own texture which can then be similarly adjusted and applied.

## Filters: Video and other

6.**172 Custom Filter** Accessed through the Filter menu under Other submenu. A filter that allows a user to create their own filter effect. The brightness value of each pixel in an image can be altered by applying a convolution, a mathematical operation in which the pixel values are altered according to those of neighbors. One or more custom filters, created using this command, can be saved for future use. → 6.172 OTHER (FILTERS); 2.057 FILTER MENU

6.**173 De-Interlace filter** Accessed through the Filter menu under Video > De-Interlace. Detects interlaced lines in a moving video image and discards them to give a smoothed image. The discarded lines can be replaced by interpolation or by duplicating the neighboring scan lines.

6.**174 Ditherbox™ Filter** Specialized filter (found in the Filter menu under the Other submenu) designed to create customized dither patterns for a specific RGB color. → 6.172 CUSTOM (FILTERS); 6.007 DITHER(ING)

6.**175 High Pass Filter** The high pass filter is found in the Other submenu of the Filter menu. It is designed specifically to remove the low-frequency data in an image. This has the effect of retaining edge details within an image (for a radius specified in the corresponding dialog box) while suppressing the remainder of the data. A typical use of this filter would be to create line-art images from scanned images. The effect is, effectively, the opposite of that of the Gaussian Blur filter → 6.172 CUSTOM (FILTERS); 6.089 GAUSSIAN BLUR FILTER

6.**176 Maximum filter** Filter from the Other submenu of the Filter menu. Along with the Minimum filter this can be used for modifying masks. Using the Maximum filter the mask is choked (spreading out the white areas and reigning in the black) while the Minimum filter spreads out the black areas and reduces the extent of the white. → 6.172 CUSTOM (FILTERS)

6.**177 Minimum filter** Cross refer to Maximum filter

6.**178 NTSC Colors filter** Accessed through the Filter menu under Video > NTSC Colors. The purpose of this filter is to alter the color gamut to that of NTSC color television. This restricted gamut prevents oversaturated colors of the original image from bleeding when displayed using the NTSC color television system.

6.**179 Offset filter** Accessed through the Filter menu under Other > Offset. This selection-based filter moves the selection a specified amount horizontally and/or vertically. An empty space is left at the original selection location that can be filled with the current background color or another selected part of the image.

6.**180 Tile Maker filter** ImageReady filter from the Other submenu group, currently only in ImageReady. Filter designed to modify an image or image selection for use as a tiled background for a website page. The edges of the tile can be made "soft" to blend with the adjacent copy of the tile when multiple tiles are pasted together. Images can also be flipped horizontally and vertically to create a "kaleidoscopic" effect. → 6.172 CUSTOM (FILTERS)

6.**181 Video filters** Accessed through the Filter menu under Video. A pair of specialized filters designed for video-based work. Comprises De-Interlace and NTSC Colors.

6.071 **Artistic**—*Original*

6.072 **Colored Pencil filter**

6.073 **Cutout filter**—*5, 4, 1*

6.073 **Cutout filter**—*5, 2, 2*

6.074 **Dry Brush filter**

6.075 **Film Grain filter**—*20, 9, 5*

6.075 **Film Grain filter**— *1, 20, 7*

6.076 **Fresco filter**

6.077 **Neon Glow filter**

6.077 **Neon Glow filter**

6.078 **Paint Daubs filter**—*Sparkle*

6.078 **Paint Daubs filter**—*Wide Blurry*

6.078 *Paint Daubs filter*—Wide Sharp

6.079 *Palette Knife filter*

6.080 *Plastic Wrap filter*

6.081 *Poster Edges filter*

6.082 *Rough Pastels filter*

6.082 *Rough Pastels filter*

6.082 *Rough Pastels filter*

6.083 *Smudge Stick filter*

6.084 *Sponge filter*—10, 2, 12

6.084 *Sponge filter*—2, 14, 4

6.085 *Underpainting filter*

6.086 *Watercolor filter*

6.087 **Blur**—Original

6.087 **Blur filter**

6.088 **Blur More filter**

6.089 **Gaussian Blur filter**

6.090 **Motion Blur filter**

6.091 **Radial Blur filter**

6.096 **Smart Blur**—Normal

6.096 **Smart Blur**—Edge Only

6.096 **Smart Blur**—Overlay Edge

6.093 **Sharpen**—Original

6.093 **Sharpen filter**

6.095 **Sharpen More filter**

6.092 *Sharpen Edge filter*

6.097 *Unsharp Mask filter*

6.097 *Unsharp Mask filter—0, 0, 0*

6.097 *Unsharp Mask—250, 1, 0*

6.097 *Unsharp Mask—250, 3, 0*

6.097 *Unsharp Mask—350, 1, 25*

6.100 *Brush strokes—Original*

6.098 *Accented Edges—5, 39, 5*

6.098 *Accented Edges—2, 33, 11*

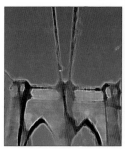

6.099 *Angled Strokes—10, 15, 3*

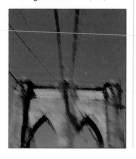

6.099 *Angled Strokes—82, 3, 10*

6.101 *Crosshatch filter*

6.102 *Dark Strokes filter*

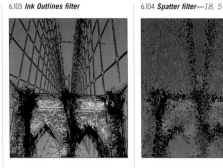

6.103 *Ink Outlines filter*

6.104 *Spatter filter—18, 5*

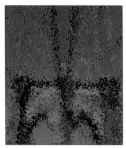

6.104 *Spatter filter—4, 8*

6.105 *Sprayed Strokes—Right Diagonal*

6.105 *Sprayed Strokes—Horizontal*

6.105 *Sprayed Strokes—Left Diagonal*

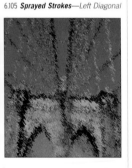

6.105 *Sprayed Strokes—Vertical*

6.106 *Sumi-e filter*

171

6.107 *Distort—Original*

6.107 *Diffuse Glow filter*

6.108 *Displace filter—Stucco*

6.108 **Displace filter**—*Weave*

6.108 **Displace filter**—*Bricks*

6.110 **Glass filter**

6.111 **Ocean Ripple filter**

6.112 **Pinch filter**

6.113 **Polar Coordinates filter**—
*Rectangular to Polar*

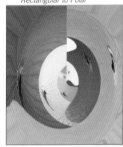

6.113 **Polar Coordinates filter**—
*Polar to Rectangular*

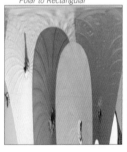

6.114 **Ripple filter**—*282, Medium*

6.114 **Ripple filter**—*998, Large*

6.115 **Shear filter**

6.116 **Spherize filter**

6.117 **Twirl filter**

.118 *Wave filter*—Sine

6.118 *Wave filter*—Square

6.119 *Zigzag filter*

.120 *Add Noise*—Original

6.120 *Add Noise*—Gaussain

6.120 *Add Noise*—Monochromatic

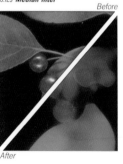

.5.121 *Despeckle filter*

Before

After

6.122 *Dust & Scratches filter*

Before

After

6.123 *Median filter*

Before

After

6.131 *Pixellate*—Original

6.125 *Color Halftone filter*

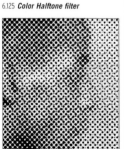

6.126 *Crystallize filter*

6.127 *Facet filter*

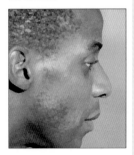

6.128 *Fragment filter*

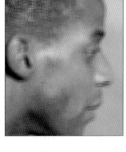

6.129 *Mezzotint filter*

6.130 *Mosaic filter*

6.132 *Pointillize*—*White Background*

6.132 *Pointillize*—*Color Background*

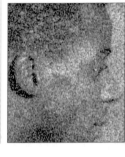

6.137 *Lighting Effects*—*Original*

6.137 *Lighting Effects palette*

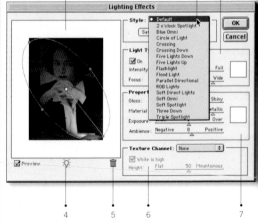

6.137 *2 o'clock spotlight*

1 *Preview*
2 *Style selection menu*
3 *Lighting type selector*
4 *Add light*
5 *Delete light*
6 *Texture channel adjustment/selector*
7 *Lighting properties*

6.137 *Blue omni*

6.137 *Circle of light*

6.137 *Crossing*

6.137 *Parallel directional*

6.137 *Five lights down*

6.137 *Five lights up*

6.137 *Flashlight*

6.137 *Floodlight*

6.137 *Parallel Directional*

6.137 *RGB lights*

6.137 *Soft directional*

6.137 *Soft omni*

6.137 *Soft spot*

6.137 *Three down*

6.137 *Triple spotlight*

6.134 *Clouds filter*

6.135 *Difference Clouds filter*

6.136 *Lens Flare filter*

6.151 *Sketch—Original*

6.140 *Bas Relief—6, 1, Bottom Right*

6.140 *Bas Relief—11, 2, Top Left*

6.141 *Chalk and Charcoal filter*

6.142 *Charcoal filter*

6.143 *Chrome filter*

6.144 *Conté Crayon filter*

6.145 *Graphic Pen filter*

6.146 *Halftone Pattern filter*

6.146 *Halftone Pattern*—2, 19, Circle

6.146 *Halftone Pattern*—2, 19, Line

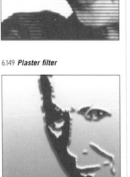

6.147 *Note Paper filter*

6.148 *Photocopy filter*

6.149 *Plaster filter*

6.150 *Reticulation filter*

177

6.152 *Stamp filter*

6.153 *Torn Edges filter*

6.154 *Water Paper filter*

6.161 *Stylize*—original

6.155 *Diffuse filter*

6.156 *Emboss filter*

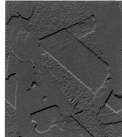

6.156 *Emboss filter*

6.157 *Extrude filter*

6.158 *Find Edges filter*

6.159 *Glowing Edges filter*

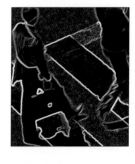

6.160 *Solarize filter*

6.162 *Tiles filter*—10, 10, Background Color

6.162 *Tiles filter*—70, 30, Foreground Color

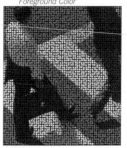

6.167 *Mosaic Tiles filter*

6.163 *Trace Contour filter*

6.164 *Wind filter*

6.157 *Extrude filter*

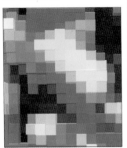

6.157 *Extrude filter*

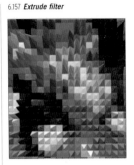

6.162 *Tiles filter*

6.165 *Texture*—*Original*

6.166 *Craquelure filter*

6.166 *Grain filter*

6.166 *Grain filter*

6.168 *Patchwork filter*

179

6.169 *Stained Glass filter*

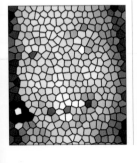

6.170 *Texturizer filter*—*Noise*

6.170 *Texturizer filter*—*Brick*

2.064 **3D transfrm tools**

1 *Selection Tool*
2 *Direct Selection Tool*
3 *Cube Tool*
4 *Sphere Tool*
5 *Cylinder Tool*
6 *Convert Anchor Point Tool*
7 *Add Anchor Point Tool*
8 *Delete Anchor Point Tool*
9 *Pan Camera Tool*
10 *Trackball Tool*
11 *Hand Tool*
12 *Zoom Tool*

2 •
1 •
3 •
5 •
7 •
9 •
11 •
12 •
10 •
8 •
6 •
4 •

6.133 **Mapped to cuboid surface**

6.133 **Mapped to sphere**

6.133 **Mapped to cylinder**

6.133 **Mapped to sphere and displaced**

6.133 **3Mapped to cylinder and displaced**

6.133 **3D Transform filter**

6.181 *Video and other—Original*

6.173 *De-Interlace filter*

6.178 *NTSC Colors filter*

6.172 *Custom—Original*

6.172 *Custom settings dialog box*

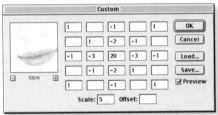

*This creates a unique filter effect in which pixel brightness is altered (multiplied) by entering multipliers (from –999 to +999) in the spaces on the grid.*

6.172 *Custom—Result 1*

6.172 *Custom—Result 2*

6.175 *High pass*

6.177 *Minimum*

6.176 *Maximum*

6.179 *Offset*

# IMAGEREADY & WEB

## ImageReady commands

7.**001 Align (slices)** ImageReady feature. Selected from the Slices menu, the Align command permits selected slices to be aligned according to options provided in a submenu: Top aligns the top edges of all the selected slices to the top edge of the selections; Vertical Center aligns the vertical center of each selected slice with the vertical midpoint of all the selected slices; Bottom aligns the bottom edges of all selected slices with the bottom edge of the lowest selected slice; Left [Right] aligns the left [right] edges of the selected slices with the left [right] edge of the left-most [right-most] selected slice; Horizontal Center aligns the horizontal center of all selected slices with the horizontal midpoint of these slices.

7.**002 Cascade** Item on the ImageReady Window menu. Arranges multiple open windows in a stacked cascade diagonally across the workspace from the top left. → 7.042 TILE

7.**003 Combine Slices** ImageReady Slices menu item that combines two (or more) slices. The combined slice will be rectangular and bound the outer edges of all original slices. It will also be a user slice, irrespective of whether the originals were auto-slices, user-slices, or a combination of both. → 7.082 SLICES

7.**004 Copy Foreground Color as HTML** ImageReady Edit menu item. Copies the current foreground color as a hexadecimal value to the clipboard, from where it may be pasted into an HTML file.

7.**005 Copy HTML Code** ImageReady Edit menu item. Copies HTML code to the clipboard. Submenu choices are: Copy All Slices: copies the HTML code for all slices in the document, whether or not they are selected; Copy Selected Slices: copies the HTML code for the selected slices; Copy Preloads: copies the JavaScript part of the HTML code for the slices in the document.

7.**006 Copy Preloads** ImageReady command. An option of Copy HTML Code command on the Edit menu, it copies the JavaScript part of the HTML code for document slices.

7.**007 Create Droplet** ImageReady command on the Optimize palette menu. To create a droplet you must first choose a compression format for a selected image and set the compression options in the Optimize palette. When Create Droplet is selected you will be

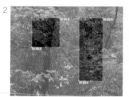
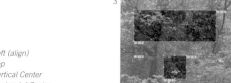

**1** *Left (align)*
**2** *Top*
**3** *Vertical Center*
**4** *Horizontal Center*

prompted for a name and a save location.>
→ 7.059 DROPLET

7.**008 Create Selection from Slices** ImageReady Select menu item. Converts a selected slice (or slices) into a conventional selection.

7.**009 Create Slices from Guides** ImageReady Slices menu item. Creates user slices from the bounds of the guides. All previous slices in the document are deleted. Slice selections can be made hard-edged or feathered.

7.**010 Create Slices from Selection** ImageReady Slices menu item. Uses the bounds of a rectangular selection as the basis of a user slice. If the selection is not rectangular a rectangular slice will be created that includes the full extent of the selection.

7.**011 Delete Channel (2)** ImageReady Select menu item. Deletes selection edges but pixels within the selection are preserved.

7.**012 Delete Slices** ImageReady Slices menu item that deletes selected slices. To delete all slices select Delete All from the Slices menu.

7.**013 Divide Slices** ImageReady Slices menu item that opens the Divide Slices dialog box. Here, a selected slice (or the default full-image auto-slice) may be divided along horizontal or vertical axes (or both). If the resulting slices are smaller than the original when combined any orphaned areas will be converted into auto-slices.

7.**014 Duplicate Optimized** ImageReady Image menu item. Duplicates an optimized image.

7.**015 Duplicate Slices** ImageReady Slices menu item. Duplicates a selected slice. The new slice is laid over the original but offset by ten pixels down and to the right.

7.**016 Export Original** ImageReady File menu item. Flattens the original image (if appropriate) then allows the image to be saved in a range of formats. Formats supported include: BMP, PCX, Pixar, Targa, and TIFF for Windows and Mac OS; PICT and QuickTime movie (Mac OS only); and FlashPix (Windows only). Saving to a format other than Photoshop will result in the loss of some image information, particularly slices and optimizations.

7.**017 HTML background** ImageReady File menu item. Specifies the current image as the background image for your web graphic.

7.**018 Link Slices** ImageReady Slices menu item. Links slices selected with the slice selection tool. Linked sets of user-slices are indicated by different colored markers.

7.**019 Master Palette** ImageReady Image Menu item. Enables the building, clearing, saving of master palettes. Also use this option to make additions to a master palette. Master palettes are typically created to accompany collections of GIF or PNG-8 images. With a master palette included all images will be displayed with the same colors.

7.**020 Matte menu** ImageReady Optimize palette pop-up menu. If you know the background color of a web page the matte feature enables a fill or blend of transparent pixels with a matte color that matches that background (note that the web page background must be a continuous tone, not patterned). The Matte menu lets you select foreground or background colors, or one of a selection in the pop-up.

183

7.010 *Create slices from selection*

1 *Rectangular Selection*
2 *User slice 03 created from selection*

**7.021 Preview In** ImageReady Preview in is a file menu item. It permits the document currently being worked on to be viewed in a web browser chosen by the user. The browser's toolbar Stop and Reload commands can be used to play animated sequences. You can specify a preferred browser by placing square brackets around the name of that browser in the Preview In folder, which is located in the Helpers folder within the Photoshop folder.

**7.022 Promote to User-Slices** ImageReady Slices menu item. "Promotes" selected auto-slices to user-slices. → 7.040 SLICES

**7.023 Recent Files** ImageReady File menu item. Displays the most recently opened files.

**7.024 Repopulate Views** ImageReady command, selected from the Optimize palette pop-up menu. Repopulate Views lets you select a version of an image in either the 2-up or 4-up views and automatically create new optimized versions of that selection. → 7076 REGENERATE

**7.025 Reset Palettes** ImageReady Window menu item. Resets all open palettes to their default position. You can set the palettes to their default position every time ImageReady opens by deselecting the Save Palette button in the File menu under Preferences > General.

**7.026 Resize Window to Fit** ImageReady View Menu item. Resizes the current image window to show the whole image, unless the image is zoomed. In this case the window area will show the maximum possible image area.

**7.027 Save Optimized** ImageReady File menu item. Saves a file that has been optimized for web delivery in its current edit state. The alternate Save Optimized As command can be used to save a copy of the file with a different filename.

**7.028 Save Optimized As** ImageReady File menu item. Saves a copy of the current optimized file with a different filename.

**7.029 Set Layer Position** ImageReady Layer menu item. Enables a selected layer to be positioned within the image. Vertical and horizontal offset options can be set via the respective pop-up menus.

**7.030 Show Original/Optimized/2-up/4-up** ImageReady View menu item. Shows image alternates (toggles round Original, Optimized, 2-up, or 4-up).

**7.031 Show Slices** Slices menu item. Displays slices in image.

**7.032 Show/Hide Animation** ImageReady Window menu item. Shows or hides the Animation palette. → 7.051 ANIMATION PALETTE

**7.033 Show/Hide Color Table** ImageReady Window menu item. Shows or hides the Color Table palette.

**7.034 Show/Hide Layer Options/Effects** ImageReady Window menu item. Shows or hides the Layer Options palette.

**7.035 Show/Hide Optimization Info** ImageReady View menu item. Shows or hides the optimization annotations to images in 2-up and 4-up views.

**7.036 Show/Hide Optimize** ImageReady Window menu item. Displays or hides the Optimize Options palette.

7.024 *Repopulate Views*

**7.037 Show/Hide Rollover** ImageReady Window menu item. Shows or hides the Rollover palette. The window will be empty if there are no rollovers for the selected image.

**7.038 Show/Hide Slice** ImageReady Window menu item. Shows or hides the Slices palette.

**7.039 Show/Hide Styles** (**2**) ImageReady Window menu item. Shows or hides the Styles palette. → 7.086 STYLES PALETTE (2)

**7.040 Slices** ImageReady menu for slice manipulations. → 7.082 SLICES

**7.041 Snap to Slices** ImageReady Slices menu item. Enables slices to be snapped to other slices.

**7.042 Tile** ImageReady Window menu item. Tiles multiple open windows across the workspace, from the left to the right edge. → 7.002 CASCADE

**7.043 Tween command** Tween command is an animation palette feature that enables the addition of new frames or modification of existing frames. Layer attributes such as positions, opacities, and effects are interpolated between the start and end points to ensure an even flow throughout. The Tween command can be considered as a short cut to achieving certain animation effects such as fades or transitions. After new frames have been created by this process they can be further modified, either collectively or individually.

**7.044 Unlink Sets** ImageReady Slices menu item. Unlinks all user-slices in a selected group (or groups). → 7.040 SLICES; 7.045 UNLINK SLICES

**7.045 Unlink Slices** ImageReady Slices menu item. Unlinks slices previously selected with the Slice Selection tool. To unlink all user-slice sets select Unlink All from the Slices menu.

**7.046 Update HTML** ImageReady File menu item. Once you have pasted the HTML code for an image into an HTML file you can update that code after subsequent image edits using the Update HTML command.

**7.047 Web Shift** ImageReady command. In the Color Table palette use the Web Shift button to shift the chosen color to its closest web palette equivalent. Alternatively select Web Shift/Unshift Selected Colors from the Color Table palette menu. → 7.090 WEB SNAP SLIDER

**7.048 Web Shift/Unshift Selected Colors** ImageReady command. Shifts (or unshifts) selected colors to the closest web palette equivalents. → 7.090 WEB SNAP SLIDER

## ImageReady features

**7.049 Adaptive Color Table** ImageReady color table option. It creates a custom color table based on samples from the spectrum elements occurring most frequently in a selected image. As most images' color elements tend to be skewed toward certain colors, an adaptive table echoes this.

**7.050 alpha transparency** ImageReady feature limited to PNG-24 images. Images created in the PNG-24 format can preserve variable transparency using the alpha transparency feature. Up to 256 levels of transparency can be preserved, enabling an appropriate image

7.043 *Tween command*

Frames 1, 2, and 8 are original images
Frames 3 to 7 were "tweened" using the tween command

7.047 *Web Shift*

Before

After

to blend seamlessly with any web background. This feature is enabled by first selecting PNG-24 from the Optimize palette, then selecting Transparency and "None" from the Matte menu. Note that this feature is also available in later versions of Photoshop, and is accessed by selecting PNG-24 from the Optimize panel in the Save For Web dialog box. → 3.045 PNG-24

**7.051 Animation palette** ImageReady palette. Displays the sequence of frames comprising the current animation. Palette buttons like those on a video recorder let you play and navigate an animation; you can also select whether the animation should be played once or "forever" (as a closed loop).

**7.052 application dither** Application dither is an artifact that occurs when ImageReady (or Photoshop) tries to simulate colors from the original image using nonexact colors in the palette specified for the optimized image. It happens with PNG-8 and GIF images, and the degree of application dither, the dithering pattern and color range can all be specified. To specify the degree of application dither applied select a dithering method from the Dither menu on the Optimize palette, then drag the dither slider to set a percentage dither.

**7.053 Bounding Box Optimization** ImageReady animated GIF specific optimization option. Choose Optimize by Bounding Box from the Optimize Animation option in the Animation palette menu. Each successive frame is cropped to include only those regions that have changed from the preceding frame.

This optimization tends to create the smallest files but ones that are not compatible with GIF editors. → 7.075 REDUNDANT PIXEL OPTIMIZATION

**7.054 Color Palette, ImageReady** Like its Photoshop counterpart, this displays the color values for the current selection of foreground and background colors. Sliders enable the colors to be changed (edited) based on different color models. These models can be selected from the pop-out menu. A color bar enables foreground and background colors to be selected directly.

**7.055 Color Table palette** Displays the current color table, enabling colors to be selected, added to, and deleted; some or all of the colors can be shifted to their web-safe equivalents.

**7.056 Custom Color Table** ImageReady color table option. Treats the current table (adaptive, selective, or perceptual) as fixed; changes to the image are not posted as updates to the table.

**7.057 Diffusion dither** Option in the Dithering Algorithm pop-up menu. Applies a random pattern of dither that is less obvious than the halftone type used by Pattern dither. Slices should be linked when using this method to avoid visible seams that sometimes affect slice boundaries. → 7.052 APPLICATION DITHER; 7.069 PATTERN DITHER

**7.058 Document Window** ImageReady display option. The document window allows you to select alternate views. As well as the original image you can opt for the web-optimized display and multiple windows. Selection

7.051 *animation palette*

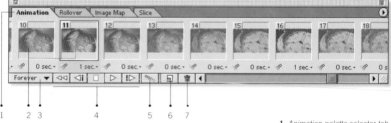

1 *Animation palette selector tab*
2 *Frames*
3 *Looping options*
4 *Frame navigation controls*
5 *Tweening option*
6 *Duplicate current frame*
7 *Trash*

between original and optimized displays can be made at any point, but most tools can only be used with the original image and not the optimized version.> You can select 2-up or 4-up displays to display two or four versions of the image in the same window. In these multiple displays versions of the image based on the current Optimize palette settings are generated; the 2-up display features the original image and the optimized version; the 4-up display adds two further optimizations. Using the Optimize palette new optimizations can be applied to any of the displayed images. Optimization information can be displayed below the 2-up and 4-up images using the Show Optimization command from the View menu.

7.**059 Droplet** A small application, or applet, that can be used to apply optimization settings to an image, or series of images. Once created a droplet can be left on the desktop so that images dragged onto it have the appropriate settings applied, or it can be saved to a folder. You can specify when creating a droplet the location in which processed images will be stored.

7.**060 hard-edged transparency** GIF or PNG-8 files can be given hard-edged transparency so that any pixels that in the original image were less than 50% transparent become totally opaque, and those more than 50% transparent become totally so. Use hard-edged transparency to prevent edge halos.

7.**061 hexadecimal color value** In ImageReady, a unique numeric value for a particular color expressed in hexadecimal form (base 16).

Colors are typically expressed as hexadecimal values for copying across to HTML files via the clipboard. → 10.079 HEX(ADECIMAL)

7.**062 Line Color option** A Slices preference option. It is accessed from File menu under Preferences > Slices, and allows a color for the slice lines to be selected from the pop-up.

7.**063 locking colors** Colors in the Color Table palette can be locked to prevent their loss when the number of colors is reduced and thus prevent them from being created by dithering. → 7.055 COLOR TABLE palette

7.**064 Looping option** Animation palette feature that enables an animation created in ImageReady to be played once, a specific number of times or indefinitely ("forever").

7.**065 Mac OS Color Table** ImageReady color table option. Color table based on the Mac OS's default eight-bit color table. This table, like the Windows Color Table, is based on the uniform sampling of RGB colors; for most practical purposes these two color tables are identical.

7.**066 Noise dither** Option in the Dithering Algorithm pop-up menu. Applies a random pattern of dithering that does not cause visible seams across slice boundaries, unlike Diffusion dither. → 7.052 APPLICATION DITHER

7.**067 Out state** Rollover state. Selecting an Out state determines the rollover state when the mouse is rolled out and away from the slice. → 7.078 ROLLOVERS

7.**068 Over state** Rollover state. Selecting an Over state determines the rollover state when the

7.060 *hard edged transparency*

*Note the obvious hard edge, and lack of gradation in the transparency on the left in the boundary of the image elements.*

*Soft*

*Hard*

mouse is rolled over a slice (mouse button released). → 7.078 ROLLOVERS

7.**069 Pattern dither** Option in the Dithering Algorithm pop-up menu. Applies a pattern of squares similar to halftone screens to simulate "missing" colors. → 7.052 APPLICATION DITHER

7.**070 Perceptual Color Table** ImageReady color table option. Color table biased towards colors to which the human eye has greater sensitivity.

7.**071 Photoshop Compensation** ImageReady color option. Choose this color display option, selected from the View > Preview menu, to show the current image with the colors adjusted to emulate their appearance in Photoshop. Note that this option is not available if the current image has no ICC profile embedded. → 4.116 ICC PROFILE

7.**072 Precision option** Slice option, enabling the precise position or dimensions of a slice to be specified. Select Show Options on the Slice palette menu.

7.**073 Progressive option** JPEG file option, selected from the Optimize palette. Selecting Progressive creates an image that appears in a web browser window at increasingly higher resolutions. Note that not all browsers support progressive JPEGs and that more RAM is needed to view such images.

7.**074 Rectangle tool** ImageReady tool. Enables bitmapped shapes (rectangle, rounded rectangle, and ellipse are available) to be drawn on an image.

7.**075 Redundant Pixel Optimization** ImageReady animated GIF specific optimization option. Choose Optimize by Redundant Pixel Removal from the Optimize Animation option in the Animation palette menu. This optimization makes all the pixels in a frame that are identical to those in the previous frame transparent. This is the default optimization. → 7.053 BOUNDING BOX OPTIMIZATION

7.**076 Regenerate** Process of recreating an optimized image, for example in the 2-up or 4-up displays. Regeneration can be triggered by clicking on the Optimized, 2-up or 4-up tabs at the top of the document. You can disable this feature from the Optimize palette by deselecting Auto Regenerate. A warning Regenerate button will appear in the lower right-hand corner of the image and can be clicked on to optimize the image. → 7.024 REPOPULATE VIEWS

7.**077 Rollover palette** Palette for creating rollover effects. → 7.078 ROLLOVERS

7.**078 rollovers** The rapid substitution of one (or more) image for another when the mouse pointer is rolled over the original image. Used extensively for navigation buttons on web pages and in multimedia presentations. The different image "states" can be defined (and hence different imagery presented to the viewer) for certain mouse movements such as Over (rolling the mouse over the slice), Down (dragging, with the mouse button down, over the slice), Click (a stationary mouse click over the slice), Out (mouse rolled out from the slice), Up

7.077 *Rollover palette*

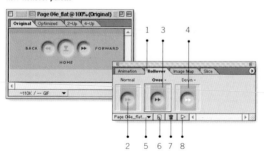

1  *Select Rollover palette tab*
2  *"Normal" image*
3  *Image when mouse is rolled over*
4  *Image when mouse is dragged over*

5  *Selects slice or image map for rollover*
6  *Create new rollover state*
7  *Selected rollover state*
8  *Preview behavior of rollover*

(releasing the mouse button over the slice), and Custom (for a custom effect). For the Custom option JavaScript code needs to be created. → 7.179 NAVIGATION BUTTON

7.**079 Selective Color Table** ImageReady color table option. The default color table, because it tends to lead to images with the best color integrity. Though similar to the Perceptual Color Table it gives increased emphasis to web-safe colors.

7.**080 Slice Select tool** ImageReady tool. Permits the selection of a slice or slices. Selections can be made either by clicking on a slice then shift-clicking on additional slices or by clicking on an auto-slice (or outside the image area) and dragging over the slices to be selected.

7.**081 Slice tool** (**2**) ImageReady tool. Illustrated by a scalpel icon, it enables the creation of slices. It is dragged over the slice area in a similar manner to the rectangular marquee. The slice created is a user-slice. The Slice tool also appears in the Photoshop menu from version 6 of that program. → 7.082 SLICES

7.**082 slices** Slices enable complex graphics and imagery to be created from and within a single document. A slice is a distinct rectangular area of an image that is assigned as a cell in an HTML table. When a slice is created using ImageReady, further slices are created automatically so that the entire image is assigned to cells in the HTML table. Slices drawn in an image are known as "user-slices." Auto-generated slices created by ImageReady are called "auto-slices." Every file contains one auto-slice, by default. From Version 6 slices also became a feature of Photoshop.

7.**083 Standard Macintosh Color** ImageReady color option selected from the View > Preview menu. Choose this color display option from a Windows PC to show the current image with the color adjusted to simulate a Mac OS display.

7.**084 Standard Windows Color** ImageReady color option selected from the View > Preview menu. Choose this color display option from a Mac OS computer and to show the current image with the color adjusted to simulate a Windows display.

7.**085 Styles** (**2**) Layer effects that can be saved and applied to other layers or images. Some predefined styles are included in ImageReady for immediate application. They can be selected by double-clicking on the appropriate icon shown in the Styles palette. Styles also appear in Photoshop 6.

7.**086 Styles palette** (**2**) ImageReady palette that displays currently available styles. Styles can be drag and dropped onto an image from this palette. A pull-out menu lets you add, change, remove, and edit styles or style sets. → 2.045 STYLES (1)

7.**087 Target Option** Image Slice option. The target indicates the browser frame in which a selected slice (or slices) with a specified URL will appear. Frames are flexible display tools that enable more than one web page to be displayed onscreen at one time; each frame hence comprises a separate page and the linked file needs a distinct URL.

7.082 *slices*

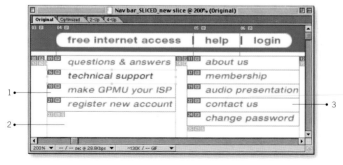

**1** *User slice*
**2** *Auto slice*
**3** *Individual rollovers*

### 7.088 *Tool options bar—image ready*

### 7.088 *Toolbar—image ready*

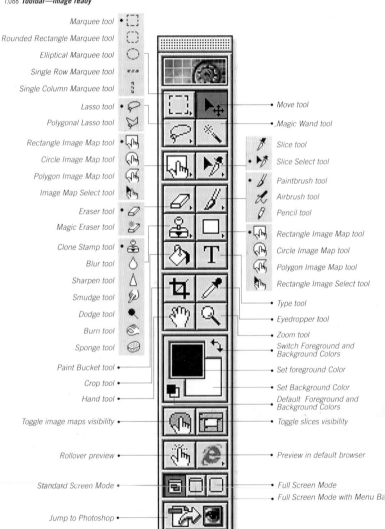

Marquee tool
Rounded Rectangle Marquee tool
Elliptical Marquee tool
Single Row Marquee tool
Single Column Marquee tool
Lasso tool
Polygonal Lasso tool
Rectangle Image Map tool
Circle Image Map tool
Polygon Image Map tool
Image Map Select tool
Eraser tool
Magic Eraser tool
Clone Stamp tool
Blur tool
Sharpen tool
Smudge tool
Dodge tool
Burn tool
Sponge tool
Paint Bucket tool
Crop tool
Hand tool
Toggle image maps visibility
Rollover preview
Standard Screen Mode
Jump to Photoshop

Move tool
Magic Wand tool
Slice tool
Slice Select tool
Paintbrush tool
Airbrush tool
Pencil tool
Rectangle Image Map tool
Circle Image Map tool
Polygon Image Map tool
Rectangle Image Select tool
Type tool
Eyedropper tool
Zoom tool
Switch Foreground and Background Colors
Set foreground Color
Set Background Color
Default Foreground and Background Colors
Toggle slices visibility
Preview in default browser
Full Screen Mode
Full Screen Mode with Menu Ba

7.088 **Toolbar** (**2**) ImageReady interface item. The main feature of the ImageReady workspace, which holds the major tools and controls, and by default appears down the left-hand edge of the workspace. Also known as the Toolbox, it shares its principal features with its Photoshop counterpart.

7.089 **Uncompensated Color** ImageReady color option. Choose this color display option, selected from the View > Preview menu, to show the current image with no color-based adjustments. This is the default option.

7.090 **Web Snap slider** Optimize palette feature. Use the slider to specify a tolerance for shifting colors to the closest web palette equivalents. A tolerance can also be set as a percentage in the Web Snap window.

7.091 **Web-Safe Color Table** ImageReady feature. Color table featuring only the standard 216 web-safe colors compatible with Mac OS eight-bit and Windows palettes. Use of this color table ensures that no dithering is used by web browsers when displaying the image. The drawback is that use of colors from this table can result in large file sizes.

7.092 **Web-Shifted Colors** ImageReady color option. Colors that have been shifted from their original value to a web-safe equivalent. → 7.047 WEB SHIFT; 7.048 WEB SHIFT/UNSHIFT SELECTED COLORS

7.093 **Windows Color Table** ImageReady color table option. This color table is based on the Windows default eight-bit color table. This table, like the Mac OS Color Table, is based on the uniform sampling of RGB colors; for most practical purposes, the two tables are identical.

## Web terms

7.094 **absolute URL** A complete web address, or "uniform resource locator" (URL), which takes you to a specific location within a web site rather than just to the home page of the site. Each absolute URL contains the full file path to the page document location on the host server and will appear, for example, as "http://www.yoursite.com/extrainfo/aboutyou/yourhouse.htm". → 7.220 URL

7.095 **active hyperlink** The currently selected link in a web browser, which is often differentiated from other links that appear on the same page by being displayed in another color.

7.096 **ActiveX Controls** Microsoft's proprietary technology for enhancing interactive web pages. Like Java "applets" ActiveX Controls can be downloaded from the Internet, but unlike Java applets they are not platform-independent and are mainly supported only in Microsoft Windows environments. → 1.225 JAVA

7.097 **address** (**2**) A string of letters or numbers used by Internet users to communicate with each other via e-mail. Also an informal name for a web site URL. → 7.125 E-MAIL; 7.234 WORLD WIDE WEB (WWW); 7.220 URL

7.098 **anchor** A text or graphic element with an HTML tag, which either links it to another location or acts as a destination for an incoming link. → 7.151 HTML; 7.213 TAG

7.099 **AOL** America Online. An Internet service provider (ISP). → 7.164 INTERNET SERVICE PROVIDER (ISP)

7.100 **associative linking** Hyperlinks organized by association rather than by formal classification.

7.101 **Asynchronous Digital Subscriber Line** (**ADSL**) A high-speed communications link capable of transmitting large amounts of data (such as a TV picture) in one direction and a small amount (such as a telephone call) in the other. Speeds of around 2 mbps (megabits per second) can be achieved – sixteen times faster than ISDN. → 7.156 ISDN

7.102 **attachment** An external file such as an image or text document "attached" to an e-mail message for electronic transmission. → 7.125 E-MAIL

7.103 **attribute** (**2**) A characteristic of an HTML tag, which is identified alongside the tag in order to describe it. → 7.151 HTML; 1.013 ATTRIBUTE (1); 7.213 TAG

7.104 **banner** An image on a web page, often animated, and designed to attract attention; usually an advertisement.

7.105 **baud** (pron.: bord) The number of signal changes transmitted per second during data transmission by modem. → 7.106 BAUD RATE

7.106 **baud rate** The speed at which a modem transmits data, or the number of "events" it can handle per second. Often used to describe the transmission speed of data itself, but since a single event can contain two or more bits, data speed is more correctly expressed in "bits per second" (bps). → 7.105 BAUD; 1.016 BIT

191

**7.107 bit rate** The speed at which data is transmitted across communications channels, measured in bits per second (bps). Modem speeds typically range from 2,400 bps to 56,000 bps, but higher speeds are measured in kilobits (kbps) or even megabits (mbps) per second – ISDN connections, for example, are usually either 65 kbps or 128 kbps. "Bit rate" is sometimes erroneously referred to as "baud rate." → 7.106 BAUD; 1.016 BIT; 7.106 BAUD RATE; 7.106 BPS; 7.156 ISDN

**7.108 Bookmark** A feature of Netscape's Navigator web browser, which remembers frequently visited web sites. The equivalent in Microsoft's Internet Explorer is called "Favorites." → 7.109 BROWSER

**7.109 browser** An application enabling you to view or "browse" World Wide Web pages across the Internet. The most widely used browsers are Netscape's "Navigator" and Microsoft's "Internet Explorer." Version numbers (sometimes referred to as "generations") are important, since these indicate the level of HTML that the browser supports. → 7.158 INTERNET; 7.234 WORLD WIDE WEB (WWW); 7.151 HTML

**7.110 bulleted list** An HTML style for web pages in which a bullet precedes each item on a list.

**7.111 bulletin board service (BBS)** A facility, usually noncommercial, which enables you to use a modem and telephone line to share information and exchange files on specialist subjects with other computer users of like mind. As distinct from commercial online service providers, which offer a wider range of services. → 7.164 ISP

**7.112 channel** A feature of web technology whereby information is automatically transmitted to your web browser, as distinct from having to request it yourself. → 7.191 PUSH (TECHNOLOGY)

**7.113 character shape player (CSP)** Software inside a web browser that enables you to view—or "play back"—the character shapes of embedded fonts in a "PFR" (portable font resource). → 10.200 TRUEDOC; 7.114 CHARACTER SHAPE RECORDER (CSR)

**7.114 character shape recorder (CSR)** Software inside an "authoring" (multimedia) application that enables you to define—or "record"—the character shapes of a font for embedding in a "PFR" (portable font

resource). → 10.200 TRUEDOC; 7.113 CHARACTER SHAPE PLAYER (CSP)

**7.115 CIX** Acronym for Commercial Internet Exchange, an alliance of Internet service providers (ISPs). → 7.164 INTERNET SERVICE PROVIDER (ISP)

**7.116 Common Gateway Interface (CGI)** A programming technique for transferring data between web server software and other applications, such as databases.

**7.117 cookie** A small piece of information deposited in your web browser (and thus on your hard disk) by a WWW site, storing such things as custom page settings or even personal information (e.g. your address or your password for that site). → 7.234 WORLD WIDE WEB (WWW)

**7.118 cyberspace** The notional environment in which communication takes place; particularly the Internet but also general telecommunication links and computer networks. → 10.163 VIRTUAL REALITY

**7.119 deprecated** The term applied to versions of HTML technology which are gradually being replaced or eradicated. → 7.151 HTML

**7.120 dial-up** A connection to the Internet or to a network which is made by dialing a telephone number for access.

**7.121 document** The entire contents of a single HTML file. HTML documents are generally referred to as "web pages," since this is how they are rendered for display by browsers. → 7.151 HTML; 7.109 BROWSER; 7.234 WORLD WIDE WEB (WWW)

**7.122 Document Type Definition (DTD)** A formal SGML specification for a document which lays out structural elements and markup definitions.

**7.123 dynamic HTML/DHTML** Dynamic hypertext markup language. A development of the basic HTML code that enables you to add such features as basic animations and highlighted buttons to web pages without relying on browser plug-ins. DHTML is built into version 4.0 or later web browsers. → 7.151 HTML; 7.109 BROWSER

**7.124 e-commerce** Contraction of electronic commerce. Commercial transactions conducted electronically over a network or the Internet. Used by business-to-business (B2B) transactions for some time, it is now becoming commonplace with business-to-consumer (B2C) transactions. → 7.125 E-MAIL

**7.125 e-mail** Contraction of electronic mail. Messages sent from your computer to someone else with a computer, either locally through a network or transmitted over telephone lines using a modem, usually via a central computer ("server"), which stores messages in the recipient's "mailbox" until they are collected. → 7.158 INTERNET; 7.209 SPAM/SPAMMING; 7.117 MIME; 1.107 SERVER

**7.126 e-tailing** Contraction of electronic retailing. The selling of goods to consumers via the Internet. → 7.124 E-COMMERCE

**7.127 e-text** Contraction of electronic text. A "text-only" file transmitted via the Internet.

**7.128 element** The items comprising a web page, for example text, graphics, animations.

**7.129 embedded program** A command or link written within text or lines of code on web pages. → 7.234 WORLD WIDE WEB (WWW)

**7.130 Extensible Markup Language (XML)** A probable successor to HTML (the underlying language used on web pages), offering more sophisticated control and formatting. XML allows the creation of user-defined tags, which expands the amount of information that can be provided about the data held in documents.

**7.131 extranet** The part of an organization's internal computer network or intranet, which is available to outside users; for example, information services for customers. Extranet hosting is a service provided by third parties to deliver resources by the Internet (or sometimes extranet) and managed either by that third party or by the organization. → 7.165 INTRANET

**7.132 Favorite** A feature of Microsoft's Internet Explorer web browser, which remembers frequently visited web sites. The equivalent in Netscape's Navigator is called "Bookmarks." → 7.109 BROWSER

**7.133 File Transfer Protocol (FTP)** A standard system for transmitting files between computers across the Internet or a network. Although web browsers incorporate FTP capabilities, dedicated FTP applications provide greater flexibility.

**7.134 forum** An online service that enables users to post messages which other users may respond or add to. These message "threads" are usually organized around special interests, such as software user groups or popular cultural themes. → 7.233 USENET; 7.184 NEWSGROUP

**7.135 global area network (GAN)** A worldwide network of computers, similar to the Internet but linking "wide area networks" (WANs). → 7.223 WIDE AREA NETWORK (WAN)

**7.136 global renaming** Software that updates all occurrences of a name throughout a web site when one instance of that name is altered. A cousin of the "Find" and "Replace" commands found in word processors.

**7.137 Gopher** A software "protocol" developed at the University of Minnesota that provides a means of accessing information across the Internet using services such as WAIS and Telnet. → 7.215 TELNET

**7.138 header file** Files that contain information identifying incoming data transmitted via the Internet.

**7.139 helper application** An application that assists a web browser in delivering or displaying information such as movie or sound files. → 7.109 BROWSER; 6.060 PLUG-IN

**7.140 history (list)** A list of visited web pages logged by your browser during a session on the Web. It provides a means of speedy access to pages already visited during that session. → 7.234 WORLD WIDE WEB (WWW)

**7.141 home page** On the World Wide Web, the term originally applied to the page that your own browser automatically links to when you launch it. It is now, however, more commonly used to describe the main page or contents page on a particular site, which provides links to all the other pages on that site.

**7.142 host** A networked computer that provides services to anyone who can access it, such as for e-mail, file transfer, and access to the Web. When you connect to the Internet, and thence to a web site, you'll be downloading information from that site's host.

**7.143 hostname** The name which identifies the computer hosting a web site.

**7.144 HotJava** A web browser developed by Sun Microsystems and written in Java programming language. → 1.225 JAVA; 7.109 BROWSER

**7.145 hotlist, hot list** A theme-related list on a web page that provides links to other pages or sites dedicated to that theme.

**7.146 HTTPd** Hypertext Transfer Protocol daemon. A collection of programs on a web server that provide web services, such as request handling. → 7.195 REQUEST

**7.147 HTTPS** Hypertext Transfer Protocol, Secure. Synonymous with "HTTP," but providing a secure link for such things as commercial transactions (online shopping with credit cards, for example) or accessing password-protected information.

**7.148 hyperlink** A contraction of "hypertext link." An embedded link to other documents, usually identified by being underlined or highlighted in a different color. Clicking on or selecting a hyperlink takes you to another document, part of a document or web site. → 7.095 ACTIVE HYPERLINK; 7.150 HYPERTEXT

**7.149 hypermedia** The combination of graphics, text, movies, sound, and other elements accessible via hypertext links in an online document or web page. → 7.148 HYPERLINK

**7.150 hypertext** A programming concept that links any single word or group of words to an unlimited number of others, typically text on a web page, which has an embedded link to other documents or web sites. Hypertext links are usually underlined and/or in a different color to the rest of the text, and are activated by clicking on them. Web browsers are normally configured so that the hypertext link changes color after a visit to indicate that the visit has occurred.> → 7.148 HYPERLINK

**7.151 Hypertext Markup Language (HTML)** A text-based "page description language" (PDL) used to format documents published on the World Wide Web, and which can be viewed with web browsers. → 9.112 PDL

**7.152 Hypertext Transfer Protocol (HTTP)** A text-based set of rules by which files on the World Wide Web are transferred, defining the commands that web browsers use to communicate with web servers. The vast

majority of World Wide Web addresses, or "URLs," are prefixed with "http://". → 7.151 HTML; 7.220 URL; 7.109 BROWSER

**7.153 ID selector** A style sheet rule for a web page element. → 1.114 STYLE SHEET

**7.154 image map** An image that contains a series of embedded links to other documents or web sites. These links are activated when the appropriate area of the image is clicked on. For example, an image of a globe may incorporate an embedded link for each visible country which, when clicked, will take the user to a document giving more information about that country.

**7.155 index page** The first page of any web site, which is selected automatically by the browser if it is named "index.htm" or "index.html".

**7.156 Integrated Services Digital Network (ISDN)** A telecommunication technology that transmits data on special digital lines rather than standard analog lines and is thus much faster. Note that ADSL (Asynchronous Digital Subscriber Line) links are even faster than ISDN lines. → 7.101 ADSL

**7.157 interlacing (2)** A technique of displaying an image on a web page so that the image reveals increasing detail as it downloads. Interlacing is usually offered as an option when saving images in GIF, PNG, and JPEG ("progressive") formats in image-editing applications. → 3.025 INTERLACED GIF; 3.045 PNG; 3.047 PROGRESSIVE JPEG

**7.158 Internet** The world-wide network of computers linked by phone (or other

**7.145 hotlist, hot list**

**7.154 image map**

*Here the embedded links are shown by the rectangle and circle (above); they would not normally be visible but the cursor would change to a "hand" when placed over either.*

*The list (left) gives hotlist of websites associated with (in this case) the question posed at the start.*

connections), providing individual and corporate users with access to information, companies, newsgroups, discussion areas, and more. → 7.234 WORLD WIDE WEB (WWW)

7.**159 Internet access provider** (**IAP**) → 7.164 Internet service provider (ISP)

7.**160 Internet Explorer** A cross-platform web browser produced by Microsoft. → 7.109 BROWSER; 7.180 NAVIGATOR

7.**161 Internet Protocol** (**IP**) The networking rules that tie computers together across the Internet. → 7.162 INTERNET PROTOCOL (IP) ADDRESS; 7.158 INTERNET

7.**162 Internet Protocol** (**IP**) **address** The unique numeric address of a particular computer or server on the Internet (or any TCP/IP network). Each one is unique and consists of a dotted decimal notation, for example 194.152.64.68. → 7.161 IP; 7.218 TCP

7.**163 Internet Relay Chat** (**IRC**) An Internet facility provided by some ISPs that allows multiple users to type messages to each other in real-time on different "channels" sometimes referred to as "rooms." → 7.164 INTERNET SERVICE PROVIDER (ISP)

7.**164 Internet service provider** (**ISP**) Any organization that provides access to the Internet. At its most basic this may merely be a telephone number for connection, but most ISPs also provide other services such as e-mail addresses and space for your own web pages. Also called "Internet access providers (IAP)." → 7.111 BBS

7.**165 intranet** A network of computers similar to the Internet but to which the general public do not have access. A sort of in-house

Internet service, intranets are used mainly by large corporations, governments, and educational institutions to share resources and distribute information that is normally classified or to which the organization does not want widespread access. → 7.158 INTERNET

7.**166 ISOC** Acronym for the Internet Society, a governing body to which the Internet Architecture Board (IAB) reports.

7.**167 kermit** An older (and slow) communications protocol.

7.**168 layout element** Any component in the layout of an HTML document—a web page, for example—such as a graphic, list, rule, or paragraph. → 7.151 HTML

7.**169 link** A pointer, such as a highlighted piece of text, in an HTML document (a web page, for example) or multimedia presentation. It takes the user to another location, page, or screen by clicking on it. → 7.148 HYPERLINK

7.**170 MacTCP** Acronym for Macintosh transmission control protocol, the Mac OS version of TCP. → 7.218 TCP

7.**171 mailto:** A hyperlink code used in web pages or e-mail applications which, when prefixed to an e-mail address and double-clicked, creates a new e-mail message for sending direct to the addressee. → 7.125 E-MAIL

7.**172 Majordomo** A system of automated multiple electronic mailing lists that users can subscribe to or unsubscribe from at will.

7.**173 markup** (**1**) The technique of embedding "tags" (HTML instructions) within special characters, which tell a program such as a web browser how to display a page. → 7.151 HTML; 7.174 MARKUP LANGUAGE

195

7.157 *interlacing*

*The total image appears with increasing detail (left, far left from 1 to 3) on a web page as it downloads when saved using the "Progressive" option.*

**7.174 markup language** A defined set of rules describing the way files are displayed by any particular method. HTML is one such language, used for creating web pages. → 7.151 HTML; 7.153 MARKUP (1)

**7.175 meta-information** This is the optional information provided in an HTML document to help search engine databases place web sites in the correct category. This facility is often abused by less scrupulous web sites and is therefore generally falling out of favor with search engine providers whose "spider" programs trawl the Web to add sites to their databases. → 7.210 SPIDER

**7.176 moving banner** An animated advertisement used within web pages. → 7.104 BANNER

**7.177 multipurpose Internet mail extensions (MIME)** A format for conveying web documents and related files across the Internet, typically via e-mail.

**7.178 navigation bar** A special bar in a web browser, web page, or multimedia presentation that helps you to "navigate" through pages by clicking on buttons or text. → 1.079 NAVIGATE

**7.179 navigation button** A button in a web browser, web page, or multimedia presentation that links you to a particular location or page. → 1.079 NAVIGATE; 7.178 NAVIGATION BAR

**7.180 Navigator** A cross-platform web browser produced by Netscape. → 7.160 INTERNET EXPLORER; 7.109 BROWSER; 7.182 NETSCAPE

**7.181 netiquette** A contraction of the words "net" and "etiquette" describing the notional rules for polite behavior by users of the Internet.

**7.182 Netscape** Company responsible for pioneering the web browser with its Navigator and Communicator products. Now part of AOL.

**7.183 Network News Transfer Protocol (NNTP)** A standard for the retrieval and posting of news articles. → 7.223 USENET; 7.184 NEWSGROUP

**7.184 newsgroup** A group of like-minded individuals who "post" and collect articles of common interest on the Internet. → 7.223 USENET

**7.185 node (2)** A basic object, such as a graphic within a scene, used in the VRML environment. → 7.226 VRML

**7.186 orphan file** A file on a web site that is not referred to by any link or button and thus cannot be reached by any means other than through its absolute URL—in other words, to find it you must know its exact pathname.

**7.187 page flipping** An HTML structure for web pages which allows users to see successive screens without needing to scroll. → 7.151 HTML

**7.188 Point-to-Point Protocol (PPP)** The most common means of establishing dial-up connections to the Internet. It provides a method for transmitting packets over serial point-to-point links. It also allows you to use other standard protocols (such as IPX and TCP/IP) over a standard telephone connection and can be used for local area networks (LAN) connections.

**7.189 portal** An Internet "front page" that provides controlled access to users. Users accessing the Internet from a portal are given quick links to relevant sites. Some

7.151 *Hypertext Markup Language (HTML)*

```
HTML: www.honestjohn.co.uk/pages/3_latest_news/news.php

<html>

<head>
    <meta http-equiv="content-type" content="text/html;charset=iso-8859-1">
    <title>
    2001-04-20 : Restyled Clio on the way
    </title>
<STYLE TYPE="text/css">
body { color: black; font-style: normal; font-weight: normal; font-size: 8pt; line-height: 11pt; font-family: Verdana, Aria
h3 { color: #696969; font-size: 10.5pt; font-family: Verdana, Arial, Helvetica, Geneva, Swiss, SunSans-Regular }
a { color: #988d06 }
h4 { color: #ff4500; font-size: 8pt; font-family: Verdana, Arial, Helvetica, Geneva, Swiss, SunSans-Regular }
p { color: black; font-style: normal; font-weight: normal; font-size: 8pt; line-height: 11pt; font-family: Verdana, Arial,
td { color: black; font-style: normal; font-weight: normal; font-size: 8pt; line-height: 11pt; font-family: Verdana, Arial,
</style>

<style type="text/css"><!--
.date { color: #ff4500; font-weight: normal; font-size: smaller }
.news_item { color: #696969; font-weight: bold }-->
</style>

</head>

<body bgcolor="white">
    <table border="0" cellpadding="0" cellspacing="0" width="99%">
    <tr align="left" valign="top">
        <td>
        <h3>Restyled Clio on the way</h3>
<span class="date">20 April 2001</span><p>
A revamped Clio will be on sale in June. Although the basic design remains the same, with the big bum back-end complete wit
<br>

<br>
Inside, the dashboard and centre console have been revised to take a double-clock binnacle and optional climate control and
<br>

<br>
The Clio will be powered by a choice of seven units (five petrol, two diesel), including Renault's new 67.3mpg 1.5dCi commo
<br>

<br>
Safety features include Emergency Brake Assist, fitted as standard across the range except in the Clio Renaultsport 172.
```

restrict access only to those sites while others provide unrestrained access to the Web. Used to gather resources in one place: Perhaps for educational purposes or to limit children's web access to preferred sites.

7.190 **Post Office Protocol (POP)** An e-mail protocol for retrieval and storage—a "POP account" is what you tell your e-mail software to use to send and retrieve your mail.

7.191 **push (technology)** A web-based technology by which information, distributed to designated groups of users via "channels," can be updated immediately whenever changes are made. As distinct from the normal web activity of browsing and requesting information at will ("pull").

7.192 **readability** The ease and comfort with which a text can be read, particularly in the context of web pages.

7.193 **RealAudio** A proprietary helper application that enables audio playback in web browsers.

7.194 **relative URL** A link that is connected to the current web page's URL so that a browser looks for the link in the same location—i.e. web site—as the web page currently being displayed.

7.195 **request** The act of clicking on a button or link in a web browser. You are, in fact, making a request to a remote server for an HTML document to be sent to you.

7.196 **response** On a network, the server's reply to a user's request for information. → 7.195 REQUEST

7.197 **robot** Referred to colloquially as a "bot," a robot is a program which roams the World Wide Web, gathering and cataloging information, usually for use by search engines such as Yahoo and AltaVista. → 7.198 SEARCH ENGINE; 7.210 SPIDER

7.198 **search engine** The part of a program, such as a database, that seeks out information in response to requests made by the user. On the Web, search engines such as Yahoo, HotBot, and AltaVista provide sophisticated criteria for searching, and provide summaries of each result as well as the web site addresses for retrieving more information. → 7.197 ROBOT; 7.199 SEARCH TOOL

7.199 **search tool** A program which enables specific web pages to be searched. → 7.198 SEARCH ENGINE

7.200 **secure area** The area of a web site in which personal or sensitive information can be entered by users. Secure areas are usually identified by the prefix "https://" in the URL and are particularly important for commercial transactions made via the Web. → 7.147 HTTPS

7.201 **serial line Internet protocol (SLIP)** A communications protocol that supports an Internet connection over a dial-up line. Now superseded by PPP. → 7.188 PPP

7.202 **service provider** → 7.164 Internet service provider (ISP).

7.203 **shocked** The term applied to web pages that contain material prepared with Macromedia's Shockwave technology, and thus require the Shockwave plug-in to be downloaded or installed prior to any shocked documents being viewed. → 7.204 SHOCKWAVE

7.204 **Shockwave** A proprietary technology developed by Macromedia for creating Director presentations, which can be delivered across the Internet and viewed with a web browser. The Shockwave plug-in (often called the Flash plug-in), which enables Shockwave material to be viewed on a computer, must be loaded on the viewing machine.> → 7.203 SHOCKED

7.205 **Simple Mail Transfer Protocol (SMTP)** A text-based TCP/IP protocol used to transfer mail messages over the Internet. → 7.218 TCP; 7.161 IP; 7.190 POP

7.206 **sitemap** An outline view of all the pages on a particular web site. → 7.234 WORLD WIDE WEB (WWW)

7.207 **source code** An alternative name for HTML. → 7.151 HTML

7.208 **spacer** A blank, transparent GIF, one pixel wide, used to space elements on a web page.

7.209 **spam/spamming** A colloquial term for an unsolicited e-mail or newsgroup posting, usually advertising material. The term derives from the television comedy show "Monty Python's Flying Circus" where, in one sketch, a restaurant menu lists food items which can only be ordered if accompanied by "spam," e.g. sausage and spam, egg and spam, spam and spam, etc. → 7.125 E-MAIL; 7.184 NEWSGROUP

7.210 **spider** A program that tirelessly roams the World Wide Web, gathering and cataloging information, typically for use by search engines. → 7.197 ROBOT; 7.198 SEARCH ENGINE

7.211 **SSL** Secure Sockets Library. A programming "library" devised by Netscape to help programmers add secure areas to web sites. Also denotes the Secure Sockets Layer, the software "layer" that encrypts important and confidential information. → 7.200 SECURE AREA; 7.147 HTTPS

**7.212 Standard Generalized Markup Language (SGML)** An ISO markup standard for defining documents that can be used by any computer, regardless of platform. → 10.092 ISO

**7.213 tag** The formal name for a markup language formatting command. A tag is switched on by placing a command inside angle brackets and switched off again by repeating the same command but inserting a forward slash before the command. For example "<bold>" makes text that follows appear in bold and "</bold>" switches bold text off.

**7.214 Tags Case Option** An HTML preference, selected from File menu > Preferences > HTML. Choose the case for all HTML tags, such as all uppercase, initial capitalization, or all lowercase.

**7.215 Telnet** The Internet standard protocol that enables you to connect to a remote computer and control it as if you were there, even if you are thousands of miles away from it. → 1.402 DUMB TERMINAL

**7.216 thread** Postings to an online newsgroup or e-mail distribution list on a theme in which a group of subscribers have a particular interest. The messages are usually followed by any replies, and the replies to those replies.

**7.217 title** Text that appears in the titlebar of a web page.

**7.218 Transmission Control Protocol (TCP)** The industry standard developed by the US Department of Defense for providing data communication between computers, such as across the Internet. It ensures reliability by retransmitting lost and corrupted data packets, and ensures that an application on the receiving end of a TCP connection will receive bits and bytes in the same order in which they were sent.

**7.219 Uniform Resource Identifier (URI)** A routine that identifies resources available to the Web, such as a URL. → 7.220 URL

**7.220 Uniform Resource Locator (URL)** The Uniform Resource Locator, or URL, is the unique address of a page on the Web. Each resource on the Internet has a unique URL that begins with letters that identify the resource type (and thus the protocol to be used), such as "http" or "ftp", followed by a colon and two forward slashes, after which comes the "domain name" ("host"), which can have several parts to it, then, after a slash, the directory name followed by path names to any particular file; for example, http://www.digiwis.com/home.htm. Usually if a file name is not stated, the browser will default to the file name "index.html" and/or "index.htm", which is usually the home page. → 7.152 HTTP; 7.094 DNS; 7.094 ABSOLUTE URL; 7.194 RELATIVE URL

**7.221 Uniform Resource Name (URN)** A permanent name for a web resource. → 7.220 URL

**7.222 URL-encoded text** A method of encoding text for passing requests from your web

7.206 *sitemap*

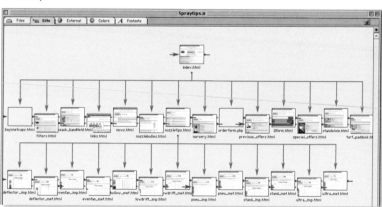

browser to a server. → 7.220 URL; 7.195 REQUEST

7.**223 Usenet** The accepted acronym for the user's network, in which a vast number of articles, categorized into newsgroups, are posted by individuals on every conceivable subject. These articles are hosted on servers throughout the world on which you can post your own articles to people who subscribe to those newsgroups. Special "newsreader" software is required to view the articles. → 7.184 NEWSGROUP; 7.134 FORUM

7.**224 user group** A group who share their experiences, their knowledge and problems, etc., either generally or in relation to a specific software application or a type of computer.

7.**225 ViewMovie** A Netscape plug-in for viewing animations. → 6.060 PLUG-IN; 7.182 NETSCAPE

7.**226 VRML** Virtual Reality Modeling Language, an HTML-type programming language designed to create 3D scenes called "virtual worlds."

7.**227 watermarking** The technique of applying a tiled graphic to the background of a web page that remains fixed, no matter what foreground materials scroll across it.

7.**228 web authoring** The process of creating documents (usually in HTML or XML format) suitable for publishing on the World Wide Web. → 2.151 HTML; 7.130 XML; 7.234 WORLD WIDE WEB (WWW)

7.**229 web master** The person responsible for managing a web site.

7.**230 web page** A published HTML document on the World Wide Web. → 7.151 HTML; 7.234 WORLD WIDE WEB (WWW)

7.**231 web server** A computer ("host") that is dedicated to web services.

7.**232 web site** The address, location (on a server), and the collection of documents and resources for any interlinked set of web pages.

7.**233 wide area network (WAN)** A series of local area networks (LANs) connected together by terrestrial or satellite links. A WAN is often a series of LAN installations at the separate sites of an organization. → 1.146 LAN; 1.152 NETWORK; 7.135 GAN

7.**234 World Wide Web (WWW)** The term used to describe the entire collection of web servers all over the world, which are connected to the Internet. The term also describes the particular type of Internet access architecture, which uses a combination of HTML and various graphic formats, such as GIF and JPEG, to publish formatted text that can be read by web browsers. Also called "the Web" or "W3." → 7.158 INTERNET; 7.109 BROWSER

7.**235 XMODEM** A standard communications protocol that transfers data in blocks of 128 K. → 7.236 YMODEM; 7.237 ZMODEM

7.**236 YMODEM** A standard communications protocol that provides error-checking while transferring data. → 7.235 XMODEM; 7.237 ZMODEM

7.**237 ZMODEM** A standard communications protocol that can provide continuous data transfer despite interruptions or pauses. → 7.235 XMODEM; 7.236 YMODEM

7.227 *Watermarking*

# PHOTOGRAPHY

## Techniques

8.**001 astrophotography** Photography of any astronomical body.

8.**002 bracketing** A series of exposures of the same subject, each one varying progressively to either side of the estimated exposure which allows for uncertainties in exposure and processing. Bracketed shots usually involve altering exposure times (so that depth of field is maintained) but they can also be made by altering the f-number. → 8.073 EXPOSURE; 8.074 EXPOSURE LATITUDE; 8.078 F-NUMBER

8.**003 burn** Giving additional exposure to regions of an enlarged print to make those regions darker on the finished print. Masks with apertures are usually employed to control the position and extent of any such actions. Duplicated in Photoshop by the Burn tool. → 2.069 BURN TOOL

8.**004 camera shake** The term describing usually undesirable movement of a camera at the moment a photograph is taken, resulting in a blurred or ghosted image. Usually occurs when a camera is hand-held and not mounted on a rigid support.

8.**005 candids** Photos of people taken without their obvious knowledge that capture them in natural, unposed activities.

8.**006 closeup** Photograph taken with the camera close to the lens' closest focusing distance. Normally applies to shots taken at distances of between several inches and a yard.

8.**007 composition** The effective arrangement of elements within a scene. This can be achieved in-camera or subsequently by cropping the original scene, or even by digital manipulation. Various rules exist with regard to composition, but many of the most powerful photographs are so because they break the same rules. → 8.162 IN-CAMERA

8.**008 differencing** A process of subtracting the pixel information of one image from another, usually of the same subject, from the same position. The difference image that results shows only the changes (in position, color, or other parameters) that have occurred between the shots. Used in forensic and medical applications.

8.**009 direct reading** The common term for taking a meter-reading directly from light reflected from a subject.

8.002 *bracketing*

8.003 *burn*

*original print*

*sky burned in*

8.**010 follow focus** A camera focusing technique used with a moving subject, in which the focusing ring is turned at exactly the rate necessary to maintain constant focus on the moving subject.

8.**011 high key** An image comprising predominantly light tones. → 8.012 LOW KEY

8.**012 low key** A photographic image that is given overall dark tones either by lighting or by processing. → 10.023 CONTRAST

8.**013 macrophotography** The photography of large-scale objects, often used erroneously to describe "photomacrography," which is close-up photography. → 8.019 PHOTOMICROGRAPHY

8.**014 multiple exposure** Two or more photographic images, which may be the same or different, superimposed during exposure or processing to form a single image.

8.**015 panning** Technique of moving the camera such that a moving object maintains the same position relative to the viewfinder when taking the picture. The net result is a sharp image of the moving subject against a blurred background.

8.**016 panorama** Term used to describe an image with an aspect ratio of at least 2:1 but not necessarily (in photographic terms) of a landscape.

8.**017 photogram** A photographic image made by placing an object (which might be opaque, translucent, or transparent) on a sheet of emulsion and briefly exposing it to light, resulting in a kind of shadow picture.

8.**018 photomacrography** → 8.013 macrophotography

8.**019 photomicrography** Photography at great magnifications using a microscope. → 8.013 MACROPHOTOGRAPHY

8.**020 posterize** Originally a "traditional" photographic technique where the number of shades of gray (or colors) in an image is reduced to a specified number. The result is more effective if this number is low. Photoshop can produce the same effect instantly. From the Image menu choose Adjust > Posterize to call up the Posterize dialog box, and enter the required number of levels. For a color image the number of levels set will apply to each of the channels. So choosing four levels for an RGB image will give twelve colors—four red, four green, and four blue. → 2.319 POSTERIZE

8.**021 stereography** A type of photograph in which two simultaneous exposures are made in such a way as to give the impression of three-dimensional depth.

## Processing

8.**022 back printing** Data printed on the reverse of a print by automated printing equipment. Typical data includes date of processing and frame number and any compensations applied. APS cameras can provide more detailed information, such as actual time and date of exposure and even selected text titles. → 8.109 APS

8.**023 blowup** Colloquial term for an enlargement made from a small negative or slide.

8.**024 chemical reversal** Chemical treatment of a photographic image to convert it from

8.004 *camera shake*

8.014 *multiple exposure*

negative to positive, or vice versa. In reversal films and original monochrome images the colur layers are reversed by chemical reversal to give the final positive image.

8.**025 clip test** A small piece cut from the end of an exposed roll of film which is processed in advance to determine whether any adjustment may be necessary in processing.

8.**026 contact print / contact** Photographic print made by placing an original negative or positive film in direct contact with the photographic paper. A contact sheet comprises (usually) an entire film contact-printed onto a single sheet of paper.

8.**027 darkroom** Any light-tight room used for the processing and handling of light-sensitive materials. The term "digital darkroom" has been applied to a computer system that includes image input and output devices and is equipped with image-editing software.

8.**028 developer** The chemical solution used to convert an invisible latent image (on a film emulsion or photographic paper) into a visible image.

8.**029 developing tank** A light-tight (usually) tank used for processing rolls of film. Allows the processor to work with economical amounts of chemicals and in daylight. There are also tanks capable of fully automatic operation and for paper processing.

8.**030 dodge / dodging** A method of obtaining lighter areas in a photographic print by the selective use of masking (hiding relevant areas from light). The Dodge tool in Photoshop digitally simulates this mechanical technique. The opposite effect—darkening areas of an image—is called burning. → 6.041 MASKING; 8.003 BURN

8.**031 easel** Baseboard of an enlarger that holds photographic paper flat during exposure. Usually incorporates a masking frame for setting print borders and cropping.

8.**032 enlargement** A reproduction that is greater than 100% of its original size. Usually applied to prints (or copy transparencies/negatives) made from a medium format (or smaller) original. → 8.023 BLOWUP

8.**033 enlarger** Device for enlarging photographic negatives or transparencies to print them. Comprises a light source, negative/slide holder, lens assembly, and easel. Adjustments for focus, image size, and (where appropriate) color are also provided.

8.**034 fixer / fixing bath** Usually the penultimate processing solution (prior to washing) for a film emulsion. Removes any light-sensitive material not affected by the developer. Sometimes called "hypo" in black and white photography.

8.**035 grade** The classification of photographic printing paper by the degree to which it affects the contrast of an image. Although not all makes are the same, the most common range from 0 (the lowest contrast, for use with high-contrast negatives) to 5 (the highest contrast, for use with low-contrast negatives). → 10.023 CONTRAST

8.**036 intensification** A technique for chemically adjusting the density of developed photographic emulsion. The chemicals are known as "intensifiers."

8.015 *panning*

8.016 *panorama*

**8.037 latent image** An image that lies dormant until something happens to it to make it appear. In photography, this is used to describe an image recorded on film at the point of exposure that only becomes apparent after it is processed.

**8.038 minilab** A machine capable of processing and printing unexposed film. Normally operated by photofinishers in retail applications, they offer the now ubiquitous "one hour service."

**8.039 negative carrier, holder** The physical support for negatives, or negative strip, when placed in enlarger. Smaller formats are normally supported by their edges, though carriers for larger formats often have glass plates to prevent negative curvature. Similar devices are used to perform the same function in film scanners.

**8.040 positive** An image emulating an original scene, made photographically on paper or film, usually from a negative. Photoshop can achieve the same result from a negative image using the Invert command. → 8.131 NEGATIVE/NEG; 2.313 INVERT

**8.041 print** A photographic image, traditionally made from a negative but now equally likely to come from a transparency or be a computer output.

**8.042 printing in** Alternate term for the darkroom technique of burning in areas of a print. → 8.003 BURN

**8.043 processing** The developing, fixing, and washing of photographic media to produce prints, negatives, or transparencies.

**8.044 pull-processing** Giving film a shorter development time than normal to compensate for overexposure or to reduce contrast. → 8.045 PUSH-PROCESSING

**8.045 push-processing** Giving film a longer development time than normal to compensate for underexposure or to increase contrast. → 8.044 PULL-PROCESSING

**8.046 reticulation** A variously desirable or undesirable effect of photographic processing in which the film emulsion adopts a disrupted, "crazed" pattern. Usually a result of temperature changes in processing or incorrect chemical formulations. From the Greek meaning "netlike."

**8.047 Sabattier effect** The partial reversal of tone or color in a photographic emulsion due to brief exposure to light during development. → 8.024 CHEMICAL REVERSAL

**8.048 safelight** A lamp used in darkrooms designed to allow the user to see his or her way around but without fogging film or paper. In truth, apart from some esoteric film emulsion/light combinations, there is no true safelight.

**8.049 sepia toning** A process of making sepia prints from standard black-and-white prints. Various bleaches and dyes are employed in the process. Similar effects can be achieved with Photoshop. → 4.059 SEPIA

**8.050 spotting** Physical retouching of a photographic print with dyes or watercolor stains to remove blemishes due to dust or scratches on the original negative. Digitally a tool such as Rubber Stamp could be used to remove blemishes. The Dust & Scratches filter can remove large numbers of blemishes, but can compromise detail in the image.

**8.051 stop bath** Processing solution (normally acetic acid) that is used between the developer and the fixer to arrest development and extend the life of the fixer.

**8.052 toning** Adding a brown or blue (usually) tone to a photographic print, supplanting the usual black silver halide component.

**8.053 unsharp masking (USM)** A traditional film compositing technique used for "sharpening" an image. An image is combined with a slightly defocused positive of the same image. In this image pair the extremes of brightness are reduced allowing fine detail in the original (sharp) image to be discerned. This can also be achieved digitally, with image-editing applications which use filters to enhance the details in a scanned image by increasing the contrast of pixels, the exact amount depending on various criteria such as the "threshold" specified and the radius of the area around each pixel. → 8.099 SHARPNESS; 6.039 INTERPOLATION

**8.054 variable contrast (VC) paper** Specialized printing paper whose contrast grade can be altered using colored filters. → 8.035 GRADE

## Photography terms

**8.055 acutance** The quality of an edge in a photographic image.

**8.056 angle of view** The amount of a scene included in a photographic picture, determined by a combination of the focal length of the lens and the film format. It is conventionally measured in degrees across the diagonal of the film format. → 8.079 FOCAL LENGTH; 8.122 FILM FORMAT

8.**057 aperture** The opening in a camera lens through which the imaging light passes en route to the film plane. The size of the aperture is usually described using f-numbers. → 8.078 F-NUMBER

8.**058 aperture priority** Camera exposure mode which allows the user to set the aperture; a corresponding shutter speed is set automatically. → 8.100 SHUTTER PRIORITY; 8.175 PROGRAM EXPOSURE

8.**059 autofocus (AF)** Method by which a camera lens can automatically focus on a selected element or position in the field of view.

8.**060 background (2)** Description of those elements visible in a scene that are behind the subject of the scene.

8.**061 brightness range** The range of tones in a photographic subject, from darkest to lightest.

8.**062 bulb (setting)** Shutter speed setting that allows the shutter to remain open as long as the shutter release is pressed. Compare with the time (T) exposure setting, which opens the shutter on the first press of the shutter release and closes it on the second press. → 8.106 TIME EXPOSURE

8.**063 camera angle** A general term describing the viewpoint of the camera, but also specifically used with reference to its angle from the horizontal. Converging verticals can occur if camera angles relative to the horizontal are used (particularly) for architectural subjects, causing obvious image distortion.

8.**064 center-weighted exposure** In automatic "through-the-lens" (TTL) metered cameras, the method of measuring exposure whereby the calculation is based on the tones in the center of the picture. → 8.185 THROUGH-THE-LENS (TTL) METER

8.**065 Cibachrome** A proprietary process for obtaining photographic color prints directly from transparencies, developed by Ilford under its then-parent Ciba-Geigy. Characterized by powerful color (due to embedded dyes) and a high-gloss finish (the original Cibachrome "paper" was a plastic film). Now marketed as Ilfochrome.

8.**066 circle of confusion** Illuminated area produced by a lens when a point source is focused. For extended sources the overlapping circles of confusion result in a "blurred" effect.

8.**067 color fringing** Effect that manifests itself as a colored rim or halo around an object. Can be due to lens aberrations, CCD artifacts, or poor convergence in the CRT monitor. → 8.208 CCD; 1.365 CRT

8.**068 coma** A photographic lens aberration that causes blurring at the edge of a picture.

8.**069 dense** A too dark description of an image.

8.**070 depth of field** The range—in front of or behind the point of focus—in a photograph in which the subject remains acceptably sharp or focused. Depth of field is controlled by the lens aperture—the smaller the aperture, the greater the depth of field or sharpness. → 8.057 APERTURE; 8.082 FOCUS; 8.079 FOCAL LENGTH

8.057 *aperture*

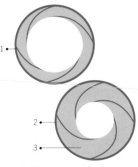

1 *Wide aperture*
2 *Narrow aperture*
3 *Diaphragm*

8.070 *depth of field*

8.**071 depth of focus** The distance through which the film plane can be moved from the point of focus and still record an acceptably sharp image. → 8.082 FOCUS; 8.079 FOCAL LENGTH; 8.070 DEPTH OF FIELD

8.**072 diopter / dioptre** The measurement of the refractive properties of a lens, such as those used for closeup photography. A concave lens is measured in negative diopters, a convex lens in positive diopters. → 8.164 LENS

8.**073 exposure** The amount of light that is permitted to reach a photosensitive material, such as photographic film, so that an image is recorded. This is usually a combination of the length of time and the intensity at which the light shines upon the material.

8.**074 exposure latitude** A range of exposure settings appropriate for a given photographic film that will still provide an acceptable result.

8.**075 field curvature** A lens aberration in which the plane of sharpest focus is curved rather than the flat surface needed at the film plane.

8.**076 filter factor** The amount of compensation required (lengthening) of a photographic exposure if a filter is used. → 8.147 COLOR FILTERS

8.**077 flat** Image that lacks sufficient color or contrast and consequently lacks perceived "depth." A subjective rather than quantitative parameter.

8.**078 f-number** The calibration of the aperture size of a photographic lens. This is the ratio of the focal length ("f" = focal) to the diameter of the aperture. The numbers are marked on the equipment. For example, a camera lens normally calibrated in a standard series would include the following numbers: f1, f1.4, f2, f2.8, f4, f5.6, f8, f11, f16, f22, f32, and so on, and these set the aperture size. The maximum amount of light that can be transmitted through a lens determines the "speed" of a lens—a lens with a minimum aperture of e.g. f1 is a "fast lens" (it lets in more light), while a lens with a minimum aperture of f3.5 is described as a "slow lens." → 8.057 APERTURE; 8.150 DIAPHRAGM

8.**079 focal length** The distance between the optical center of a lens and its point of focus (usually the film plane) when the lens is focused on infinity. It is normally measured in millimeters. → 8.056 ANGLE OF VIEW; 8.078 F-NUMBER

8.**080 focal plane** The plane at which a camera lens forms a sharp image; also the "film plane," the point at which the image is recorded.

8.**081 focal range** The range over which a camera or lens is able to focus on a subject. On interchangeable lenses the range is usually marked on the lens barrel and might be, for example, 0.5 m to infinity.

8.**082 focus** The point at which light rays converge to produce a sharp image. In a camera this is achieved by the lens. → 8.070 DEPTH OF FIELD; 8.079 FOCAL LENGTH

8.**083 foreground** The visible area or objects between the camera and the main subject.

8.**084 grain** The density of tiny light-sensitive silver bromide crystals—or the overlapping

8.079 *focal length*

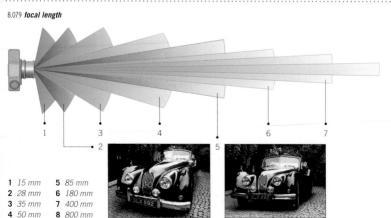

| | | | |
|---|---|---|---|
| **1** | *15 mm* | **5** | *85 mm* |
| **2** | *28 mm* | **6** | *180 mm* |
| **3** | *35 mm* | **7** | *400 mm* |
| **4** | *50 mm* | **8** | *800 mm* |

clusters of crystals—in a photographic emulsion; the finer the grain the better the detail but the slower (less light-sensitive) the film. Noticeably coarse grain can be used for graphic effect.

**8.085 halation** In the highlights of a photographic image, an unwanted spread of light beyond its natural boundary, caused by overexposure or (in platemaking) poor plate contact during exposure.

**8.086 hybrid photography, imaging** Photography that uses elements of both conventional and digital technologies. The Advanced Photo System and PhotoCD both employ hybrid technology. ➔ 8.109 ADVANCED PHOTO SYSTEM (APS); 1.538 PHOTOCD

**8.087 hyperfocal distance** The closest distance at which a lens records a subject sharply when focused at infinity. Will vary with aperture.

**8.088 Ilfochrome** Name for reversal printing paper from Ilford which was formerly marketed as Cibachrome. ➔ 8.065 CIBACHROME

**8.089 key tone** The most important tone in a photographic scene that must be recorded accurately.

**8.090 lens aberration** A fault in a photographic lens in which light rays are improperly passed through the lens, causing degraded images. With chromatic aberration light of different colors comes to different focal planes, resulting in colored halos around objects. In spherical aberration imprecise (or incorrect) curvature of the lens surface prevents light from coming to a single focal point; instead there is a focal patch from which the "best point of focus" must be selected. Though not strictly aberrations, distortions can also blight lenses. Barrel distortion causes objects to "bulge," with rectangles appearing barrel-like. Pincushion distortion is the converse, with rectangles appearing "pinched" along their sides.

**8.091 lens speed** The widest setting to which a lens can be set. Corresponds to the smallest f-number.

**8.092 multipattern metering** An exposure metering system in which areas of the image are measured separately, and assessed according to a predetermined program.

**8.093 off-the-film (OTF) metering** Technique pioneered and exploited by Olympus. Light readings are taken from the light reflected from the film emulsion during the actual exposure. The principal benefit is responsiveness: changes in light levels during the exposure can be compensated for by changes in exposure time. The drawback is the need for a second exposure meter system to advise the photographer of the approximate exposure time prior to exposure.

**8.094 overexpose / overexposure (1)** A condition wherein too much light reaches the film, resulting in a very dense negative or light slide (or print).

**8.095 reciprocity failure** An exception to the mathematical reciprocity law in photographic processing. A short exposure under a bright light does not produce the same result as a long exposure in a dim light, although

8.084 *grain*

8.085 *halation*

mathematically it should. In other words, at very short and very long exposures, the reciprocity law ceases to hold true, and an extra exposure is needed. The effect produced varies with film types, but on color film the three dye layers suffer differently and a color caste may occur, so only the exposure range that the film was designed for should be used. → 8.096 RECIPROCITY LAW

8.**096 reciprocity law** A law that states that photographic exposure is the result of both the intensity of light and the time taken to make the exposure. If you double one, you need to halve the other to achieve the same exposure. → 8.095 RECIPROCITY FAILURE

8.**097 redeye** Defect in photographic portraits taken with flash due to the flash light reflecting off the subject's retina resulting in the characteristic red irises. Can be relieved in-camera by moving the flash away from the subject–camera axis or using bounce flash. Redeye in existing images can be removed digitally.

8.**098 resolving power** The ability of a photographic emulsion or lens to record fineness of detail.

8.**099 sharpness** A measure of the clarity of focus present in a photographic image. → 10.033 DEFINITION

8.**100 shutter priority** An exposure mode in automatic cameras that lets the user select the shutter speed manually, the aperture then being set automatically according to the camera's metering system. If the user subsequently changes the shutter speed, or the ambient light levels change, the camera compensates automatically. The opposite of aperture priority. → 8.101 SHUTTER SPEED; 8.058 APERTURE PRIORITY

8.**101 shutter speed** A measure of the time a shutter remains open when an exposure is made. Most cameras have shutter speeds based on the sequence 1/1000 s, 1/500 s, 1/250 s, 1/125 s, 1/60 s, etc., where each shutter speed is approximately twice the previous. → 8.100 SHUTTER PRIORITY

8.**102 soft focus** An effect that "softens" or slightly diffuses the lines and edges of an image without altering the actual focus. Slightly opaque "softening" filters are employed. Usually used to confer a "romantic" feel to portraits and landscapes, but also useful for hiding minor skin blemishes. → 8.197 DIFFUSE

8.**103 spherical aberration** The failure of a lens to exactly focus light rays at its center and at its edges. → 8.090 LENS ABERRATION

8.**104 stop** The aperture size of a camera lens. → 8.078 F-NUMBER

8.**105 stop down** The action of closing down the aperture of a lens, e.g. from f/4 to f/5.6.

8.**106 time exposure** An exposure whose duration is measured in seconds (rather than fractions of seconds) or longer time intervals. A "time" setting on some cameras makes time exposures easier: Pressing once on the shutter release opens the shutter, and it remains open until the shutter release is pressed again.

8.**107 underexpose, underexposure** Insufficient light to effect the correct exposure of a

8.101 *shutter speed*

*Slow shutter speed*

*Fast shutter speed*

photosensitive material. The result is a print or transparency that is too dark and a negative that is too "thin" (resulting in a dark print).

8.**108 vignetting** A reduction in the light levels at the edge of an image or print due to deficiencies in the lens used for taking or enlarging the print. The use of an incorrect lens hood or too many filters can also cause vignetting.

## Film

8.**109 Advanced Photo System** (**APS**) A film format using 24-mm-wide cartridge-loaded film. A magnetic coating allows the transfer of photographic data to viewing and processing devices using information exchange (IX) circuitry. Such information advises the photofinishing lab of, for example, the film format used (classic, wide HDTV, or ultrawide panoramic) and exposure information.

8.**110 C format** One of the three print formats for the Advanced Photo System. Short for Classic format, it trims the shorter edges of the image to give a conventional 4:3 aspect ratio. → 8.109 ADVANCED PHOTO SYSTEM (APS); 8.127 H FORMAT; 8.134 P FORMAT

8.**111 cartridge** Film container for loading directly into a camera, such as those 35-mm film is produced in.

8.**112 cassette** Name given to the film container for APS film that is loaded with no film leader exposed. A casette also contains indicators to advise whether the film inside is exposed, partially exposed, unexposed, or processed. → 8.109 APS

8.**113 color negative film** Photographic film in which the image, after processing, is formed in negative colors, from which positive color prints are made. As distinct from color transparency film which is positive and which is not generally used for making prints. Also referred to as "color negs." → 8.114 COLOR TRANSPARENCY FILM

8.**114 color transparency film** A photographic image on transparent film generated, after processing, as a positive image. Color transparencies are ideal as originals for color separations for process color printing, because they provide a greater range of colors than do reflective prints. Color transparency film is supplied for a variety of camera formats, typically 35 mm, 2¼ in square, and 4 x 5 in. Color transparencies are also known variously as "trannies," "color trannies," "slides" (which generally refers to 35-mm film only), and "color reversal film." → 8.113 COLOR NEGATIVE FILM

8.**115 daguerrotype** The first practical method of creating and fixing a photographic image. Invented by Louis J. M. Daguerre in 1833, the process involved exposing a silvered copper plate to iodine or bromine vapor, which made it light-sensitive.

8.**116 diapositive** A photographic transparency in which the image is positive.

8.**117 D-max** D-max is the term for maximum density that can be achieved in a photographic original or by a photomechanical system. → 8.118 D-MIN

8.097 *redeye*

8.108 *vignetting*

8.**118 D-min** Minimum density that can be achieved in a photographic original or by a photomechanical system. → 8.117 D-max

8.**119 emulsion** The light-sensitive coating of a photographic material which, when exposed and processed, reveals the image. Colloquially (but incorrectly) called "the film."

8.**120 film** A cellulose acetate base material which is coated with light-sensitive emulsion so that images can be recorded photographically. Photographic film can be color or black and white, line or tone, negative or positive.

8.**121 film base** A transparent substrate used as a carrier for such things as light-sensitive photographic emulsion.

8.**122 film format** Standard measurements for sheet and roll photographic film, corresponding to film widths and standard camera sizes. Typical formats include 35 mm, APS, 12on120, 5 x 4 inches, and 10 x 8 inches. Less common (or defunct) formats include 110, 126, 127, and Disc.

8.**123 film negative** A photographic image in which highlights and shadows are transposed. It is used in printing to make plates or film positives, and in photography to make prints.

8.**124 film speed** A measure of the sensitivity of a film or emulsion to light. Measured in ISO. Films with ratings of less than ISO100 are considered "slow" (less light sensitive), while those rated ISO400 and over are "fast." Some speeds are still denoted by ASA (such as 50ASA). The ASA and ISO ratings are equivalent.

8.**125 frame** (1) Individual image on a film strip.

8.**126 graininess** The granulated effect present in a negative, print, or slide. The degree to which it is visible depends on such things as film speed (it increases with faster films), enlargement, and processing. Graininess can be introduced into images for creative effect using Photoshop filters.

8.**127 H format** This is one of the three Advanced Photo System print formats. Short for HDTV (so-named because its aspect ratio of 16:9 echoes that of wide-screen high-definition television screens), the H format uses the entire area of an APS frame. → 8.109 Advanced Photo System (APS); 8.110 C format; 8.134 P format .

8.**128 index print** An "electronic contact sheet" comprising small thumbnails of a set of images. Index prints generally accompany processed 35-mm films, APS films, PictureCDs, and PhotoCDs, or image memory cards submitted to photofinishers.

8.**129 interneg(ative)** A photographic negative used as the intermediate step when making a copy (usually a print) from a transparency or flat original. Internegatives were more common when photographic papers suitable for printing direct from transparencies tended to be very high contrast.

8.**130 line film** Negative or positive photographic film in which the image consists of solid elements, such as lines or text matter, with no continuous tones or halftones (actually, halftones are usually printed to line film as they consist entirely of solid dots). → 8.132 orthochromatic

8.111 *cartridge/cassette*

The 35mm film cartridge has been popular with professional and amateur photographer alike for many years. Will it soon be replaced by digital equipment?

8.122 *film format*

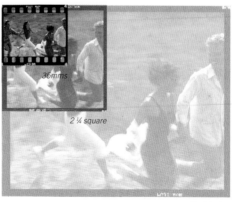

36mms

2 ¼ square

5 x 4 inches

8.**131 negative / neg** Photographic film or paper in which all the dark areas appear light and vice versa. Negative film is used extensively in the reproduction process and is either made directly from originals, or produced by an imagesetter.

8.**132 orthochromatic** A photographic emulsion that is sensitive to all colors except red, and used extensively in conventional reproduction. Also called "lith film." → 8.133 ORTHOGRAPHIC

8.**133 orthographic** Photographic emulsion that is sensitive only to green, blue, and ultraviolet light. → 8.132 ORTHOCHROMATIC

8.**134 P format** One of the three Advanced Photo System formats. The Panoramic setting uses only the central band of the APS frame to create a wide print with an aspect ratio of 5:2. The small image area used can sometimes lead to grainy or ill-defined images. → 8.109 ADVANCED PHOTO SYSTEM (APS); 8.110 C FORMAT; 8.127 H FORMAT

8.**135 panchromatic** Photographic emulsion that is sensitive to all colors in the visible spectrum Most readily available "consumer" emulsions are panchromatic. → 8.133 ORTHOGRAPHIC

8.**136 reversal film** Film emulsion that produces a positive image, as in color transparencies ("slides").

8.**137 tungsten film** A photographic film that is used where the scene is to be illuminated by tungsten lamps (versions appropriate for use with normal, domestic lamps or special tungsten based-photographic lamps are available).

8.**138 universal film** A general term for consumer film that is suitable for all occasions. Usually denotes fast film (ISO400). Also a descriptive term for color separation film that produces the same results on both litho plates and on gravure cylinders.

### Cameras and accessories

8.**139 Advantix** Brand name for Advanced Photo System cameras produced by Kodak.

8.**140 automatic camera** Camera with built-in coupled exposure meter that automatically adjusts the aperture and/or shutter speed to achieve correct exposure. → 8.057 APERTURE

8.**141 bellows** The accordian-like folding fabric section of some cameras (or lenses) that provides a light-tight link between the lens and the camera body. Typically found with monorail cameras, closeup lens systems, and in Hasselblad's ArcBody. → 8.169 MONORAIL

8.**142 between the lens shutter** A shutter whose blades are placed between elements of the lens.

8.**143 camera** A device in which light passes through a lens to record an image. The image can be recorded onto presensitized film or paper, or by means of electronic sensors (CCDs) which digitally "write" the image to a storage device such as a memory card or hard disk. → 8.208 CCD; 8.174 PROCESS CAMERA; 8.186 VERTICAL CAMERA

8.**144 catadioptric lens** A type of mirror lens in which a supplementary lens is employed (usually at the aperture) to correct aberrations in the prime mirror. The Schmidt design, for example, uses a simple (and cheap) spherical mirror coupled with a lens of complex form to remove spherical aberrations from the mirror. → 8.168 MIRROR LENS

8.**145 closeup lens** A subsidiary lens fitted to the filter ring of a conventional lens to enable close-up shots to be taken at a distance less than that which the lens alone would allow.

8.**146 coated lens** A photographic lens coated with a thin film which reduces "flare" (undesirable scattered light); sometimes referred to as a bloomed lens. A multicoated lens has multiple coatings applied to further reduce reflection and internal reflection. → 8.210 FLARE

8.**147 color filters** Thin sheets of transparent material such as glass or gelatin placed over a camera lens to modify the quality of light or colors in an image for corrective or creative purposes.

8.**148 compound lens** A photographic lens made up of more than one lenses (elements). The use of compound lenses enables the lens to be optically adjusted for aberrations and distortion.

8.**149 condenser (lens)** A photographic lens which concentrates light into a beam. Used in enlargers and process cameras (a camera used for preparing film and plates for printing). → 8.174 PROCESS CAMERA

8.**150 diaphragm** An adjustable opening, or "aperture," behind a camera lens that controls the amount of light that reaches the film. The aperture opening is calibrated on the camera lens by f-stop numbers. Also called an "iris diaphragm." → 8.078 F-NUMBER

8.**151 disposable camera** → 8.180 single-use camera

8.**152 diverging / divergent lens** A camera lens which causes light rays to bend outward from the optical axis. Also called a "negative element."

8.**153 exposure meter** A device, used in photography to calculate the correct exposure, that measures the light generated by, reflected off, or falling on, a subject. Also called a "light meter." It can be a hand-held or camera mounted device, or an integral unit.

8.**154 exposure setting** The combination of shutter speed and amount of aperture (lens opening). Because different combinations result in the same amount of light reaching the film (for example, 1/30s at f/8 is the same as 1/60s at f/5.6) exposure settings are sometimes calibrated in exposure values (EV).

8.**155 finder** Part of a camera that illustrates to the photographer the view that will be recorded on film. Can be a direct vision viewfinder, frames (often used e.g. for underwater photography where it is difficult to use a conventional viewfinder), or a separate viewer.

8.**156 fish-eye lens** A camera lens with an extremely wide angle of view, producing a distorted image with an exaggerated apparent curve. → 8.187 WIDE-ANGLE LENS

8.**157 fixed focus** Description of a lens (or camera) which has a fixed, predetermined focus set for a particular subject distance (normally around 9 ft, in order to have group shots and middle distance objects in best focus). The use of small apertures on such cameras generally means there is reasonable depth of field.

8.**158 fixed-focus lens** A photographic lens with no variable focus adjustment. A feature of very cheap or specialized cameras.

8.**159 focal plane shutter** A camera shutter located close to the focal plane, in which two blinds form an adjustable gap which moves across the film determining the exposure.

8.**160 gelatin filter** A colored filter made from dyed gelatin on an optically transparent polyester base, placed over a camera lens to add a color bias (or some other effect) to a shot with no significant effect on the optical quality of the final image.

8.**161 hot shoe** The mounting point situated on the top of a camera that supports a small flashgun (or an appropriate cable running to a separately mounted gun), which provides a direct connection to trigger the flash at the same time as the exposure is made. There can also sometimes be additional contacts on the mount to enable dedicated flashguns to communicate directly with the camera. → 8.202 FLASH SYNCHRONIZATION; 8.196 DEDICATED FLASH

8.**162 in-camera** The creation of effects within the camera, rather than at postproduction, processing, or otherwise. Filter effects and multiple exposures are typical examples of in-camera effects. Photographic processing that takes place inside the camera, such as with Polaroid products, is also referred to as in-camera.

8.**163 LCD panel** Display panel on some cameras used to relay information regarding camera settings, remaining exposures, and battery condition to the user.

8.**164 lens** The name describing a cylindrical tube containing one or more glass "elements" which collect and focus light rays to create an image.

8.**165 lens shade** A hood placed over the front of a lens to prevent extraneous light from entering the lens and causing flare. Different lenses generally require individual lens shades to ensure that no unwanted light enters but also that the shade never appears in shot.

8.**166 long-focus lens** A camera lens with a focal length longer than the diagonal measurement of the film format. Thus, for 35-mm film, a lens longer than about 50 mm is considered long-focus. → 8.184 TELEPHOTO LENS; 8.177 SHORT-FOCUS LENS

8.**167 macro lens** Lens with a focusing range from infinity to extreme closeup. Normally macro lenses are capable of reproducing objects at a 1:1 scale on film (i.e. life size). Some macro lenses use supplementary closeup lenses to achieve even greater magnifications.

8.**168 mirror lens** A camera lens that forms an image by reflecting it from curved mirrors rather than by refraction through a series of lenses. A mirror lens is more compact than a traditional lens of the same focal length (a telephoto lens, for example). → 8.184 TELEPHOTO LENS

8.**169 monorail** A type of studio support for standard-view cameras to which the lens plate and film holder are attached and aligned. Also the name given to such cameras.

8.**170 neutral density filter** A filter that uniformly reduces all colors of light during an exposure. It effectively reduces the film speed so that larger apertures (with their more restricted depth of field) can be used.

8.**171 PC cord** Connecting cable between a PC socket on a camera and a flashgun. Enables synchronization between camera and gun. Performs same function as a basic hot shoe. → 8.161 HOT SHOE

8.**172 perspective control (PC) lens** A camera lens used mainly to correct converging verticals in architectural photography. Also called a "shift lens."

8.**173 polarizing filter** Filter comprising Polaroid material designed to remove polarized light from an image. Polarized light tends to include reflected light, and use of a polarizing filter can remove reflections resulting in brighter colors and richer skies. A single layer polarizer is known as a linear polarizer. Most autofocus and digital cameras need a circular polarizer: This is a two-stage filter that polarizes the light at the first stage then "rescatters" it. This prevents the focusing and other electronic monitoring elements from receiving an incorrect exposure reading.

8.**174 process camera** A specially designed graphics art camera used in photomechanical reproduction. Also called a "repro camera" or "reproduction camera." → 8.186 VERTICAL CAMERA

8.**175 program exposure** An exposure mode wherein the camera determines both the aperture and shutter speed. Programs are usually biased toward the hand-holding of cameras so, light levels permitting, tend to keep shutter speeds high at the expense of the aperture size. Many cameras have multiple program modes that offer special shutter speed/aperture combinations suited for, say, sports photography, portraits, or landscapes.

8.**176 rangefinder** A focusing aid in many non-autofocus cameras that aids precise focusing.

8.**177 short-focus lens** A camera lens with a focal length shorter than the diagonal measurement of the film format. Thus for 35-mm film, a lens shorter than 35 mm is short-focus. → 8.166 LONG-FOCUS LENS

8.**178 shutter** The mechanical device in a camera that is used to control the length of time a film is exposed to the light. → 8.101 SHUTTER SPEED

8.**179 single lens reflex (SLR)** A camera in which the lens used for the photograph also transmits, via a mirror, the same image to the viewfinder.

8.**180 single-use camera** Camera designed to be used only for the enclosed film. Once exposed the camera is broken open to remove and process the film. Think of it as a film cartridge with a lens attached. Helpful where use of a conventional camera might be risky.

8.169 *monorail camera*

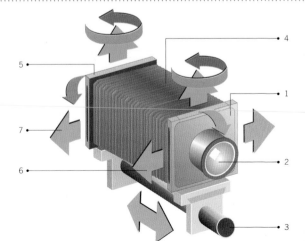

1 *Lens board*
2 *Lens*
3 *Monorail*
4 *Bellows*
5 *Film/plate back*
6 *Front movements*
7 *Back movements*

8.**181 standard lens** The fixed focus lens normally sold with SLR cameras and boasting a focal length of between 45 mm and 55 mm. This gives a view that most closely echoes the proportions and perspective of the original scene, although often has too narrow a field of view for use with interiors and is not selective enough for longer range views. Also known as a "normal lens."

8.**182 standard zoom** A zoom lens including the range of a standard lens (around 50 mm) in its focal range. Although this might apply to some of the "superzooms" (with focal ranges from 28 mm to 300 mm) it normally applies to more modest ranges (typically 28–80 mm, for example).

8.**183 starburst (filter)** A photographic filter inscribed with one or more series of fine, parallel lines. This creates the effect of "streaks" from any highlights in a direction perpendicular to the rulings. By inscribing multiple sets of lines, starbursts with 2, 4, 8, or more points are possible.

8.**184 telephoto lens** A photographic lens with a long focal length that enables distant objects to be enlarged. Telephoto lenses have a limited depth of field. ➔ 8.168 MIRROR LENS; 8.188 ZOOM LENS; 8.166 LONG-FOCUS LENS

8.**185 through-the-lens (TTL) meter** An exposure meter built into a camera that calculates an exposure based on the amount of light passing through the camera lens.

8.**186 vertical camera** A camera used for reproduction, typically with a fixed position camera and a horizontal copyboard that is moved up or down. ➔ 8.174 PROCESS CAMERA

8.**187 wide-angle lens** A photographic lens with wider field of view than a standard lens, so that more of the subject can be included. For 35-mm cameras the term wide angle usually applies to focal lengths of 35 mm or less. ➔ 8.156 FISH-EYE LENS; 8.177 SHORT-FOCUS LENS; 8.166 LONG-FOCUS LENS

8.**188 zoom lens** A camera lens with a focal length that can be adjusted over a wide range giving, in effect, a set of lenses of different focal length in one body. Useful for framing a subject. ➔ 8.184 TELEPHOTO LENS

## Lighting

8.**189 ambient light** Also known as available light. This is the light (natural, artificial, or both) in the environment of, and lighting, the photographic subject. It is specifically that illumination not provided by the photographer.

8.**190 axial lighting** The technique of lighting a photographic subject by shining a light along the lens axis. The result is little or no shadow, which can create very "flat" results in the finished image.

8.**191 back projection** The technique of projecting an image behind a photographic subject from an appropriate projector.

8.**192 backlighting** In this technique the principal light sources originate behind the subject and are directed (broadly) toward the camera lens. It tends to produce results that have a lot of contrast, with silhouettes. A specific form of backlighting is called contre jour. ➔ 8.195 CONTRE JOUR

8.179 *single lens reflex (SLR)*

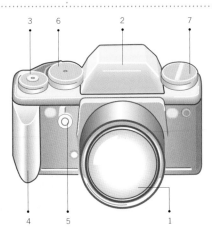

1 *Lens*
2 *Pentaprism housing*
3 *Shutter release*
4 *Grip*
5 *Self tuner*
6 *Shutter speed control*
7 *Manual rewind*

213

8.**193 base lighting** The technique of lighting a photographic subject from beneath by projecting the light upward. Also known as "ground lighting." Often used for still-life photography of glassware and metallic objects to provide full lighting but without the flash highlights of front or sidelighting.

8.**194 bounce lighting** Lighting (flash or otherwise) that indirectly lights a subject or background, having first been reflected from a dedicated reflector, or the walls or ceiling, to give a more natural effect.

8.**195 contre jour** Literally "against the light"; this describes a specific form of backlighting in which the picture is taken with the camera lens pointing toward the light source. → 8.192 BACKLIGHTING

8.**196 dedicated flash** A flash system designed to work with specific makes or models of camera. Dedicated flash systems often incorporate special circuitry to communicate with the camera, enabling camera settings to be detected by the flash and vice versa. Often the camera's light sensors can be used to control flashgun output.

8.**197 diffuse** A softened effect in an image, created by scattered light giving an object the appearance of, for example, being viewed through translucent glass. → 8.102 SOFT FOCUS

8.**198 diffuse lighting** Light that has low contrast and no obvious highlights. Bounce lighting can be diffuse if well spread. Overcast skies also represent diffuse light sources.

8.**199 existing light** Also called available light; the term describes all natural and environmental light sources (i.e. those not specifically employed for the purpose of photography).

8.**200 fill-in light** Additional lighting added to a scene to soften, lighten, or remove shadows or dark regions due to the main light source.

8.**201 flare** Scattered light which degrades the quality of a photographic image, usually caused by too much light being reflected. In some situations flare can be used for beneficial effect. Photoshop provides the Lens Flare filter to emulate the effect in controllable and adjustable ways. → 8.146 COATED LENS

8.**202 flash** A split-second, intense burst of artificially generated light used in photography to light a subject. Called electronic flash if it originates from an electronic flashgun.

8.**203 flash synchronization** A camera system in which the peak output from the flash unit occurs when the shutter is fully open.

8.**204 flat lighting** Lighting that is usually low in contrast and shadows. → 8.198 DIFFUSE LIGHTING

8.**205 sidelighting** Lighting that hits the subject from the side, causing sharp, dichotomous shadows.

8.**206 tungsten lighting** Conventional filamentary domestic lighting. Photoflood bulbs are brighter and more consistent forms of tungsten lighting.

## Digital

8.**207 CCD array** A collection of CCDs arranged in a line. → 8.208 CHARGE-COUPLED DEVICE (CCD)

8.**208 charge-coupled device (CCD)** A tiny light sensor ("photosite")—that is sensitized by giving it an electrical charge prior to exposure—used in flatbed scanners and digital cameras for converting light into data. → 8.143 CAMERA

8.**209 CoolPix** Proprietary name for digital cameras produced by Nikon.

8.**210 dark current** Noise that builds up on a CCD (charge-coupled device) when it is not exposed to light and which is due to small background charges. All CCDs suffer from this effect to a degree but it is not normally significant until very dim subjects are imaged. Then the signal-to-noise ratio (the ratio of the image charge levels to the dark current) will become small and poor (usually grainy or blotchy) results will ensue. → 8.208 CHARGE-COUPLED DEVICE (CCD)

8.**211 data exchange (DX)** A method of passing data from a 35-mm film cassette to a camera. A pattern of black and metallic squares on the cassette makes contact with contacts in the film chamber that pass information to the camera with regard to film speed, film type, and film length. Not all cameras so equipped (usually denoted as "DX compatible") make use of all the data available with the DX coding regime: More basic cameras default to ISO 100 settings for films that are not recognized as either ISO 100 or ISO 400. → 8.109 INFORMATION EXCHANGE (IX)

8.**212 digital camera** A photographic device that captures and records images using a digital imaging chip and consequently stores the image data in digital form on an onboard memory block, removable memory card, or directly connected computer. → 8.124 ELECTRONIC CAMERA

8.**213 digital photography** The process either of capturing an image with digital equipment or of manipulating photographic images on a computer, or both. In either case the term describes photographs that are recorded or manipulated in binary form rather than on conventional film. Not synonymous with electronic photography. → 8.212 DIGITAL CAMERA; 1.016 BIT

8.**214 electronic camera** Camera that uses electronic techniques and hardware in order to deliver an image. Generally applies to early electronic imaging cameras producing images as analog still video. The first (c.1989) Sony Mavica and Canon iON cameras are examples of electronic cameras. Though digital cameras are electronic, the term is not usually used to describe digital devices.

8.**215 electronic photography, electronic still photography** Photography using electronic cameras (as distinct from digital cameras). → 8.214 ELECTRONIC CAMERA

8.**216 FinePix** Proprietary name for digital cameras produced by Fujifilm, mainly for the "consumer" market.

8.**217 Image Magic** Proprietary name for many of Kodak's "consumer-level" imaging products including PictureCD and some services delivered via the Internet.

8.**218 Image Pac** Kodak's proprietary system for PhotoCD image storage, including all the PhotoCD resolutions from base/16 through to 64base. The latter, used only in the Pro PhotoCD, is contained within the IPE (Image Pac Extension). → 1.538 PHOTOCD

8.**219 iON** An early type of electronic camera that was developed by Canon and was first released c. 1989. It used an electronic imaging element but stored images on small disks using analog technology. The name is an abbreviation for image online network.

8.**220 linear array CCD** A single row of CCD imaging elements that scan the "film plane" in some high-end, high-performance digital cameras. Because the scan (much in the same manner as a flatbed scanner's CCD array) takes a finite time (sometimes running to minutes) it is suitable only for studio-based photography of inanimate objects. → 8.208 CCD

8.**221 Mavica** Acronym for magnetic video camera. The name given to electronic stills cameras that were produced by Sony during the 1980s. After a break, the name was resurrected once more and used for their digital cameras that use floppy disks (and more recently for recordable 8-cm CDs) for image storage.

8.**222 still video** Description of early electronic stills camera. The image is formed by a focal plane CCD but recorded as an analog signal (rather than digital) on disk, tape, or card. The term is occasionally used now to describe the video camera feature enabling a "snapshot" to be taken and recorded on video tape.

8.212 *digital camera*

1 *Hot shoe (clip to hold devices such as electronic flash)*
2 *LCD*
3 *Mode dial*
4 *Viewfinder*
5 *Auto exposure*
6 *Auto focus*
7 *Lens*
8 *Digital control buttons*
9 *Lower LCD, to set digital values*

# PRINTING

## Prepress

9.**001 black generation** Technique to create the black-component plate of a CMYK color separation.

9.**002 Color-Key** A proprietary dry proofing system developed by 3M. → 9.050 DRY PROOF

9.**003 contact film** "Continuous tone" film used to produce a same-size negative image from a film positive original, or vice versa, when the two are placed in direct contact with each other. Also called "color-blind film."

9.**004 etch** To dissolve away an area of printing plate to produce a relief or intaglio image (depending on the printing method) or, on film, to reduce the size of halftone dots. The term is also used to describe the process of desensitizing the nonimage areas (which are protected by a "ground") of a litho plate to make them receptive to water instead of ink. → 9.091 DESENSITIZE

9.**005 film positive** A record of an image on clear film, emulating the original. Used for film assembly and for making printing plates.

9.**006 finished art**(**work**) Any illustrative matter prepared specifically for reproduction. Artwork which includes or is comprised entirely of text is usually described as "camera-ready art" or "mechanicals."

9.**007 halftone screen** Conventionally, a sheet of glass or film cross-hatched with opaque lines, used to convert a continuous tone image into halftone dots so that it can be printed. Computer applications generate a halftone screen digitally without the need for a physical halftone screen, by generating each halftone dot as an individual "cell," itself made up of "printer" dots. Also called a "crossline screen" or "contact screen." → 9.053 HALFTONE (1)

9.**008 imagesetter** A high-resolution output device used to generate reproduction-quality copy for printing, either as film negatives or positives or on photographic bromide paper for use as camera-ready artwork.

9.**009 inspection copy** Copy of a book given to decisionmakers, for example teachers, lecturers, and library staff to solicit purchasing or referral interest. Sometimes called a "desk copy."

9.**010 markup** (**2**) A set of instructions and specifications usually marked on a hard copy for any material prepared for typesetting, reproduction, or printing.

9.017 *progressive proofs/progs*

1

2

3

4

9.**011 old-tech** A colloquial expression referring to prepress technology which has largely been replaced by new, mostly computer-based, technology.

9.**012 overexpose / overexposure** (**2**) A fault in platemaking caused when the light source is too close or too bright.

9.**013 page proofs** A proof of pages that have been paginated (put into the correct page sequence). Traditionally, this is the secondary stage in proofing, i.e. after galley proofs and before machine proofs, although there may be other stages of proofing either before or after page proofs, such as the "blues" used to check imposition. Also called "made-up pages."

9.**014 pass for press** A printing job that has had corrections approved and is ready for press.

9.**015 pasteup** The physical layout of a design, including all elements such as text and illustrations. A pasteup for layout and markup purposes is called a "rough," while one which will be used to make film for reproduction is called "camera-ready" (or a "mechanical"). Digital (on screen) pasteups can be produced in DTP systems.

9.**016 prepress** Any or all of the reproduction processes that may occur between design and printing, but often specifically used to describe color separation and planning. Also called "origination."

9.**017 progressive proofs / progs** Proofs used in color printing to show each color printed separately, and progressively combined—in the order in which they will be printed—with each other.

9.**018 proof** A prototype of a job, taken at various stages from laser printers, imagesetters, inked plates, stones, screens, block, type, etc., in order to check the progress and accuracy of the work. Also called a "pull."

9.**019 proofing** The production/correction of a prototype or simulation of a print job prior to its subsequent reproduction in quantity.

9.**020 registration marks** Marks that can be printed on the margins of a Photoshop image to determine whether, when printed as color separations, all four components print in register. → 9.043 REGISTER

9.**021 trap** An overlap introduced to a CMYK image to allow for misregistration between color plates when that image is printed. This avoids unsightly "gaps" between areas of color. A set of rules governs the trapping conditionality: 1. All colors spread under black; 2. Light colors spread under dark; 3. Yellow spreads under cyan, magenta, and black; 4. Pure cyan and pure magenta spread under each other equally. → 2.326 TRAP

## Inks

9.**022 absorbency / absorption** The property of a paper, or other substrate, to absorb liquids such as ink. In desktop printing, absorption is not only determined by the fiber structure of the paper, but also by the surface coating properties and constituency of the ink. Incorrect absorption can lead to printing problems such as strike through and drying failure. Visually this leads to effects

1  *Yellow*
2  *Magenta*
3  *Yellow plus magenta*
4  *Cyan*
5  *Yellow, magenta plus cyan*
6  *Black*
7  *Yellow, magenta, cyan, plus black*

such as surface blooming, reticulation, and poor definition.

9.**023 color burnout** An undesirable and unintentional change in the color of printing inks due to chemical reactions when the ink is mixed or as it dries after printing.

9.**024 double-tone ink** A printing ink that produces a secondary tone as it dries, creating the illusion of two-color printing in a single pass.

9.**025 dye-based ink** Inks that derive their colors from aniline dyes. The name distinguishes them from the more permanent (though often more problematic) pigment-based inks.

9.**026 flat color** A uniform color of consistent hue. In printing, this usually means a specially mixed color which is printed apart from any other colors.

9.**027 grayness** A quality of yellow, magenta, and cyan process color inks relating to the degree of contamination. An increase in the grayness value indicates a decrease in purity or saturation.

9.**028 ink penetration** The degree to which ink penetrates a substrate; more acute during the moment of impression than after it, and important if smudging or "setoff" is to be avoided.

9.**029 ink receptivity** The degree to which a substrate such as paper or plastic/plastic-coated film will absorb printing ink.

9.**030 medium** A substance, such as linseed oil or gum arabic, into which pigment is mixed to create printing ink or artist's paint. Also called a "vehicle."

9.**031 process ink gamut (PIG) chart** A chart which compares the colors that can be obtained from a variety of ink and substrate combinations. Useful for confirming/establishing those colors that might be incorrectly printed.

9.**032 rich black** A percentage of another color—usually 20–40% black or magenta—which is printed under solid black in color printing to produce a more dense black.

9.**033 secondary color** Color produced by overprinting two primary colors. Also called "overprint color."

9.**034 solid** An area printed with 100% of a color.

9.**035 spot color** Any color used for printing which has been "custom mixed" for the job, as opposed to one of the four standard process colors.

9.**036 toner** The plastic powder used in laser and LED page printers and photocopiers to produce an image. Normally black, color lasers use yellow, cyan, and magenta toners also.

9.**037 total ink limit** The maximum ink density achievable by a printer (or printing press). The Photoshop defaults are Black 100% and Total Ink Limit 300%.

9.**038 varnish** A liquid that dries with a hard surface and is generally insoluble in water. It is used in the manufacture of printing inks, in some drying agents, and as a surface protector.

## Separations

9.**039 color bar** The color device printed on the edge of color proofs or in the trim area of press sheets that enables the repro house and printer to check—by eye or with instruments—the fidelity of color separations and the accuracy of printing. The color bar helps to monitor such things as ink density, paper stability, dot gain, trapping, and so on. → 9.040 COLOR SEPARATION; 9.125 TRAPPING

9.**040 color separation** The process of dividing a multicolored image into the four individual process colors—cyan, magenta, yellow, and black (by using red, green, and blue filters)—so that the image can be reproduced on a printing press. Conventionally, this was done using the filters in a "process" camera, but color separations can now be prepared from within Photoshop. Photoshop color separations are produced by first converting the image to CMYK color mode, then from the File menu selecting Print > Space: Separations prior to printing. → 1.438 SCANNER; 4.009 CMYK

9.**041 color separations** The set of four films, one for each of the four process colors—cyan, magenta, yellow, and black—generated as a result of the color separation process. → 9.040 COLOR SEPARATION; 1.453 PRINTER; 4.009 CMYK

9.**042 Grayscale Component Replacement (GCR)** One of two methods (the other is Undercolor Removal) used in prepress to produce black in print. Black ink is substituted for some of the cyan, magenta and yellow in both neutral and colored image areas. This leads to deep saturated

### 9.042 *Grayscale Component Replacement (GCR)*

*1 Image separated without any color replacement or removal*

C+M+Y, no black

Black only

All four colors (CMYK)

*2 Image separated with neutral values (grays) of CMY replaced with black*

C+M+Y, no black

Black only

All four colors (CMYK)

### 9.046 *Undercolor removal (UCR)*

*3 Image separated with color under the black removed*

C+M+Y, no black

Black only

All four colors (CMYK)

colors that are more accurately defined than with Undercolor Removal and have a better gray balance. The ultimate choice of methods will be determined by the twin requirements of the paper stock to be printed on and the requirements of the print shop. ➔ 9.046 UNDERCOLOR REMOVAL (UCR)

9.**043 register** The accurate positioning of color plates when printed one over another. When a plate is mispositioned the result is said to be "out of register."

9.**044 separation artwork** Artwork that consists of separate layers for each of the colors used. ➔ 9.040 COLOR SEPARATION

9.**045 separation filters** The filters used to separate colors so that they can be printed individually. They each transmit about one third of the spectrum. ➔ 9.040 COLOR SEPARATION

9.**046 Undercolor Removal** (**UCR**) Alternate method of generating black in a printed image (the other is Grayscale Component Removal). Undercolor Removal uses black ink to replace cyan, magenta and yellow in areas determined to be "neutral" (i.e. comprising equal components of all three colors). This method tends to be used in undemanding situations, since the lower ink usage means more rapid drying times with little compromise in image quality. ➔ 9.042 GRAYSCALE COMPONENT REMOVAL (GCR)

## Types

9.**047 compound printing** The process of printing two or more colors in a single pass. To do this different areas of the forme (in letterpress printing) or different sections of the inking system (in offset printing) are separately inked but then run at the same time. ➔ 9.061 PRINTING PROCESSES

9.**048 Cromalin** A proprietary dry-proofing system from DuPont which uses toners on light-sensitive paper. Also known as "offpress proofs" or "prepress proofs."

9.**049 dry litho** A lithographic printing technique in which the nonprinting areas of the plate are etched to leave a relief printing area, thus avoiding the need for water. Dry litho is a variation of the "letterset" printing technique.

9.**050 dry proof** Any color proof made without printing ink, such as a Cromalin or Matchprint, but particularly proofs produced digitally—from a laser printer, for example. ➔ 9.048 CROMALIN; 9.002 COLOR-KEY

9.**051 dye sub**(**limation**) A printing process in which vaporized ink dyes are bonded to a substrate by heat, producing near-photographic-quality proofs. Dye sublimation allows digital printing of large images onto fabric, metal, and other substrates, and is thus particularly suitable for fashion, architectural, and other large-format display items, since size is no limitation and runs can be as low as a single item. Also known as "dye diffusion."

9.**052 four-color process** Any printing process that reproduces full-color images which have been separated into the three basic "process" colors—cyan, magenta, and yellow —with the fourth color, black, added for extra density. ➔ 9.066 THREE-COLOR PROCESS; 9.040 COLOR SEPARATION

9.**053 halftone** (**1**) The reprographic technique, developed in the 1880s, of reproducing a continuous tone image on a printing press by breaking it up into a pattern of equally spaced dots of varying size. This determines tones or shades—the larger the dots, the darker the shade. ➔ 4.026 CONTINUOUS TONE IMAGE

9.**054 halftone** (**2**) Any image reproduced by the halftone process. ➔ 9.053 HALFTONE (1)

9.**055 intaglio** Printing process wherein the image to be printed is below the surface level of the plate used for the printing.

9.**056 lithography** A "planographic" printing process invented in 1798 by the German Aloys Senefelder, in which an image is produced from a dampened, flat surface, using greasy ink, based on the principle of the mutual repulsion of oil and water.

9.**057 mezzotint** Traditional engraving printing technique for reproducing tones rather than lines. An Intaglio-type technique.

9.**058 PhotoGrade** A technology introduced by Apple Computers in the 1980s to improve the quality of graphic and photographic images reproduced by laser printers, then the only credible economic source of high-quality output.

9.**059 photorealistic** A description applied to output devices, including computer printers and monitors, that are capable of producing results equivalent to or comparable with those from a standard photographic source. Generally refers to monitors capable of 24-

bit color and printers capable of four-color 720 dpi resolution. Some printers include the word "photorealistic" in their name or description, although this is not a precisely defined term.

9.**060 Pictrography** Printing system introduced by Fuji that uses a laser-printer-like system to transfer an image onto a "donor sheet" that has been dipped in silver halide and other chemicals. This donor sheet is combined with a transfer sheet that accepts the chemicals when heated in the presence of a small amount of water. Donor sheets remain in the printer where the unused impregnated chemicals can be removed along with the silver halide.

9.**061 printing processes** There are four generic printing processes: "intaglio" (e.g. gravure), "planographic" (e.g. lithography), "relief" (e.g. letterpress), and "stencil" (e.g. screen printing). → 9.083 COLOR PRINTING

9.**062 screen printing** A printing process in which ink is forced through a porous mesh screen stretched across a frame. The image is formed by means of a hand-cut or photomechanically-generated stencil bonded to the screen that blocks the nonimage areas.

9.**063 Thermal Autochrome** (**TA**) Printing system that uses special paper featuring three dye layers under a surface layer. The dyes are held in microcapsules that release color when a specific level of heat is received from the printing head. Different heat profiles release different colors and color saturations.

9.**064 thermal printing** General term for any printing methods that use heat as part of the image-forming process. Includes thermal transfer printers and Thermal Autochrome.

9.**065 thermal wax transfer printer** Printer that operates by melting dyed wax sheets onto a paper surface using fine heating elements that melt pinpoints of wax. Prints are produced by passing the image over the heating elements four times, once for each color. → 9.063 THERMAL AUTOCHROME (TA)

9.**066 three-color process** Printing method that uses only cyan, magenta, and yellow inks, synthesizing black from a combination of all three. Used now only on the most basic of inkjet papers due to the inability to achieve a perfect deep black.

## Finishing

9.**067 cameo coated paper** A paper with a dull finish. The UK equivalent is "matt art paper."

9.**068 coated paper** A paper which has had a mineral coating applied to its surface after the body paper was made; examples include art, chromo, and enamel papers. Coated paper is also known as "surface paper."

9.**069 corner marks** Marks in the corner of an image or page which usually indicate its final size after trimming or cropping, but can also be used as a guide for positioning or for registration during makeup or printing. Also called "crop marks," "trim marks" or "cut marks." → 9.020 REGISTRATION MARKS

9.**070 deckle edge** The rough, uneven edge of untrimmed handmade paper. Deckle edge

9.053 *halftone*

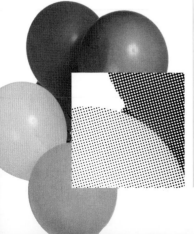

9.066 *three color process*

9.052 *four color process*

221

effects are also applied mechanically to machine-made paper.

9.**071 dry mounting** To mount items such as traditional photographs onto board using heat-sensitive adhesive tissue. Incongruously named "dry mounting sprays" provide a similar adhesive that can be used hot or cold, depending on formulation. Some inkjet papers are available with adhesive backs that can be peeled after printing.

9.**072 enamel** A coating that provides a glossy surface on paper.

9.**073 film coating** A lightweight film applied to paper. Also called "wash coating."

9.**074 film lamination / laminating** A thin, plastic, protective film that is bonded to a printed paper under pressure and heat. Laminates can have a glossy or matte finish and have a variable effect on UV/sunlight resistance.

9.**075 finishing** All operations that take place after printing, such as collating, folding, gathering, trimming, binding, and packing.

9.**076 heat sealing** A technique in which two materials, usually plastic, are fused together under heat and pressure. → 9.073 FILM LAMINATION/LAMINATING

9.**077 matt / matte** A flat, slightly dull surface. Matt finish paper is typically used as a flat alternative to glossy surfaces where surface reflections might be an issue.

### Print terms

9.**078 background printing** A computer printing option that allows the computer to print an image or document while work is continuing with another operation in the foreground. → 1.460 BUFFER

9.**079 banding** An artifact of some printers where a continuous tonal gradient is represented by discontinuous levels of tone. Tends to occur more with printers that are not specifically designed for photographic or photorealistic output. Can emulate posterization effects. → 8.020 POSTERIZE

9.**080 Calibration Bars** Photoshop printing option. Adds calibration bars to an image printed from Photoshop. From the File menu select Page Setup and then Calibration Bars. Note that this option may not be available, or may be disabled, with some printers.

9.**081 color chart** A printed reference chart used in color reproduction in order to select or match color tints made from percentage variations of the four process colors. For absolute accuracy when using a color chart, you should use one that has been prepared by your chosen printer and printed on paper which is at least similar to the paper that will be used for the job. → 4.019 COLOR PICKER (1); 4.021 COLOR SWATCH; 4.009 CMYK

9.**082 color correction** The process of adjusting color values in reproduction in order to achieve the desired result. Although this can occur at the scanning or image-manipulation stages, color correction is generally carried out after wet proofing (proofs created using process color inks) and, as a very last resort, on press.

9.069 *deckle edge*

9.079 *banding*

9.**083 color printing** Printing in inks other than black. The major commercial printing processes today are offset lithography (either sheet- or web-fed) and web gravure. Screen printing is also widely used, although generally for specialist work in small runs. Color letterpress printing—the oldest method —has all but died out except for very specialist work. → 9.061 PRINTING PROCESSES

9.**084 comprehensive** → 9.109 mock-up

9.**085 continuous feeder** On an automatic sheet-fed printing press, the mechanism which supplies the sheets of paper—and which can be replenished—without interrupting the printing process.

9.**086 contrast ratio** Measure of the opacity of paper, 100% being totally opaque.

9.**087 crop marks** Short lines that can be included on a proof print (or other prints) to indicate to a print shop where the page should be trimmed. → 9.068 CORNER MARKS

9.**088 cutout** A halftone image in which the background has been removed to provide a freeform image. Also known as an "outline halftone" or "silhouette halftone." → 9.053 HALFTONE (1)

9.**089 dark field illumination** A method of checking the quality of halftone dots on a piece of film by holding the film at an angle against a dark background.

9.**090 descreen(ing)** The technique of removing a halftone dot pattern from an image to avoid an undesirable "moiré" pattern which may occur when a new halftone screen is applied. This can be achieved in image-editing applications using built-in "filters" (effects) to slightly blur the image and then sharpen it. Other peripherals, such as scanners, feature descreening routines that will remove the pattern during the image acquisition process. → 9.053 HALFTONE (1); 10.112 MOIRÉ; 6.039 INTERPOLATION

9.**091 desensitize** Chemical treatment of a lithographic plate to make the nonimage areas water-receptive so that they repel ink. The chemical solution used is called an "etch." → 9.004 ETCH

9.**092 diffraction** The scattering of lightwaves as they strike the edge of an opaque surface. In the conventional preparation of halftones, this can affect dot formations. → 9.053 HALFTONE (1)

9.**093 diffuse highlight** An area of highlight on a halftone image that bears the smallest printable dot. → 9.053 HALFTONE (1)

9.**094 direct digital color proof** (**DDCP**) Any color proof made directly from digital data without using separation films, such as proofs produced directly on an inkjet printer. → 1.446 INKJET PRINTER

9.**095 dot pattern** The pattern created by halftone dots after all colors are printed. A halftone image printed in register, and with the correct halftone screen angles, will produce a "rosette" pattern, while incorrectly angled halftone screens will produce a pattern known as "moiré." → 10.112 MOIRÉ

9.**096 double image** A printing aberration caused by additional or duplicated halftone dots.

9.**097 double-dot halftone** Two halftone films made from a single original image, one

9.095 *dot pattern*

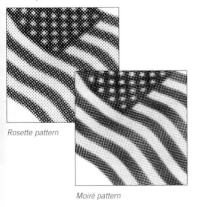

Rosette pattern

Moiré pattern

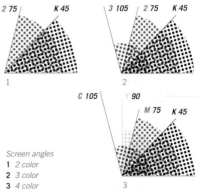

1

2

*C 105*  *Y 90*

*M 75*  *K 45*

3

Screen angles
1 *2 color*
2 *3 color*
3 *4 color*

exposed to accommodate midtones, the other to reproduce highlights and shadows, and which, when combined, produce a printed image with a greater tonal range than would be possible with a single exposure. → 9.053 HALFTONE (1); 6.064 DUOTONE

9.**098 drum** An alternative term for the cylinder of a printing press or papermaking machine.

9.**099 elliptical dot** (**screen**) A halftone screen in which the dots are elliptical in shape. → 9.007 HALFTONE SCREEN

9.**100 finished page area** The area on a computer layout or printed sheet that will form the page after the sheet is trimmed. Once printed, the finished page area is delineated by corner marks ("trim," or "crop" marks).

9.**101 full color** Synonymous with "four color," the term usually used to describe process color reproduction wherein the end result can include full color imagery. → 9.052 FOUR-COLOR PROCESS

9.**102 grayscale** (**printing**) A tonal scale printed in steps from white to black and used for controlling the quality of both color and black-and-white photographic processing, and also for assessing quality in a halftone print. A grayscale (also called a "step wedge," "halftone step scale" or a "step tablet") is sometimes printed on the edge of a sheet.

9.**103 halftone dot** The smallest basic element of a halftone. It may be round, square, elliptical, or any other shape. The frequency of halftone dots is measured in lines per inch (lpi) or lines per centimeter (lpc).

9.**104 indeterminate color** A trapping term which describes an area of color comprised of many colors, such as a picture. → 9.125 TRAPPING

9.**105 knockout** An area of background color that has been masked ("knocked out") by a foreground object, and thus does not print. The opposite of "overprint."

9.**106 lap** Contraction of overlap, describing colors that overlap to avoid registration problems ("trapping"). → 9.125 TRAPPING

9.**107 lines per inch** (**lpi**) The measurement of the resolution, or coarseness, of a halftone, being the number of rows of dots to each inch.

9.**108 mesh marks** In screen printing, a cross-hatch pattern on the printed surface, left by the mesh of the screen fabric and caused by incorrect ink consistency. Also called "screen marks."

9.**109 mock-up** A preliminary rendering of a composite image or project wherein the principal elements are represented by simulations of the finished artwork to imply the final effect rather than show it in full detail. Also known as a "comprehensive," "presentation visual" or "finished rough."

9.**110 nonimpact printing** Printing processes in which the printing surface does not strike the surface of the substrate, when using plotters, laser, and inkjet printers, for example.

9.**111 output resolution** The resolution of a computer printer, monitor, imagesetter, or similar device, usually measured in dpi (dots per inch). The relationship between output resolution and halftone screen ruling determines the tonal range that can be printed. The following formula should be

9.103 *Halftone dot—dot shape*

*round*

*line*

*elliptical*

*square*

*ordered dither*

used to calculate the optimum number of grays that can be achieved (remembering that 256 is the PostScript maximum):

(output resolution ÷ screen ruling) 2 + 1 = shades of gray. Therefore an image output at 1,200 dpi and printed with a screen ruling of 90 lpi will produce 178 shades of gray. Increasing the screen ruling creates smaller halftone dots and adds detail to an image. However, this also reduces the number of grays, so the same image output at 1,200 dpi and printed with a screen ruling of 175 lpi will produce only 48 shades of gray. The screen ruling in four-color process work is usually 150 lpi, so for an image to print with the maximum number of 256 grays it will need to be output with an imagesetter resolution of 2,400 dpi. The typical resolution for a monitor is 72–90 dpi, for a laser printer 600 dpi, and for an imagesetter anything upward of 1,000 dpi. → 6.016 INPUT RESOLUTION

9.**112 page description language** (**PDL**) A programming language, such as Adobe's PostScript, that uses program instructions to construct graphics and characters on a printed page. Typically PDLs are machine independent however they do rely on output devices that have substantial quantities of memory.

9.**113 photoresist** A coating selectively applied to a printing plate to protect it from etching chemicals.

9.**114 pixels per inch** (**ppi**) A measure of the resolution in an image (or, less commonly used now, in a CCD imaging chip). Normally measured horizontally. Also a measurement of the ability of a scanner to discern detail in a scanned image. → 1.095 PIXEL

9.**115 plate** A metal, plastic, or paper sheet from which an image is printed by a commercial printer.

9.**116 press** Any machine that transfers (prints) an impression, traditionally from a forme, block, plate or blanket onto paper or other material.

9.**117 printer description file** A file that defines the specific characteristics of individual printers. → 3.046 POSTSCRIPT PRINTER DESCRIPTION (PPD)

9.**118 purity** The degree of saturation of a color, usually applied to printing inks.

9.**119 registration color** In many graphics applications, a default color that, when applied to items such as crop marks, will print on every separation plate.

9.**120 rotary press** Any printing press in which the printing surface is on a rotating cylinder. Paper can be delivered to rotary presses in either sheet or web form.

9.**121 Rubylith** Proprietary name for a widely used type of peelable masking film used for film makeup. Photoshop's mask is sometimes colloquially referred to as a rubylith. → 6.041 MASKING

9.**122 screen tester** A piece of equipment used to identify the screen resolution, or number of lines per inch, of a printed halftone image. → 9.007 HALFTONE SCREEN

9.**123 service bureau** A company that provides digital image services such as color scanning and high-resolution imagesetting.

9.107 *lines per inch*

*150 lpi*

*100 lpi*

*60 lpi*

9.**124 spread / choke** Two "trapping" techniques used in print preparation to ensure that two abutting areas of ink print without gaps. A spread traps a light foreground object to a surrounding dark background by expanding the edge of the inner object so that the two colors overlap. A choke, on the other hand, does precisely the opposite. It traps a dark foreground object to a surrounding light background. Because the darker of the two adjacent colors defines the visible edge of the object, it is always preferable to extend the lighter color into the darker. Traditionally, spreads and chokes were achieved by slightly overexposing the film so that the image areas expanded. The piece of film used for the spread was termed a "fatty," whereas the film used for the choke was termed a "skinny." Nowadays, software applications provide automatic trapping features. ➔ 9.125 TRAPPING

9.**125 trapping** The slight overlap of two colors to eliminate gaps that may occur between them due to the normal fluctuations of registration during printing. Also refers to printing an ink color before the previous one has dried ("wet trapping"). ➔ 9.124 SPREAD/CHOKE

9.**126 ultraviolet (UV) light** Light waves that lie beyond the visible violet part of the spectrum. Because they can be absorbed by certain photosensitive materials, they are used for platemaking, printing inks, etc. UV light also has a detrimental effect on inks used in many printing processes, especially inkjets.

9.**127 web offset** A rotary printing press that uses a continuous reel-fed paper "web" where the impression (image) from the plate is offset onto a blanket (usually rubber) before being printed onto the paper. There are three main systems: "blanket to blanket," in which two plates and two blanket cylinders on each unit print the web; three-cylinder systems, in which plate blanket and impression cylinders print one sie of the paper only; and satellite or planetary systems, in which two, three or four plate and blanket cylinders are arranged around a common impression cylinder, printing one side of the web in as many colors as there are plate cylinders. ➔ 9.128 WEB (PRINTING) PRESS

9.**128 web (printing) press** A rotary printing press that uses continuous paper from a large roll that is fed through a series of rollers (cylinders) on which the plates are mounted. The impression from the plate is offset onto a blanket before being printed onto the paper. ➔ 9.127 WEB OFFSET

9.**129 watercolor printing** A printing process using water-soluble inks on porous paper that results in the blending of overlapping layers of color.

9.**130 work and tumble** A printing technique in which pages from both sides of the sheet are printed in one side using a single plate. After printing the first side the sheet is then turned, with the back edge becoming the front edge, and passed through the press for a second time. The technique produces two copies of each page. A similar result is achieved with work and turn.

9.124 *spread*

*Yellow overprints cyan*

*spread*

9.125 *trapping*

*without trapping*

*with trapping*

9.124 *choke*

*Cyan overprints yellow*

*choke*

# GENERAL

## General terms

**10.001 absolute value** The magnitude of a number irrespective of its sign (+ or –). The number –15 has an absolute value of 15.

**10.002 American National Standards Institute (ANSI)** An organization devoted to defining standards, such as those used for programming languages. ANSI represents the United States at the International Organization for Standardization (ISO).

**10.003 American Standards Association (ASA)** The association that defined the scale used for rating the speed (light-sensitivity) of photographic film.

**10.004 animation** The process of creating a moving image by rapidly moving from one still image to the next. Traditionally this was achieved through a laborious process of drawing or painting each "frame" (a single step in the animation) manually onto cellulose acetate sheets (which were known as "cels," or "cells"). However, animations are now more commonly created by means of specialist software which renders sequences in a variety of formats, typically QuickTime, AVI, and animated GIF.

→ 10.067 FRAME; 1.242 QUICKTIME; 3.003 AVI; 3.001 ANIMATED GIF

**10.005 archive quality** A print, mounting board, or storage medium that is designed to last (almost) indefinitely. In practice it describes printing inks that are unlikely to fade rapidly, and mounting boards and storage materials (particularly plastics) that will not give off gases or seep acids that will be detrimental to the imagery that is mounted on (or stored in) them.

**10.006 artifact** A visible flaw in an electronically prepared image, usually occurring as a result of the imaging technique employed. JPEG compression, for example, reduces image data in square blocks of pixels that can become clearly visible, particularly when high contrast or color effects are applied.

**10.007 aspect ratio** The ratio of the width of an image to its height, expressed as x:y. For example, the aspect ratio of an image measuring 200 x 100 pixels is 2:1.

**10.008 bas relief** An image that is embossed and stands out in shallow relief from a flat background, designed to give the illusion of further depth.

10.007 *aspect ratio*

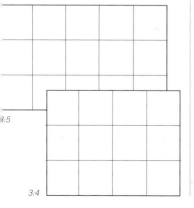

3:5

3:4

10.008 *bas relief*

10.**009 bevel** A chamfered edge applied to type, buttons, or selections to emphasize a three-dimensional effect.

10.**010 bilevel, bileveled** Black-and-white images containing no intermediate gray levels.

10.**011 binary** Literally, two outcomes or two components. The binary number system has the base 2 and so all values are expressed as combinations of 1 and 0, including logical states (true/false). These states can be represented in computers as on/off or circuit closed/circuit open, hence the binary system underpins digital computing.

10.**012 black box** A colloquial term for a piece of equipment which converts data or performs other automatic tasks, but which does not have a keyboard attached.

10.**013 blooming** Optical term for applying an antireflective coating to camera (and other optical equipment) lenses. Such lenses are then said to be bloomed. Also a defect in early CCD (charge-coupled device) imaging chips that caused charge from a pixel to "leak" to neighboring pixels when imaging an object that produced charge levels larger than its nominal maximum. This resulted in smeared highlights and blurred haloes.

10.**014 Blue Book** The document which specifies all parameters for Enhanced Music CD (CD Extra) interactive technology; this technology creates multisession CDs that contain audio tracks in one session as well as a data track.

10.**015 calibrate, calibration** The process of adjusting a machine or piece of hardware to conform to a known scale or standard so that it performs more accurately. In graphic reproduction it is important that the various devices and materials used in the production chain—such as scanners, monitors, imagesetters, and printing presses—conform to a consistent set of measures in order to achieve true fidelity, particularly where color is concerned. Calibration of reproduction and display devices is generally carried out with a "densitometer." ➔ 10.035 DENSITOMETER

10.**016 capture** The action of "getting" an image, by taking a photograph, scanning an image into a computer, or "grabbing" an image using a frame grabber. ➔ 1.383 SCREEN CAPTURE

10.**017 clip art / clip media** Collections of (usually) royalty-free photographs, illustrations, design devices, and other precreated items, such as movies, sounds, and 3D wireframes. Clip art is available in three formats: on paper, so it can be cut out and pasted onto camera-ready art; on CD or floppy disk; or, increasingly, via the Web. The quality of clip art collections can vary enormously, as can the licensing requirements, so you are advised to check both before purchasing. Clip art collections are often referred to as "copyright-free," but your purchase of the material merely grants you the license to use the images without payment of further fees, this is a bit of a misnomer and care should be exercised over your subsequent use of the images. ➔ 10.086 IMAGE RESOURCE; 10.027 COPYRIGHT-FREE

10.**018 clipping** Limiting an image or piece of art to within the bounds of a particular area. ➔ 5.043 CLIPPING PATH

10.**019 collage** An image assembled from elements drawn from different sources. Originally used to describe those pieces produced by pasting together images culled from magazines (say) or fabric swatches. It now also describes images built by image editing but with the disparate nature of the separate components still obvious. Also known as a montage or (for photographic subjects) a photomontage.

10.**020 color temperature** A measure of the composition of light. This is defined as the temperature—measured in degrees Kelvin—to which a black object would need to be heated to produce a particular color of light. The color temperature is based on a scale that sets zero as absolute darkness and increases with an object's—for example a light bulb filament's—brightness. A tungsten lamp, for example, has a color temperature of 2,900 K, while the temperature of direct sunlight is around 5,000 K and is considered the ideal viewing standard in the graphic arts.

10.**021 comb filter** Electronic filter which splits an incoming video signal into brightness (luminance) and color (chrominance).

10.**022 constrain** (1) A facility in some applications to contain one or more items within another. For example, in a page layout application, a picture box (the "constrained item") within another picture box (the "constraining box").

10.**023 contrast** The degree of difference between adjacent tones in an image (or computer monitor) from the lightest to the darkest. "High contrast" describes an image with light highlights and dark shadows, but with few shades in between, while a "low contrast" image is one with even tones and few dark areas or highlights. → 8.011 HIGH KEY; 8.012 LOW KEY

10.**024 copy** (**1**) Any manuscript, typescript, transparency, or computer disk that is used for reproduction. Also called the "original."

10.**025 copyright** The right of a person who creates an original work to protect that work by controlling how and where it may be reproduced. This does not mean that ownership of the work automatically signifies ownership of copyright (or vice versa)—ownership of copyright is transferred if the creator of the work assigns it in writing. While certain aspects are controlled by international agreement, as defined by the Universal Copyright Convention (UCC), there are some differences from country to country, particularly when it comes to the period, or "term," for which a work is protected (in most countries this is 50 years after its creator's death). In the United States, the Pan American agreement decrees that ownership of an "intellectual property" (the legal description of copyright ownership) be established by registration, whereas in the United Kingdom it exists automatically by virtue of the creation of the work. There is often confusion between copyright in a work and the "right" to publish it—ownership of the right to publish a work in one country may not extend to other countries, and it does not necessarily signify ownership of copyright. Equally, ownership of copyright may be shared—the author of a book, for example, may own copyright in the text, while copyright in the design of the book may be owned by its designer or publisher. → 10.026 COPYRIGHT NOTICE/LINE

10.**026 copyright notice / line** The indication of ownership of copyright in a work ("form of notice"), particularly one that is reproduced, as required by the Universal Copyright Convention. This states that all the first and subsequent editions of a work bear the word "Copyright" or the symbol "©" (most publishers include both), the year of publication (or of first publication if it is a straight reprint), and the name of the owner of the copyright in the work. Thus a notice would appear: "Copyright © 2001 A. N. Author." → 10.025 COPYRIGHT

10.**027 copyright-free** A misnomer used to describe ready-made resources such as clip art. In fact, resources described as such are rarely, if ever, "copyright free"—it is generally only the license to use the material which is granted by purchase. The correct description would normally be "royalty-free"—that is, material which you can use—under license—that is free from payment of further fees or royalties. → 10.025 COPYRIGHT; 10.017 CLIP ART; 10.086 IMAGE RESOURCE

10.**028 crop** To trim or mask an image so that it fits a given area, or to discard unwanted portions of an image.

10.**029 data bank** Any place or hardware device where large amounts of data are stored for ready access.

10.**030 data warehouse** A large repository of data (usually corporate) that is stored either at a company's location or by a third party so it is accessible but away from data that is used day-to-day.

10.**031 datum** A piece of information. Its plural, "data," is nowadays erroneously used as a singular noun in place of "datum." → 1.034 DATA

10.**032 decryption** The process of removing the protection given to data or a document by encryption. Usually, the software used to encrypt data must be the same as that used to decrypt it. → 10.059 ENCRYPTION

10.**033 definition** The overall quality—or clarity—of an image, determined by the combined subjective effect of graininess (or resolution in a digital image) and sharpness. → 10.139 RESOLUTION

10.**034 degrade / degradation** A decrease in quality (usually signal quality), generally caused by physical erosion. Though analog systems are prone to signal degradation, digital systems too can be affected.

10.**035 densitometer** A precision instrument used to measure the optical density and other properties of color and light in positive or negative transparencies, printing film, reflection copy, or computer monitors. Also called a "color coder." → 10.015 CALIBRATE, CALIBRATION

10.**036 density** The darkness of tone or color in any image. In a transparency this refers to the amount of light which can pass through it, thus determining the darkness of shadows and the saturation of color. A printed highlight cannot be any lighter in color than the color of the paper it is printed on, while the shadows cannot be any darker than the quality and volume of ink that the printing process will allow.

10.**037 density range** The maximum range of tones in an image, measured as the difference between the maximum and minimum densities (the darkest and lightest tones). → 10.036 DENSITY

10.**038 detail** The degree to which individual features of an image are defined.

10.**039 Deutsche Industrie-Norm (DIN)** A code of standards established in Germany and used widely throughout the world to standardize such things as size, weight, and other properties of particular materials and manufactured items—for example computer connectors and photographic film speed—so that they are universally compatible.

10.**040 diffuser** Any material that scatters transmitted light, thus increasing the area of the light source. → 8.197 DIFFUSE (IMAGE)

10.**041 digit** Any numeral from 0 to 9. → 1.016 BIT

10.**042 digital** Anything operated by or created from information represented by binary digits, such as digital recording. Distinct from analog, in which information is a physical variable. → 1.016 BIT

10.**043 digital data** Information stored or transmitted as a series of 1s and 0s ("bits"). Because values are fixed (so-called discrete values), digital data is more reliable than analog data, as the latter is susceptible to sometimes uncontrollable physical variations. → 10.050 DISCRETE VALUE; 1.016 BIT

10.**044 Digital Data Exchange Standard (DDES)** An ANSI/ISO approved standard that allows equipment produced by different manufacturers to communicate ("interface"). → 10.002 ANSI; 10.092 ISO; 1.325 INTERFACE

10.**045 digital device** Any piece of equipment that operates by means of instructions or signals represented by binary digits, such as a computer. → 10.042 DIGITAL; 1.016 BIT

10.**046 digital domain** General term to denote information handling or activity that takes place digitally. Thus Photoshop image manipulation is in the digital domain.

10.**047 digital image** Image converted to (or created in) the digital domain. Elements of the image are represented by pixels with discrete color and brightness values. → 10.046 DIGITAL DOMAIN

10.**048 digitize** To convert anything, for example text, images, or sound, into binary form so that it can be digitally processed, manipulated, stored, and reconstructed. In other words, transforming analog to digital. → 1.016 BIT; 10.042 DIGITAL

10.**049 direct access** Access to an item by a direct path. For example, a computer, when connected to another by means of a continuous, dedicated telephone line rather than via modems and regular telephone lines, has direct access. → 1.150 MODEM

10.**050 discrete value** A value which is individually distinct and varies only by whole, defined units, as distinct from a value which is infinitely variable ("nondiscrete value").

10.**051 dots per inch (dpi)** A unit of measurement used to represent the resolution of devices such as printers and imagesetters and also, erroneously, monitors and images, whose resolution should more properly be expressed in pixels per inch (ppi). The closer the dots or pixels (the more there are to each inch) the better the quality. Typical resolutions are 72 ppi for a monitor, 600 dpi for a laser printer, and 2450 dpi (or more) for an imagesetter. → 10.139 RESOLUTION

10.**052 dots per square inch (dpsi / dpi2)** A numerical value representing the number of dots that are printed (or could be printed) over one square inch of paper.

10.**053 downtime** A period of time in which a person, machine, or device is idle, for any reason.

10.**054 draft** The initial stage of a manuscript, text, or illustration that will be refined, rewritten, or edited. A draft design is called a "rough," "visual" or "scamp." When a manuscript is ready for typesetting, it is called a "final draft." → 10.142 ROUGH

10.**055 dupe** A duplicate of anything, although generally used to describe a copy of an original transparency.

10.**056 dynamic range** In electronic imaging, the range of light levels recordable by a CCD (charge-coupled device) or other electronic imaging device.

10.**057 electronic media** General term to describe media that uses electronic means for dissemination and delivery of information. CD-ROMs and the Internet would qualify but newspapers would not, even though electronic means are used to gather and produce them.

**10.058 electronic publishing (EP)** General term that describes information distributed by electronic media. → 10.057 ELECTRONIC MEDIA

**10.059 encryption** Method of scrambling data using complex algorithms to protect information from unauthorized access. Encrypted files usually require a password or code to "unlock" the data. → 10.032 DECRYPTION

**10.060 error-checking** A way of ensuring the integrity of data. This can occur either when the data is input—via a keyboard for example (a spellchecker is a type of error-check)—or when it is transmitted via a device such as a modem.

**10.061 error / result code** A number that sometimes accompanies error messages to show the nature of the problem. → 1.043 ERROR MESSAGE

**10.062 export** A feature provided by many applications to allow you to save a file in an format so that it can be used by another application or on a different operating system. For example, an illustration created in a drawing application may be exported as an EPS file so that it can be used in a page-layout application. → 10.089 IMPORT; 1.057 IMPORT/EXPORT FILTER

**10.063 factory settings** Settings to which a device (computer, peripheral, or software) has been set at the factory or assembly plant. Also known as "defaults" and "presets." These settings can be changed but there is generally an option to "restore factory settings" or "restore defaults."

**10.064 first generation copy** A duplicate of an item, such as a photograph, made directly from the original (as distinct from a copy made from another copy of the original). → 10.055 DUPE

**10.065 flow chart** A diagrammatic representation of a process. Also used as a diagrammatic representation of a computer program's actions.

**10.066 fractal;** Infinitely variable shapes characterized by (often) extreme irregularity and defined by complex but precisely defined mathematical expressions. A principal characteristic is self-similarity, wherein a magnified part of a fractal appears identical to the "parent" shape and has identical visual and mathematical properties. Fractals are categorized into sets, including Mandelbrot and Julia sets. Some Photoshop filters (notably Kai's Power Tools, version 5 and 6) make extensive use of fractal mathematics and patterning, allowing users to make bold graphics from scratch and use image elements as the basic element. Fractal routines are being used in proprietary image compression routines to enable dramatic reductions in size but with limited effect on image quality.

**10.067 frame (2)** A single still picture from a movie or animation sequence. Also a single complete image from a TV picture (which normally comprises two interlaced fields, each carrying alternate line information).

**10.068 frame grab(bing)** The capture of a single still frame from a video sequence.

**10.069 frames per second (FPS)** The number of individual still images required to make each second of an animation or movie sequence.

231

10.066 *fractal*

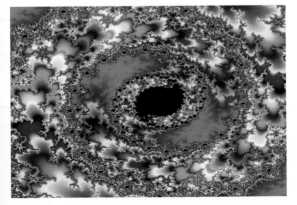

10.**070 frequently asked question (FAQ)** A method of delivering technical support to users of software, hardware, and the Internet—and, increasingly, to users of virtually any product or service—by means of a database of answers to commonly asked questions.

10.**071 FYI** abb.: for your information. A frequently used shorthand, particularly in e-mail correspondence.

10.**072 generation** Successive copies of data. Theoretically digital data can be copied for multiple generations with no loss of quality, but the introduction of file compressions often compromises image quality cumulatively over successive generations.

10.**073 graduation / gradation** The smooth transition from one color or tone to another.

10.**074 graphic** A general term describing any illustration or drawn design.

10.**075 graphic arts** The general term encompassing the entire craft of reproduction by means of any of the many printing processes. As distinct from "graphic design," which involves providing a graphic solution to a specific problem and the implementation of that solution by whatever means.

10.**076 Green Book** The document which specifies all parameters for CD-I (compact disc-interactive) technology. Little used now, as the CD-I format has been substantially, if not totally, superseded. → 1.495 CD-I

10.**077 hard copy** A physical copy of something, such as a printout of an image document. The same document stored on disk or in memory is known as a soft copy. → 10.197 SOFT COPY

10.**078 hertz (Hz)** A measurement of frequency. One hertz is one cycle, or occurrence, per second.

10.**079 hex(adecimal)** The use of the number 16 as the basis of a counting system, as distinct from our conventional decimal (base ten) system or the binary (base two) system used by basic computer processes. The figures are represented by the numbers 1 to 9, followed by the letters A to F. Thus decimal 9 is still hex 9, while decimal 10 becomes hex A, decimal 16 becomes hex 10, decimal 26 becomes hex 1A, and so on.

10.**080 highlight** To mark an item, such as a section of text, icon, or menu command, to indicate that it is selected or active.

10.**081 hologram** An image created by lasers to give an illusion of three dimensions, used commonly in security printing, but also as a novelty. → 10.100 LASER

10.**082 IBM** International Business Machines, a major manufacturer of computing hardware. → 1.053 IBM PC

10.**083 icon** A graphical representation of an object (such as a disk, file, folder, or tool) or of a concept or message used to make identification and selection easier. → 1.322 GUI

10.**084 image area** The area within which a particular image or group of images is to fit in a final document. Also the description of the area in a program interface (such as Photoshop) where the image to be manipulated sits.

10.**085 image library** A source of original transparencies and pictures that can be used for virtually any purpose on payment of a fee, which usually varies according to usage—a picture to be used in an advertisement will invariably cost a great deal more than the same picture for use in a school textbook. Many libraries specialize in various subjects, such as garden plants, wildlife, and fine art. (In the last case be aware that while the library may own the copyright in the photograph of a painting, the ownership of copyright in the painting itself may belong elsewhere.) → 10.086 IMAGE RESOURCE; 10.025 COPYRIGHT

10.**086 image resource** A source of ready-made material such as royalty-free image libraries, clip art, and mapping resources distributed digitally on various media such as CD-ROM and the Web; as distinct from "image libraries," which supply original transparencies and pictures. → 10.017 CLIP ART/CLIP MEDIA; 10.085 IMAGE LIBRARY

10.**087 image size** A description of the dimensions of an image. Depending on the type of image being measured, this can be in terms of linear dimensions, resolution, or digital file size.

10.**088 imaging device** A general term describing any dedicated piece of equipment that either captures an image from an original such as a scanner or camera, or generates an image from a previously captured original such as a contact printing frame or imagesetter.

10.**089 import** To bring text, pictures, or other data into a document. → 10.062 EXPORT

10.**090 input** Generally, anything that is put in or taken in to something else, but usually used with reference to entering information into a computer by whatever means.

10.**091 interactive** Any activity that involves an immediate and reciprocal action between a person and a machine (for example, driving a car), but more commonly describing dialog between a computer and its user. → 1.059 INTERACTIVE MODE

10.**092 International Organization for Standardization (ISO)** A Swiss-based body responsible for defining many elements common to design, photography, and publishing, such as paper size, film speed rating, and network protocol (ISO/OSI protocol).

10.**093 International Press Telecommunications Council (IPTC)** A body responsible for defining the standards for image and image text transmission. The standard defines categories such as caption, credit, and keyword for text annotation to images. Photoshop conforms to this standard. → 2.227 FILE INFO

10.**094 ISO equivalent** A term for relating the sensitivity of a digital camera to that of conventional film stock. Giving an ISO equivalent rating (which, in a digital camera, may be switchable over a considerable range) enables users to use familiar aperture and exposure values.

10.**095 Julia set** Fractal set. Along with the Mandelbrot set, a feature of certain fractal pattern generators in later versions of Kai's Power Tools. → 10.066 FRACTAL

10.**096 Kelvin temperature scale (K)** A unit of measurement that describes the color of a light source, based on absolute darkness rising to incandescence. → 10.020 COLOR TEMPERATURE

10.**097 key frame** A single animation frame in a QuickTime sequence in which information is stored as a reference, so that subsequent frames only store changes in the frame ("differences") rather than storing the whole frame each time; this making the file smaller. The frames based on changes are called "delta frames" or "difference frames."

10.**098 kilo** A unit of metric measurement representing 1,000 (from the Greek "khilioi" for "thousand"). However, although the term is widely used as a measure of computer data ("kilobyte," for example), computers use a binary system (pairs of numbers) in which each number is doubled: 2; 4; 8; 16; 32; 64; 128; 256; 512; 1,024; etc. Thus "kilo" in a data context does not mean 1,000, but 1,024 (210). → 10.111 MEGA

10.**099 landscape format** An image or page format in which the width is greater than the height. Also called "horizontal format." → 10.125 PORTRAIT FORMAT

10.**100 laser** Acronym for light amplified by stimulated emission of radiation. A light source of almost pure wavelength.

10.**101 layout** A drawing that shows the general appearance of a design, indicating, for example, the position of text and illustrations. The term is also used when preparing a design for reproduction, where it is called a "tissue" or "overlay," the terms deriving from the transparent paper often used for drawing layouts.

10.**102 library** A feature of some applications which provides a facility for storing frequently used items or attributes (such as colors) that you have created so that you can access them immediately from within any document.

10.**103 light-emitting diode (LED)** An electronic component providing miniature light sources which are used to display alphanumeric characters on some hardware devices.

10.**104 light sensitive** Any material or device that responds either chemically or digitally to light striking it, such as a photographic emulsion or a photosite (the light sensor of a CCD). → 8.208 CCD; 8.119 EMULSION

10.**105 light table / box** A table or box with a translucent glass top lit from below, giving a color-balanced light suitable for viewing color transparencies and for color-matching them to proofs.

10.**106 line art** Diagrams and graphics comprising (normally) black lines on a white background.

10.**107 line weight** The thickness of a line or rule.

10.**108 Mandelbrot set** Fractal set. Along with the Julia set, a feature of certain fractal pattern generators in later versions of Kai's Power Tools. → 10.066 FRACTAL

10.**109 master** An original item from which all copies are made, or upon which any changes are marked or made.

10.**110 mean noon sunlight** An arbitrary color temperature to which most daylight color films are balanced, based on the average color temperature of direct sunlight at midday in Washington DC (5,400K).

10.**111 mega** A unit of metric measurement representing 1,000,000. Although the term is used as a measure of computer data ("megabyte," for example), computers use a binary system (pairs of numbers) in which each number is doubled: 2; 4; 8; 16; 32; 64; 128; 256; 512; 1,024; etc., thus "mega" in a data context does not mean 1,000,000 but 1,048,576 (230). → 10.098 KILO

10.**112 moiré** An unintended pattern that occurs in halftone reproduction when two or more colors are printed and the dot screens are positioned at the wrong angles. The correct angles at which screens should be positioned depends on the number of colors being printed, but the normal angles for four-color process printing, and thus the default setting in many computer applications, are: cyan 105°; magenta 75°; yellow 90°; black 45°. A moiré pattern can also be caused by scanning or rescreening an image to which a halftone screen has already been applied. → 9.090 DESCREEN(ING); 9.095 DOT PATTERN

10.**113 mono(chrome) / monochromatic (2)** An image of varying tones reproduced in a single color. Not necessarily black and white. → 6.066 MONOTONE

10.**114 Motion Picture Experts Group (MPEG)** A compression format for squeezing full-screen, VHS-quality digital video files and animations, providing huge compression ratios of up to 200:1. MPEG-2 is commonly used for digital television transmissions.

10.**115 mottling** An image artifact that can appear when an image containing large areas of flat color, or gentle gradients, is sharpened. The sharpening algorithm adds perceived detail but also acts on small fluctuations in these areas and accentuates them. It is most virulent with images originally compressed using the JPEG routines.

10.**116 multimedia** Any combination of various digital media, such as sound, video, animation, graphics, and text, incorporated into a software product or presentation.

10.**117 near letter quality (NLQ)** A description of the quality offered by early low-cost printers (usually dot matrix printers).

10.**118 Orange Book** The document which specifies all parameters for recordable CD (CD-R) technology, developed by Sony and Philips. → 1.498 CD-R

10.**119 orientation** The print direction of a page, or format of an image (portrait or landscape).

10.**120 origin** The fixed or zero point of horizontal and vertical axes, or of the rulers featured in Photoshop (and most applications) from which measurements can be made.

10.**121 perspective** A technique of rendering 3D objects on a 2D plane, duplicating the "real world" view by giving the same impression of the object's relative position and size when viewed from a particular point—the shorter the distance, the wider the perspective; the greater the distance, the narrower the perspective.

10.**122 photomechanical transfer (PMT)** A method of transferring images onto paper, film, or metal litho plates by means of photography.

10.107 *line weight:*

| Points: | Pixels at 300 dpi: | Pixels at 72 dpi: |
| --- | --- | --- |
| hairline | 1 pixel | |
| 1pt | 4 pixels | 1 pixel |
| 2pt | 8 pixels | 2 pixels |
| 4pt | 17 pixels | 4pixels |
| 6pt | 25 pixels | 6 pixels |
| 8pt | 33 pixels | 8 pixels |
| 12pt | 50 pixels | 12 pixels |

An image that has been produced by this method is also known as a PMT. Also called "diffusion transfer," "chemical transfer," or "velox."

10.**123 pictogram / pictograph** A simplified, pictorial symbol distilled to its salient features to represent an object or concept.

10.**124 picture skew** The distortion of an image by slanting the two opposite sides of a rectangle away from the horizontal or vertical. → 10.121 PERSPECTIVE

10.**125 portrait format** An image or page in a vertical format. Also called "upright format." → 10.099 LANDSCAPE FORMAT

10.**126 proprietary** A design, product, or format developed, marketed, and owned by a company or person, rather than one defined by a standards organization.

10.**127 public domain** (**PD**) A description of "intellectual property" that is free of all copyrights, meaning that it can be used by anyone for any purpose, either because the copyright period has lapsed or because, as is sometimes the case with computer software, its author has declared it so. Not to be confused with "shareware," for which a fee is usually required.

10.**128 raster image** An image defined as rows of pixels or dots.

10.**129 raster(ization)** Deriving from the Latin word "rastrum," meaning "rake," the method of displaying (and creating) images employed by video screens, and thus computer monitors, in which the screen image is made up of a pattern of several hundred parallel lines created by an electron beam "raking" the screen from top to bottom at a speed of about one–sixtieth of a second. An image is created by varying the intensity of the beam at successive points along the raster. The speed at which a complete screen image, or frame, is created is called the "frame" or "refresh" rate. → 1.102 RASTER IMAGE PROCESSOR (RIP)

10.**130 real-time** The actual time in which things happen; on your computer, therefore, an event that corresponds to reality. For example, at its simplest, a character appearing on screen at the moment you type it is said to be real-time, as is a video sequence that plays back as it is being filmed. Also called "interactive mode." → 1.059 INTERACTIVE MODE

10.**131 Red Book** The document which specifies all parameters for the original compact disc digital audio (CD-DA) technology developed by Sony and Philips. As well as defining the format in which an audio CD must be recorded so that it is playable in every CD player, it also specifies what the CD player must do to play CDs correctly.

10.**132 reflection copy** Any flat item reproduced photographically by light reflected from its surface. As distinct from a "transparency" or "slide" original in which the light is passed through it. → 8.114 TRANSPARENCY

10.**133 reflective art** Artwork or imagery with opaque backing: Viewed from reflected light, rather than transmitted light in the case of a transparency.

10.**134 refraction** Light that is bent, typically when passing through one medium to

235

10.121 *perspective*

10.124 *picture skew*

10.123 *pictogram/pictograph*

another, such as air to water. → 10.135
REFRACTIVE INDEX

10.**135 refractive index** The measurement of the degree to which light is bent by passing through one medium to another, expressed as a ratio of the speed of light between the two. → 10.134 REFRACTION

10.**136 render** Wrapping a surface texture over a three-dimensional body created as a "wire frame." Typically used to create realistic landscapes or turn wire-frame figures into "characters." The wrapping is usually combined with other effects (such as lighting effects) to increase the realism. The Render Photoshop filters create effects such as clouds and lighting effects. → 6.138 RENDER FILTERS

10.**137 replication** This technique is used when an image is enlarged by resampling, but specifically when the resolution is being increased by factors of two in each direction. Rather than being interpolated, new pixels are added automatically take on the exact color and brightness values of their neighbors.

10.**138 rescale** Amending the size of an image by proportionally reducing its height and width. → 6.047 SCALE/SCALING

10.**139 resolution** The degree of quality, definition, or clarity with which an image is reproduced or displayed, for example in a photograph, or via a scanner, monitor screen, printer, or other output device. → 9.111 OUTPUT RESOLUTION; 6.016 INPUT RESOLUTION

10.**140 restore (revert)** To restore something to its original state or, in the case of a document, to its last "saved" version. Also called "revert."

10.**141 retouching** Altering an image, artwork, or film to modify or remove imperfections. Can be done using mechanical methods (knives, inks, and dyes) or digitally, using Photoshop. → 8.050 SPOTTING

10.**142 rough** A preliminary drawing showing a proposed design. Also called a "scamp," or "visual." → 10.101 LAYOUT

10.**143 scan(ning)** An electronic process that converts a hard copy of an image into digital form by sequential exposure to a moving light beam such as a laser. The scanned image can then be manipulated by a computer or output to separated film. → 1.424 DRUM SCANNER; 1.421 DESKTOP SCANNER; 10.100 LASER

10.**144 scanned image** An image that has been recorded by a scanner and converted to a suitable form for reproduction, such as film or a digital file. → 10.143 SCAN(NING)

10.**145 selector** The rules applied to a set of properties and values by which you make a selection.

10.**146 sensitize** To make something, such as a piece of paper, sensitive to something else, such as light. In printing, this includes making the image areas of a printing plate ink-receptive by applying a special coating to an aluminum printing plate.

10.**147 smearing** Image artifact of some early CCDs and early TV picture tubes. Overexposure of a group of pixels results in halation and solarization effects to the source and a bright line (following the pixel columns of the overexposed pixels) above and below the source.

10.**148 snail mail** Derogatory term for the standard postal system, compared with e-mail.

10.**149 source document** Any original used as a master for reproduction.

10.**150 specular highlight** The lightest highlighted area in a reproduced photograph, usually reproduced as unprinted white paper.

10.**151 string** All characters within a given sequence, including spaces and special characters.

10.**152 tear sheet** A page removed from a publication and used or filed for future reference. Often used by published photographers as part of a portfolio of their work or as collection of inspirational imagery gleaned from magazines.

10.**153 throughput** A unit of time measured as the period elapsing between the start and finish of a particular activity. For example, the amount of data that is passed along a communications line in a given period of time.

10.**154 thumbnail** A small representation of an image used mainly for identification purposes in an image directory listing or, within Photoshop, for illustrating channels and layers. Thumbnails are also produced to accompany PictureCDs, PhotoCDs and most APS and 35-mm films submitted for processing.

10.**155 tile / tiling** The repetition of a graphic item, with the repetitions placed side-by-side in all directions so that they form a pattern—

just like tiles. The Displace filter in Photoshop can create tiled images and ImageReady includes a Tile Maker filter that creates seamlessly blended tiles for use in web backgrounds.

10.**156 tone compression** The inevitable consequence of printing an image, resulting in a reduction of the range of tones from light to dark.

10.**157 tracking** The adjustment or fine-tuning of space between multiple text characters in a selected piece of text. The multiple adjustment distinguishes tracking from "kerning," which only involves pairs of characters.

10.**158 transmissive art** Artwork produced on a transparent or translucent backing, such as transparencies. Designed to be viewed with a light source behind the image.

10.**159 transpose / transposition** To exchange the position of any two images, either by design or because they are in the wrong order. For example, image layers may be transposed when a lower layer and higher one are positionally reversed. Animation cells can be transposed in a similar way.

10.**160 value** A particular tint of color. Also a quantity assigned to a parameter, variable, or symbol that will change with application and circumstance.

10.**161 vector** A mathematical description of a line that is defined in terms of physical dimensions and direction. Vectors are used in drawing packages (and Photoshop 6) to define shapes (vector graphics) that are position- and size-independent.

10.**162 videoconferencing** The facility to conduct conferences over a computer network using sound and video pictures.

10.**163 virtual** Not physically existing, but made to appear as though it does. For example, virtual memory is memory (usually on a hard disk) that is perceived to the user and the current application to be an extension of the computer's RAM. ➔ 1.480 VIRTUAL MEMORY

10.**164 virtual reality** A simulated 3D environment that the user can explore on screen or using special virtual reality peripherals. Users can sometimes interact with the virtual environment by using these peripherals to point, or "move around" the environment.

10.**165 wireframe** A three-dimensional shape with no "surface" or texture applied. Because they are built from multiple polygons they resemble shapes built from chicken wire. ➔ 10.136 RENDER

10.**166 working white (space) (ww, wws)** The term describing areas of white space in a design or layout that contain no text or images, but which form an integral part of the design.

10.**167 Yellow Book** The document that specifies all parameters for CD-ROM technology, guaranteeing that discs can be read by all CD-ROM drives. ➔ 1.496 CD-ROM

## Text terms

10.**168 aligned left / right / center** Text positioned such that the left edge, right edge, or center point of each line is aligned to the vertical left, right, or center line of the text box.

10.169 *bitmapped font*

Cozy

10.173 *character space*

ba

10.174 *character width*

aa

10.176 *extended character set*

1234567890-=
ABCDEFGHIJKLMNOPQRSTUVWXYZ
abcdefghijklmnopqrstuvwxyz
!@£$%^&*()_+±⌀◇fifl‡°·,—
±Œ,,‰ÂÊÁËÈØ∏''ÅÍÎÏÌÓÔ●ÒÚÆ»ŸÛÙÇ◊₁^˜-˜¿

10.**169 bitmapped font** A bitmapped font is one in which the characters are made up of dots, or pixels, as distinct from an outline font which is drawn from vectors. Bitmapped fonts generally accompany PostScript Type 1 fonts and are used to render the fonts' shape on screen (they are sometimes also called screen fonts). To draw the character shape accurately on screen your computer must have a bit map installed for each size (they are also called "fixed-size" fonts), although this is not necessary if you have ATM installed, since this uses the outline, or "printer" version of the font (the file that your printer uses in order to print it). TrueType fonts are "outline" and thus do not require a bitmapped version. ➔ 10.160 VECTOR; 1.197 ADOBE TYPE MANAGER (ATM); 10.202 TYPE 1 FONT; 10.201 TRUETYPE font (TTF)

10.**170 case sensitive** The term used to indicate that the case (upper or lower) of characters input into a field, such as a "Find" dialog, or an e-mail address, is significant and will determine the outcome of the request.

10.**171 center-aligned** ➔ 10.168 aligned left/right/center

10.**172 character set** The complete repertoire of letters, numbers, and symbols in a font design. ➔ 10.186 ISO/ADOBE CHARACTER SET

10.**173 character space** The distance between each character as determined by the font designer, as distinct from "kerning" and "tracking," which are modifications of that distance. ➔ 10.188 KERNING;

10.**174 character width** The width of each character, determined from the origin of one to the origin of the next (where the origin is the bottom left-hand corner of the space occupied by each character). ➔ 10.173 CHARACTER SPACE

10.**175 dingbat** The modern name for fonts of decorative symbols, traditionally called printer's "flowers," "ornaments," or "arabesques."

10.**176 extended character set** The characters available in a font other than those that appear on the keyboard, such as accents, symbols, etc., and which are accessed by combinations of key strokes. ➔ 10.172 CHARACTER SET

10.**177 face** Traditionally the printing surface of any metal type character, but nowadays used as a series or family name for fonts with similar characteristics, such as "modern face" or "old face."

10.**178 FON** A bitmap font format used on Windows computers.

10.**179 font** Set of characters sharing the same typeface and size.

10.**180 font family** The complete set of characters of a typeface design in all its sizes and styles. A typical font family contains four individual fonts: roman, italic, bold and bold italic. As distinct from a "typeface" or "font." Also known as a "type family."

10.**181 font file** The file of a bitmapped or screen font, usually residing in a suitcase file on Mac OS computers. ➔ 10.169 BITMAPPED FONT; 10.198 SUITCASE FILE

10.**182 font substitution** A facility of some printers to substitute outline fonts for the basic system bitmapped fonts. On Macintosh

10.184 *horizontal scaling*

hori

10.184 *vertical scale*

verti

10.175 *dingbats*

computers, for example, Helvetica is substituted for Geneva, and Courier for Monaco.

10.**183 font / type series** The identification of a typeface by a series number, for example "Univers 55." → 10.205 TYPEFACE; 10.179 FONT; 10.180 FONT FAMILY

10.**184 horizontal scaling** Text manipulation term. Horizontal scaling retains the exact attributes of the source font but distorts its appearance. Although the feature can sometimes be used advantageously it can also produce ugly typography; in these cases the specially designed condensed or expanded versions of the font, if available, may look more aesthetic.

10.**185 hyphenation and justification (H&J, H / J)** The process of distributing space in a line of type to achieve the desired measure in justified text. When the space between words or characters is too great, and therefore unaesthetic, the word at the end of the line may be "broken" by placing a hyphen at a suitable point in the word.

10.**186 ISO / Adobe character set** The industry standard character set for PostScript type faces. Access to characters depends on which operating system and application is being used. → 10.172 CHARACTER SET

10.**187 italic** The sloping version of a roman type design deriving from cursive handwriting and calligraphic scripts, intended for textual emphasis. The first italic type was cut by Aldus Manutius in about 1499. A version of italic, often called oblique or sloped roman, can be generated digitally by most applications, but this merely slants the roman style to the right so is a poor substitute for the real thing.

10.**188 kerning** The adjustment of spacing between two characters (normally alphanumeric) to improve the overall look of the text.

10.**189 keyboard map** Characters as displayed on a monitor, which correspond with the arrangement on a keyboard. Useful for "finding" nonstandard characters and characters from symbol fonts, such as dingbats. → 10.175 DINGBAT

10.**190 Linotype** A type foundry and manufacturer of typesetting equipment and digital fonts. The original Linotype machine was the first keyboard-operated composing machine to employ the principle of a "matrix," which cast hot metal type in solid lines, or "slugs." It was invented by the German-born American engineer Ottmar Mergenthaler and patented in 1884. The Monotype machine was invented almost simultaneously, in 1885. → 10.191 MONOTYPE

10.**191 Monotype** The name of a type foundry, Monotype Corporation, which designs and supplies digital fonts. Originally, Monotype was the manufacturer of a typesetting process invented in 1885 by Tolbert Lanston of Ohio (one year after the invention of the Linotype machine), which employed a keyboard-operated composing machine to cast type as individual letters. → 10.190 LINOTYPE

10.**192 OpenType** A development of Microsoft's "TrueType Open" font format that adds

---

10.188 *kerning:* variable spacing between pairs of characters

10.157 *tracking:* equal spacing between several characters

10.198 *suitcase file*

📋 Venetian 301 BT

   ⓐ Venetian301 Bd BT

   ⓐ Venetian301 BdIt BT

   ⓐ Venetian301 BT

   ⓐ Venetian301 Dm BT

   ⓐ Venetian301 DmIt BT

   ⓐ Venetian301 It BT

support for Type 1 font data. An OpenType font can have Type 1 data only, TrueType data only, or both. The Type 1 data can be rendered ("rasterized") by a utility such as Adobe Type Manager, or converted to TrueType data for rasterization by the TrueType rasterizer. This font format is a superset of the existing TrueType and Type 1 formats, and is designed to provide support for type in print and onscreen and, with its compression technology, is also relevant to the Internet and the World Wide Web, since it allows fast downloading of type.

10.**193 PostScript font** → 10.202 Type 1 font

10.**194 right-aligned / justified** → 10.168 aligned left/right/center

10.**195 roman** (**type**) A font design in which the characters are upright, as distinct from italic.

10.**196 slash** An obliquely sloping line, or "forward slash" (/). Reversal forms a "backslash" (\). Also called a "solidus."

10.**197 soft copy** Text matter appearing on a computer monitor screen. → 10.077 HARD COPY

10.**198 suitcase file** On computers running the Mac OS, a font file (TrueType), screen font file (PostScript "Type 1"), or collection of sound files, represented by an icon of a suitcase. → 10.201 TRUETYPE FONT (TTF); 10.202 TYPE 1 FONT

10.**199 text path** An invisible line, either straight, curved, or irregular, along which text can be forced to flow.

10.**200 TrueDoc** A font format devised by the Bitstream Corporation which is completely independent of platform, operating system, application, resolution, and device.

10.**201 TrueType font** (**TTF**) This font was originated by Apple Computer's digital font technology, which was developed as an alternative to PostScript and is now used by both Apple and Microsoft for their respective operating systems. A single TrueType file is used for both screen rendering and printing, unlike PostScript fonts, which require a screen font file as well as a printer font file. → 10.192 OPENTYPE; 10.202 TYPE 1 FONT

10.**202 Type 1 font** The Adobe PostScript outline font technology containing "hints" for improved rendering on-screen. Type 1 fonts come as two files: an outline printer file and a bitmapped screen file.

10.**203 Type 3 font** A PostScript font format that does not contain reproduction improvement hints and is now virtually obsolete. → 10.202 TYPE 1 FONT

10.**204 type family** → 10.180 font family

10.**205 typeface** The term (based on "face"—the printing surface of a metal type character) describing a type design of any size, including weight variations on that design such as light and bold, but excluding all other related designs such as italic and condensed. As distinct from "type family," which includes all related designs, and "font," which is one design of a single size, weight, and style. Thus "Baskerville" is a type family, while "Baskerville Bold" is a typeface and "9 pt Baskerville Bold Italic" is a font.

10.**206 Unicode** A character set system which makes provision for 65,000 characters, thus accommodating the languages of the world. → 10.172 CHARACTER SET

10.180 *font family*

| | |
|---|---|
| Light | Light Condensed |
| *Light italic* | *Light Italic Condensed* |
| Medium | Medium Condensed |
| *Medium Italic* | *Medium Italic Condensed* |
| **Bold** | **Bold Condensed** |
| ***Bold Italic*** | ***Bold Italic Condensed*** |
| **Ultra Bold** | **Ultra Bold Condensed** |
| ***Ultra Bold Italic*** | ***Ultra Bold Italic Cond.*** |

# Part 3

# KEYBOARD
# SHORTCUTS

| Operation | Photoshop 6 Macintosh | Photoshop 6 Windows |
|---|---|---|
| Adobe online | Help | - |
| Auto levels | Cmd+Shift+L | Ctrl+Shift+L |
| Clear | Delete (or Backspace) | Delete (or Backspace) |
| Close | Cmd+W | Ctrl+W |
| Color Balance | Cmd+B | Ctrl+B |
| Color Balance, use previous settings | Cmd+Option+B | Ctrl+Alt+B |
| Copy | Cmd+C or F3 | Ctrl+C or F3 |
| Copy Merged | Cmd+Shift+C | Ctrl+Shift+C |
| Curves | Cmd+M | Ctrl+M |
| Curves, use previous settings | Cmd+Option+M | Ctrl+Alt+M |
| Cut | Cmd+X or F2 | Ctrl+X or F2 |
| Desaturate | Cmd+Shift+U | Ctrl+Shift+U |
| Deselect | Cmd+D | Ctrl+D |
| Exit | Cmd+Q | Ctrl+Q |
| Extras, show or hide | Cmd+H | Ctrl+H |
| Fade Filter | Cmd+Shift+F | Ctrl+Shift+F |
| Feather Selection | Cmd+Option+D r Shift+F6 | Ctrl+Alt+D or Shift+F6 |
| Fill | Shift+Delete or Shift+F5 | Shift+Backspace or Shift+F5 |
| Fill from History | Cmd+Option+Delete | Ctrl+Alt+Backspace |
| Filter, repeat last | Cmd+F | Ctrl+F |
| Filter, repeat with new settings | Cmd+Option+F | Ctrl+Alt+F |
| Fit on Screen | Cmd+0 (zero) | Ctrl+0 (zero) |
| Free Transform | Cmd+T | Ctrl+T |
| Gamut Warning | Cmd+Shift+Y | Ctrl+Shift+Y |
| Grid, show or hide | Cmd+Option+' (quote) | Ctrl+Alt+' (quote) |
| Group with Previous Layer | Cmd+G | Ctrl+G |
| Guides, show or hide | Cmd+' (quote) | Ctrl+' (quote) |
| Help contents | Cmd+? | Ctrl+? |
| Hide Path | Cmd+Shift+H | Ctrl+Shift+H |
| Hue/Saturation | Cmd+U | Ctrl+U |
| Hue/Saturation, use previous settings | Cmd+Option+U | Ctrl+Alt+U |
| Inverse Selection | Cmd+Shift+I or Shift+F7 | Ctrl+Shift+I or Shift+F7 |
| Invert | Cmd+I | Ctrl+I |
| Jump to ImageReady | Cmd+Shift+M | Ctrl+Shift+M |
| Layer Via Copy | Cmd+J | Ctrl+J |
| Layer Via Cut | Cmd+Shift+J | Ctrl+Shift+J |

| Operation | Photoshop 6 Macintosh | Photoshop 6 Windows |
|---|---|---|
| Levels | Cmd+L | Ctrl+L |
| Levels, use previous settings | Cmd+Option+L | Ctrl+Alt+L |
| Lock Guides | Cmd+Option+; (semicolon) | Ctrl+Alt+; (semicolon) |
| Merge Down | Cmd+E | Ctrl+E |
| Merge Visible | Cmd+Shift+E | Ctrl+Shift+E |
| Menu commands Auto Levels | Cmd+Shift+L | Ctrl+Shift+L |
| Moves target layer down/up | Cmd+[ or ] | Ctrl+[ or ] |
| Moves target layer back/front | Cmd+Shift+[ or ] | Ctrl+Shift+[ or ] |
| New | Cmd+N | Ctrl+N |
| New Layer | Cmd+Shift+N | Ctrl+Shift+N |
| New, with default settings | Cmd+Option+N | Ctrl+Alt+N |
| Open | Cmd+O | Ctrl+O |
| Page Setup | Cmd+Shift+P | Ctrl+Shift+P |
| Paste | Cmd+V or F4 | Ctrl+V or F4 |
| Paste Into | Cmd+Shift+V | Ctrl+Shift+V |
| Preferences | Cmd+K | Ctrl+K |
| Preferences, last panel | Cmd+Option+K | Ctrl+Alt+K |
| Preview CMYK | Cmd+Y | Ctrl+Y |
| Print | Cmd+P | Ctrl+P |
| Quit | Cmd+Q | – |
| Reselect | Cmd+Shift+D | Ctrl+Shift+D |
| Revert | F12 | F12 |
| Rulers, show or hide | Cmd+R | Ctrl+R |
| Save | Cmd+S | Ctrl+S |
| Save for web | Cmd+Shift+Option+S | Ctrl+Shift+Alt+S |
| Save As | Cmd+Shift+S | Ctrl+Shift+S |
| Select All | Cmd+A | Ctrl+A |
| Snap | Cmd+; (semicolon) | Ctrl+; (semicolon) |
| Snap to Grid | Cmd+Shift+' (quote) | Ctrl+Shift+' (quote) |
| Snap to Guides | Cmd+Shift+; (semicolon) | Ctrl+Shift+; (semicolon) |
| Step Backwards | Cmd+Option+Z | Ctrl+Alt+Z |
| Step Forwards | Cmd+Shift+Z | Ctrl+Shift+Z |
| Transform Again | Cmd+Shift+T | Ctrl+Shift+T |
| Undo/Redo, toggle | Cmd+Z or F1 | Ctrl+Z |
| Zoom In | Cmd++ (plus) | Ctrl++ (plus) |
| Zoom Out | Cmd+- (minus) | Ctrl+- (minus) |

| Painting | Photoshop 6 Macintosh | Photoshop 6 Windows |
|---|---|---|
| **Brush size, decrease/increase** | [ or ] | [ or ] |
| **Brush softness/hardness, decrease/increase** | Shift+[ or ] | Shift+[ or ] |
| **Create new brush shape** | Click in empty area of Brushes palette | Click in empty area of Brushes palette |
| **Cycle through Eraser functions** | Option+click Eraser tool icon or Shift+E | Alt+click Eraser tool icon or Shift+E |
| **Cycle through Focus tools** | Option+click Focus tool icon or Shift+R | Alt+click Focus tool icon or Shift+R |
| **Cycle through Rubber Stamp options** | Option+click Rubber Stamp tool icon or Shift+S | Alt+click Rubber Stamp tool icon or Shift+S |
| **Cycle through Toning tools** | Option+click Toning tool icon or Shift+O | Alt+click Toning tool icon or Shift+O |
| **Delete shape from Brushes palette** | Option+click brush shape | Alt+click brush shape |
| **Display crosshair cursor** | Caps Lock | Caps Lock |
| **Display Options palette** | Return | Enter |
| **Display Fill dialog box** | Shift+Delete | Shift+Backspace |
| **Edit brush shape** | Double-click brush shape | Double-click brush shape |
| **Paint or edit in a straight line** | Click and then Shift+click | Click and then Shift+click |
| **Reset to normal brush mode** | Shift+Option+N | Shift+Alt+N |
| **Restore image with Magic Eraser** | Option+drag with eraser | Alt+drag with eraser |
| **Rename brush** | Double-click brush | Double-click brush |
| **Select Airbrush tool** | J | J |
| **Select Paintbrush tool** | B | B |
| **Select background tool** | Option+Eyedropper tool+click | Alt+Eyedropper tool+click |
| **Set opacity, pressure, or exposure** | Any painting or editing tool+number keys (e.g. 0=100%, 1=10%, 4 then 5 in quick succession=45%) | Any painting or editing tool+number keys (e.g. 0=100%, 1=10%, 4 then 5 in quick succession=45%) |

| Applying colors | Photoshop 6 Macintosh | Photoshop 6 Windows |
|---|---|---|
| **Add new swatch to palette** | Click in empty area of palette | Click in empty area of palette |
| **Color palette, show/hide** | F6 | F6 |
| **Cycle through color choices** | Shift+click color bar | Shift+click color bar |
| **Delete swatch from palette** | Cmd+click swatch | Ctrl+click swatch |
| **Display Fill dialog box** | Shift+Delete or Shift+F5 | Shift+Backspace or Shift+F5 |
| **Fill layer with background color but preserve transparency** | Shift+Cmd+Delete | Shift+Ctrl+Backspace |
| **Fill layer with foreground color but preserve transparency** | Shift+Option+Delete | Shift+Alt+Backspace |
| **Fill selection on any layer with background color** | Cmd+Delete | Ctrl+Backspace |

| Applying colors | Photoshop 6 Macintosh | Photoshop 6 Windows |
|---|---|---|
| **Fill selection or layer with foreground color** | Option+Delete | Alt+Backspace |
| **Fill selection with source state in History palette** | Cmd+Option+Delete | Ctrl+Alt+Backspace |
| **Lift background color from color bar at bottom of Color palette** | Option+click color bar | Alt+click color bar |
| **Lift background color from Swatches palette** | Option+click swatch | Alt+click swatch |
| **Lift foreground color from color bar at bottom of Color palette** | Click color bar | Click color bar |
| **Lift foreground color from Swatches palette** | Click swatch | Click swatch |
| **Replace swatch with foreground color** | Shift+click swatch | Shift+click swatch |
| **Specify new color bar** | Ctrl+click for dialog box | Ctrl+click for dialog box |

| Type | Photoshop 6 Macintosh | Photoshop 6 Windows |
|---|---|---|
| **Align left, center, or right** | Horizontally orient type tool +Shift+Cmd+L, C, or R | Horizontally orient type tool +Shift+Ctrl+L, C, or R |
| **Align top, center, or bottom** | Vertically orient type tool +Shift+Cmd+L, C, or R | Horizontally orient type tool +Shift+Ctrl+L, C, or R |
| **Edit text layer** | Double-click on 'T' in Layers palette or Option+click with Type tool | Double-click on 'T' in Layers palette or Option+click with Type tool |
| **Move type in image** | Cmd+drag type when Type is selected | Cmd+drag type when Type is selected |
| **Leading, increase/decrease by 2 pixels** | Option+arrow key | Alt+arrow key |
| **Leading, increase/decrease by 10 pixels** | Cmd+Option+_ or _ (left or right arrow) | Ctrl+Alt+_ or _ (left or right arrow) |
| **Select all text** | Cmd+A | Ctrl+A |
| **Select word, line, paragraph, or story** | Double-click, triple-click, quadruple-click, or quintuple-click | Double-click, triple-click, quadruple-click, or quintuple-click |
| **Select word to left or right** | Cmd+Shift+_ or _ (left or right arrow) | Ctrl+Shift+_ or _ (left or right arrow) |
| **Toggle Underlining on/off** | Cmd+Shift+U | Ctrl+Shift+U |
| **Toggle Strikethrough on/off** | Cmd+Shift+/ | Ctrl+Shift+/ |
| **Toggle Uppercase on/off** | Cmd+Shift+K | Ctrl+Shift+K |
| **Toggle Small Caps on/off** | Cmd+Shift+H | Ctrl+Shift+K |
| **Toggle Superscript on/off** | Cmd+Shift++ (plus) | Ctrl+Shift++ (plus) |
| **Toggle Subscript on/off** | Cmd+Option+Shift++ (plus) | Ctrl+Alt+Shift++ (plus) |
| **Type size, increase/decrease by 2 pixels** | Cmd+Shift+< or > | Ctrl+Shift+< or > |
| **Type size, increase/decrease by 10 pixels** | Cmd+Shift+Option+< or > | Ctrl+Shift+Alt+< or > |

| Making Selections | Photoshop 6 Macintosh | Photoshop 6 Windows |
|---|---|---|
| **Add point to Magnetic selection** | Click with Magnetic Lasso tool | Click with Magnetic Pen tool |
| **Add or subtract from selection** | Any Selection tool+Shift or Option+drag | Any Selection tool+Shift or Alt+drag |
| **Cancel Polygon or Magnetic selection** | Escape | Escape |
| **Change lasso tool to irregular Polygon tool** | Option+click with Lasso tool | Alt+click with Lasso tool |
| **Clone selection** | Option+drag selection with Move tool or Cmd+Option+drag with other tool | Alt+drag selection with Move tool or Ctrl+Alt+drag with other tool |
| **Clone selection in 1-pixel increments** | Cmd+Option+arrow key | Ctrl+Alt++arrow key |
| **Clone selection in 10-pixel increments** | Cmd+Shift+Option+arrow key | Ctrl+Shift+Alt+arrow key |
| **Clone selection to different image** | Cmd+drag selection from one window and drop it into another | Ctrl+drag selection from one window and drop it into another |
| **Close magnetic selection with straight segment** | Option+double-click or Option+ Return | Alt+double-click or Alt+Enter |
| **Close polygon or magnetic selection** | Double-click with respective Lasso tool or press Return | Double-click with respective Lasso tool or press Enter |
| **Constrain marquee to square or circle** | Press Shift while drawing shape | Press Shift while drawing shape |
| **Constrain movement vertically or horizontally** | Press Shift while dragging selection | Press Shift while dragging selection |
| **Copy empty selection outline to different image** | Drag selection from one window into another with selection tool | Drag selection from one window into another with selection tool |
| **Cycle through Lasso tools** | Option+click Lasso tool icon or Shift+L | Alt+click Lasso tool icon or Shift+L |
| **Cycle through Marquee tools (including Crop tool)** | Option+click Marquee tool icon | Alt+click Marquee tool icon |
| **Delete last point added with Magnetic Lasso tool** | Delete | Backspace |
| **Deselect all** | Cmd+D | Ctrl+D |
| **Draw out from center with Marquee tool** | Option+drag | Alt+drag |
| **Feather selection** | Cmd+Option+D or Shift+F6 | Ctrl+Alt+D or Shift+F6 |
| **Hide or show marquee** | | |
| **Increase or reduce magnetic lasso detection width** | [ or ] (square brackets) | [ or ] (square brackets) |
| **Move copy of selection** | Drag with Move tool+Option | Drag with Move tool+Alt |
| **Move selection in 1-pixel increments** | Move tool+arrow key | Move tool+arrow key |
| **Move selection in 10-pixel increments** | Move tool+Shift+arrow key | Move tool+Shift+arrow key |
| **Move selection area in 1-pixel increments** | Any selection+arrow key | Any selection+arrow key |
| **Move selection area in 10-pixel increments** | Any selection+Shift+arrow key | Any selection+Shift+arrow key |

| Selection | Photoshop 6 Macintosh | Photoshop 6 Windows |
|---|---|---|
| Move selection outline independently of its contents | Drag with Selection tool | Drag with Selection tool |
| Paste image behind selection | Cmd+Shift+Option+V | Ctrl+Shift+Alt+V |
| Paste image into selection | Cmd+Shift+V | Ctrl+Shift+V |
| Reselect after deselecting | Cmd+Shift+D | Ctrl+Shift+D |
| Reverse selection | Cmd+Shift+I or Shift+F7 | Ctrl+Shift+I or Shift+F7 |
| Select all | Cmd+A | Ctrl+A |
| Select Move tool | V | V |
| Subtract from selection | Option+drag | Alt+drag |
| Toggle between rectangular and elliptical marquees | Shift+M | Shift+M |

| Layers and channels | Photoshop 6 Macintosh | Photoshop 6 Windows |
|---|---|---|
| Add spot color channel | Cmd+click page icon at bottom of Channels palette | Ctrl+click page icon at bottom of Channels palette |
| Add to current layer selection | Shift+Cmd+click layer or thumbnail in Layers palette | Shift+Ctrl+click layer or thumbnail in Layers palette |
| Clone selection to new layer | Cmd+J | Ctrl+J |
| Convert floating selection to new layer | Cmd+Shift+J | Ctrl+Shift+J |
| Copy merged version of selection to Clipboard | Cmd+Shift+C | Ctrl+Shift+C |
| Create new layer, show layer options dialog box | Option+click page icon at bottom of Layers palette or Cmd+Shift+N | Alt+click page icon at bottom of Layers palette or Ctrl+Shift+N |
| Create new layer below target layer | Cmd+click page icon at bottom of Layer Palette | Ctrl+click page icon at bottom of Layer Palette |
| Create new layer below target layer, show layer options dialog box | Cmd+Option+click page icon at bottom of Layers palette | Ctrl+Alt+click page icon at bottom of Layers palette |
| Display or hide Layers palette | F7 | F7 |
| Disable specific layer effect/style | Option+choose command from Layer > Effects submenu | Alt+choose command from Layer > Effects submenu |
| Duplicate layer effect/style | Shift+drag effect/style to target layer | Shift+drag effect/style to target layer |
| Edit layer style | Double click layer | Double click layer |
| Edit layer effect/style | Double-click on layer effect/style | Double-click on layer effect/style |
| Go to background | Shift+Option+[ | Shift+Alt+[ |
| Go to top layer | Shift+Option+] | Shift+Alt+] |
| Group neighboring layers | Option+click horizontal line in Layers palette or Cmd+G | Alt+click horizontal line in Layers palette or Ctrl+G |
| Intersect with current layer selection | Shift+Option+Cmd+click layer or thumbnail in Layers palette | Shift+Alt+Ctrl+click layer or thumbnail in Layers palette |
| Load layer as selection | Cmd+click layer or thumbnail in Layers palette | Ctrl+click layer or thumbnail in Layers palette |

| Layers and channels | Photoshop 6 Macintosh | Photoshop 6 Windows |
|---|---|---|
| Merge all visible layers | Cmd+Shift+E | Ctrl+Shift+E |
| Merge layer with next layer down | Cmd+E | Ctrl+E |
| Merge linked layers | Cmd+E | Ctrl+E |
| Move contents of a layer | Drag with Move tool or Cmd+drag with other tool | Drag with Move tool or Ctrl+drag with other tool |
| Move contents of a layer in 1-pixel increments | Cmd+arrow key | Ctrl+arrow key |
| Move contents of a layer in 10-pixel increments | Cmd+Shift+arrow key | Ctrl+Shift+arrow key |
| Move shadow when Effect dialog box is open | Drag in image window | Drag in image window |
| Move to next layer above | Option+] | Alt+] |
| Move to next layer below | Option+[ | Alt+[ |
| Moves target layer down/up | Cmd+[ or ] | Ctrl+[ or ] |
| Moves target layer back/front | Cmd+Shift+[ or ] | Ctrl+Shift+[ or ] |
| Preserve transparency of active layer | / | / |
| Retain intersection of transparency mask and selection | Cmd+Shift+Option+click layer name | Ctrl+Shift+Alt+click layer name |
| Save flattened copy of layered image | Cmd+Option+S | Ctrl+Alt+S |
| Send layer backward one level | Cmd+[ | Ctrl+[ |
| Send layer to back, just above the background layer | Cmd+Shift+[ | Ctrl+Shift+[ |
| Subtract transparency mask from selection | Cmd+Option+click layer name | Ctrl+Alt+click layer name |
| Subtract from current layer selection | Option+Cmd+click layer or thumbnail in Layers palette | Alt+Ctrl+click layer or thumbnail in Layers palette |
| Switch between independent color and mask channels | Cmd+1 through Cmd+9 | Ctrl+1 through Ctrl+9 |
| Switch between layer effects in Effects dialog box | Cmd+1 through Cmd+0 palette | Ctrl+1 through Ctrl+5 |
| Switch to composite color view | Cmd+~ (tilde) | Ctrl+~ (tilde) |
| Ungroup Layers | Cmd+Shift+G | Ctrl+Shift+G |
| Ungroup neighboring layers | Option+click dotted line in Layers palette or Cmd+Shift+G | Alt+click dotted line in Layers palette or Ctrl+Shift+G |
| View single layer by itself | Option+click eyeball icon in Layers palette | Alt+click eyeball icon in Layers palette |

| Masks | Photoshop 6 Macintosh | Photoshop 6 Windows |
|---|---|---|
| Add channel mask to selection | Cmd+Shift+click channel name | Ctrl+Shift+click channel name |
| Add layer mask to selection | Cmd+Shift+click layer mask thumbnail | Ctrl+Shift+click layer mask thumbnail |
| Change Quick Mask color overlay | Double-click Quick Mask icon | Double-click Quick Mask icon |

| Masks | Photoshop 6 Macintosh | Photoshop 6 Windows |
|---|---|---|
| Convert channel mask to selection outline | Cmd+click channel name in Channels palette or Cmd+Option+ number (1 through 0) | Ctrl+click channel name in Channels palette or Ctrl+Alt+number (1 through 0) |
| Convert layer mask to selection outline | Cmd+click layer mask thumbnail or Cmd+Option+\ (backslash) | Ctrl+click layer mask thumbnail or Ctrl+Alt+\ (backslash) |
| Create channel mask filled with black | Click page icon at bottom of Channels palette | Click page icon at bottom of Channels palette |
| Create channel mask filled with black and set options dialog | Option+click page icon at bottom of Channels palette | Alt+click page icon at bottom of Channels palette |
| Create channel mask from selection outline | Click mask icon at bottom of Channels palette | Click mask icon at bottom of Channels palette |
| Create channel mask from selection outline and set options dialog | Option+click mask icon at bottom of Channels palette | Alt+click mask icon at bottom of Channels palette |
| Create layer mask from selection outline | Click mask icon | Click mask icon |
| Create layer mask that hides selection | Option+click mask icon | Alt+click mask icon |
| Disable layer mask | Shift+click layer mask thumbnail | Shift+click layer mask thumbnail |
| Enter or exit Quick Mask mode | Q | Q |
| Intersect a channel mask and selection | Cmd+Shift+Option+click channel name | Ctrl+Shift+Alt+click channel name |
| Subtract channel mask from selection | Cmd+Option+click channel name | Ctrl+Alt+click channel name |
| Subtract layer mask from selection | Cmd+Option+click layer mask thumbnail | Ctrl+Alt+click layer mask thumbnail |
| Switch focus from image to layer mask | Cmd+\ (backslash) | Ctrl+\ (backslash) |
| Switch focus from layer mask to image | Cmd+~ (tilde) | Ctrl+~ (tilde) |
| Toggle link between layer and layer mask | Click between layer and mask thumbnails in Layers palette | Click between layer and mask thumbnails in Layers palette |
| View channel mask as Rubylith overlay | Click eyeball of channel mask in Channels palette | Click eyeball of channel mask in Channels palette |
| View layer mask as Rubylith overlay | Shift+Option+click layer mask thumbnail or press \ (backslash) | Shift+Alt+click layer mask thumbnail or press \ (backslash) |
| View layer mask independently of image | Option+click layer mask thumbnail in Layers palette or press \ (backslash) then ~ (tilde) | Alt+click layer mask thumbnail in Layers palette or press \ (backslash) then ~ (tilde) |
| View Quick Mask independently of image | Click top eyeball in Channels palette or press ~ (tilde) | Click top eyeball in Channels palette or press ~ (tilde) |

| Paths | Photoshop 6 Macintosh | Photoshop 6 Windows |
|---|---|---|
| Add cusp to path | Drag with Pen tool, then Option+ drag same point | Drag with Pen tool, then Alt+drag same point |
| Add point to magnetic selection | Click with Magnetic Pen tool | Click with Magnetic Pen tool |
| Add smooth arc to path | Drag with Pen tool | Drag with Pen tool |

| Paths | Photoshop 6 Macintosh | Photoshop 6 Windows |
|---|---|---|
| Cancel magnetic or freeform selection | Escape | Escape |
| Clone path | Cmd+Option+drag with pen | Ctrl+Alt+drag with pen |
| Close magnetic selection | Double-click with Magnetic Pen tool or click on first point in path | Double-click with Magnetic Pen tool or click on first point in path |
| Close magnetic selection with straight segment | Option+double-click or Option+Return | Alt+double-click or Alt+Enter |
| Deactivate path | Click in empty portion of Paths palette | Click in empty portion of Paths palette |
| Delete last point added with Pen tool or Magnetic Pen tool | Delete | Backspace |
| Draw freehand path segment | Drag with Freeform Pen tool or Option+drag with Magnetic Pen tool | Drag with Freeform Pen tool or Alt+drag with Magnetic Pen tool |
| Hide path (it remains active) | Cmd+Shift+H | Ctrl+Shift+H |
| Increase or reduce magnetic pen width | [ or ] (square brackets) | [ or ] (square brackets) |
| Move selected points | Drag point with Arrow tool or Cmd+drag with Pen tool | Drag point with Arrow tool or Ctrl+drag with Pen tool |
| Save path for future use | Double-click Work Path item in Paths palette | Double-click Work Path item in Paths palette |
| Select arrow (direct selection) tool | A | A |
| Select entire path | Option+click path with arrow or Cmd+click with pen | Alt+click path with arrow or Ctrl+Alt+click with pen |
| Select Insert Point tool or Remove Point tool | +(plus) or - (minus) | +(plus) or - (minus) |
| Select multiple points in path | Cmd+Shift+click with pen | Ctrl+Shift+click with pen |
| Subtract path from selection | Cmd+Option+click path | Alt+Enter on keypad |
| Select Pen tool | P | P |
| Make active path a selection | Cmd+Return | Ctrl+Enter |

| Crops and transformations | Photoshop 6 Macintosh | Photoshop 6 Windows |
|---|---|---|
| Accept transformation | Double-click inside boundary or press Return | Double-click inside boundary or press Enter |
| Cancel crop | Escape | Escape |
| Cancel transformation | Escape | Escape |
| Constrained distort for perspective effect | Cmd+Shift+drag corner handle | Ctrl+Shift+drag corner handle |
| Constrained distort for symmetrical perspective effect | Cmd+Shift+Option+drag corner handle | Ctrl+Shift+Alt+drag corner handle |
| Freely transform with duplicate data | Cmd+Option+T | Ctrl+Alt+T |
| Replay last transformation with duplicate data | Cmd+Shift+Option+T | Ctrl+Shift+Alt+T |

| Crops and transformations | Photoshop 6 Macintosh | Photoshop 6 Windows |
|---|---|---|
| Freely transform selection or layer | Cmd+T | Ctrl+T |
| Replay last transformation | Cmd+Shift+T | Ctrl+Shift+T |
| Rotate image (always with respect to origin) | Drag outside boundary | Drag outside boundary |
| Select Crop tool | C | C |
| Skew image | Cmd+drag side handle | Ctrl+drag side handle |
| Skew image along constrained axis | Cmd+Shift+drag side handle | Ctrl+Shift+drag side handle |
| Skew image with respect to origin | Cmd+Option+drag side handle | Ctrl+Alt+drag side handle |
| Skew image along constrained axis with respect to origin | Cmd+Shift+Option+drag side handle | Ctrl+Shift+Alt+drag side handle |
| Distort corner | Cmd+drag corner handle | Ctrl+drag corner handle |
| Symmetrically distort opposite corners | Cmd+Option+drag corner handle | Ctrl+Alt+drag corner handle |

| Rulers, measurements and guides | Photoshop 6 Macintosh | Photoshop 6 Windows |
|---|---|---|
| Create guide | Drag from ruler | Drag from ruler |
| Display or hide grid | Cmd+Option+" (quote) | Ctrl+" (quote) |
| Display or hide guides | Cmd+" (quote) | Ctrl+; (semicolon) |
| Display or hide Info palette | F8 | F8 |
| Display or hide rulers | Cmd+R | Ctrl+R |
| Lock or unlock guides | Cmd+Option+; (semicolon) | Ctrl+Alt+; (semicolon) |
| Snap guide to ruler tick marks | Press Shift while dragging guide | Press Shift while dragging guide |
| Toggle grid magnetism | Cmd+Shift+; (semicolon) | Ctrl+Shift+" (quote) |
| Toggle horizontal guide to vertical or vice versa | Press Option while dragging guide | Press Alt while dragging guide |

| Slicing and optimizing | Photoshop 6 Macintosh | Photoshop 6 Windows |
|---|---|---|
| Draw square slice | Shift+drag | Shift+drag |
| Draw from center outward | Option+drag | Alt+drag |
| Draw square slice from center outward | Option+Shift+drag | Alt+Shift+drag |
| Open slices contextual menu | Control+click on slice | Right mouse button on slice |
| Reposition slice while creating slice | Spacebar+drag | Spacebar+drag |
| Toggle snap to slices on/off | Control while drawing slice | Ctrl while drawing slice |
| Toggle between Slice tool and Slice selection tool | Cmd | Ctrl |

| Filters | Photoshop 6 Macintosh | Photoshop 6 Windows |
| --- | --- | --- |
| Adjust angle of light without affecting size of footprint | Cmd+drag handle | Ctrl+drag handle |
| Clone light in Lighting Effects dialog box | Option+drag light | Alt+drag light |
| Delete Lighting Effects light | Delete | Delete |
| Delete selected 3D Transform shape | Delete | Backspace |
| Edit 3D transform shape with pan camera or trackball | E or R | E or R |
| Select 3D cube, sphere, or cylinder tool | M, N, or C | M, N, or C |
| Repeat filter with different settings | Cmd+Option+F | Ctrl+Alt+F |
| Repeat filter with previous settings | Cmd+F | Ctrl+F |
| Reset options inside Corrective Filter dialog boxes | Option+click Cancel button or Option+Escape | Alt+click Cancel button |

| Hide and undo | Photoshop 6 Macintosh | Photoshop 6 Windows |
| --- | --- | --- |
| Display or hide Actions palette | F9 | F9 |
| Display or hide all palettes, toolbox, status bar | Tab | Tab |
| Display or hide palettes except toolbox | Shift+Tab | Shift+Tab |
| Hide toolbox and status bar | Tab, Shift+Tab | Tab, Shift+Tab |
| Move a panel out of a palette | Drag panel tab | Drag panel tab |
| Revert to saved image | F12 | F12 |
| Undo or redo last operation | Cmd+Z | Ctrl+Z |

| Viewing | Photoshop 6 Macintosh | Photoshop 6 Windows |
| --- | --- | --- |
| 100% magnification | Double-click Zoom tool or Cmd+Option+0 (zero) | Double-click Zoom tool or Ctrl+Alt+0 (zero) |
| Applies zoom percentage and keeps zoom percentage box active | Shift+Return in Navigator palette | Shift+Enter in Navigator palette |
| Fits image in window | Double-click Hand tool or Cmd+0 (zero) | Double-click Hand tool or Ctrl+0 (zero) |
| Moves view to upper left corner or lower right corner | Home or End | Home or End |
| Scrolls image with hand tool | Spacebar+drag or drag view area box in Navigator palette | Spacebar+drag or drag view area box in Navigator palette |
| Scrolls up or down 1 screen | Page Up or Page Down | Page Up or Page Down |
| Scrolls up or down 10 units | Shift+Page Up or Page Down | Shift+Page Up or Page Down |
| Zooms in or out | Cmd++ (plus) or - (minus) or Cmd+Spacebar or Option+Spacebar | Ctrl++ (plus) or - (minus) or Ctrl+Spacebar or Alt+Spacebar |
| Zooms in on specified area of an image | Cmd+drag over preview in Navigator palette | Ctrl+drag over preview in Navigator palette |